THE ULTIMATE FOOTBALL
FACT AND QUIZ BOOK

Henry Russell

Cartoons by
Peter Coupe

STOPWATCH

Published by Stopwatch Publishing Limited
For Bookmart Limited
Registered Number 2372865
Trading as Bookmart Limited
Desford Road
Enderby
Leicester
LE9 5AD

This edition published 1998

Printed and bound in Finland

The views and opinons of the writer not necessarily
those of Bass Brewers Limited

Compiled by Henry Russell

1st Floor
1–7 Shand Street
London SE1 2ES

info@stopwatch.co.uk

ISBN 1 900032 43 0

CARLING

THE ULTIMATE FOOTBALL

FACT AND QUIZ BOOK

CONTENTS

FOOTBALL
Quiz Book

QUIZ CONTENTS

Quiz 1   ### Also Known As...

Identify the following:

1 **A 1960s' goalkeeper known as the Flying Pig.**

2 The winger known as the Kosher Garrincha.

3 **The Welsh Wizard or the Prince of Wingers.**

4 Der Kaiser.

5 **Der Bomber.**

6 The Ambassador of Football - the England player who objected most strongly to giving the Nazi salute before the match against Germany in Berlin in 1938.

7 **Bald Eagle, a successful manager of Oxford United, Queen's Park Rangers, Newcastle United and Derby County.**

8 Someone known as The Cat when he was at home and the Mexico Fumbler when he was away.

9 **Thomas the Book.**

10 The Boy, until recently Arsenal's all-time leading scorer.

11 **The Tipton Terror.**

12 Budgie.

13 **The Vulture.**

14 Captain Marvel.

15 **The Gentle Giant.**

---

1 **Tommy Lawrence (Liverpool and Tranmere Rovers)** 2 Mark Lazarus (Queen's Park Rangers) 3 **Billy Meredith (Manchester City and Manchester United)** 4 Franz Beckenbauer 5 **Gerd Müller** 6 Eddie Hapgood 7 **Jim Smith** 8 Peter Bonetti (Chelsea and England) 9 **Referee Clive Thomas** 10 Cliff Bastin 11 **Steve Bull (Wolverhampton Wanderers)** 12 Johnny Byrne (Crystal Palace, West Ham, Fulham and England) 13 **Emilio Butragueño (Real Madrid and Spain)** 14 Bryan Robson (WBA, Manchester United and England) 15 **John Charles (Leeds United and Wales)**

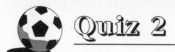

Quiz 2

Also Known As...

What are the real names of the following Scottish teams?

1 **The Red Lichties (English: Red Lights), after the town's Stevenson-built Bell Rock lighthouse.**

2 The Bairns, from the line:
'Better meddle wi' the Devil than the Bairns o' .....

3 **The Sons, as in 'The Sons of the Rock', a name thought to be derived from the hill on which the local castle stands.**

4 The Binos.

5 **The Jags.**

6 The Wee Jags.

7 **Bully Wee (a reference to their most famous forward line, the members of which, though short in stature, more than made up for it in toughness).**

8 The Diamonds, after their team strip, white with red diamonds.

9 **The Terrors - a name which might be frightening if it were not shared with gentle little Tooting and Mitcham United.**

10 The Pars.

11 **The Loons.**

12 The Honest Men, from Tam O'Shanter, the poem by Burns which contains the lines:
*'Auld ——, wham ne'er a town surpasses,
For honest men and bonnie lasses.'*

13 **The Gers.**

14 The Jammies.

15 **The Spiders, after the black and white hoops they play in.**

 **Quiz 3**   **Also Known As...**

1   Which team is sometimes known as The Addicks, a term originally derived from the haddocks served at the fish and chip shop over which the team first met?

2   Which team is known as the Chairboys, after the furniture-making industry for which their town was famous?

3   Which team takes one of its nicknames from the thrush or throstle on its badge and the other from the baggy shorts once favoured by its players?

4   Who are the Stags?

5   Who were hubristically called 'The Team of the Eighties' by Terry Venables, their manager from 1976-80?

6   Who are variously known as the Colliers or the Tykes?

7   The most famous Irons are West Ham United. With which other team do they share this nickname?

8   Who are the Seasiders?

9   Who are the Seagulls?

10 Who are called the Quakers because of the strength of the Society of Friends in that part of the country?

11 If you shouted 'Allez les verts!', who would you be supporting?

12 Which team are known as the Terriers and have this type of dog on their badge?

13 Who are known as The Lions?

14 Who are called the Imps after a gargoyle in the local cathedral?

15 Who are nicknamed the Bantams because their colours - claret and amber shirts, black shorts and black stockings - are supposed to resemble those of the farm bird?

 **Quiz 4**　　　　**Also Known As...**

1　Who are known as the Trotters - not for their piggishness, but because, for much of their early history, they were constantly on the move from one ground to another?

2　What are Fulham popularly known as?

3　Who are nicknamed the Rams, after their county emblem?

4　Who are the Foxes?

5　Who are, famously, the Toffees, and less famously, the Moonlight Dribblers, after their penchant for training at night?

6　Why are Sheffield Wednesday called the Owls?

7　Who are the Pirates, after their city's maritime traditions?

8　If Leeds United are the Peacocks, why don't they play in blue?

9　Who are known as the Pilgrims because it was from the city in which they play that the Pilgrim Fathers set out to found the United States of America?

10　Who are the Merry Millers?

11　Who are the Lilywhites?

12　Who are the Shrimpers?

13　Which Silkmen entered the Football League in 1997?

14　Which town - long famous as the home of the Huntley and Palmer's factory - has a team known as the Biscuitmen?

15　Which town, famous for the manufacture of leather products, has a team nicknamed the Saddlers?

14 Reading 15 Walsall
10 Rotherham United 11 Preston North End 12 Southend United 13 Macclesfield Town
if they used the same strip as the great Spanish team of the 1950s 9 Plymouth Argyle
Rovers 8 They used to, until manager Don Revie decided they would play more like Real Madrid
6 Because the district in which their ground stands used to be called Owlerton 7 Bristol
1 Bolton Wanderers 2 The Cottagers 3 Derby County 4 Leicester City 5 Everton

Quiz 5

Also Known As...

1 For no good reason, many Brazilian players are known only by a single name. What was Eduardo Gonçalves de Andrade better known as in the 1970 World Cup?

2 What was Jairzinho's full name?

3 **What are the forenames of the player known only as Falcao?**

4 Manoel Francisco dos Santos was universally known as Garrincha. What does Garrincha mean?

5 **What is Pele's real name?**

6 What was the nickname of Waldir Pereira, the architect of Brazil's triumph in the 1958 World Cup?

7 **What was the real name of his midfield partner, Zito?**

8 Juninho means 'junior' in Portuguese. What is his full real name?

9 **And what does Mrs Emerson fill in under 'Name of Spouse'?**

10 What was the full name of Gerson, midfield general and chain-smoker, who contributed enormously to the 1970 World Cup triumph without, as memory tells it, breaking into a run?

11 **What is Ronaldo's full name?**

12 Who is Artur Antunes Coimbra, a.k.a 'The White Pele'?

13 **Which Brazilian was nicknamed The Little Ant?**

14 Who was Joe Mercer referring to in the 1970 World Cup when he said that, despite his name, he was 'no cat'?

15 **What is the real name of Middlesbrough's Branco?**

 ## Quiz 6   Also Known As...

1   Which Republic of Ireland international was known as Chippy, reputedly because of his preferred food?

2   Who was known as Chopper, no doubt because of his robust tackling?

3   Which Liverpool star of the '60s, who also played for Dundee United in the '50s and Tranmere Rovers in the '70s, was known as the Colossus?

4   Which great Scottish international was known Corky, apparently because he always carried a lucky champagne cork which he had kept since Rangers' victory over Morton in the 1948 Scottish FA Cup Final?

5   Which England midfielder was known as the Crab because, as Tommy Docherty said: 'The only time he comes forward is to toss the coin'?

6   Which Cockney hero, who played for Millwall during the 1960s and '70s, was nicknamed the Dog for his tenacity?

7   Who was the Mad Dog of West Ham United in the early '90s?

8   The winner of League Championship medals for both Heart of Midlothian and Everton, who was known as the Golden Vision?

9   By what sobriquet was Tom Finney sometimes known?

10 Who was the Galloping Major?

11 Which former Aston Villa, Chelsea, Arsenal, Manchester United, Portsmouth and Crystal Palace midfielder was known as Stroller?

12 Which Welsh international forward is nicknamed Sparky?

13 Which players with degrees were known as Big Bamber and Little Bamber (after Bamber Gascoigne, once the host of the Granada TV quiz show University Challenge)?

14 Which three England players shared goalkeeping duties during the 1965-66 season, became close friends and were known as the Marx Brothers?

15 What is the nickname of Nottingham Forest, Newcastle and England left back Stuart Pearce?

Quiz 7

Also Known As...

Identify the following:

1 **The White Feather.**

2 Safe Hands.

3 **The Blue Brazil.**

4 Trigger.

5 **Razor.**

6 Juke Box.

7 **The Governor.**

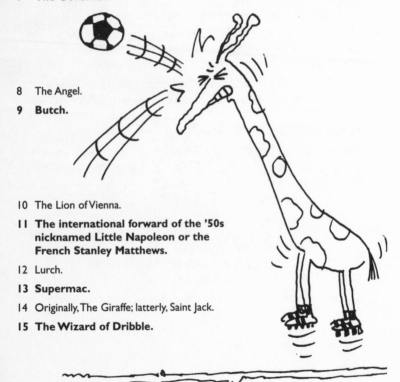

8 The Angel.

9 **Butch.**

10 The Lion of Vienna.

11 **The international forward of the '50s nicknamed Little Napoleon or the French Stanley Matthews.**

12 Lurch.

13 **Supermac.**

14 Originally, The Giraffe; latterly, Saint Jack.

15 **The Wizard of Dribble.**

1 **Fabrizio Ravanelli** (ex-Middlesbrough) 2 David Seaman (Arsenal) 3 **Cowdenbeath** 4 Jason McAteer (Liverpool) 5 **Neil Ruddock (Liverpool)** 6 Gordon Durie (Rangers) 7 **Paul Ince (Liverpool)** 8 Gabriel Batistuta (Fiorentina) 9 **Ray Wilkins** 10 Nat Lofthouse (Bolton Wanderers) 11 **Raymond Kopa (Real Madrid and Reims)** 12 Dave Beasant (ex-Wimbledon) 13 **Malcolm Macdonald** 14 Jack Charlton: the first as a Leeds United player; the second during his time as manager of the Republic of Ireland 15 **Stanley Matthews (Stoke City and Blackpool)**

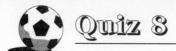

Quiz 8

Also Known As...

1 **What was the nickname of Patsy Gallagher, the star inside forward of Celtic and Sunderland in the 1920s and '30s?**

2 Which English international, European Footballer of the Year in 1978 and 1979, was known to the press as Mighty Mouse?

3 **Which Rangers and Scotland outside left of the 1920s was known as The Wee Blue Devil?**

4 Who was Wor Jackie?

5 **Who is Skippy?**

6 Who are The O's?

7 **Who were The Old Invincibles?**

8 Who was Pop to thousands of fans at Newcastle United, West Ham United, Sunderland, Carlisle and Chelsea?

9 **Who is Toto?**

10 What was the collective nickname of 1950s' Bolton Wanderers defenders Roy Hartle, Derek Henning, Eddie Hopkinson, John Higgins, Bryan Edwards and Tom Banks?

11 **Who were The Lions of Lisbon?**

12 What nickname did the tabloid press use to describe collectively that club's next generation of stars, players such as Kenny Dalglish, Lou Macari and David Hay?

13 **Who was The Godfather to English footballers of the '60s and early '70s?**

14 Which centre forward, star of Brazil's 1938 World Cup campaign, was variously known as The Black Diamond or The Rubber Man?

15 **From which Italian forward, in the '60s and '70s, might you have heard The Rumble of Thunder?**

 Quiz 9

Also Known As...

1   What was the nickname of 1930s Italian striker Giuseppe Meazza
    (1910-1979) who played for Internazionale, AC Milan and Juventus
    and helped his country to two World Cups (1934 and 1938).

2   Which leading Portuguese team are nicknamed The Dragons?

3   **Which Newcastle United and England inside forward of the '40s
    and '50s was known as The Clown Prince of Soccer?**

4   Which famous manager was known as The Tank during his playing days at
    Oxford United?

5   **Who are the Saints?**

6   Who is the Saint?

7   **Mrs David Beckham may be Posh, but who are The Posh?**

8   What nickname, a reference to their highly organised and precise style of
    play, was given to the Championship-winning Everton side of the 1930s?

9   **Nicknamed Slim Jim, who was the Raith Rovers, Rangers,
    Sunderland and Nottingham Forest forward who played 34 times
    for Scotland in the 1960s?**

10 The Italian league side Torino is affectionately known by the name of the
    fruit which is thought to have roughly the same colour as their strip of red
    shirt, white shorts and red socks. What is their nickname?

11 **Who, in the'60s and '70s, was Anfield Iron?**

12 Why is Southampton, Blackburn Rovers, Newcastle and England striker Alan
    Shearer known as Smokey?

13 **Why are Charlton Athletic sometimes known as The Valiants?**

14 What was the codename of Danish goalkeeper Eric Sorensen, whose identity
    Morton wanted to keep under wraps in 1964?

15 **Which Yugoslav midfielder, who became a star with Dynamo
    Zagreb and AC Milan in the late '80s, was known as Zorro, partly
    because of his rapier-like skills, and partly because of his first
    name, Zvonimir?**

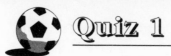

Quiz 1

Book That Man!

Which footballers are the authors and/or subjects of the following books:

1 **'Tales From The Boot Camps'?**
2 'Soccer My Battlefield'?
3 **'Bonzo'?**
4 'From St Tropez to St James"?
5 **'Achieving The Goal'?**
6 'Goals From Nowhere'?
7 **'Never Afraid To Miss'?**
8 'The Goal Machine'?
9 **'Return Of The Little Villain'?**
10 'Call The Doc'?

11 **'The Red And The Black'?**
12 'Three Of The Best'?
13 **'Rock Bottom'?**

14 'The Good, The Bad And The Bubbly'?
15 **'Heading For Victory'?**

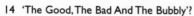

 # Quiz 1   Brothers On The Ball

Identify the following pairs of brothers:

1 **Both played for Arsenal, the elder until 1951, the younger until 1949. The younger was also a great cricketer.**

2 One played for Middlesbrough and Spurs; he died in 1991 aged 47. The other played for Wolves until quitting to become a Jehovah's Witness.

3 **One made his England debut in 1995 against Japan; the other won his first international cap the following year against China.**

4 One made 53 England appearances and a pop record; the other played for Barnet.

5 **One led his team to their first Championship for 25 years; the other played for Bradford City.**

6 One began at Preston and played 106 times for England; the other was at Leeds throughout his career and then led a country to the World Cup finals.

7 **One was an England international and an FA Cup winner with Chelsea in 1970; the other kept goal and played for Wales.**

8 Twins who played on opposite wings for Queen's Park Rangers.

9 **Leeds United and Scotland stars of the '60s, '70s, '80s and '90s. The elder went on to manage his old club; the younger ran Darlington.**

10 Paul and Ron, who started at Chester City in the '70s, then went to Luton Town and Manchester City together.

11 **One played for Bradford, Wolves, Coventry and Bristol Rovers between 1967 and 1988 and later became Director of Football at Cardiff. The other won a Fairs Cup runners' up medal with Leeds in 1968 and also played for Newcastle and Birmingham.**

12 Goalkeeping brothers who both played for Queen's Park Rangers and Sheffield Wednesday. The elder also played 33 times for England.

13 **Welsh internationals of the '40s and '50s who began and ended their careers with Swansea City.**

14 Barnardo's boys who started at Norwich City. The elder then went to Nottingham Forest, the younger to Wimbledon.

15 **One played for Arsenal, Brighton and Hove Albion and Charlton Athletic between 1977 and 1993; the other captained England.**

---

1 Denis and Leslie Compton 2 Cyril and Peter Knowles 3 Philip and Gary Neville 4 Glenn and Carl Hoddle 5 Bryan and Gary Robson 6 Jack and Bobby Charlton 7 John and David Hollins 8 Ian and Roger Morgan 9 Eddie and Frankie Gray 10 Futcher 11 Kenny and Terry Hibbitt 12 Ron and Peter Springett 13 Ivor and Len Allchurch 14 Justin and John Fashanu 15 Steve and Mike Gatting

THE ULTIMATE FOOTBALL FACT AND QUIZ BOOK

Quiz 1

Celebrity Fans

Which teams do the following support:

1 **Comedian Tommy Trinder?**

2 Comedian Jimmy Tarbuck?

3 **Pop group Oasis?**

4 Pop singer David Essex?

5 **Conservative politicians John Major and David Mellor?**

6 Pop star Elton John?

7 **Television chef Delia Smith?**

8 Television sports presenter Des Lynam?

9 **Comedian Frank Skinner?**

10 'They Think It's All Over' compere Nick Hancock?

11 **Alf Garnett actor Warren Mitchell?**

12 Nick Hornby, author of 'Fever Pitch'?

13 **Actor Sean Bean (he even has a tattoo to this effect)?**

14 Comedian Jasper Carrott?

15 **Prime Minister Tony Blair?**

1 **Fulham** 2 Liverpool 3 **Manchester City** 4 West Ham United 5 **Chelsea** 6 Watford
7 **Norwich City** 8 Brighton and Hove Albion 9 **West Bromwich Albion** 10 Stoke City
11 **Tottenham Hotspur** 12 Arsenal 13 **Sheffield United** 14 Birmingham City
15 Newcastle United

 # Quiz 2   **Celebrity Fans**

Which teams do the following support:

1   **Journalist and television interviewer Michael Parkinson?**

2   Actor Kevin Lloyd, best known at the time of his death in May 1998 as Detective Constable Alfred 'Tosh' Lines in 'The Bill'?

3   **Leyton-born Manchester United star David Beckham?**

4   Liverpool midfielder Jason McAteer?

5   **BBC Radio One Breakfast Show presenter Zoe Ball?**

6   Newcastle United and England midfielder Robert Lee?

7   **1998 World Snooker Champion John Higgins?**

8   Classical violinist Nigel Kennedy?

9   **Comedian David Baddiel?**

10 Comedian Phil Jupitus?

11 **Talk show host Clive Anderson?**

12 West Ham MP and Sports Minister Tony Banks?

13 **King Olaf of Norway?**

14 Children's television presenter Kirsten O'Brien?

15 **Sporty Spice (Mel C)?**

1 **Barnsley** 2 Derby County 3 **Manchester United** 4 Liverpool 5 **Manchester United** 6 West Ham United 7 **Celtic** 8 Aston Villa 9 **Chelsea** 10 West Ham United 11 **Arsenal** 12 Chelsea 13 **West Ham United** 14 Middlesbrough 15 **Liverpool**

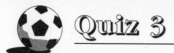 # Quiz 3   **Celebrity Fans**

Which teams do the following support:

1 **Eric Morecambe of the celebrated comic double act Morecambe and Wise?**

2 Mikhail Gorbachev, the last leader of the USSR?

3 **Actor and 'Have I Got News For You' presenter Angus Deayton?**

4 Singer and Labour Party member Billy Bragg?

5 **Roman Catholic Cardinal Basil Hume?**

6 Yorkshire and England fast bowler Darren Gough?

7 **Education Secretary David Blunkett?**

8 Comedian and cross-dresser Eddie Izzard?

9 **Formula One Racing Team boss Eddie Jordan?**

10 Time-defying pop singer Engelbert Humperdinck?

11 **George Carey, Archbishop of Canterbury?**

12 Jim Bowen, the host of television quiz-and-darts show 'Bullseye'?

13 **Former World Snooker Champion John Parrott?**

14 Johnny Rotten, former lead singer of the Sex Pistols?

15 **'Terry and June' star June Whitfield?**

1 **Luton Town** 2 Wigan Athletic 3 **Manchester United** 4 West Ham United 5 **Newcastle United** 6 Barnsley 7 **Sheffield Wednesday** 8 Crystal Palace 9 **Coventry City** 10 Leicester City 11 **Arsenal** 12 Blackburn Rovers 13 **Everton** 14 Arsenal 15 **Wimbledon**

Quiz 4

Celebrity Fans

Which teams do the following support:

1 **Former world snooker champion Ken Doherty?**

2 Leslie Phillips, actor and film star?

3 **Actor and film director Lord Richard Attenborough?**

4 Former England cricket captain Mike Atherton?

5 **Actor Neil Pearson, star of 'Drop The Dead Donkey' and 'Between The Lines'?**

6 Richard Whiteley, host of the television quiz show 'Countdown'?

7 **Journalist and Labour MP Roy Hattersley?**

8 Scary Spice (Mel B)?

9 **Richard Branson, chairman of the Virgin group of companies?**

10 Swedish former Wimbledon champion and London resident Stefan Edberg?

11 **Comedian Tim Brooke-Taylor?**

12 Former Manchester United and England goalkeeper Alex Stepney?

13 **Athlete Steve Cram?**

14 Television horse racing commentator Julian Wilson?

15 **Champion jockey Walter Swinburn?**

1 **Manchester United** 2 Tottenham Hotspur 3 **Chelsea** 4 Manchester United
5 **Tottenham Hotspur** 6 Leeds United 7 **Sheffield Wednesday** 8 Leeds United
9 **Southampton** 10 Leeds United 11 **Derby County** 12 Manchester City 13 **Sunderland**
14 Swindon Town 15 **Manchester United**

Quiz 5

Celebrity Fans

Which teams do the following support:

1 **Russian President Boris Yeltsin?**

2 Former Labour leader Michael Foot?

3 **Composer Michael Nyman?**

4 World champion 10,000 metres runner Liz McColgan?

5 **Athlete David Moorcroft?**

6 Former World Snooker Champion Steve Davis?

7 **Snooker star Jimmy White?**

8 John Lloyd, former tennis player and husband of Chris Evert?

9 **Wales Rugby Union and Rugby League international Jonathan Davies?**

10 Television racing pundit John McCririck?

11 **Former Celtic great Kenny Dalglish?**

12 Controversial Liverpool politician Derek Hatton?

13 **England's 1998 World Cup referee Paul Durkin?**

14 Spanish operatic tenor Placido Domingo?

15 **Catalan operatic tenor Jose Carreras?**

 ## Quiz 1   Cricketing Footballers

Identify the following all rounders:

1 **Shrewsbury Town, Sheffield United and Doncaster Rovers defender between 1960 and 1968 who also batted regularly in the middle order for Worcestershire.**

2 Another Worcestershire player, for many years the county captain, who also played for Lincoln City from 1974-84.

3 **The Yorkshire, Leicestershire and England Test cricketer who made over 500 League appearances for Huddersfield Town, Carlisle United and Doncaster Rovers between 1959 to 1975.**

4 The Yorkshire and England fast bowler who also played in defence for Manchester United in the 1970s.

5 **The West Ham goalkeeper, winner of FA Cup and European Cup Winners' Cup medals, who also played for Worcestershire.**

6 Tranmere Rovers, West Bromwich Albion, Aston Villa and Southport goalkeeper and Worcestershire fast bowler.

7 **Scottish international goalkeeper who also represented his country at cricket in the NatWest Trophy.**

8 Yorkshire, Somerset and England captain who played six games and scored two goals for Bradford City in 1952.

9 **League Championship winner with Arsenal in 1948 and brilliant Middlesex and England batsman.**

10 Tory MP who played cricket for Gloucestershire and Warwickshire and was on the books of Aston Villa. Later a controversial chairman of Luton Town.

11 **Won the League Championship with Arsenal, managed Chelsea and played county cricket for Hampshire.**

12 Surrey and England cricketer, later England manager, who was a pro at Charlton Athletic in 1956.

13 **From Norfolk, this Middlesex and England batsman was a pro with Tottenham Hotspur just after the Second World War.**

14 Sussex and England great who played football for Corinthians and in one international for England, against Northern Ireland in 1901.

15 **Double international who played for Gloucestershire and Arsenal. Won one England football cap against Austria in 1952.**

1 **Ted Hemsley** 2 Phil Neale 3 **Chris Balderstone** 4 Arnie Sidebotham 5 **Jim Standen** 6 Jim Cumbes 7 **Andy Goram** 8 Brian Close 9 **Denis Compton** 10 David Evans 11 **Ted Drake** 12 Mickey Stewart 13 **Bill Edrich** 14 C.B. Fry 15 **Arthur Milton**

Quiz 1 European Cup Winners' Cup

1 **Which Italian team were the first winners of the Cup Winners' Cup in 1961?**

2 Which British club did they beat, in the only Cup Winners' Cup Final to have been played over two legs?

3 **Which was the first English team to participate in the Cup Winners' Cup?**

4 Which was the first English team to win the Cup Winners' Cup?

5 **Which three teams have won Cup Winners' Cup finals in their home cities?**

6 Who became the first German winners of the Cup Winners' Cup when they beat Liverpool in the 1966 Final?

7 **Which member of this German team created a Cup Winners' individual goal-scoring record, with 14 goals in 1965-66?**

8 Who, in 1969, became the first Eastern European club to win the Cup Winners' Cup?

9 **Which club reached three consecutive Cup Winners' Cup finals in the 1970s?**

10 Which Dutch international scored twice for this club in both the 1976 and 1977 Cup Winners' Cup finals?

11 **What was unusual about the atmosphere during the second leg of West Ham United's 1981 Cup Winners' Cup match against Castilla of Spain?**

12 The 1981 Cup Winners' Cup Final was the only one ever to have been contested by two teams from Eastern Europe - name them.

13 **Which manager has led two British clubs to Cup Winners' Cup victory?**

14 Which Italian Serie B club reached the Cup Winners' Cup semi-final in 1988?

15 **Which Belgian team won the 1988 Cup Winners' Cup in their first season in European competition?**

1 Fiorentina 2 Rangers 3 Wolverhampton Wanderers 4 Tottenham Hotspur 5 West Ham United (1965), Anderlecht (1976), Barcelona (1982) 6 Borussia Dortmund 7 Lothar Emmerich 8 Slovan Bratislava 9 Anderlecht 10 Robbie Rensenbrink 11 The match was played behind closed doors because of crowd trouble in the first leg 12 Dynamo Tbilisi (USSR) and Carl Zeiss Jena (East Germany) 13 Alex Ferguson (Aberdeen and Manchester United) 14 Atalanta 15 Mechelen

Quiz 2 European Cup Winners' Cup

1 **Who scored both goals for Sampdoria in their 2-0 victory over Anderlecht in the 1990 Cup Winners' Cup Final?**

2 Who scored both goals for Manchester United in their 2-1 victory over Barcelona in the 1991 Cup Winners' Cup Final?

3 **Which Spanish club knocked holders Manchester United out of the 1991-92 Cup Winners' Cup in the second round?**

4 One of Werder Bremen's goals in their 1992 Cup Winners' Cup Final victory over Monaco was scored by Wynton Rufer. Which country did he play for at international level?

5 **Who played for Parma against Antwerp from his native Belgium in the 1993 Cup Winners' Cup Final?**

6 In which city was the 1994 Cup Winners' Cup Final between Arsenal and Parma played?

7 **Name the Real Zaragoza player who scored in every round of the 1994-95 Cup Winners' Cup?**

8 Which Welsh international scored Arsenal's goal in their 2-1 defeat by Real Zaragoza in the 1995 Cup Winners' Cup Final?

9 **Whose shot from the halfway line won the 1995 European Cup Winners' Cup Final?**

10 Which English club reached the semi-finals of the 1996-97 Cup Winners' Cup?

11 **Which Brazilian scored the only goal of the 1997 Final for Barcelona against Paris St Germain?**

12 Name any of the three teams from the former East Germany that played in Cup Winners' Cup finals.

13 **Which seven English teams have won the Cup Winners' Cup?**

14 Which club has won the Cup Winners' Cup most often?

15 **In which city has the Final been played most often?**

Quiz 1 European Championships

1 **By what name were the European Football Championships formerly known?**

2 How often are the European Championship finals held?

3 **In which year was the European Championship first contested?**

4 Who were the first champions, winning the Cup for the only time in their entire history as a nation?

5 **Which is the only nation to have won the European Championship more than once?**

6 Who is the secretary of the French Football Federation after whom the European Championship trophy was named?

7 **Which three countries have won the European Championship on their home soil?**

8 Who was the goalkeeper for Czechoslovakia when they beat West Germany on penalties in the 1976 Final in Belgrade?

9 **Which two neighbouring countries met for the first time in September 1978 in a qualifying match for the 1980 European Championship finals?**

10 Who scored both West Germany's goals in their 2-1 victory over Belgium in the 1980 European Championship Final?

11 **Which Danish international broke his leg in the opening match of the 1984 finals?**

12 Who won the 1988 European Championship, beating the USSR 2-0 in the Final?

13 **Who was captain of the 1988 European Champions?**

14 1992 European Champions Denmark originally failed to qualify for the finals but were brought in eight days before the tournament began to fill the gap created by the expulsion of which country?

15 **Which Brondby and future Arsenal player scored the opening goal for Denmark in the 1992 Final against Germany?**

Quiz 2   European Championships

1 Who scored the goal for Sweden that finally put paid to England's hopes in the 1992 European Championship finals?

2 Which member of the Scotland squad in the 1992 European Championship finals in Sweden was born in Sweden?

3 In which four Swedish cities were European Championship finals matches played in 1992?

4 In which of these cities was the 1992 Final played?

5 Who was the captain of winners Germany in Euro '96?

6 Who scored Germany's match-winner in the Final against the Czech Republic?

7 What was historic about this goal?

8 Who took the first four kicks for England in their penalty shoot-outs against both Spain and Germany?

9 Who took England's fifth penalty against Germany?

10 After Gareth Southgate's famous England miss, who scored the winning spot-kick for Germany?

11 Who was the leading scorer in Euro '96, with five goals in the tournament?

12 Which club was he playing for at this stage of his career?

13 Who scored three goals for Croatia during their first appearance in the finals of an international tournament?

14 Three other players - one Bulgarian, one Dane and one German - scored three goals in Euro '96. Name them.

15 Apart from England, which other country took part in two penalty shoot-outs in Euro '96?

Quiz 3 European Championships

1. Which outfield player saved on the line with his hands in the Scotland v Holland group match in Euro '96?

2. Which club was he playing for at this stage of his career?

3. Whose penalty for France was saved in the semi-final shoot-out against the Czech Republic?

4. When Germany and the Czech Republic met during the group stage of Euro '96, ten players were shown the yellow card. Who was the English referee who booked them?

5. At which grounds were the quarter-finals of Euro '96 played?

6. Who scored Scotland's only goal of Euro '96?

7. Which Englishman scored against his own club keeper in Euro '96?

8. Which member of the Italian squad for Euro '96 played his club football in the USA?

9. Who scored from the penalty spot to give the Czech Republic the lead in the Euro '96 Final against Germany?

10. Who had been fouled in the penalty area?

11. Give the name and/or the nationality of the referee who pointed to the spot?

12. Who was the French goalkeeper, man of the match in the quarter-final victory over Holland?

13. Which country won the Euro '96 tournament Fair Play Award?

14. At the time of Euro '96, for which Italian club was star Bulgarian striker Hristo Stoichkov playing club football?

15. Where will the finals of the 2000 European Championship be held?

Quiz 1 — The European Cup

1 As what did the early stages of the European Cup become known in 1991?

2 In which season had the European Cup first been held?

3 Which Spanish team were the first winners of the trophy?

4 As holders of the trophy, this team automatically entered the competition the following season. When were they eventually knocked out?

5 Before the adoption of the league system, what was the lowest number of matches required to win the European Cup?

6 Where was the first European Cup Final held?

7 The attendance at this match was a mere 38,000. Which ground holds the record for the highest European Cup gate - 135,000 for the Real Madrid v Eintracht Frankfurt Final in 1960?

8 Which team has won the European Cup most often?

9 Benfica have played in seven European Cup Finals. How many times have they won the trophy?

10 What outstanding feat in the European Cup has been achieved by all the following teams: AC Milan, Ajax, Bayern Munich, Benfica, Internazionale, Liverpool, Nottingham Forest and Real Madrid?

11 Which is the only team to have won the European Cup more often than its own domestic Championship?

12 To date, there has only ever been one European Cup match between teams from the same city. Which were the clubs involved in this local derby in the 1958-59 semi-finals?

13 Who was the Spanish international who played in European Cup Finals for both Barcelona and Inter Milan in the 1960s?

14 Who scored both AC Milan's goals when they won the Cup in 1963 and also played for Juventus when they lost the 1973 Final to Ajax?

15 Velibor Vasovic appeared in the European Cup Finals of 1966 and 1969 and finished on the losing side on both occasions. Which teams did he play for?

---

1 The Champions' League 2 1955-56 3 Real Madrid 4 1960-61, after winning it five times running 5 Nine (three two-legged rounds, a semi-final at home and away and a one-off Final) 6 Paris 7 Hampden Park, Glasgow 8 Real Madrid (seven times) 9 Twice 10 They have all retained the trophy 11 Nottingham Forest 12 Real Madrid and Atletico Madrid 13 Luis Suarez 14 Jose Altafini 15 Partizan Belgrade and Ajax

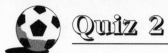 **Quiz 2**　　　　　　The European Cup

1　In 1967, who became the first British team to win the **European Cup?**

2　Who did they beat in the Final?

3　**Who scored the goals in their 2-1 victory?**

4　Who scored for the opposition from the penalty spot?

5　**Where was the 1967 Final played?**

6　Which was the first English team to take part in the European Cup?

7　**Who was manager of Manchester United when they won the European Cup in 1968?**

8　Who were their opponents in the Final?

9　**Where was the 1968 Final played?**

10　In which year did Liverpool become the next British team to win the European Cup?

11　**Who scored for Liverpool in their 3-1 victory over Borussia Moenchengladbach in Rome?**

12　Borussia Moenchengladbach's goal was scored by Danish international Alan Simonsen. For which English League club did he later play?

13　**Which German international was twice a loser to Liverpool in European Cup Finals?**

14　In 1979, who became the first Swedish team to reach the Final of the European Cup?

15　**Who scored on his European Cup debut in the 1979 Final?**

1 **Celtic (1967)** 2 Internazionale Milan 3 **Tommy Gemmell and Steve Chalmers**
4 Sandro Mazzola 5 **Lisbon** 6 Manchester United 7 **Matt Busby** 8 Benfica (Portugal)
9 **Wembley** 10 1977 11 **Terry McDermott, Tommy Smith and Phil Neal (penalty)**
12 Charlton Athletic 13 **Uli Stellike** 14 Malmo 15 **Trevor Francis (Nottingham Forest)**

 Quiz 3   European Cup

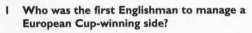

1 **Who was the first Englishman to manage a European Cup-winning side?**

2 Which team won the only European Cup Final to date to have gone to a replay?

3 **Which England international played against Nottingham Forest in the 1980 European Cup Final?**

4 Which was the last team to win the European Cup in their first ever season in the competition?

5 **After English teams had won the European Cup for six years in succession, which German club interrupted their domination of the tournament in 1983?**

6 Which was the only Eastern European or Iron Curtain team ever to win the European Cup?

7 **With which two clubs did Dutch international star Ronald Koeman win European Cup medals?**

8 Which Dutchman scored the winning goal for AC Milan in the 1990 European Cup Final?

9 **Which England international played for Marseille in the 1991 European Cup Final?**

10 Which two British clubs played each other in the European Cup in 1992?

11 **Why did the second leg of Leeds United's 1992 first round tie against Stuttgart have to be replayed?**

12 Which French international played in three consecutive European Cup Finals in 1993, 1994 and 1995?

13 **Who scored twice for AC Milan in the 1994 European Cup Final?**

14 Before Borussia Dortmund in 1997, which was the last team to win the European Cup Final in their own country?

15 **Who scored for Juventus in their 1997 European Cup Final defeat by Borussia Dortmund?**

 ## Quiz 1 — European Football

1 Apart from Athens and Thessaloniki, which is the only other city in Greece to have been home to winners of the Greek League Championship?

2 In which Austrian city do FC Tirol play their home games?

3 In which European nation does the football season usually run from April to October?

4 In which Italian city do Atalanta play their home matches?

5 In which Russian city do Zenit play their home matches?

6 In which Swiss city do Servette play their home matches?

7 Name the Atletico Madrid goalkeeper who kept a clean sheet for 1,275 minutes (more than 14 games) in March 1991.

8 To what did Dinamo Zagreb change their name in 1991?

9 Under Communism, what was the name of the Polish police team?

10 What is the real forename of the German goalkeeper universally known as 'Sepp' Maier?

11 What nationality is Jean-Marc Bosman, of the European Court's famous 1995 'Bosman ruling'?

12 What, to English-speakers at least, is the more familiar Flemish name of the Belgian club known in French as FC Malines?

13 Which Ajax star of the '70s was Holland's first full-time soccer professional?

14 Which are the two leading football clubs in Munich?

15 Which Austrian international striker has played club football for Torino (Italy), Seville (Spain) and FC Koln (Germany)?

 # Quiz 2   European Football

1 **Which Austrian striker has scored in European Cup Winners' Cup finals for both Barcelona and Rapid Vienna?**

2 Which German city is home to St Pauli?

3 **Which club from Madeira plays in the Portuguese league?**

4 Which club has won the Austrian League Championship most often?

5 **Which club has won the Spanish Cup most often?**

6 Which club shares a stadium with Real Madrid and is traditionally their 'B' team or feeder?

7 **Which club won the French League Championship seven times between 1967 and 1976?**

8 Which German city is home to FC Schalke '04?

9 **Which goalkeeper is the most capped Swedish international?**

10 Which is the only Hungarian club to have won a European trophy?

11 **Which is the only Irish team to have won both the Northern Irish and the Irish championships?**

12 Which is the only leading team from the former East Germany to have stayed in the top flight of the Bundesliga since reunification?

13 **Which Portuguese club wears black and white chequered shirts?**

14 Which Swiss club did the League and Cup double in 1997?

15 **Which Swiss club is named after the forward Max Abegglen?**

Quiz 3   European Football

1 **Which team has won the Bulgarian League Championship most often?**

2 Which team has won the Irish League Championship most often?

3 **Which team won ten successive League titles in East Germany?**

4 Which team won the first Bundesliga championship in Germany in 1963?

5 **Which team won the first Czech League Championship after the split with Slovakia in the 1993-94 season?**

6 Which two Belgian clubs share the Jan Breydel Stadium?

7 **Which two Polish clubs play at home in the city of Lodz?**

8 Which two Polish clubs play at home in the city of Poznan?

9 **Which Ukrainian played in Britain for Ipswich Town and St Johnstone?**

10 Who has managed Czechoslovakia, Slovakia and Aston Villa?

11 **Who kept goal for Belgium in the 1994 World Cup?**

12 Who made the most international appearances for the former Yugoslavia?

13 **Who took over from Richard Moller-Nielsen as Denmark manager in 1996?**

14 Who was captain of the Denmark team that won the 1992 European Championship in Sweden?

15 **Who was Spain's coach in Euro '96?**

Quiz 1   FA Charity Shield

1 **What are the usual qualifications for the two teams that contest the FA Charity Shield?**

2 In which year was the FA Charity Shield first played?

3 **In the 74 fixtures up to 1997, how many different teams had appeared in it?**

4 Which team has appeared in it most often?

5 **In which year was the Charity Shield first played at Wembley?**

6 How many times has the match not been decided in 90 minutes?

7 **Until 1974, what happened to the Shield when the matches were drawn?**

8 How did that change in 1974?

9 **Which team was the first to win the Charity Shield on penalties?**

10 Who did they beat?

11 **Of the teams in questions 9 and 10, which one won the Championship and which the FA Cup?**

12 To date, which is the only other team to have won the Charity Shield on penalties?

13 **Who were their opponents on that day?**

14 What do the following teams have in common? Blackpool; Bolton Wanderers; Brighton and Hove Albion; The 1950 Canadian Touring Team; Cardiff City; The Corinthians; Coventry City; Derby County; An FA XI; Huddersfield Town; Leicester City; Northampton Town; Portsmouth; Preston North End; Southampton; Swindon Town; Wimbledon; The England 1950 World Cup Team

15 **Despite never having won either the League Championship or the FA Cup, Leicester City won the 1971 Charity Shield. How come?**

---

1 **League Champions versus FA Cup winners** 2 1908 3 40 4 **Liverpool** (18 times) 5 **1974** 6 11 times 7 **The trophy was shared for six months each** 8 Shield decided on penalties 9 **Liverpool** 10 Leeds United 11 **Leeds were champions; Liverpool were the Cup winners** 12 Manchester United in 1993 13 **Arsenal** 14 They have all appeared in only one Shield 15 Arsenal won the double that year, so the Shield was contested between Liverpool, the Cup runners-up and Leicester City, Division Two champions

 Quiz 2   FA Charity Shield

1   What was the highest score in a Charity Shield?

2   Which team appeared in four consecutive Shields in the years 1933-36, winning twice and losing twice?

3   Which two teams played each other in four consecutive Charity Shields in the years 1923-26, each winning it twice?

4   Which team won the Charity Shield four times running between 1984 and 1987?

5   Which two internationals were sent off in the 1974 match?

6   Name the three teams that have shared the trophy but never won it outright.

7   For various reasons, the Charity Shield has not always been between the Champions and the Cup winners. Of the times that these two teams have played each other, how many times have the Champions won the trophy outright?

8   How many times have the Cup winners won it outright?

9   What was unique about the first Charity Shield match, a 1-1 draw between Manchester United and Queen's Park Rangers?

10 When Tottenham Hotspur became the first modern team to win the double in 1961, who did they push and overrun in the Charity Shield?

11 There have to date there have been only two 0-0 draws, in 1977 and 1991. Which teams were involved?

12 In 1996, Manchester United won the double. Why were Newcastle United chosen to play them in the Charity Shield?

13 Who won the Charity Shield in 1938 and then again in 1948, the next time it was played, thus becoming the longest-ever holders of the trophy?

14 What is the common link between Blackpool, Bolton Wanderers, Brighton and Hove Albion, Cardiff, Coventry City, Derby County, Huddersfield Town, Leicester City, Northampton Town, Portsmouth, Preston North End, Southampton, Swindon Town and Wimbledon?

15 Who were the first Cup winners to win the Charity Shield?

 # Quiz 1   **Fanzines**

Which club would you probably support if you spent good money on the following fanzines:

1 **'Thorne In The Side' and 'Beesotted'?**

2 'The Hanging Sheep', 'The Square Ball', 'Till The World Stops' and 'To Ell And Back'?

3 **'Brian Moore's Head Looks Uncannily Like London Planetarium' and 'Light At The End of The Tunnel'?**

4 'A Love Supreme' and 'It's The Hope I Can't Stand'?

5 **'A Load of Cobbolds', 'Dribble', 'Without A Care In The World' and 'Those Were The Days'?**

6 'On A Mission', 'Over Land And Sea', 'The Water In Majorca' and 'The Ultimate Dream'?

7 **'Cheat!', 'Spitting Feathers', 'The Blue And White Wizard' and 'War of the Monster Trucks'?**

8 'Pie Muncher' and 'The Silence Of The Lamb'?

9 **'The Mag' and 'The Number Nine'?**

10 'The 69er' and 'Randy Robin'?

11 **'Liverpool Are On The Tele Again', 'Ferry Across The Wensum', 'I Can Drive A Tractor!', 'Cheep Shot' and 'Love Shaq'?**

12 'Loadsamoney' and '4,000 Holes'?

13 **'The Tricky Tree' and 'Garibaldi'?**

14 'Rub Of The Greens' and 'Hoof!'?

15 **'Blazing Saddlers' and 'Moving Swiftly On'?**

 # Quiz 2 **Fanzines**

Which club would you probably support if you spent good money on the following fanzines:

1 **'When You're Smiling' and 'Where's The Money Gone?'**

2 'One More Point' and 'Eastern Eagles'?

3 **'Hanging On The Telephone' and 'A Slice of Kilner Pie'?**

4 'Our Days Are Numbered' and 'All Day And All Of The Night'?

5 **'Sour Grapes', 'Hoof The Ball Up!' and 'Route One'?**

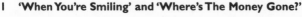

6 'Fly Me To The Moon' and 'The Boys From Brazil'?

7 **'Greasy Chip Buttie' and 'The Red And White Wizaaard'?**

8 'Kicker Conspiracy' and 'Bob Lord's Sausage'?

9 **'Deranged Ferret' and 'The Yellow Belly'?**

10 'Follow The Yellow Brick Road' and 'Iffy Haircut - The Journal'?

11 **'Exceedingly Good Pies' and 'The Dale Blues'?**

12 'All Quiet On The Western Avenue' and 'A Kick Up The Rs'?

13 **'And Smith Must Score'?**

14 'Grorty Dick'?

15 **'One Nil Down Two One Up'?**

Quiz 3

Fanzines

Which club would you probably support if you spent good money on the following fanzines:

1 **'Speke From The Harbour' and 'When Skies Are Grey'?**

2 'No One Likes Us', 'Tales From Senegal Fields' and 'The Lion Roars'?

3 **'The Holy Trinity' and 'Witton Wisdom'?**

4 'White Love'?

5 **'Sing When We're Fishing'?**

6 'Come In No 7 - Your Time Is Up' and 'The Cider'ed'?

7 **'Rage On' and 'Yellow Fever'?**

8 'The Small Heathen'?

9 **'The Ugly Inside'?**

10 'The Seadog Bites Back!'?

11 **'The Hatchet'?**

12 'The Adams Family'?

13 **'Better Red Than Dead'?**

14 'The Sheeping Giant'?

15 **'What A Load of Cobblers'?**

 # Quiz 1   **Fathers and Sons**

Identify the following family firms:

1 **Father and son played for the same club and have the same first name. Dad played twice for England, against Yugoslavia in 1973 and Australia in 1980. Son made England B debut in 1998 v Chile.**

2 Dad played for a London club and later, after ten years picking Cherries, returned to manage it. Son was a Cherry who got thrown into a bigger Pool.

3 **From 1958-1973, Dad played for seven clubs, including Chelsea. Son played for Rangers and 32 times for England (1984-92).**

4 Son played for Southend and Cambridge between 1981 and 1984. Dad scored 220 goals for Spurs and played 57 times for England.

5 **Dad was with Colchester when he hung up his gloves in 1982. Son plays for Spurs and made his England debut against Italy in 1998.**

6 Dad played for Scunthorpe, Liverpool, Tottenham Hotspur and 61 times for England. Son broke into the Spurs first team during the 1997-98 season.

7 **Dad played for Derby, Forest and 43 times for Scotland. Son plays for Forest and made his Scotland debut against Japan in 1995.**

8 An elegant defender, Dad won 27 England caps while with Derby County between 1972 and 1977. Son plays for the club his father currently manages.

9 **The father is the only man to have managed the Champions on both sides of the border. The son now plays for Wolves.**

10 Dad is Scotland's most capped player; Son is currently on loan from Dad's present club to Bury.

11 **Dad was a nine-club man who later managed Wimbledon to their 1988 FA Cup triumph. Son keeps goal for Celtic.**

12 Dad played for Middlesbrough and Sunderland and twice for England in 1962. Son started at Forest and won 14 England caps.

13 **Dad scored 27 goals for Spurs in their double year. Two of his sons played football, and one was 1987 PFA Player of the Year.**

14 Both achieved fame with Manchester City, Dad as a wing half in the '50s, Son on the wing in the '70s. Son was capped 22 times by England.

15 **Dad played for Liverpool and was later their chief scout. Son played for Preston and Bristol Rovers between 1983 and 1993. Both have the same name.**

Senior and Junior

1 **Frank Lampard Senior and Junior** 2 Harry and Jamie Redknapp 3 **Tony and Mark Hateley** 4 Danny and Jimmy Greaves 5 **Mike and Ian Walker** 6 Ray and Stephen Clemence 7 **Archie and Scott Gemmill** 8 Colin and Andy Todd 9 **Alex and Darren Ferguson** 10 Kenny and Paul Dalglish 11 **Bobby and Jonathan Gould** 12 Brian and Nigel Clough 13 **Les and Clive and Bradley Allen** 14 Ken and Peter Barnes 15 **Geoff Twentyman**

Quiz 1

Football Rules, OK?

1 **What is the maximum length of a soccer pitch?**

2 What is the maximum width of a soccer pitch?

3 **What is the minimum length of a soccer pitch?**

4 What is the minimum width of a soccer pitch?

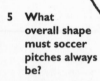

5 **What overall shape must soccer pitches always be?**

6 What must be the radius of the centre circle?

7 **How high must the goals be?**

8 How wide must the goals be?

9 **Must the goalposts be rounded?**

10 What should be the minimum height of the corner flags?

11 **Measured along the goal line, what must be the distance from the inside of the goalpost to the edge of the six yard area?**

12 What are the dimensions of the penalty area?

13 **Measured along the goal line, what must be the distance from the edge of the six yard box to the nearest edge of the penalty area?**

14 Is an offence committed on the line inside or outside the penalty area?

15 **How far must the penalty spot be from the goal line?**

1 **130 yards** 2 100 yards 3 **100 yards** 4 50 yards 5 **Oblong - the length must always exceed the width** 6 10 yards 7 **8 feet** 8 8 yards 9 **No - they may also be square, elliptical or rectangular** 10 At least 5 feet 11 **6 yards** 12 18 yards into the field by 44 yards along the goal line 13 **12 yards** 14 Inside 15 **12 yards**

Quiz 2

Football Rules, OK?

1 **What must be the radius of the semi-circle in front of the corner flag?**

2 What is the significance of the semi-circle at the edge of the penalty area?

3 **A penalty taker slips and kicks the ball only a yard. One of his team mates runs into the area and puts the ball in the net. Is this a goal?**

4 A penalty taker slips and kicks the ball only a yard. He recovers quickly and kicks the ball into the net himself. Is this a goal?

5 **Can a substitute be brought on to take a penalty?**

6 What should happen if the penalty taker hits the referee and the ball rebounds into the goal?

7 **Does the goalkeeper need to be told which of the opposing side will take the penalty?**

8 A penalty kick hits the post and the ball rebounds to the penalty taker who then puts it into the net. Is this a goal?

9 **In a penalty shoot-out, which team takes the first kick?**

10 Which end is used?

11 **Where, in general, must all 20 players other than the penalty taker and the defending goalkeeper stand?**

12 Which player might be excepted?

13 **Where might he stand?**

14 In which year was a penalty shoot-out first used to settle a first-class match in England?

15 **What is the minimum number of goals required to win a penalty shoot-out?**

1 **One yard** 2 It marks a radius of 10 yards from the penalty spot. At a penalty kick, all players apart from the taker must be outside it 3 **Yes** 4 No 5 **Yes** 6 The kick should be retaken 7 **Yes** 8 No: the penalty taker is offside 9 **The team that wins the toss** 10 Whichever the referee wants 11 **In the centre circle** 12 The other goalkeeper 13 **Outside the penalty area, out of the line of sight of the goalkeeper facing the penalty** 14 1970 15 **Three**

 ## Quiz 3   **Football Rules, OK?**

1   **What is the maximum permitted width of a touch-line marking?**

2   What must be the circumference of a football?

3   **What must a football weigh?**

4   To what pressure - in atmospheres - must the ball be inflated?

5   **At the kick-off, what should the referee do if the player who takes it then kicks it again before anyone else?**

6   Does it count if the ball goes straight into the goal from a throw-in?

7   **Can a goal be scored direct from a goal kick?**

8   Can a defender taking a free kick score an own goal?

9   **What is the punishment for offside?**

10   How does the referee indicate such a kick?

11   **For how long should he do this?**

12   Where should a free kick for offside be taken from if the offence is committed outside the penalty area?

13   **Where should a free kick be taken for offside if the offence is committed inside the penalty area?**

14   Must a goal kick be taken from the same side of the goal as that on which the ball went out of play?

15   **What action should the referee take if a player handles the ball unintentionally but derives an advantage from it?**

---

1 5 inches 2 27-27.5 inches **3 14.5-16 ounces** 4 0.6-1.1 atmospheres **5 Award an indirect free kick to the opposition** 6 No 7 **No** 8 No 9 An indirect free kick to the opposition 10 By holding his arm up vertically **11 Until the ball has gone out of play or another player has touched it** 12 From the spot on which the player was judged when standing when judged to be offside **13 Anywhere in the penalty area** 14 Not any more: in the interests of keeping the game moving, it is now permissible to take the goal kick from anywhere on the six-yard line **15 He should wave play on: the nub of the handball rule is intention**

Quiz 4 — Football Rules, OK?

1. What should the referee do if a goalkeeper handles a ball from a backpass from the foot of one of his fellow team members?

2. Is a goalkeeper who dribbles the ball around his area wasting time according to the rules?

3. What should the referee do if a defender deliberately handles the ball in a successful attempt to deny an obvious goalscoring opportunity?

4. What should the referee do if a defender deliberately handles the ball in an unsuccessful attempt to deny an obvious goalscoring opportunity, and the ball goes into the net?

5. What should the referee do if he hears a player shout 'my ball' or 'mine' in a way which might distract or mislead an opponent?

6. What should the referee do if a player dissents from a decision while the ball is still in play?

7. One player hits another, who hits him back. The referee sends them both off. How should play be restarted?

8. Can a player be cautioned or sent off for misconduct during half time?

9. A player punches an opponent in his own penalty area while the play is at the other end of the field. What should the referee do?

10. What is the penalty for a foul throw?

11. What happens if the ball does not enter the field of play after a throw-in?

12. What should the referee do if a throw-in goes straight into the opponent's goal?

13. What should the referee do if a throw-in goes straight into the thrower's own goal?

14. What should the referee award if a player takes a throw-in and then kicks it himself before anyone else has touched it?

15. What should the referee do if a properly taken throw-in goes straight back out of play further along the touchline?

---

1 Award an indirect free kick to the opposition 2 No: he is wasting time only if he picks it up and holds it for too long 3 Send the offending player off and award a penalty or direct free kick to the opposition 4 Award the goal and caution the offending player 5 Award an indirect free kick to the opposition; if it is thought to have been done with the intention of putting the opponent off, the offender should also be cautioned 6 Stop the game, caution the player, then award an indirect free kick to the opposition from the place where the offence took place 7 With an indirect free kick to the side of the player who suffered the first blow 8 Yes 9 Award a penalty 10 Awarding the throw in to the other side 11 Retake the throw 12 Award a goal kick 13 Award a corner 14 Award an indirect free kick to the opposition from the place where the player kicked the ball 15 Award a throw-in to the opposition

Quiz 1   Formerly Known As...

Which English League teams were originally known by the following names:

1 **Abbey United?**

2 Ardwick?

3 **Belmont?**

4 Boscombe St Johns?

5 **Christ Church FC?**

6 Dial Square?

7 **Headington?**

8 Heaton Norris Rovers?

9 **New Brompton?**

10 Newton Heath?

11 **Pine Villa?**

12 Purdown Poachers?

13 **Riverside?**

14 Shaddongate United?

15 **Singers FC?**

BORING, BORING DIAL SQUARE!

1 **Cambridge United** 2 Manchester City 3 **Tranmere Rovers** 4 AFC Bournemouth
5 **Bolton Wanderers** 6 Arsenal 7 **Oxford United** 8 Stockport County 9 **Gillingham**
10 Manchester United 11 **Oldham Athletic** 12 Bristol Rovers 13 **Cardiff City**
14 Carlisle United 15 **Coventry City**

 ## Quiz 2   **Formerly Known As...**

Which English League teams were originally known by the following names:

1 **Small Heath Alliance?**

2 St Domingo?

3 **St Jude's?**

4 St Luke's, Blakenhall?

5 **Thames Ironworks?**

6 West Herts?

7 **The Black Arabs?**

8 Glyn FC?

9 **Stanley?**

10 Thornhill United?

11 **When did Swansea cease to be a Town and become a City?**

12 Who began as Rovers, tried their hand at being Athletic, but ended up just plain FC?

13 **To what did the English League Cup change its name in 1986-87?**

14 And to what did this name change in 1990-91?

15 **And as what has the League Cup been known since 1992-93?**

 ## Quiz 1

Great Quote, Barry

Who said:

1 'I'm the best goalkeeper in the country - it's the towns I have trouble in'?

2 'The moment I saw Middlesbrough I felt it was a strange, terrible place. I had never seen anything like it. It seemed so dark and quiet outside and it was always windy or raining'?

3 'We've signed five foreigners over the summer. But I'll be on hand to learn them a bit of English'?

4 'If we played the team of '68, we'd beat them 10-0'?

5 'The only thing that's ten times better about the current United team is their salaries'?

6 'I realise now that computer games have affected my performance badly'?

7 'I'm not a believer in luck, but I do believe you need it'?

8 'If you want someone to track back as well as do what I do, he would cost about £25 million'?

9 'If history is going to repeat itself, I should think we can expect the same thing again'?

10 'I've only taken one penalty before - for Crystal Palace. It was 2-2 in the 90th minute. I hit the post and we went down that year'?

11 'The Bosman ruling doesn't affect me. I don't have any trouble losing money on transfer fees'?

12 'English football can end the millennium as it started it - as the greatest football nation in the world'?

13 'A goalkeeper is a goalkeeper because he can't play football'?

14 'The trouble is he speaks about as much English as I do'?

15 And who suggested to whom that he would get into the England team if he let his hair grow?

 # Quiz 2

Great Quote, Barry

Who said:

1   After scoring six times on his debut for Newcastle United in their 13-0 defeat of Newport County: 'And they were lucky to get nil'?

2   'We don't need people like Vinnie Jones who is just a self-hyped personality - fine for him, but he isn't a good player and no benefit to the game'?

3   '[Lineker] has the charisma of a jellyfish - a jellyfish without a sting'?

4   'You've beaten them once. Now go out and bloody beat them again'?

5   'He [Diego Maradona] is the best one-footed player since Puskas'?

6   'They [Osvaldo Ardiles and Ricardo Villa] can't expect not to be tackled just because Argentina won the World Cup'?

7   'I've got a little black book in which I keep the names of all the players I've got to get before I pack up playing. If I get half a chance they will finish up over the touchline'?

8   'Say nowt, win it, then talk your head off'?

9   'Then my eyesight started to go and I took up refereeing'?

10 'I am amazed by how many vultures there are out there trying to peck my eyes out'?

11 'The last player to score a hat trick in the Cup Final was Stan Mortensen. He even had a Final named after him - the Matthews Final'?

12 'A penalty is a cowardly way to score'?

13 'Football is the opera of the people'?

14 'I was born close to Dracula's castle but I'm no relation. I just like scaring defences'?

15 'Do I not like that'?

 # Quiz 1   Guess Who?

1 **Former Northern Ireland international and European Cup winner, later a Coca-Cola Cup winning manager, whose wife told him: 'Your ego will always be bigger than your bank balance'.**

2 Arsenal captain, 1950 footballer of the year, who briefly managed England for a short and glorious period in 1974, between Sir Alf Ramsey and Don Revie.

3 **Norwegian international bought from Bayern Munich to replace Larry Lloyd, but played only 20 games for Forest in 1980-81.**

4 The successor to Sir Stanley Rous, who took over as President of FIFA just before the 1974 World Cup.

5 **Scottish international defender who played for both Arsenal and Tottenham Hotspur under Terry Neill in the 1970s.**

6 A Tottenham Hotspur player from 1968 to 1979, when his career ended he became assistant manager at White Hart Lane. After getting the sack there, he later took up a coaching job in Nigeria.

7 **Sunderland hero who saved them from Leeds United on an unforgettable summer afternoon in 1973.**

8 For a time in the '70s, the only regular Liverpool first team player who was not a full international. He later played for Southampton and managed Brighton and Hove Albion.

9 **Scorer of the goal that took the FA Cup to Coventry for the first time in 1987.**

10 European Cup winner and Aston Villa captain who played more than 700 matches in a career that began in 1969 and ended in 1984.

11 **Munich air crash survivor who played on until 1966 then went to run a hotel in his native Northern Ireland.**

12 Glaswegian hardman who started at Birmingham City but really made his name under Brian Clough at Nottingham Forest in the late '70s.

13 **Goalkeeper capped seven times by Scotland while at Kilmarnock then bought by West Ham United. Later emigrated to Australia.**

14 Promotion-winning Bradford City manager at the time of the disastrous fire in the stand there in 1985, this defender started at Huddersfield Town in 1966 then moved to Leeds United, with whom he won 27 caps for England.

15 **Ron Atkinson protege who emerged from the big man's shadow to manage Hereford United in 1972, the year they won election to the Football League.**

 **Quiz 2**

Guess Who?

1 Capped 10 times by England as a semi-pro, he later managed Wimbledon, Watford, Sheffield United and Nottingham Forest.

2 Began in 1969 at Hull City; moved to Manchester United in 1974; won 15 England caps; moved to West Ham in time for their 1980 FA Cup victory.

3 **Midfielder who joined Liverpool from Manchester University; won FA Cup, League Championship and UEFA Cup medals at Anfield; later played for Plymouth Argyle and Burnley; retired in 1979.**

4 Attacking midfielder who played five times for Scotland, he started at Chelsea in 1964, then moved to Sheffield Wednesday, Wolves, Manchester United, Southampton and Lincoln City, where he was player coach in 1978.

5 **Joined Manchester City from Leeds Polytechnic in 1975; made 350 appearances at Maine Road before moving to Everton, where he won a League Championship medal; retired in 1987.**

6 Inside forward with Reading from 1958 to 1965. Later drove a taxi, coached QPR, and twice managed Spurs (1984-86 and 1991-92).

7 **Seventies Chelsea defender who also played for Derby, QPR (two spells) and Crystal Palace before returning to Stamford Bridge, where he ended his career in 1987.**

8 Winner of 63 international caps for Northern Ireland and the scorer of the goal that beat host nation Spain in the 1982 World Cup finals.

9 **England youth winger who played League football for Fulham, Forest and Portsmouth between 1953 and 1966. Coached Portsmouth before being appointed manager of Aston Villa in 1982, the year they won the European Cup. Died in August 1993.**

10 Don't be misled by the Polish surname, the eight international caps won by this West Bromwich Albion and Huddersfield Town midfielder between 1970 and 1972 were for Wales.

11 **1964 Cup Winners' Cup winner with West Ham, this full back moved to South Africa in 1974 as player coach of Durban City.**

12 Birdwatcher who kept goal for Arsenal and Everton and won four caps for Scotland between 1979 and 1982.

13 **Central defender who made his name with Crystal Palace, then moved to Southampton where he won an FA Cup winner's medal.**

14 Eccentric goalkeeper bought by Chelsea from Partizan Belgrade in 1978. Left London in 1981 to run a controversial duty free shop in his native Yugoslavia.

15 **Oldham Athletic wing half of the 1940s who married actress Dora Bryan.**

Quiz 3

Guess Who?

1   Everton defensive stalwart also played for Sheffield Wednesday and Grimsby Town between 1970 and 1986. Later managed Grimsby, then went to coach the national team of Brunei.

2   Played for Sunderland and Peterborough, which he also managed (1983-86), but was most famous during his 500 appearances for West Brom.

3   The holder of the record for the number of goals scored in an FA Cup match - nine for Bournemouth against Margate in 1971-72.

4   Bolton Wanderers defender who also played for seven other clubs in a career that began in 1973 and ended in 1989. Manager of Blackpool from 1994-96.

5   Charlton and Leicester winger between 1962 and 1975 who later managed Harlow Town and a pub in Kibworth, Leics.

6   Played more than 400 games for Wolverhampton Wanderers between 1973 and 1986, as well as a few for Burnley. Later became a constable in the West Midlands police.

7   Dundee striker who moved to Spurs in the early '60s. Played 22 times for Scotland. Retired in 1973, then spent time in South Africa before returning to England to go into the haulage business.

8   Bearded striker who scored 148 goals in 312 League appearances for Luton, Charlton, Derby, West Ham and Gillingham between 1972 and 1985.

9   Former Bournemouth and Norwich City player who was sold to Manchester City in 1980 for £1.25 million. Played twice for England in the same year. Finished his career at Burnley.

10   Oxford United defender for much of the '80s who ended his playing career at Barnsley in 1995 and then became their reserve team coach.

11   Played a record number of games (671) for Blackburn Rovers between 1970 and 1986. Later coach at Newcastle United and back at Ewood Park.

12   Norwich player who retired in 1977 and then managed Manchester City (1987-89), Barnsley (1989-93) and went to Bournemouth in August 1994.

13   Charlton Athletic's amazing signing from Barcelona in 1982 who later became the manager of the Faroe Islands.

14   Norwich City goalkeeper of the 1960s who retired in 1979 and went to sell contact lenses in Florida.

15   Middlesbrough and Southampton midfielder. Played three times for England between 1980 and 1984, but many thought he might have won more caps if his premature baldness hadn't made him look older than his years.

1 Mick Lyons 2 John Wile 3 Ted MacDougall 4 Sam Allardyce 5 Len Glover
6 Geoff Palmer 7 Alan Gilzean 8 Derek Hales 9 Kevin Reeves 10 Malcolm Shotton
11 Derek Fazackerley 12 Mel Machin 13 Allan Simonsen 14 Kevin Keelan
15 David Armstrong

 # Quiz 4

Guess Who?

1 'Wee' left winger who played over 500 times for Arsenal in the 1960s before moving on to Leicester City in 1977.

2 A doctor of medicine who played for Arsenal and Brentford between 1945 and 1949 and represented Ireland at both football and rugby union.

3 A good luck charm as much as a player, this right back won 50 caps for Ireland while at Shamrock Rovers, Chelsea, Palace and WBA.

4 A League Cup winner with Stoke City in 1972, this player won four England caps in 1974. He retired in 1979 then coached in Kuwait and managed Chester City from 1994 to 1995.

5 A playing career which began at Morton in 1975 and ended at Reading in 1993 was less noteworthy than his times as a manager - taking over at Leicester in 1994, he controversially left Filbert Street in December 1995 for Wolves.

6 A Manchester United player from 1968 to 1971, he later returned to his native Italy where he won a Cup winner's medal with Bologna in 1974.

7 A scouser who went to the London School of Economics and then signed for Fulham in 1972. Played in the 1975 FA Cup Final, then moved to Spurs in 1978 before ending his career at Palace in 1983.

8 African Leeds United winger with a Nordic name who in 1965 became the first black player in an FA Cup Final. Died in 1995.

9 After scoring 44 goals in a season for Bradford Park Avenue, they sold him for £40,000 to Derby County, with whom he won two Championship medals. Retired in 1981 and became a postman.

10 After starting at Dundee United in 1975, he moved to West Ham United, where he was nicknamed 'Tonker'. Capped 10 times by Scotland.

11 An identical twin, a former England Under-23 international who played over 250 games for QPR and Spurs before retiring in 1971 at the age of 25. Later a community officer at West Ham United.

12 Arsenal and Leicester City midfielder who played from 1962 to 1977. Later became a driving instructor in Leicestershire.

13 Arsenal double-winner who won 17 England caps and also played for Liverpool, Swansea and Hartlepool. Now suffers from Parkinson's disease.

14 Arsenal player who later became Finance Minister of Iceland.

15 Attacking full back for Leeds and England who managed Bristol City (1982-88), Exeter (1988-91) and Birmingham (1991-93). Returned to Exeter in 1994, but resigned the following year because of ill health.

 Quiz 5   **Guess Who?**

1 **Attacking player who never quite made it at Tottenham Hotspur so moved to Millwall, where he became a legend. Emigrated to Canada in 1977, where he played for Vancouver Whitecaps.**

2 Attacking West Brom left back who won three England caps in 1983.

3 **Began and ended at Orient, his finest hour was at QPR, for whom he played in the 1982 FA Cup Final. Manager of Watford from 1993 to 1996, later a scout for England coach Glenn Hoddle.**

4 Blackburn Rovers, Everton and Burnley full back who played 27 times for England between 1966 and 1970.

5 **Blond winger who was the only Birmingham-born player in Aston Villa's 1981 Championship- and 1982 European Cup-winning sides.**

6 Booked 60 times in his career, this player began at Birmingham City in 1978 and ended at Crystal Palace in 1990. His golden period was at Southampton.

7 **Britain's first million pound footballer.**

8 Burnley and Bristol City centre half between 1964 and 1971 who became Southampton manager in 1995 after the departure of Alan Ball but lost the job the following year on the arrival of Graeme Souness.

9 **Capped 43 times by Northern Ireland, this striker scored 219 goals in 532 League games between 1957 and 1974. He played for six clubs, but his greatest times were at Molineux, where he later became Chairman and Chief Executive.**

10 Capped 56 times by Northern Ireland, he played for Sunderland, Luton Town, Everton and Port Vale between 1950 and 1964. Everton manager 1973-77.

11 **Captain of Southampton when they won the FA Cup in 1976, the year a knee injury forced him to retire.**

12 Celtic goalkeeper in the year they won the European Cup, he won his first Scotland cap at the age of 36. Later sat on the Pools Panel.

13 **Celtic's leading post-war scorer with 273 goals. One of the 1967 Lions of Lisbon. Awarded the MBE.**

14 Centre half who won an FA Cup winner's medal with Newcastle United in 1955 and then managed Sunderland when they won the trophy in 1973. Managed Bury in 1977-78.

15 **Chelsea's all-time leading scorer, he played for them from 1958 to 1973 before moving to Crystal Palace. Retired in 1973 and later went bankrupt.**

Quiz 6

Guess Who?

1　**Clyde, Aberdeen, Tottenham Hotspur, Barcelona, Blackburn Rovers and Reading striker who played 27 times for Scotland. Later became manager of East Fife, but left in 1996.**

2　Coventry City and Hereford United goalkeeper whose career was curtailed by illness. Presented BBC television sports programmes for a while; now widely ridiculed for his religious beliefs.

3　**Danish international who came to Manchester United from Ajax in 1984. Retired in 1988 and settled in Cheshire.**

4　Defender who was Manchester United's Player of the Year in 1973-74, the season they were relegated. Retired in 1982 and became a publican in Coventry. Died in 1993.

5　**Defender who won the European Cup Winners' Cup with Aberdeen and played once for Scotland before moving south to Chelsea.**

6　Despite having played for England, he was dropped by Chelsea manager Tommy Docherty to make room for Peter Osgood. Moved on to Birmingham City, Queen's Park Rangers, Millwall and Brighton and Hove Albion but never quite recovered from the earlier setback. Retired in 1973.

7　**Doncaster Rovers stalwart from 1949-58 who later became a well-loved television comedian.**

8　Double-winning captain of Arsenal who later managed Leicester City (1977-78), coached at Queen's Park Rangers and managed Brentford (1984-87).

9　**Dundee, Arsenal, Manchester United and St Mirren defender from 1953 to 1973. Later managed Stirling Albion, coached in Iceland and then became a prison social worker.**

10　Eight years a Sunderland left back in the 1970s, he moved to Middlesbrough in 1981 and is now a Sheffield-based lorry driver.

11　**Eldest of three footballing brothers, a goalkeeper for Birmingham City and Bury who later became a cemetery curator.**

12　England international goalkeeper who now works as a sports presenter on South African television.

13　**Ever-present goalkeeper in both Derby County's Championship-winning sides (1971-72 and 1974-75).**

14　Everton and Wales goalkeeper who also played for Swansea City, Wrexham and Tranmere Rovers in a career that ended in 1983. Later ran a natural healing centre in Llangollen, Wales.

15　**FA Cup finalist with Sheffield Wednesday in 1966 who retired in 1980 and later ran a pub close to the Hillsborough ground.**

1 **Steve Archibald** 2 David Icke 3 **Jesper Olsen** 4 Jim Holton 5 **Doug Rougvie** 6 Barry Bridges 7 **Charlie Williams** 8 Frank McLintock 9 **Ian Ure** 10 Joe Bolton 11 **Dave Latchford** 12 Gary Bailey 13 **Colin Boulton** 14 Dai Davies 15 **Graham Pugh**

 Quiz 7   **Guess Who?**

1   **For 10 years the regular keeper for Middlesbrough and Northern Ireland, he retired in 1982 and managed Darlington in 1995-96.**

2   Former Reading player who scored the winner for Wimbledon in the 1988 FA Cup Final.

3   **The Fulham keeper in the 1975 FA Cup Final, he now coaches in the USA.**

4   Hearts and Rangers star of 1965-82 and the holder of the record number of Scottish League appearances.

5   **His goal for Arsenal in 1971 was the first ever scored by a substitute in an FA Cup Final.**

6   His playing career began at Sheffield United in 1975 and took in Oldham Athletic, Queen's Park Rangers, Sheffield Wednesday, Aston Villa, Stoke City and Strasbourg. After retiring in 1988, he became manager of Ayr United.

7   **In a career spanning the years 1962-79, this defender played 745 games for Leeds United and three times for England. Later moved to Bradford City.**

8   In a career that began in 1962 and ended in 1976, he played for Huddersfield Town, Carlisle United, Torquay United, Bristol Rovers and Bournemouth. Became manager of Port Vale in March 1984, a post he still held in 1998.

9   **Ipswich Town and Arsenal midfielder who played in three successive FA Cup finals and was capped six times by England between 1977 and 1980. Managed West Bromwich Albion, then Aldershot, then Hibernians of Malta.**

10   Leading scorer for Leeds United in 1976, famously photographed jumping over a mini 'because he could'.

11   **Leeds United and Birmingham City goalkeeper who won 37 caps for Wales between 1964 and 1975.**

12   Leicester City, Grimsby Town, Charlton Athletic and Middlesbrough player from 1978 to 1992 who later managed Ayssriska in Sweden and then came home to join the police force.

13   **Made 400 League appearances and played in the 1975 FA Cup for Fulham. Ended his career in 1977 at Millwall and later ran Magdalen Florists in Earlsfield, London SW.**

14   Made 595 appearances for Scunthorpe (1950-65) and was described by Bill Shankly as the best full back never to have played for England.

15   **Made over 200 League appearances for Spurs between 1935 and 1948. Then became manager of West Bromwich Albion, who came second in the First Division and won the FA Cup in his first season.**

1 Jim Platt 2 Lawrie Sanchez **3 Peter Mellor** 4 Sandy Jardine **5 Eddie Kelly** 6 Simon Stainrod **7 Paul Reaney** 8 John Rudge **9 Brian Talbot** 10 Duncan McKenzie **11 Gary Sprake** 12 Andy Peake **13 Les Barrett** 14 Jack Brownsword **15 Vic Buckingham**

 **Quiz 8**   **Guess Who?**

1 Manchester City and England winger who also played for Swindon, Burnley, Blackpool and Stockport. Retired in 1979 and now makes shirts for the stars.

2 Manchester City player of the late '70s who went to Oldham, returned to Maine Road, then went on to Bury and Shrewsbury. Retiring in 1990, he was manager of Limerick for a while, but has since become a driving instructor.

3 **Manchester United and Everton shooting star who was forced to retire through injury in 1990 at the age of 26. The winner of 38 caps for Northern Ireland, he is now a qualified chiropedist.**

4 Manchester United player who won two England caps between 1960 and 1962. Ended his career at Stoke City in 1967; later emigrated to the USA, where he runs soccer camps in Florida.

5 **Millwall winger who went on to win six England caps and an FA Cup winners' medal with Manchester United in 1977.**

6 South African who swapped the Veld for the Valley, playing for Charlton and then managing them (1967-70). Later coached in New York-New Jersey.

7 **Newcastle United and Middlesbrough right back who played from 1970 to 1985 then became a horse breeder.**

8 Newcastle player who managed Carlisle, Hearts and Plymouth. A dedicated sailor who has taken part in the Fastnet race and crossed the Atlantic.

9 **Newport, Oxford, Liverpool and Tranmere striker who scored nearly 400 goals in his career. After winning 69 caps for Ireland, he became manager of Tranmere in April 1996.**

10 Nigerian international who played 20 League games for Orient between 1977-81. Now a London bus driver.

11 **Nigerian international who started his League career at Orient in 1976, then played for Notts County and Spurs. Now runs a bouncy castle company in Hampshire.**

12 Nottingham Forest striker for whom Manchester United paid £1.25 million in 1980. Now a fishmonger in Grimsby.

13 **Britain's most expensive player when West Brom manager Ron Atkinson bought him from Middlesbrough for £516,000 in 1979.**

14 Played 269 games for Liverpool between 1955 and 1971 and then managed Brighton and Hove Albion in the year they reached the FA Cup Final.

15 **Played for Arsenal, Nottingham Forest and Sheffield United in a career that began in 1956 and ended in 1970. Later managed Peterborough United (1977-78), Wolverhampton Wanderers (1978-81) and Northampton Town (1993-95).**

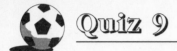 **Quiz 9**   **Guess Who?**

1 Played for Liverpool and Everton between 1957 and 1972, then moved to Oldham, where his career was cut short by injury.

2 Played for Plymouth, Everton, Portsmouth and Torquay from 1962 to 1972 and scored two goals in the 1966 FA Cup Final. Later emigrated to Australia.

3 Played for River Plate in Buenos Aires before signing for Sheffield United in 1978. Then went to Leeds United before returning to his native Argentina in 1980.

4 Played more than 400 games for West Brom and won five England caps. Retired in 1961 and later managed Wolves, Athletic Bilbao, Sporting Lisbon, Walsall, West Brom and Panathinaikos.

5 Played one game for Liverpool in 1953 then almost 300 for Workington Town. Manager of Tottenham Hotspur from 1976-84.

6 Played only 31 games for West Ham between 1959 and 1962, but later became one of their most successful managers. Sacked in 1989, then went to Ipswich Town, which he managed until 1994.

7 Played over 500 League games between 1967 and 1982 for Cardiff, Aston Villa, Swansea, Charlton and Exeter. Won 58 caps for Wales.

8 Player-manager of Marlow when they knocked his previous club Chelsea out of the FA Cup in 1995.

9 Plymouth Argyle, Arsenal, Crystal Palace, West Bromwich Albion, Stoke City, Queen's Park Rangers and Reading goalkeeper between 1976 and 1986. Now a fitness consultant in the West Midlands.

10 Prolific Portsmouth striker who managed Aston Villa from 1974 to 1982.

11 Rangers legend who played only one game for Chelsea after his £35,000 transfer to London in 1983. Later returned to Scotland where he became manager of Partick Thistle.

12 Republic of Ireland international who played for Fulham, Chelsea and Philadelphia Furies in a career that lasted from 1954 to 1975.

13 Right back who played over 300 league games for Sheffield Wednesday, Doncaster rovers and Lincoln City between 1965 and 1977. Later managed Reading (1984-89), Southampton (1991-94) and Fulham (1994-96).

14 Said by some Sunderland supporters to be their best ever player, this man won 40 caps for the Republic of Ireland between 1957 and 1969.

15 Scored 43 goals in 112 League appearances for Chelsea between 1968 and 1975. Best remembered for his long throw-ins.

15 Ian Hutchinson
11 Derek Johnstone 12 John Dempsey 13 Ian Branfoot 14 Charlie Hurley
6 John Lyall 7 Leighton Phillips 8 Peter Rhodes-Brown 9 Paul Barron 10 Ron Saunders
1 John Morrissey 2 Mike Trebilcock 3 Alex Sabella 4 Ronnie Allen 5 Keith Burkinshaw

 Quiz 10   **Guess Who?**

1 **Scored for Spurs in their 1967 FA Cup Final victory over Chelsea and was capped once by Scotland against Wales in 1965.**

2 Scorer of the only goal in the 1978 FA Cup Final, this Ipswich Town stalwart later drove a lorry for his family fruit and vegetable firm.

3 **Scorer of the winning goal in the 1967 FA Cup Final, his career also included spells at Southampton, QPR and Millwall.**

4 Scorer of the winning goal in the 1969 League Cup Final, this skilful forward played made over 400 appearances for Swindon Town.

5 **Signed from Zeljeznicar in 1979, this Bosnian Serb played 42 times for Middlesbrough then went home to practise as a lawyer. Killed in the Yugoslav wars.**

6 Son of a Swiss restaurateur, he made 600 League appearances for his only club between 1959 and 1978. Retired to the Isle of Mull, where he became a postman. Later moved to Birmingham.

7 **South African-born midfielder with Ipswich Town, Manchester City and Chelsea who played twice for England in 1975. Retired in 1981 and went to run a pub near Heathrow Airport.**

8 Starting at Plymouth Argyle in 1973, this striker went on to win 35 England caps while with Ipswich Town and Arsenal between 1977 and 1985. Later became football coach at the University of Arizona.

9 **Sunderland legend who also played for Norwich City, Middlesbrough, Brighton and Hove Albion and Carlisle. He ended his career at Burnley in 1988.**

10 The first black footballer to play for England.

11 **The first ever PFA Player of the Year in 1974, this defender won 28 England caps between 1966 and 1975. Played for Leeds United. Said to have been a leg-biter.**

12 The first man to captain FA Cup-winning sides on both sides of the border, he played 34 times for Scotland between 1972 and 1979. He retired in 1984 and the following year was briefly manager of Burnley.

13 **The highlight of a distinguished career was 93 goals in 144 games for Arsenal. Despite having played for Scotland Schoolboys, he won eight England caps between 1960 and 1966.**

14 The man who missed the supposedly open goal for Brighton and Hove Albion at the end of the 1983 FA Cup Final against Manchester United.

15 **The only Bermudian international to have played for West Ham United, he now runs a dry cleaning business in Portland, Oregon.**

1 **Jimmy Robertson** 2 Roger Osborne 3 **Frank Saul** 4 Don Rogers 5 **Bozo Jankovic** 6 Peter Bonetti 7 **Colin Viljoen** 8 Paul Mariner 9 **Gary Rowell** 10 Viv Anderson 11 **Norman Hunter** 12 Martin Buchan 13 **Joe Baker** 14 Gordon Smith 15 **Clyde Best**

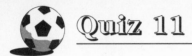 # Quiz 11

Guess Who?

1   The only Englishman to have managed the same club three times.

2   The only man ever to have scored two own goals in a game for Leicester City, for whom he played during the 1960s.

3   **Scored for both sides in the 1981 FA Cup Final.**

4   This Huddersfield-bred full back made 501 appearances for Wolverhampton Wanderers between 1967 and 1982, more than any other player in the history of the club. Later became a gardener.

5   **Watford goalkeeper in the 1984 FA Cup Final - later went to Grimsby Town.**

6   Watford player of the late '50s and early '60s who managed Wolverhampton Wanderers (1976-78) and Doncaster Rovers (1994-96).

7   **Welsh international with 29 caps between 1964 and 1974 who played his finest club football for Norwich City and Southampton. Now lives near Orlando, Florida, where he paints and coaches the local semi-professional side.**

8   Welsh winger who played for Burnley and won 54 caps between 1972 and 1983. Later ran a sweetshop near Turf Moor.

9   **West Ham wing half and 1964 FA Cup winner, he later moved into women's clothing - by running Jays Fashion Discount Market at Archway, London N.**

10 Widely known as 'Sarge', because of his involvement in the Boys' Brigade, West Ham bought this striker from QPR in 1980.

11 **Winger in Chelsea's 1970 Cup winning side who was later transferred to Oxford United. He was killed with his family in a car accident on the outskirts of Oxford in 1977 at the age of 32.**

12 Winner of 13 Scotland caps, he started at Ipswich Town in 1977, moved first to Spurs in 1983 and then to Manchester United in 1984. Later played for Coventry and QPR. Now sometimes heard on Radio Five Live.

13 **Winner of 23 Scotland caps, an East Stirlingshire boy who found fame with Chelsea, of which he was captain and manager. Later became manager of Memphis Rogues and still lives in the USA.**

14 Winner of three FA Cup winner's medals with Manchester United and capped 14 times by Scotland, this full back retired in 1993 and became manager of Droylesden in the North West Counties League.

15 **Wolverhampton Wanderers defender; the second black player to be capped by Wales, he made his international debut against West Germany, the country of his birth.**

Quiz 1 — Longest-Serving Players

1 Between 1970 and 1980, which Swindon Town player made more appearances (770) than any Football League player has ever made for any club?

2 Who made 764 appearances for Portsmouth between 1946 and 1965?

3 **Who made 764 appearances for Port Vale between 1950 and 1972?**

4 Who made 713 appearances for Southampton between 1956 and 1974?

5 **Which defender made a record 663 appearances for West Ham United between 1967 and 1988 and later managed the club?**

6 Who played 655 times for Tottenham Hotspur between 1969 and 1986?

7 **Who made exactly the same number of appearances (655) in the Chelsea defence between 1962 and 1980?**

8 Who is Liverpool's longest serving player, with 640 appearances between 1960 and 1978?

9 **Who was Leeds United's longest-serving player - a centre half in 629 games between 1953 and 1973.**

10 Who made 629 League appearances for Sheffield United between 1948 and 1966?

11 **For which club did Bob Mc Kinley play 614 League games between 1951 and 1970?**

12 Who played a record 613 games for Chesterfield between 1948 and 1967?

13 **And who played exactly the same number of games (613) for Colchester United between 1969 and 1984?**

14 Who scored a record number of League goals (199) in a record number of appearances (606) for Manchester United between 1956 and 1973?

15 **For which west country team did John Ayteo play a record number of games - 597 - between 1951 and 1966?**

Quiz 2   ## Longest-Serving Players

1 **For which Lancashire club did Derek Fazackerley make a record number of League appearances - 596 - between 1970 and 1986?**

2 Between 1946 and 1964, Harold Bell made 595 appearances for his club, including 401 in succession - an all-time record. For which club did he play?

3 **Meanwhile, in another part of the country, from 1950 to 1965, who was making the same number of appearances for Scunthorpe United?**

4 Which England player made a record number of appearances (594) for Fulham between 1952 and 1970?

5 **For which Welsh club did Arfon Griffiths make 592 League appearances between 1959 and 1979?**

6 And for which East Anglian club did Ron Ashman play exactly the same number of League games between 1947 and 1964?

7 **For which team did left back Mick Mills play 591 times?**

8 For which club does Wilfred Milne hold the record number of League appearances in a career that stretched from 1919 to 1937?

9 **Who has played more games than anyone else for Charlton Athletic?**

10 For which team did Tony Brown play 574 times between 1963 and 1980?

11 **Who played 571 times for Gillingham from 1957 to 1972?**

12 And who played the same number of games (571) for Crystal Palace between 1973 and 1988?

13 **Which England international played 568 times for Blackpool between 1952 and 1971?**

14 Which Welsh international holds the record for the highest number of League appearances (566) for Everton?

15 **Who has made more appearances (565) than any other player for Manchester City?**

Quiz 3   Longest-Serving Players

1   For which club did Albert Iremonger play 564 times between 1904 and 1926?

2   Despite having a career disrupted by the First World War, Tim Williamson still managed to play in 563 League games for which club?

3   Who has played most often for Aston Villa - 561 League games between 1961 and 1976?

4   Who has made more League appearances than anyone else for Arsenal - 558 League games between 1975 and 1993?

5   For which team did Stuart Taylor make 546 appearances between 1966 and 1980?

6   Who played in 537 League games for Sunderland between 1962 and 1977?

7   With 530 League appearances between 1978 and 1992, Kevin Hodges holds which club's appearance record?

8   Who played 528 games for Leicester City between the Wars?

9   Who has made the highest number of appearances in the League for Oldham Athletic (525 between 1966 and 1980)?

10   Who played 523 games for Millwall between 1967 and 1982 and then joined the police?

11   For which Lancashire club did Jerry Dawson play 522 League games between 1907 and 1928?

12   Who has played more matches than anyone else for Northampton Town?

13   For which Yorkshire club did Andy Davidson make 520 League appearances between 1952 and 1967?

14   And for which other Yorkshire club did Billy Smith play the same number of League games - 520 - between 1914 and 1934?

15   Who holds the record for the number of League appearances for QPR, having played 519 times between 1950 and 1963?

 ## Quiz 4   Longest-Serving Players

1 With 519 League appearances between 1956 and 1970, who has played most matches for Bolton Wanderers?

2 For which team did Ken Coote make 514 League appearances between 1949 and 1964?

3 For which team did Barry Murphy make exactly the same number of League appearances (514) between 1949 and 1964?

4 Who made more appearances than any other player in the history of Brighton and Hove Albion in a career that spanned the years 1922-36?

5 Who has made most League appearances for Stoke City (506 between 1958 and 1976)?

6 For which Lancashire team did Norman Bullock make 506 appearances between 1920 and 1935?

7 For which Yorkshire team did Andy Wilson make 502 League appearances between 1900 and 1920?

8 With 502 appearances between 1970 and 1984, who has played more games than anyone else for Bradford City?

9 Who has made the most League appearances for Reading (exactly 500 between 1978 and 1991)?

10 Which west country club had Arnold Mitchell in their team 495 times between 1952 and 1966?

11 Who made 494 appearances for Luton Town between 1948 and 1964?

12 For which Midlands' club did Frank Womack make 491 League appearances between 1908 and 1928?

13 Who played in 489 League matches for Stockport County in two spells with the club (1978-86 and 1988-92)?

14 Who played in more League games than anyone else for Derby County, with 486 appearances in two spells with the club (1966-78 and 1980-82)?

15 For which Midlands' club did George Curtis make 486 League appearances between 1956 and 1970?

Quiz 5   Longest-Serving Players

1 **Who made 482 League appearances for Peterborough United between 1968 and 1981?**

2 Who made 481 League appearances for York City between 1958 and 1970?

3 **Which Manor legend played 478 games for his only club, Oxford United, between 1962 and 1977?**

4 Which player made the most League appearances for Cardiff City (471 games between 1972 and 1985)?

5 **Who made 467 League appearances for Walsall between 1964 and 1982?**

6 For which club did Alan Ross make a record number of appearances - 466 - between 1963 and 1979?

7 **For which club did Danny Williams play 459 matches between 1946 and 1956?**

8 Who holds the record for the greatest number of league appearances for Southend United (451 between 1950 and 1963)?

9 **For which club did Keith Jobling play 448 League games between 1953 and 1969?**

10 For which club did Alan Kelly play 447 League games between 1961 and 1975?

11 **Who made 447 League appearances between 1948 and 1964 for what was then Hartlepools United?**

12 For which club did Dennis Lewis play 443 League games between 1947 and 1959?

13 **Who has made more League appearances than any other player for Darlington (442 between 1955 and 1968)?**

14 Who made 415 League appearances for Watford in a total of three spells at the club - 1976-83, 1984-88 and 1991-92?

15 **For which club did Mel Pejic play 412 League games between 1980 and 1992?**

 ## Quiz 1   **Managers**

1   **Before becoming manager of the Republic of Ireland, of which club had Mick McCarthy been in charge from 1992 to 1996?**

2   Before moving to Tottenham Hotspur in 1986, of which club had David Pleat been manager since 1978?

3   **In which year did Brian Clough become the manager of Nottingham Forest?**

4   For which two clubs did Wimbledon manager Joe Kinnear play his football?

5   **From their formation in 1900 to 1998, how many managers have West Ham United had?**

6   Graham Taylor went back to Watford as manager in 1997. When had he left the club?

7   **Huddersfield Town, Notts County, Plymouth Argyle - which manager has won promotion for each of these clubs through the play-offs?**

8   In March 1995, who became Sunderland's 16th manager since the Second World War?

9   **Martin O'Neill took over as manager of Leicester City in December 1995. Where had he briefly worked immediately before?**

10 Name the Derby County manager between 1984 and 1993 who was in charge at Chesterfield from 1976 to 1980.

11 **Name the four Rons who have managed West Bromwich Albion.**

12 Of which club was Bert Head manager and general manager from 1966-72?

13 **Of which Lincolnshire club was former Everton defender Mike Lyons manager from 1985-87?**

14 The League record for length of service to a single club - 46 years - is held by Fred Everiss. Which club did he manage from 1902-48?

15 **In which month and year did Alex Ferguson take over as manager of Manchester United?**

RON 4

 **Quiz 2**   **Managers**

1 In which year did Roy Evans become manager of Liverpool?

2 When was John Rudge appointed manager of Port Vale?

3 **Where did Barry Fry go after he left Birmingham City in May 1996?**

4 Where was Glenn Hoddle's first managerial appointment?

5 **Which all-time great cut his teeth in management at Hartlepool United from 1965 to 1967?**

6 Which Dane became manager of Walsall in June 1997?

7 **Which ex-Charlton striker was manager of Gillingham from 1993 to 1995?**

8 Which ex-Chelsea star was appointed player manager of Doncaster Rovers in August 1996?

9 **Which ex-Derby County and Nottingham Forest duo managed Rotherham United from 1994 to 1996?**

10 Which ex-Sunderland manager was in charge of Blackpool in 1978-79?

11 **Which former Arsenal and Republic of Ireland player managed Bradford City between 1991 and 1994?**

12 Which former Chelsea boss was manager of Cambridge United in 1985?

13 **Which former England captain managed Exeter City in 1983-84?**

14 Which former England international was Director of Football at Barnet in 1996 and 1997?

15 **Which former Leeds United and England striker had two spells as manager of Barnsley - 1978-80 and 1985-89?**

 Quiz 3   **Managers**

1 **Which former Liverpool defender went to manage Oxford United in 1988 but soon fell out with chairman Robert Maxwell?**

2 Which former Manchester United star ran Rochdale in 1983 and 1984?

3 **Which former Norwich City boss became manager of Wigan Athletic in November 1995?**

4 Which former Stoke City defender was manager of Chester City in 1994 and 1995?

5 **Which former West Ham United goalkeeper was manager of Carlisle United from 1996 to 1997?**

6 Which former Wolverhampton Wanderers player and Walsall manager became chief coach at Cardiff City in 1995 and subsequently their Director of Football?

7 **Which future Arsenal manager was in charge at Bolton Wanderers from 1992-95?**

8 Which future Aston Villa boss began his managerial career with Darlington in 1989?

9 **Which future England coach was in charge of Queen's Park Rangers from 1980 to 1984?**

10 Which future manager of Birmingham City was in charge at Hillsborough from 1991 to 1995?

11 **Which future Northern Ireland manager was in charge at Southampton from 1973-85?**

12 Which future Nottingham Forest manager managed Blackburn Rovers from 1953-58?

13 **Which goalkeeper managed Plymouth Argyle from 1992 to 1995?**

14 Which Hereford hero ran Wrexham from 1985 to 1989?

15 **Which Lion of Lisbon managed Aston Villa from 1986 to 1987?**

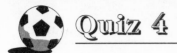

Quiz 4

Managers

1 Which Liverpool manager was in charge at Huddersfield Town from 1956 to 1959?

2 Which Munich air crash survivor was manager of Swansea City from 1972 to 1975?

3 **Which of England's 1966 World Cup winning team was manager of Sheffield United in 1981?**

4 Which Shropshire club was managed by Asa Hartford from 1990 to 1991?

5 **Which three Grahams have managed Wolverhampton Wanderers?**

6 Which two England managers were formerly in charge at Ipswich Town?

7 **Which two European Cup winning managers have briefly been in charge at Elland Road?**

8 Which two Liverpool legends have managed Tranmere Rovers since the Second World War?

9 **Which twosome managed Reading from 1994 to 1997?**

10 Which was the only League club Bobby Moore ever managed?

11 **Who became manager of Northampton Town in January 1995?**

12 Who coached Barcelona to the Spanish League title in 1985?

13 **Who has been Newcastle United's longest serving manager since the Second World War?**

14 Who has managed both Brentford and Fulham?

15 **Who has managed Leyton Orient, Luton Town and Queen's Park Rangers?**

Quiz 5 — Managers

1 **Who is the only Doctor to have managed an English First Division League club?**

2 Who is the only man to have managed both Bristol City and Inter Milan?

3 **Who managed Crewe Alexandra from 1972-73 and later led Brighton and Hove Albion to an FA Cup Final?**

4 Who succeeded Jack Charlton as manager of Middlesbrough in 1977?

5 **Who took over as Arsenal manager on the death of Herbert Chapman in 1934?**

6 Who took over from Brian Clough as Derby County manager in 1973?

7 **Who took over from Harry Redknapp when he left Bournemouth for West Ham United in 1992?**

8 Who was appointed Lincoln City manager in October 1995?

9 **Who managed Scunthorpe United for three days in 1959?**

10 Who managed Crystal Palace for four days in 1984?

11 **Who was Danny Wilson's immediate predecessor as manager of Barnsley?**

12 Who was manager of Everton from 1961-73?

13 **Who was manager of Arsenal from 1986 to 1995?**

14 Who was manager of Brighton and Hove Albion when they narrowly escaped relegation from the Football League in 1997?

15 **Who was manager of Burnley when they were last in the First Division in 1975-76?**

 Quiz 6 **Managers**

1 **Who was manager of Bury when they won the Nationwide Second Division title in 1997?**

2 Who was manager of Chelsea when they won the FA Cup in 1970?

3 **Who was manager of Coventry City in 1987 when they won the FA Cup?**

4 Who was manager of Macclesfield Town when they won promotion to the Football league in 1997?

5 **Who was manager of Manchester City in 1968, the last time they won the Championship?**

6 Who was manager of Southampton in 1966, when they won promotion to the First Division for the first time in their history?

7 **Who was manager of Stoke City when they won the League Cup in 1972?**

8 Who was manager of Tottenham Hotspur in their double-winning year?

9 **Who was manager of Wycombe Wanderers when they won promotion to the Football League in 1993?**

10 Who was sacked by Fulham to make way for Kevin Keegan?

11 **Who was the Major who commanded the men of Notts County between 1944 and 1946, Hull City between 1946 and 1948 and Leeds United from 1948 to 1953?**

12 Who was West Ham United's third manager, who served his apprenticeship at Colchester United between 1946 and 1948?

13 **Who were co-managers of Charlton Athletic from 1991 to 1995?**

14 Who, in June 1996, began his second spell as manager of Norwich City?

15 **Which manager of Zambia scored the winning goal in an English FA Cup Final?**

 # Quiz 1

Mixed Bag

1 **Who, in the 1960s and '70s, were the five Chelsea 'H's?**

2 Which is the only League club in the British Isles with the letter 'J' in its name?

3 **Name the three England internationals with three 'O's in their surnames.**

4 Who were the Blackburn Rovers 'SAS' strike force?

5 **Who were England's five 'W's in the 1984 World Cup qualifier against Turkey in Istanbul?**

6 Name the five English clubs with the letter 'X' in their name.

7 **Which three England captains played for Scunthorpe United in the 1970s?**

8 With 125 caps, who has played most games for England?

9 **If it was Sunderland in 1979 and Villa in 1981, what was it in 1980?**

10 London, Bristol, Glasgow, Dundee, Sheffield, Liverpool, Edinburgh, Manchester, Birmingham - which other British city has more than one League club?

11 **Name the only English player in the Italian League in 1998.**

12 Who was the first goalkeeper to make 200 Premier League appearances?

13 **In 1997-98, which were the only two Football League teams without a shirt sponsor?**

14 What was remarkable about Tottenham Hotspur goalkeeper Pat Jennings' performance in the 1967 Charity Shield against Manchester United?

15 **The first black player to be capped by Wales was Ted Parris of Bradford City in 1932 against Northern Ireland. Which Wolverhampton Wanderers defender became the second in 1979?**

1 **Ron Harris, Marvin Hinton, Ian Hutchinson, John Hollins, Peter Houseman** 2 St Johnstone 3 **Peter Osgood (Chelsea), Ian Storey-Moore (Nottingham Forest), Tony Woodcock (Nottingham Forest and Arsenal)** 4 Alan Shearer and Chris Sutton 5 **Steve Williams, Ray Wilkins, Peter Withe, Tony Woodcock, Mark Wright** 6 Crewe Alexandra, Exeter City, Halifax Town, Oxford United, Wrexham 7 **Ray Clemence, Kevin Keegan and Ian Botham** 8 Peter Shilton 9 **Brooking (the question refers to scorers of FA Cup-winning goals, not to clubs, geddit?)** 10 Stoke (Stoke City and Port Vale) 11 **Tony Dorigo (Torino)** 12 Neville Southall (Everton) 13 **Doncaster Rovers and West Ham United** 14 15 **George Berry**

 **Quiz 2**　　　　　　　　　　　Mixed Bag

1　For which club did Matt Busby, Denis Compton, Stan Cullis, Tommy Lawton, Wilf Mannion, Joe Mercer and Frank Swift all play during the Second World War?

2　For which three countries did Alfredo di Stefano play international football?

3　Who was Sporting Lisbon's English coach when they won the Portuguese League Championship in 1982?

4　In 1946, which Charlton Athletic player became the first player to score for both teams in an FA Cup Final?

5　In which city are the modern headquarters of FIFA?

6　Within ten, how many members does FIFA currently have?

7　In which West Midlands town does the church of St Francis have a stained glass window dedicated to the memory of Munich air crash victim Duncan Edwards?

8　In which year did FIFA decree that linesmen be called Referee's Assistants?

9　In which year was the FA Amateur Cup replaced by the FA Vase?

10　'Like a Centurion tank was our Nathan
Wi' a turn of speed like a bomb
Many a goalie's said sadly
"I wonder where that came from?"'
Who is being sung about?

11　Outside which football ground were the 1990s' northern nostalgia Hovis ads filmed?

12　Second Lieutenant Donald Bell is the only professional footballer to have won the Victoria Cross (posthumously in 1916). For which Yorkshire team did he play?

13　Plymouth Argyle takes its name from the Argyll and Sutherland Highlanders - true or false?

14　Under what name were Internazionale Milan forced to play by the Italian Fascists in the 1930s and '40s?

15　What does 'Spion Kop' mean in Afrikaans?

 # Quiz 3 **Mixed Bag**

1   **What is calcio?**

2   What is the footballing link between Pope John Paul II and Albert Camus?

3   **What is the most common scoreline in football?**

4   What is the South American equivalent of the European Cup?

5   **What mythical beast links FC Porto with Wivenhoe Town?**

6   What name did Dixie Dean give his daughter, born on the day in 1931 that his club, Everton, beat Southport 9-1?

7   **What was first broadcast on August 22, 1964?**

8   What was the name of the white horse who helped avert disaster at the first Wembley Cup Final in 1923?

9   **What was the Piccadilly Line tube station called before 1932, when Herbert Chapman arranged for its name to be changed to Arsenal?**

10   What, in managerspeak, is the POMO?

11   **When was the Red Card first brandished?**

12   And who was the first English League player to be shown it?

13   **Where, in 1878, was the first match played under floodlighting?**

14   Which British football club is named after a novel?

15   **Which British footballer had the longest professional career - 653 games for six clubs over 22 years?**

1 **The Italian word for football** 2 Both goalkeepers 3 **2-1** 4 **La Copa Libertadores**
5 **Both teams are nicknamed The Dragons** 6 Nina 7 **Match of the Day** 8 Billy
9 **Gillespie Road** 10 The Position of Maximum Opportunity 11 **1976** 12 David Wagstaffe
(Blackburn Rovers) 13 **Bramall Lane, Sheffield** 14 Heart of Midlothian 15 **Bobby Collins**

Quiz 4

Mixed Bag

1 **Which club - a League member until 1972 - imported two Argentine players in 1937?**

2 Which club did Bill Shankly nickname The Ale-House Brawlers?

3 **Which English First Division clubs comprised the so-called Big Five who threatened to break away and set up a superleague early in the 1980s?**

4 Which English First Division clubs comprised the so-called Big Ten who threatened to break away and set up a superleague later in the 1980s?

5 **Which former player and television personality took over when a linesman was injured during an Arsenal v Liverpool match in 1972?**

6 Which is the largest football stadium in the British Isles?

7 **Which Scottish team appeared as Tannochbrae in an episode of the 1960s' BBC drama serial Doctor Finlay's Casebook?**

8 Which team played at Plumstead Common from 1886-87?

9 **Which two countries went to war in 1969 over a football match?**

10 Which was the first club to achieve the so-called 'New Double' of League Championship and League Cup?

11 **Which was the first English League club to have a plastic pitch?**

12 Which was the first ground to have floodlights permanently installed?

13 **Who are sometimes called The Nearly Men of Scottish Football?**

14 Who bit yer leg?

15 Who bit yer bum?

1 Barrow 2 Southampton 3 Arsenal, Everton, Liverpool, Manchester United and Tottenham Hotspur 4 The above five plus Aston Villa, Newcastle United, Nottingham Forest, Sheffield Wednesday and West Ham United **6** Hampden Park, Glasgow **7 Alloa Athletic 8** Arsenal **9 El Salvador and Honduras 10** Nottingham Forest (1978) **11 Queen's Park Rangers (1981)** 12 The Manor, Oxford United (1950) **13 Heart of Midlothian 14** Norman Hunter (Leeds United) **15 Billy Bonds (West Ham United)**

 Quiz 5   Mixed Bag

1 Which manager is famous for the remark: 'I've had more clubs than Jack Nicklaus'?

2 Who is the only English League player to have twice been voted PFA Player of the Year (1989 and 1991)?

3 Who scored more hat-tricks in his career - 37 - than any other British footballer?

4 What was the historic achievement of A.H. Chequer (alias Morton Peto Betts)?

5 Who was the English manager of Ajax (Amsterdam) in the 1970s?

6 Who was the English trainer of Ajax Amsterdam who led them to their first Dutch Championship in 1918?

7 Who was the first - and, until the start of the 1998 tournament - the only player to score a hat-trick in a World Cup Final?

8 Who was the first player to score a hat-trick in the World Cup?

9 Who was the only Scottish winner of the Anglo-Scottish Cup, which ran from 1976 to 1981?

10 Which footballer refused to appear on This Is Your Life?

11 Who, in 1888, scored the first League hat trick (for Burnley against Blackburn Rovers)?

12 Who, in 1961, became the first British footballer to earn £100 a week?

13 Who, in 1975, broke his jaw while shouting at a team-mate?

14 Whose autobiographies are entitled 'This One's On Me' and 'It's A Funny Old Life'?

15 Whose ghost is reputed to haunt the marble halls of Highbury?

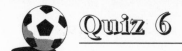

Quiz 6

Mixed Bag

1 Which year was the first season of the Premiership?

2 How long had the old Football League been going?

3 In the first season of the Premiership, what colour strip did the referees wear?

4 Under the new Premiership arrangements, the half-time interval was to be 15 minutes long. How long had it previously been?

5 How many substitutes were allowed on the bench?

6 How many substitutes could be used in the Premiership?

7 Which club has the largest pitch in England?

8 Which club has the smallest pitch in the Premiership?

9 Which Premiership ground has the largest seating capacity?

10 What was the name of the police dog that ran onto the pitch and bit Jim McNichol of Torquay United during their vital Fourth Division relegation battle against Crewe Alexandra in 1987?

11 Who is sometimes known as The Turtle because he is turtally dedicated to Newcastle United?

12 Which manager is called Harry even though that's not his name?

13 Which player is known as Chief?

14 In 1993, the FA Cup semi-finals were between Arsenal and Tottenham Hotspur and Sheffield United and Sheffield Wednesday. Where were they held?

15 Who was the first native East German to play for the unified national side?

 ## Quiz 1 — Most Capped Players

1 **Who is the only player to have won an international cap while playing for Hereford United?**

2 Who is Arsenal's most capped player, a full back who played 77 times for England while at Highbury?

3 **Who is the only player to have won an international cap while playing for Hartlepool United?**

4 The Coventry City player with the most international caps (27) has played 37 times for Zimbabwe. Who is he?

5 **With which two clubs was Peter Shilton the most capped player?**

6 Who is Aston Villa's most capped player, making 51 of his 83 international appearances while at Villa Park?

7 **Only one Torquay United player - Rodney Jack - has ever won an international cap. Which country did he represent?**

8 Brentford's most capped player, John Buttigieg, made 63 international appearances for whom?

9 **Although no one has ever won an international cap while playing for Oldham Athletic, the most capped player they have ever had on their books played 54 times for Norway. Name him.**

10 For which English League club was Alan McDonald playing throughout his 52-cap international career with Northern Ireland?

11 **Name the Bermudian who won 18 international caps while playing for Rotherham United.**

12 How many of his 108 England caps did Bobby Moore win while playing for West Ham United?

13 **Watford have two players with the same number of international caps (31). One is John Barnes, who played for England 79 times altogether. The other won all his 31 caps for Wales while at Vicarage Road. Who is he?**

14 Which Nigeria international is Leyton Orient's most capped player?

15 **Which Welshman is Crystal Palace's most capped player?**

1 **Brian Evans (Wales)** 2 Kenny Sansom 3 **Ambrose Fogarty (Northern Ireland)**
4 Peter Ndlovu 5 **Derby County and Southampton** 6 Paul McGrath (Republic of Ireland)
7 **St Vincent** 8 Malta 9 **Gunnar Halle** 10 Queens Park Rangers 11 **Shaun Goater**
12 All of them 13 **Kenny Jackett** 14 John Chiedozie 15 **Eric Young**

Quiz 2 — Most Capped Players

1 **Bobby Charlton is Manchester United's most capped international player. How many times did he play for England?**

2 Stockport County's most capped international player is Martin Nash, who played twice for which country?

3 **Who is Leeds United's most capped international, with 54 appearances for Scotland?**

4 Gordon Banks won 36 of his England caps while at Stoke City. Where was he when he won the other 37?

5 **Who is Leicester City's most capped international, with 39 appearances for Northern Ireland between 1980 and 1986?**

6 Eamonn Dunphy, Millwall's most capped player, won all but one of his 23 Republic of Ireland caps while playing at the Den. Which club was he playing for when he played his first international, against Spain in 1966?

7 **Who is Wigan Athletic's only international player to date, with a single appearance as a substitute in Northern Ireland's 1997 game against Thailand?**

8 Neville Southall is Everton's most capped player. How many times did he play in goal for Wales?

9 **Who is Chelsea's most capped player, winning 24 of his 84 England caps while at Stamford Bridge?**

10 Name Sunderland's most capped international, who won 38 of his 40 Republic of Ireland caps while at Roker Park between 1958 and 1969.

11 **Who is Swansea City's most capped international?**

12 How many times did Billy Wright, Wolverhampton Wanderers' most capped player, play for England?

13 **In a career spanning 1950-60, who became Newcastle's most capped international, with 40 appearances for Northern Ireland?**

14 Nigel Worthington won 66 Northern Ireland caps - two with Stoke City, 14 with Leeds United and 50 with whom, making him their most capped international player?

15 **Which Blackburn Rovers player made 41 England appearances between 1902 and 1914?**

 ## Quiz 3 — Most Capped Players

1 Which Northern Ireland international won 47 of his 53 caps while at Ipswich Town between 1972 and 1980?

2 For which Yorkshire team did Billy Gillespie win 25 Northern Ireland caps between 1913 and 1931?

3 With 48 England caps between 1968 and 1976, which Manchester City player made most appearances for his country?

4 Which club's most capped international is Northern Ireland's Gerry Taggart?

5 Which Welshman is Liverpool's most capped international?

6 For which club did Jimmy Armfield play throughout his international career?

7 For which club did Johnny Haynes play throughout his international career?

8 With 10 Republic of Ireland caps since 1996, Kenny Cunningham became which club's most capped international?

9 Norwich City's most capped international played for Wales between 1988 and 1995 - name him.

10 Who is Bolton Wanderers' most capped international, winning all his 33 England caps while with the club between 1951 and 1959?

11 For which north London club was Pat Jennings playing when he won 74 of his 119 Northern Ireland caps?

12 Winning 30 of his 50 caps for Wales between 1967 and 1973, which club's most capped international is Rod Thomas?

13 With 76 caps for England, which defender has made more international appearances than any other Nottingham Forest player?

14 For which club did Tom Finney play throughout his England career?

15 For which club did Wilf Mannion play throughout his England international career?

1 Allan Hunter 2 Sheffield United 3 Colin Bell 4 Barnsley 5 Ian Rush 6 Blackpool 7 Fulham 8 Wimbledon 9 Mark Bowen 10 Nat Lofthouse 11 Tottenham Hotspur 12 Swindon Town 13 Stuart Pearce 14 Preston North End 15 Middlesbrough

Quiz 1   **Names Of Grounds**

Which English Football League teams play at home at the following stadiums:

1 **The Abbey Stadium?**
2 Adams Park?
3 **Anfield?**
4 Ashton Gate?
5 **Belle Vue?**
6 The Bescot Stadium?
7 **Bloomfield Road?**
8 Blundell Park?
9 **Bootham Crescent?**
10 Boothferry Park?
11 **Boundary Park?**
12 Bramall Lane?
13 **Brisbane Road?**
14 Brunton Park?
15 **Carrow Road?**

1 **Cambridge United** 2 Wycombe Wanderers 3 **Liverpool** 4 Bristol City
5 **Doncaster Rovers** 6 Walsall 7 **Blackpool** 8 Grimsby Town 9 **York City** 10 Hull City
11 **Oldham Athletic** 12 Sheffield United 13 Leyton Orient 14 Carlisle 15 **Norwich City**

 # Quiz 2   **Names Of Grounds**

What are the names of the following clubs' grounds?

1   **Preston North End**

2   Mansfield Town

3   **Plymouth Argyle**

4   Lincoln City

5   **Stoke City**

6   Burnley

7   **Barnet**

8   Brentford

9   **Bolton Wanderers**

10 Middlesbrough

11 **Reading**

12 Oxford United

13 **Huddersfield Town**

14 Which two teams have home stadiums known as The County Ground?

15 **By what name is one of these County grounds more commonly known?**

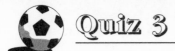 ## Quiz 3   ### Names Of Grounds

Which English Football League teams play at home at the following stadiums:

1 **The City Ground?**

2 Craven Cottage?

3 **Dean Court?**

4 The Dell?

5 **The Deva Stadium?**

6 Edgeley Park?

7 **Elland Road?**

8 Ewood Park?

9 **Feethams?**

10 Filbert Street?

11 **Fratton Park?**

12 Gay Meadow?

13 **Gigg Lane?**

14 Glanford Park?

15 **Goodison Park?**

 # Quiz 4   Names Of Grounds

What are the names of the following clubs' grounds?

1 **Arsenal**

2 Bristol Rovers

3 **Colchester United**

4 Coventry City

5 **Crewe Alexandra**

6 Luton Town

7 **Macclesfield Town**

8 Manchester City

9 **Millwall**

10 Peterborough United

11 **Queen's Park Rangers**

12 Rotherham United

13 **Scarborough**

14 Sheffield Wednesday

15 **West Bromwich Albion**

1 **The Arsenal Stadium (but popularly Highbury)** 2 The Memorial Ground 3 **Layer Road**
4 Highfield Road 5 **Gresty Road** 6 Kenilworth Road 7 **The Moss Rose Ground**
8 Maine Road 9 **The New Den** 10 London Road 11 **Loftus Road** 12 Millmoor
13 **The McCain Stadium** 14 Hillsborough 15 **The Hawthorns**

 **Quiz 5**   **Names Of Grounds**

Which English Football League teams play at home at the following stadiums:

1 **Molineux?**

2 Oakwell?

3 **Plainmoor?**

4 Portman Road?

5 **Prenton Park?**

6 Pride Park?

7 **The Priestfield Stadium?**

8 The Pulse Stadium?

9 **The Racecourse Ground?**

10 The Recreation Ground?

11 **Roots Hall?**

12 Sixfields Stadium?

13 **Spotland?**

14 Springfield Park?

15 **St Andrews?**

 ## Quiz 6   Names Of Grounds

1   **Exeter City and Newcastle United play at grounds with very similar names. What is the key difference between the two?**

2   What was the name of Middlesbrough's ground until 1995?

3   **What is Sunderland's ground correctly known as?**

4   What was the name of Sunderland's old ground, on which they played from 1898-1997?

5   **Although almost everyone says that West Ham United play their home games at Upton Park, that is the name of the area in which their stadium is situated. What is the name of the stadium itself?**

6   Name the three English League clubs that have played home games at Selhurst Park?

7   **With which temporarily exiled club did West Ham United share their home ground during the 1990-91 season?**

8   Tottenham Hotspur's ground is universally known as White Hart Lane. In which street is the main entrance?

9   **What was the name of Wimbledon's ground when they joined the Football League in 1977-78?**

10   What was the name of the ground at which Derby County played their home matches between 1895 and 1997?

11   **At which League ground did Brighton and Hove Albion play their home matches in 1997-98?**

12   Although it is universally known as Loftus Road, in which street is the main entrance to the Queen's Park Rangers ground?

13   **What are the names of the three English Football League grounds that are not in England?**

14   What is the name of the one Football League ground in England whose team does not play in the English Football League?

15   **What was the name of the ground at which Wycombe Wanderers played from 1901 to 1990?**

Quiz 7 Names Of Grounds - Scotland

Which Scottish Football League teams play at home at the following stadiums:

1 **The Almondvale Stadium?**
2 Bayview Park?
3 **Boghead Park?**
4 Which two clubs share the Broadwood Stadium?
5 **Brockville Park?**
6 Burnbrae?
7 **The Caledonian Stadium?**
8 Cappielow Park?
9 **Central Park?**
10 The Cliftonhill Stadium?
11 **The Cliftonville Stadium?**
12 Dens Park?
13 **East End Park?**
14 Easter Road?
15 **Fir Park?**

Quiz 8 Names Of Grounds - Scotland

What are the names of the following clubs' grounds?

1 **Aberdeen**
2 Alloa Athletic
3 **Arbroath**
4 Ayr United
5 **Brechin City**
6 East Stirlingshire
7 **Kilmarnock**
8 Montrose
9 **Partick Thistle**
10 Queen of the South
11 **Queen's Park**
12 Rangers
13 **St Johnstone**
14 Stenhousemuir
15 **Stirling Albion**

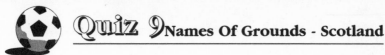

Quiz 9 Names Of Grounds - Scotland

Which Scottish Football League teams play at home at the following stadiums:

1 **Stair Park?**

2 Stark's Park?

3 **Station Park?**

4 Tannadice Park?

5 **Tynecastle Park?**

6 Victoria Park?

7 **Name the eight Scottish Football league clubs whose grounds have a Glasgow postal address.**

8 In which city did Meadowbank Thistle play their home matches?

9 **What happened to them?**

10 Which was Scotland's - and, indeed, Britain's - first all-seater stadium?

11 **Where did Clydebank play their home matches during the 1996-97 season?**

12 Which Scottish club previously had homes at Burnbank and Kinning Park?

13 **From its formation in 1945 until 1992, which Scottish club played its home matches at Annfield?**

14 Until 1917, which team played its home matches at North End Park, which was nicknamed the Colliers Den?

15 **Which team played its home matches at Cathkin Park before dropping out of the Scottish League in 1967?**

1 **Stranraer** 2 Raith Rovers 3 **Forfar Athletic** 4 Dundee United 5 **Heart of Midlothian**
6 Ross County 7 **Airdrieonians, Celtic, Clyde, Clydebank, Dumbarton, Partick Thistle,**
Queen's Park, Rangers 8 Edinburgh 9 They disbanded in 1988 10 Pittodrie, Aberdeen
11 **Boghead Park, Dumbarton** 12 Rangers 13 **Stirling Albion** 14 Cowdenbeath
15 Third Lanark

Quiz 1 — One Cap Wonders

Identify the following:

1   **The Aston Villa goalkeeper who came on as a substitute against Australia in 1983.**

2   The Arsenal defender, formerly with Coventry City, later with Leicester City, who played once against Yugoslavia in 1973.

3   **The Ipswich Town star who came on as a substitute in England's match against Luxembourg in 1978.**

4   Ted MacDougall's striking partner whose one cap game against Wales in 1976 while he was playing for Norwich City.

5   **West Bromwich Albion's record-breaking striker who played once against Wales in 1971.**

6   Came on once as a substitute against Wales in 1975. Played for Aston Villa, whom he later managed.

7   **England cricketer who played football for Corinthians and for England against Northern Ireland in 1901.**

8   Aston Villa full back who went to Everton after winning his sole England cap against Luxembourg in 1977.

9   **West Ham United's ex-QPR striker who came on once as a substitute against Iceland in 1982.**

10   Much-travelled goalkeeper who played for England against Italy in 1976 while playing club football for Arsenal.

11   **Won one cap against Malta in 1971 while playing for Everton, a club he managed between 1987 and 1990.**

12   Capped once against Holland in 1970, while in the middle of four consecutive years as Nottingham Forest's top scorer.

13   **Everton player whose one appearance came in 1965 against West Germany.**

14   Manchester United stalwart from 1952 to 1969 who made his one England appearance against Northern Ireland in 1955.

15   **Nottingham Forest starlet who never really fulfilled his potential. Played once in 1985 against the Republic of Ireland. Moved on to Manchester United, Middlesbrough, Sunderland and Airdrieonians.**

Quiz 2

One Cap Wonders

Identify the following:

1   **Chelsea player and future manager capped once against Czechoslovakia in 1963.**

2   West Ham United's other England international named Moore, who was capped against Sweden in 1923.

3   **Queen's Park Rangers goalkeeper who played once against Portugal in 1974.**

4   Member of the Tottenham Hotspur 1961 double-winning side who played against France in 1963.

5   **Blackpool goalscorer capped once against France in 1963.**

6   Arsenal player of the '50s and early '60s, capped against Wales in 1959.

7   **One-club man who played nearly 400 times for Burnley between 1955 and 1966. Capped against Austria in 1961.**

8   Home-grown Arsenal star who won his cap in 1977 against the Republic of Ireland while playing for Derby County.

9   **Sheffield Wednesday forward capped against Luxembourg in 1962.**

10 Won his cap for England against Spain in 1967 while at Chelsea. Also played for Queen's Park Rangers and Arsenal. Awarded MBE.

11 **Former Watford goalkeeper who played once for England against Mexico while at Liverpool.**

12 PFA Executive who won one England cap as a substitute against Saudi Arabia in 1989.

13 **Played almost 400 times for Burnley between 1955 and 1966. Capped by England against Austria in 1961.**

14 Played once for England against Portugal in 1951 while with Tottenham Hotspur, the club he later managed to the double.

15 **Everton, Watford, Arsenal and Real Sociedad stalwart who played for England against Greece in 1994 while with Aston Villa. Ended the 1997-98 season with Coventry City.**

1 **Ken Shellito** 2 W.G.B. Moore 3 **Phil Parkes** 4 Ron Henry 5 **Ray Charnley**
6 Daniel Clapton 7 **Brian Miller** 8 Charlie George 9 **John Fantham** 10 John Hollins
11 **David James** 12 Brian Marwood 13 **Brian Miller** 14 Bill Nicholson
15 **Kevin Richardson**

THE ULTIMATE FOOTBALL FACT AND QUIZ BOOK

 **Quiz 1** Football Pop Songs

I **Who, in the words of the song, was:**
   'As strong as a lion and never will give up,
   That's why —— is favourite for the Cup'?

2 Which Cup, and when?

3 **Who recorded this song?**

4 Who had a No I hit in 1970 with a song containing the words:
   'Once more we will meet with the best
   Like before we'll be put to the test
   Knowing we'll give all we've got to give for the folks…'?

5 **What was the title of this song?**

6 What was the name of the song sung by Glenn Hoddle and Chris Waddle
   that reached No 12 in the charts in 1987?

7 **What was the name of their follow-up single, which did nothing?**

8 Who had a hit in 1978 with a song about Scotland's World Cup prospects
   which contained the couplet:
   'Olé, olé, olé ola,
   We're gonna bring that World Cup back from over thar'?

9 **Who had a 1973 hit with the song 'Nice One Cyril'?**

10 To which Tottenham Hotspur player did this refer?

11 **The catchphrase 'Nice One Cyril' originated in a television advert**
    for a product unconnected with football. What?

12 The Cyril in the advert had nothing to do with Spurs. Where, in the words
    used, did the product originate?

13 **Complete the missing line from a 1971 hit (Tune: Rule Britannia):**
    '—— —— ———
    We're proud to say that name
    While we sing this song we'll win the game'?

14 For which World Cup was the England song 'This Time (We'll Get It Right)'?

15 **What was the title of the 1982 Liverpool song in which the talents**
    of John Barnes loomed large?

 ## Quiz 2 — Football Pop Songs

1   In which year did 'We All Follow Man United' reach No10?

2   Which group backed England on the No1 hit 'World in Motion'?

3   Which group played on the Euro '96 anthem 'Football's Coming Home'?

4   And who were the two comedians who wrote the words?

5   What was the title of Kevin Keegan's 1979 hit single?

6   Which footballer made a version of Lindisfarne's 'Fog on the Tyne'?

7   What was Arsenal striker Ian Wright's single called?

8   In which year did Leeds United have a No 10 hit with a song called - inspirationally - 'Leeds United'?

9   What was the title of the Scotland World Cup squad song that reached No 20 in 1974?

10   Who had a hit in 1985 with a song to the tune of 'Here We Go'?

11   In which year was 'I'm Forever Blowing Bubbles' a hit for West Ham United?

12   Who reached No 5 in 1982 with 'We have A Dream'?

13   In which year did Chelsea have a hit with 'Blue is the Colour'?

14   In which year did Tottenham Hotspur have a No 5 hit with 'Ossie's Dream'?

15   Which is thought to be the only professional football club in Great Britain never to have made a pop record?

Quiz 1

Season 1899-1900

1 Who were the first Champions of the 20th century, scoring a record number of goals (77) in the course of the 34-match season?

2 Who was their - and the League's - leading scorer, with 27 goals?

3 **Who was their versatile captain?**

4 Which Yorkshire team made the running for most of the season before being pipped at the post on the last day of the season?

5 **Which team from the smallest habitation ever to have been represented in English top-flight football was relegated from the First Division, never to return?**

6 Which two teams bounced straight back up to the First Division, winning promotion from Division Two the year after they had both been relegated?

7 **Which team left the League for ever, after finishing bottom of Division Two with one victory, 18 goals for and 100 against in 34 matches?**

8 Which small Lancashire club heralded the dawn of their finest era by winning the FA Cup for the first time, beating non-League Southampton 4-0 in the Final?

9 **Which three First Division sides had Southampton put out on their way to the Final?**

10 Which non-League side from London did Southampton beat in a semi-final that went to a replay?

11 **The first match - a 0-0 draw - had been played at Crystal Palace. Where in Berkshire was the replay, which Southampton won 3-0?**

12 Which Derby-winning racehorse owner talked Scotland into playing their match against England at Parkhead in his racing colours?

13 **Playing in primrose and pink had no ill-effect on the Scots, who won the match 4-1. Who was the Queen's Park amateur who scored a hat trick?**

14 Rangers won the Scottish Championship, winning all but three of their 20 matches. Which was the only team they failed to beat at home or away?

15 **Celtic retained the Scottish FA Cup. Who did they beat 4-3 in the Final, after trailing 3-1 at half time?**

 **Quiz 2** **Season 1900-1901**

1   Tottenham Hotspur became the first non-League club to win the FA Cup. Which Yorkshire club did they beat 3-1 in the Final replay, after the first match had been drawn 1-1?

2   Who was the triumphant Spurs manager?

3   The first match had been played at Crystal Palace - where was the replay held?

4   When had the FA Cup Final last gone to a replay?

5   What was the name of the Spurs centre forward who became the first man to score in every round of the Cup?

6   How many times in the 20th century did Spurs win the Cup in a year ending with the number one?

7   Who won their first League Championship, and went on to take the title 17 more times during the 20th century?

8   Who was their star Scottish international centre half?

9   Which two former League champions were relegated to the Second Division?

10 Who was the First Division's leading scorer, with 24 goals for 12th-placed Derby County?

11 Which founder member of the Football League won the Second Division title and promotion to the First Division for the first time?

12 Against which nation did Scotland record their highest ever international victory - 11-0?

13 In Scotland, who won the League Championship for the third year in succession?

14 Who were runners-up in both the Scottish League and FA Cup?

15 Who lifted the Scottish FA Cup, after a 4-3 victory in the Final?

 Quiz 3   Season 1901-1902

1   In which stadium were 25 people killed and hundreds injured when a stand collapsed during an international match?

2   What was the new maximum wage for professional footballers in England?

3   Sunderland won the League Championship for the fourth time - when had they last been champions?

4   Of the current Sunderland squad, two had played in the previous Championship-winning team. One was their Scottish international goalkeeper - what was his name?

5   The other survivor was the centre forward, another Scot who had been capped for his country while at Rangers - what was his name?

6   The First Division's leading scorers were James Settle and Fred Priest, each with 18 goals. Which teams did they play for?

7   Who won the FA Cup for the second time, beating Southampton 2-1 in the Final replay after the first match had been drawn 1-1?

8 Which great England cricketer played at right back for Southampton in the FA Cup Final?

9 Which Midlands team won the Second Division title with a record number of points (55)?

10 This was the last season in which there was a League club called Newton Heath - to what did they change their name the following season?

11 What was historic about the Home International between England and Scotland at Villa Park?

12 Rangers won the League; who won the Scottish Cup for the second time in their history?

13 Who were runners-up in both the Scottish First Division and the FA Cup?

14 Which Glasgow club won promotion from the Second Division, only to go down again the following season and out of the League altogether in 1911?

15 Which other club was promoted in readiness for the following season, when the Scottish First Division was increased from 10 clubs to 12?

---

1 **Ibrox Park, Glasgow** 2 **£4 a week** 3 **1895** 4 Ted Doig 5 **Jimmy Millar** 6 Everton and Sheffield United respectively 7 **Sheffield United** 8 C.B. Fry 9 **West Bromwich Albion** 10 Manchester United 11 **It was the first international in which all the players on both sides were professionals** 12 Hibernian 13 Celtic 14 Port Glasgow Athletic 15 **Partick Thistle**

Quiz 4 — Season 1902-1903

1 What was spotted for the first time at football grounds all around the country?

2 The Wednesday won the League Championship, the first of four times that they achieved this feat. Who was their centre forward and leading scorer, with 12 goals?

3 **Who was the local Sheffield hero who had an outstanding season at centre half?**

4 Who won the FA Cup for the second time in their history, winning the Final by the all-time record margin of 6-0?

5 **For only the second time in the history of the FA Cup, the winners did not concede a single goal throughout the tournament. Which other club had previously achieved this feat?**

6 Who were the beaten Cup finalists, the third time they had lost at this stage since 1896?

7 **Which Midlands' team were runners-up in the League and semi-finalists in the FA Cup?**

8 The other beaten FA Cup semi-finalists were a London club - then non-League - with strong North British links, taking many of their players from the Docklands factory of Scottish jam and marmalade maker Morton & Co - who were they?

9 **Who was the First Division's leading scorer, with 31 goals for fifth-placed Liverpool?**

10 Why was Roker Park closed for a week after Sunderland lost 1-0 at home to The Wednesday?

11 **Which three teams shared the Home International Championship?**

12 Who won the first of their four Scottish League Championships, the others coming in 1948, 1951 and 1952?

13 **Who were runners-up in Scotland, their best position in the League until they finally won it in 1962?**

14 Rangers won the Scottish FA Cup after the Final had gone to a second replay. Who did they beat 2-0 after the two previous matches had ended 1-1 and 0-0?

15 **Which three Scottish internationals also formed the backbone of the Sunderland defence?**

 **Quiz 5**   **Season 1903-1904**

1 **The Wednesday won their second League Championship in succession. Who was their secretary-manager?**

2 Who came second in the League and won the FA Cup?

3 **Which Second Division team did they beat 1-0 in the all-Lancashire Final?**

4 Name the great Welsh international who scored the winning goal in the 1904 FA Cup Final.

5 **What was the name of the winning team's manager?**

6 Which Lancashire team was relegated from the First Division despite having scored one more goal (49) than the Champions?

7 **Who was the First Division's leading scorer, with 20 goals for 14th-placed Derby County?**

8 Who became the first side from south of the River Trent to win promotion to the First Division?

9 **Who won the Scottish League Championship for the only time in their history?**

10 The Scottish First Division had been increased from 12 clubs to 14. Who were the two newcomers?

11 **Who scored two goals for Rangers in the Scottish FA Cup Final?**

12 Who then scored a hat-trick to make the final score Celtic 3 Rangers 2?

13 **For which established centre forward had the hat-trick hero been a last-minute replacement?**

14 Who was the Celtic manager who made this controversial selection?

15 **What is the unique link between this year's English and Scottish FA Cup winners?**

Quiz 6 — Season 1904-1905

1 Newcastle United won the League Championship for the first time in their history. Which Midlands side stopped them winning the double by beating them in the Final of the FA Cup?

2 Name the centre forward who scored both goals in their 2-0 victory in the Final at Crystal Palace?

3 In addition to making up the champions' formidable half-back line, what was the other link between Newcastle's Andy Aitken, Alex Gardner and Peter McWilliam?

4 Who was the Newcastle United centre forward?

5 Who, in February 1905, became the first £1000 player, when he moved from Sunderland to Middlesbrough?

6 With which Yorkshire club had he started his career?

7 How many times did he play for England?

8 Who was the First Division's leading scorer, with 23 goals for 13th-placed Sheffield United?

9 Which Lancashire club were runners-up in the League and beaten semi-finalists in the FA Cup?

10 After finishing seventh in the First Division, to what did Small Heath change their name?

11 Where did they finish the following season (1905-06)?

12 Celtic and Rangers finished joint top of the Scottish First Division, with both clubs on 41 points. Which club had the better goal average?

13 Which club won the Scottish title after a play-off?

14 Who came third in the League and won the Scottish FA Cup for the second time in their history?

15 Who did they beat 3-1 in the Final?

1 Aston Villa 2 Harry Hampton 3 They were all Scots 4 Bill Appleyard 5 Alf Common 6 Sheffield United 7 Three 8 Arthur Brown 9 Everton 10 Birmingham City 11 Seventh 12 Rangers 13 Celtic 14 Third Lanark 15 Rangers

 **Quiz 7**   Season 1905-1906

1 What was unprecedented about Liverpool's second League title?

2 Who was their goalkeeper, an early-season purchase from Second Division Chesterfield Town, against whom they had netted six the previous season?

3 Which old stager did he replace in goal?

4 Who was Liverpool's Scottish centre half?

5 Who was their leading scorer, with 22 League goals?

6 Whose place did he take at centre forward when the first choice broke his wrist on the opening day of the season at Woolwich Arsenal?

7 The joint leading scorers in the First Division were 'Bullet' Jones and Albert Shepherd, with 26 goals apiece. Which teams did they play for?

8 Which Lancashire club won the FA Cup for the first time in their history?

9 Who lost in the Final for the second year running?

10 Who scored the only goal of the match?

11 Which West Country won the Second Division Championship and very nearly went on to win the First Division the following year?

12 Which great name - eventually seven-time Championship winners - won promotion to the First Division as runners-up?

13 Celtic won the Scottish Championship, while the runners-up in the League had the consolation of winning the FA Cup - who were they?

14 In the Final, they beat the holders of the trophy 1-0. Who scored the winning goal?

15 Which other team finished above fourth-placed Rangers in the Scottish First Division?

1 **They were the first newly-promoted club to win the League** 2 Sam Hardy 3 **Ted Doig**
4 Alec Raisbeck 5 **Joe Hewitt** 6 Jack Parkinson 7 **Birmingham City and Bolton Wanderers respectively** 8 Everton 9 **Newcastle United** 10 Sandy Young 11 **Bristol City**
12 Manchester United 13 **Heart of Midlothian** 14 G. Wilson 15 **Airdrieonians**

THE ULTIMATE FOOTBALL FACT AND QUIZ BOOK

 **Quiz 8**   **Season 1906-1907**

1 **Who won the League Championship for the second time?**

2 Which was the only team to take a point off them at home this season?

3 **Who were runners-up, their highest ever position in the Football League, and the highest achieved to date by a team from south of the River Trent?**

4 Who was their most distinguished player, dominating the defence at centre half despite appearing overweight and being only 5 feet 4 inches tall?

5 **Which club became the first southern team ever to lead the First Division, although they faded later in the season and finished in seventh place?**

6 Who was the League's leading scorer, with 30 goals for third-placed Everton?

7 **Which lowly Southern League club from London knocked Newcastle United out of the FA Cup, beating them 1-0 at St James's Park in the first round?**

8 Which two 'W's were beaten semi-finalists in the Cup?

9 **Which Yorkshire club won the FA Cup for the second time in their history, beating Everton 2-1 in the Final?**

10 Who bounced straight back as Second Division Champions after having been relegated in 1906?

11 **Which London club came second and thus won promotion to the First Division for the first time in their history?**

12 Wales became the first country other than England and Scotland to win the Home International Championship outright. Who scored in their goal in the 1-1 draw with England at Craven Cottage?

13 **Which Lancashire club did he play for?**

14 Celtic won the Scottish League Championship for the seventh time, their third title in succession. They also became the first team to do the double - who did they beat 3-0 in the Scottish FA Cup Final?

15 **Who scored Celtic's goals in this match?**

THE ULTIMATE FOOTBALL FACT AND QUIZ BOOK

 ## Quiz 9   **Season 1907-1908**

1 **Manchester United won the first of seven League Championships - who was their captain?**

2 What was the famous habit of their great right winger, Billy Meredith?

3 **How many times did Meredith play for Wales?**

4 Enoch West, the League's leading scorer, netted 27 times in the season - for which club?

5 **Wolverhampton Wanderers won the FA Cup for the second time in their history - who did they beat 3-1 in the Final?**

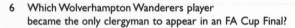

6 Which Wolverhampton Wanderers player became the only clergyman to appear in an FA Cup Final?

7 **The vicar opened the scoring; his goal was followed three minutes later with another by George Hedley. With which team had Hedley twice won the Cup before?**

8 Which London Second Division team reached the semi-final of the Cup?

9 **Which south-coast non-League side were the other beaten semi-finalists?**

10 In their first ever international on foreign soil on June 6, England won 6-1 - who were their opponents?

11 **Before moving on to their next destination, they played the same country again. What was the score in this match?**

12 Which two other countries did England beat on their summer tour?

13 **North of the border, Celtic won their fourth Championship on the trot, scoring 86 goals in 34 League games. But who were the runners-up who became the first Scottish team to score a century, with an all-time record 102 goals?**

14 Who did Celtic beat 5-1 in the Scottish FA Cup Final?

15 **Which teams shared the Home International Championship, drawing 1-1 with each other and beating the other two nations?**

 **Quiz 10**   **Season 1908-1909**

1 **Newcastle United won the League Championship for the third time this century. What was the amazing scoreline in their home fixture with Sunderland, who finished third?**

2 Who were the two main goalscorers in this game?

3 **Who was the League's leading goalscorer, with 38 goals for runners-up Everton?**

4 Which new trophy - introduced for the first time this year - was played for between Manchester United, the 1908 League Champions, and Queen's Park Rangers, winners of the Southern League?

5 **Who equalled West Bromwich Albion's record First Division victory with a 12-0 defeat of already relegated Leicester Fosse on April 21?**

6 When did Leicester Fosse change their name to Leicester City?

7 **Which other team was relegated, only to bounce straight back as Division Two champions in 1910?**

8 Manchester United won the FA Cup - which west country team did they beat 1-0 in the Final?

9 **Who scored the only goal of the match?**

10 Celtic won their fifth consecutive Scottish League Championship - what happened in the Scottish FA Cup?

11 **Which founder member of the Scottish League won the Second Division before going out of the League for ever in 1915?**

12 Who won the Olympic soccer gold medal?

13 **Who did they beat 2-0 in the Final?**

14 Who scored the goals?

15 **Where in London was the Olympic Final played?**

 # Quiz 11   Season 1909-1910

1 **Who won the League Championship for the first time in 10 years, but the sixth time in their history?**

2 Who was the First Division's leading scorer, with 25 goals for Liverpool, the runners-up?

3 **Who eventually won the FA Cup for the first time after reaching the semi-final the previous year and appearing in three out of four previous finals?**

4 Who did they beat 2-0 in the Final replay, after the first match had been drawn 1-1?

5 **Who was their centre forward who scored both goals?**

6 Who was their right half and captain?

7 **What was historic about the second goal in this match?**

8 Where was the replay held?

9 **Playing for England in an amateur international against Holland, who became the first player to score a double hat trick for the second time?**

10 In Scotland, Celtic won the Championship for the sixth year in a row. Who were runners-up, for the second time in three years?

11 **Who finished bottom of the Scottish First Division and then went out of the League?**

12 Who knocked Celtic out of the Scottish FA Cup in the semi-final?

13 **Who won the Scottish Cup for the first time, beating Clyde 2-1 in the second replay?**

14 Who scored the winning goal?

15 **Who won the Home International Championship outright for the first time in 10 years?**

 **Quiz 12**   **Season 1910-1911**

1 **Of the 20 teams in the First Division, eight were from Lancashire - name them.**

2 Which of them won the First Division for the second time in four years?

3 **Who was their manager?**

4 Who was still their captain?

5 **Which Midlands club did they beat into second place by one point?**

6 Who was the Champions' leading scorer, with 19 goals?

7 **And who chipped in with a further 18?**

8 But who was the League's leading scorer, with 25 goals for eighth-placed Newcastle United?

9 **Who won their first major honour by beating Newcastle 1-0 in the FA Cup Final replay after the first match had been drawn 0-0?**

10 The first match had been at Crystal Palace - where was the replay held?

11 **Which ex-Rangers Scottish international scored the winner?**

12 Who was the winning manager?

13 **After five consecutive Scottish League titles, Celtic finished a lowly fifth. Who were the Champions?**

14 Celtic had the consolation of victory in the Scottish FA Cup - who did they beat in the Final?

15 **Who scored the goals in their 2-0 victory?**

THE ULTIMATE FOOTBALL FACT AND QUIZ BOOK

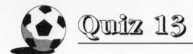 ## Quiz 13   Season 1911-1912

1 **Who won the League Championship for the first time and were beaten semi-finalists in the FA Cup?**

2 The joint top scorers in the League were Harry Hampton, George Holley and Dave McLean, with 25 goals each. Which teams did they play for?

3 **Who became the first Second Division team to win the FA Cup?**

4 Who did they beat 1-0 in a replay after the first match had been drawn 0-0?

5 **The first game was at Crystal Palace. Where was the replay?**

6 Name the inside right who scored the winning goal in the last minute of extra time.

7 **What change was made to the playing conditions as a result of the length of time it had taken to get results in the last three FA Cup Finals?**

8 Which non-League club reached the semi-finals of the FA Cup?

9 **Which Lincolnshire club finished bottom of Division Two and then disappeared for ever from the Football League?**

10 Who won the Olympic football gold medal in Stockholm?

11 **Who did they beat in the Final?**

12 Who won the Scottish League Championship for the second year running?

13 **Who won the Scottish FA Cup for the second year in succession?**

14 Who scored the goals in their 2-0 Final victory?

15 **Who came third in the League and were runners-up in the Cup?**

Quiz 14   Season 1912-1913

1   Who won the League Championship for the fifth time and lost in the Final of the FA Cup?

2   Who won the FA Cup for the fifth time and finished second in the League?

3   Who was the right half who scored the only goal of the Final with a header from a corner?

4   What happened to Final referee A. Adams after the match?

5   Who was the First Division's leading scorer, with 30 goals for third-placed Wednesday?

6   Which Lancashire team reached the semi-final of the Cup and won promotion from the Second Division?

7   Which Sheffield United centre forward scored both goals for Ireland in their 2-1 victory over England in the Home International in Belfast?

8   Which Sunderland and future Arsenal inside forward won the first of his six England caps and scored the opening goal in this game?

9   With which other players did he make one third of England's so-called 'Sunderland Triangle'?

10 Who was the Huddersfield Town inside left who went off with a knee injury in the first half, reducing the Irish to 10 men?

11 Who moved their ground, changed their name and were relegated from the First Division, all in the same season?

12 Who won the Scottish League for the third year in succession?

13 Which two teams made their first appearances in the Scottish FA Cup Final?

14 Who won the Cup, with a 2-0 victory?

15 Where was the Final played?

Quiz 15

Season 1913-1914

1 Blackburn Rovers won the League Championship for the second time in three years. Who were runners-up and semi-finalists in the FA Cup?

2 Who was the English First Division's leading scorer, with 31 goals for third-placed Middlesbrough?

3 Which Lancashire club was relegated from the First Division after having been promoted the previous year and relegated the year before that?

4 Which other Lancashire club won the FA Cup - its first major honour - beating yet another (Liverpool) 1-0 in the Final?

5 Where was the Final played?

6 Who was the victorious captain?

7 Which monarch presented him with the Cup?

8 Who won the Home International Championship for the first time?

9 On their way to the title, they beat England 3-0 away. Where was this match played?

10 Who was the leading scorer in the Scottish First Division, with 21 goals for double-winners Celtic?

11 Celtic created a Scottish First Division record for the fewest League goals against in a season - how many did they concede in their 38 matches?

12 How many times had Celtic now won the Scottish League and the Cup in the same season?

13 Who did they beat 4-1 in the replayed Final of the Scottish FA Cup, after the first match had been drawn 0-0?

14 Which two players scored twice in this game?

15 Who won the Second Division but were not promoted because of the following season's reorganisation of the Scottish League?

---

1 Aston Villa 2 George Elliott 3 Preston North End 4 Burnley 5 Crystal Palace 6 Tommy Boyle 7 King George V 8 Ireland 9 Middlesbrough 10 Patsy Gallagher 11 Fourteen 12 Three 13 Hibernian 14 McColl and Browning 15 Cowdenbeath

 ## Quiz 16   Season 1914-1915

1 Who won the League Championship for the second time in their history and retained the title for five years because of the intervention of the First World War?

2 Who was their leading scorer, with 35 goals in the season?

3 Who were runners-up, the highest position in their history, one point behind the winners?

4 Why was Oldham Athletic's game against Middlesbrough abandoned?

5 How did the War with Germany cause the FA Cup second round replay at Lincoln between Bradford City and Norwich City to be played behind closed doors?

6 Who won the FA Cup, beating Chelsea 3-0 in the Final?

7 Who scored the goals?

8 Who was the victorious captain who won his second FA Cup winner's medal after having played for Barnsley in their 1912 victory?

9 Where was the 1915 FA Cup Final played?

10 By what name is this match more commonly known, because of the large number of servicemen in the crowd of 49,557?

11 Who presented the Cup and made a speech about the need to serve King and country?

12 In Scotland, there was no FA Cup for five years after 1914 because of the War. However, the League continued right through without interruption. Who won it in 1915, 1916, 1917 and 1919?

13 And who pipped them by a point for the 1918 title?

14 In the Scottish Division B, there was a tie on points and the Championship was decided by a three-way play off. Which were the teams involved?

15 Which team was promoted?

---

1 **Everton** 2 Bobby Parker 3 **Oldham Athletic** 4 Because Billy Cook of Oldham refused to leave the field when sent off 5 **Because the ground was next door to a munitions factory, and there was thought to be a danger of an explosion** 6 Sheffield United 7 **Simmons, Kitchen and Faazackerley** 8 George Utley 9 **Old Trafford** 10 The Khaki Cup Final 11 **Lord Derby** 12 Celtic 13 **Rangers** 14 Cowdenbeath, Leith Athletic and St Bernard's 15 None of them: only the top division as previously constituted played for the rest of the War

 **Quiz 17**　　　　　**Season 1919-1920**

1　**The First Division was enlarged to 22 clubs. How many teams had previously been in the top flight of English football?**

2　Which two clubs were promoted after finishing first and second in Division Two in 1915, before the First World War brought League football to a halt?

3　**To help make up the numbers, one club was not relegated from the First Division, despite having finished next to last in 1915 - which club?**

4　Which was the other new member of the First Division, promoted despite having finished only fifth in Division Two in 1915?

5　**The First Division's bottom club in 1915 was relegated. This was much to their consternation, because the last time the number of clubs in the First Division had been increased, in 1905, no one had been relegated. Which was the club?**

6　Which Second Division club was thrown out of the League in October 1919 after the discovery of irregularities in their payments to players during the War and their subsequent refusal to produce accounts for the previous two years?

7　**Among the club officials punished by the Football League was former manager George Cripps. Which other former manager - later to win the Championship with two clubs - was also banned?**

8　Who took over their place in the Second Division and the 10 points they had gained before their expulsion?

9　**Who won the League Championship with a record number of goals scored (104)?**

10　Who was their leading individual scorer, with 37 goals?

11　**Who won the FA Cup for a record sixth time, beating Huddersfield Town 1-0 in the Final?**

12　Who scored the winning goal in extra time?

13　**From where had he been bought for £250 earlier in the season?**

14　Kilmarnock won the Scottish FA Cup for the first time. Which team - who came bottom of the First Division - did they beat 3-2 in the Final?

15　**The Scottish First Division was also increased to 22 clubs. Who won the first Championship in the new format with a record 71 points?**

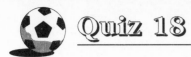 **Quiz 18**   **Season 1920-1921**

1 **Burnley won the first of their two League Championships - when was their next title?**

2 From September 4, Burnley went 30 matches without defeat, a League record. Who finally beat them on March 26?

3 **The League was increased from two divisions to three. Of the teams that played in the first ever Third Division, which is the only one to have gone on to win the League Championship?**

4 Who were the first Champions of the Third Division?

5 **The First Division's top scorer was Joe Smith, with 38 goals in the season. Who did he play for?**

6 Who won promotion to the First Division in their first season in the Football League?

7 **Which newly-promoted First Division team won the FA Cup?**

8 Which Second Division team did they beat 1-0 in the Final?

9 **Who was the winning captain and goalscorer?**

10 Which member of the 1910 Newcastle United team now became the first man to have played in and then managed a Cup-winning team?

11 **In the Third Division, the 0-0 draw at Old Trafford on May 7 between Stockport County and Leicester City was watched by fewer paying spectators than any other first class match in the history of the game. How many turned up?**

12 Who joined the League as replacements for Lincoln City, who failed to win re-election after finishing next to bottom of the Second Division in 1920?

13 **In Scotland, Rangers won the Championship; who were the only club to beat them in the League all season?**

14 Who was the League's leading scorer for the second season running, with 43 goals for fifth-placed Motherwell?

15 **Who won the Scottish FA Cup for the only time, beating Rangers 1-0 in the Final?**

 Quiz 19   Season 1921-1922

1 **Who won the English League Championship for the third time in their history?**

2 Who was their manager?

3 **Who were relegated for the first time under their present name?**

4 Their manager stayed in place for long enough to see them back into the First Division at the start of the 1925-26 season. Name him.

5 **Eighth-placed Middlesbrough had the League's leading scorer, with 31 goals. What was his name?**

6 How many new clubs joined the League when the old Third Division was enlarged and divided into Northern and Southern sections?

7 **Of these new clubs, how many have since won the League Championship, the Premiership or the FA Cup?**

8 Who won the FA Cup, beating Preston North End 1-0 in the Final?

9 **Who scored the winner from the penalty spot?**

10 Where was the match held?

11 **In Scotland, who were runners-up in both League and FA Cup?**

12 Who beat them 1-0 in the Cup Final, the only major honour in their long history?

13 **Who scored their winner at Hampden Park on April 15, in front of 75,000 people?**

14 For the first time, the Scottish League was divided into two divisions: who were the first champions of the new lower division?

15 **At the end of the season, which three clubs became the first to be relegated from the Scottish First Division?**

 ## Quiz 20   **Season 1922-1923**

1 The players' maximum wage was reduced by £1 from its 1921-22 level. What was the new rate?

2 Liverpool won the League title for the second year running. Who was their Northern Ireland international goalkeeper?

3 **Liverpool then entered the longest period in their history without a League title. When did they next win it?**

4 Who were runners-up in 1923, six points behind the champions?

5 **Which player for the second placed team was the First Division's leading scorer, with 30 goals?**

6 Which London team won promotion to the First Division for the first time in its history?

7 **Who was their centre forward who won the first of his five England caps in this year?**

8 Who was their England international goalkeeper?

9 **Who was their manager?**

10 Which three other teams from the capital did they join in the top flight?

11 **Who beat them 2-0 in this year's FA Cup Final, the first to be played at Wembley?**

12 Who scored the goals?

13 **What is this Final commonly known as?**

14 Who was the leading scorer in Scotland, with 30 of Heart of Midlothian's 51 goals in the season?

15 **Who is the leading scorer in Scottish League history, with 410 goals in a 408-game career which began in this year?**

Quiz 21

Season 1923-1924

1 **Who won the first of three successive League Championships?**

2 Who was their captain?

3 **Who did they edge into second place on goal average?**

4 Who was the First Division's leading scorer, with 28 goals for Everton?

5 **What made the Second Division game between Manchester United and Oldham Athletic unforgettable for Latics' full back Sam Wynne?**

6 Who won the FA Cup, beating Aston Villa 2-0 in the Final?

7 **Who, at 41 years and 8 months, became the oldest player ever to appear in an FA Cup Final?**

8 What was the score in the England v Scotland game, the first international to be played at Wembley?

9 **Wales won the Home International Championship for the second time and made their first clean sweep of three victories. Which Plymouth Argyle player scored from the penalty spot in their 1-0 victory over Northern Ireland in Belfast?**

10 In the Wales v Scotland match - which the home side won 2-0 - both captains - Fred Keenor (Wales) and Jimmy Blair (Scotland) - played for the same club. Which?

11 **What was the venue for the England v Wales match, which Wales won 2-1?**

12 The Scottish League launched a Third Division. Of the 16 original members, how many were still in existence in 1998?

13 **Which now defunct club were the first Champions of this division?**

14 Rangers won the Scottish Championship. Who was the League's leading scorer, with 38 goals for Dundee?

15 **Who won the Scottish FA Cup, beating Hibernian 2-0 in the Final?**

 **Quiz 22**   **Season 1924-1925**

1 **Which Midlands team were runners-up to Huddersfield Town in the English First Division?**

2 Which Huddersfield player became the first footballer to score direct from a corner (this was the first season in which it was permissible to do so)?

3 **Who were Huddersfield's opponents in this match on October 11?**

4 And who scored the first FA Cup goal from a corner, enabling Cardiff City to scrape through a fourth round tie against Leicester City?

5 **Who was the First Division's leading scorer, with 31 goals for tenth-placed Manchester City?**

6 Which south coast Second Division side lost 2-0 to Sheffield United in the semi-final of the FA Cup?

7 **Who did Sheffield United beat 1-0 in the Final?**

8 Who scored the winning goal in that match?

9 **Who won the Scottish League Championship?**

10 Willie Devlin was the leading scorer in Scotland, with 33 goals for the fifth-placed club. Which?

11 **Which now defunct Dumfries club won promotion from the Scottish Third Division?**

12 Celtic won the Scottish FA Cup, beating Dundee 2-1 in the Final. Who scored the Celtic equaliser by somersaulting into the net with the ball held between his feet?

13 **What was his nickname?**

14 This was Celtic's eleventh FA Cup triumph. Whose record of ten victories did they overtake?

15 **At the end of the season, which other law was altered leading to a glut of goals in succeeding years?**

1 **West Bromwich Albion** 2 Billy Smith 3 **Arsenal** 4 Willie Davies 5 **Fred Roberts** 6 Southampton 7 **Cardiff City** 8 Fred Tunstall 9 **Rangers** 10 Cowdenbeath 11 **Nithsdale Wanderers** 12 Patsy Gallagher 13 **The Mighty Atom** 14 Queen's Park 15 **Offside: the** number of players that had to be between the attacker and the ball when it was played to him was reduced from three to two

 **Quiz 23**   Season 1925-1926

1 **Who did Herbert Chapman succeed as manager of Arsenal?**

2 When Chapman signed Charlie Buchan from Sunderland, the fee was £2000 plus how much per goal?

3 **How much more did this cost Arsenal in the first year?**

4 Huddersfield Town became the first club ever to win the League Championship three years in a row. Who took over from Herbert Chapman as their manager at the start of the season?

5 **Which of Chapman's last signings for Huddersfield (from Aberdeen) scored 16 goals from outside right in his first season south of the border?**

6 Which Huddersfield player created a new club scoring record, with 35 goals in the League?

7 **Who was the League's leading scorer, with 43 goals in the season for twelfth-placed Blackburn Rovers?**

8 Which team became the first to reach the FA Cup Final and be relegated from the First Division in the same season?

9 **Who won the FA Cup?**

10 Which future Arsenal star scored the only goal of the match?

11 **Celtic won the Scottish League title but lost in the Final of the FA Cup. Who beat them 2-0 to win the competition for the first time?**

12 Who were runners-up in the Scottish League for the fourth year running?

13 **Bobby Skinner set a British scoring record with 53 goals for the Division Two champions in Scotland. Who were they?**

14 Why was the Scottish Third Division not completed?

15 **Which team topped the Third Division table but were not promoted and then left the League altogether?**

 **Quiz 24**   **Season 1926-1927**

1   Who won the League Championship for the first time in 18 years?

2   Who was their Scottish captain, scorer of 36 goals in the season?

3   Who was their secretary-manager?

4   On January 22, live commentary on a football match was broadcast on radio for the first time. Which teams were involved?

5   What was the famous catchphrase popularised - if not actually originated - by this and subsequent broadcasts?

6   The FA Cup left England for the only time when Cardiff City beat Arsenal in the Final. Who scored the only goal of the game?

7   What was the name of Arsenal's Welsh international goalkeeper who was widely thought to have been at fault with the goal?

8   Cardiff City were one of six Welsh clubs in the Football League at the time. Name the other five.

9   Which two Second Division clubs from the south of England were beaten FA Cup semi-finalists?

10 Which member of The Wednesday team was the First Division's leading scorer, with 37 goals?

11 Who scored 59 of Middlesbrough's 122 goals as they romped to the Second Division title?

12 Which Celtic player was Scotland's leading scorer with 49 goals despite missing five of their 38 games through injury?

13 Despite scoring 101 goals, Celtic finished third behind champions Rangers and which other club?

14 Which great Evertonian scored both goals for England in their 2-1 victory over Scotland?

15 When was the last time England had won at Hampden Park?

 **Quiz 25**   Season 1927-1928

1 Who scored the all-time record number of goals in a season - 60 - for League Champions Everton?

2 How many of the club's 42 League games did he play in?

3 Which other Lancashire club won the FA Cup?

4 Which Yorkshire club were runners-up in both the League and the Cup?

5 Which London club scored a League record 127 goals while winning the Third Division (South)?

6 What was the score when Scotland's 'Wembley Wizards' played England in the Home International Championship at Wembley?

7 Who scored a hat-trick in this match?

8 Who was the Scottish outside left - known as 'The Wee Blue Devil' - who put over the crosses for three of the goals?

9 Who was the Scotland captain in this match?

10 Which Scottish team won their first League and Cup double?

11 Who were runners-up in both the Scottish League and FA Cup?

12 Which Celtic player was the First Division's top scorer?

13 Of this player's 47 goals, a record eight came in one game, a 9-0 victory over which Fife team?

14 Jim Smith scored 66 goals in the season, a British record. Which team did he help to win the Scottish Second Division title?

15 For two Scottish Second Division clubs, this was to be the last full season of existence. Which two?

1 Dixie Dean 2 39 3 Blackburn Rovers 4 Huddersfield Town 5 Millwall 6 England 1
Scotland 5 7 Alex Jackson (Huddersfield Town) 8 Alan Morton (Rangers) 9 Jimmy
McMullan (Manchester City) 10 Rangers 11 Celtic 12 Jimmy McGrory 13 Dunfermline
Athletic 14 Ayr United 15 Arthurlie and Bathgate

 **Quiz 26**   **Season 1928-1929**

1   Who, on August 25, became the first two teams to wear numbered shirts in a League game?

2   For which great Arsenal player, now retiring, was David Jack a replacement?

3   **Where did Arsenal buy David Jack from?**

4   What was the record-breaking transfer fee?

5   **The First Division was won by The Wednesday, who then changed their name to Sheffield Wednesday during the close season. Who was their captain?**

6   Name the Wednesday manager who had bought this player from Spurs.

7   **Who won the FA Cup for the third time this decade, beating Portsmouth 2-0 in the Final?**

8   On May 15, England suffered their first-ever defeat on foreign soil. Who beat them 4-3?

9   **Who was the First Division's leading scorer, with 43 goals for fourth-placed Sunderland?**

10   Rangers won the Scottish Championship, but who beat them 2-0 in the FA Cup Final?

11   **Which Rangers player became the first man to be sent off in an FA Cup Final?**

12   For which team did Scotland's leading scorer Evelyn Morrison - with 43 goals in the season - play?

13   **Who scored a record five goals for Scotland in their 7-3 win over Northern Ireland in Belfast?**

14   This player had begun his international career in 1924 while with Airdrieonians. For which English First Division club was he now playing?

15   **Scotland won the Home International Championship with three wins out of three. What was historic about Alex Cheyne's goal in their 1-0 win over England at Hampden Park?**

---

1 Arsenal (at Hillsborough) and Chelsea (at home to Swansea Town) 2 Charlie Buchan
3 Bolton Wanderers 4 £10,890 5 Jimmy Seed 6 Bob Brown 7 Bolton Wanderers
8 Spain 9 Dave Halliday 10 Kilmarnock 11 Jock Buchanan 12 Falkirk 13 Hughie
Gallacher 14 Newcastle United 15 It was the first international goal to be scored
direct from a corner

Quiz 27   Season 1929-1930

1 **Sheffield Wednesday retained the League Championship; who was the season's leading scorer, with 42 goals for seventh-placed West Ham United?**

2 Who were runners-up in the League under George Jobey, equalling their previous best in 1895-96?

3 **Who won the FA Cup for the first time, beating Huddersfield Town 2-0 in the so-called Graf Zeppelin Final in which the German airship passed over Wembley on the afternoon of the match?**

4 Who was their manager, who had previously been the manager of the runners-up?

5 **Who scored the goals in the Final?**

6 From which club did Arsenal buy Alex James?

7 **How much was the record fee for which he was transferred?**

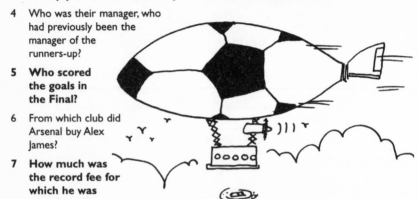

8 How many caps did James win for Scotland?

9 **Five days before the FA Cup Final, Arsenal were involved in the highest scoring draw in League history, 6-6 away to whom?**

10 Who won promotion to the Second Division after having finished second in Division Three (South) in six of the previous eight seasons?

11 **Rangers won the Scottish Championship, but the First Division's leading scorer - with 38 goals - played for third-placed Aberdeen. What was his name?**

12 Rangers also won the FA Cup; who did they beat 2-1 in the Final replay, after the first match had been drawn 0-0?

13 **Which now defunct team won the Second Division title?**

14 England beat Scotland 5-1 at Wembley to win the Home Championship outright for the first time since the First World War. Which Sheffield Wednesday player scored twice in this game on his international debut?

15 **Which Arsenal player was England captain in this match?**

---

1 Vic Watson 2 Derby County 3 Arsenal 4 Herbert Chapman 5 Alex James and Jack Lambert 6 Preston North End 7 £9000 8 Eight 9 Leicester City 10 Plymouth Argyle 11 Benny Yorston 12 Partick Thistle 13 Leith Athletic 14 Ellis Rimmer 15 David Jack

 **Quiz 28**   **Season 1930-1931**

1 **Arsenal became the first London club to win the Championship. How many goals did they score in the 42-game season?**

2 Who was their leading scorer, with 38 goals in the season?

3 **Name the Arsenal inside right who contributed another 31 goals...**

4 ...And the left winger who scored a further 28.

5 **Amazingly, Arsenal were not the top scorers in the First Division that year - that title went to the runners-up. Who were they?**

6 Who was their - and the League's - leading scorer, with 49 goals?

7 **Which team became the first to win the FA Cup and promotion from the Second Division in the same season?**

8 In the semi-final, they beat the team who beat them into second place in the Second Division. Who?

9 **Who were the runners-up in the FA Cup?**

10 Who scored both the winning side's goals in the Final?

11 **Rangers won the Scottish League Championship, but the highest scorer, with 44 goals, played for fifth-placed Heart of Midlothian. Name him.**

12 Who did Celtic beat 4-2 in the replayed Final of the Scottish FA Cup, after the first match had been drawn 2-2?

13 **In May, which country became the first to defeat Scotland on foreign soil?**

14 Which other team did Scotland lose to on this tour?

15 **Who did Scotland beat 3-2 in the final match of their 1931 summer tour?**

 # Quiz 29   **Season 1931-1932**

1   **Who won the First Division Championship?**

2   What was the real name of Dixie Dean, their leading scorer that season with 44 goals?

3   **Why was he called Dixie?**

4   How many goals did Dean score for England in his 16 international appearances between 1927 and 1933?

5   **Who were runners-up in both the League and the FA Cup?**

6   Who scored both Newcastle United's goals in their 2-1 Cup Final victory?

7   **What has the Newcastle equaliser come to be known as?**

8   Which Third Division club became the first to resign from the Football League during the course of a season?

9   **Who bounced straight back up to the First Division after having been relegated in 1931?**

10   Which Newcastle and England player made his name during the Home Internationals as perhaps the first exponent of the long throw-in?

11   **Motherwell won the Scottish League Championship for the only time in their history. When was the last time it had been won by anyone other than Celtic or Rangers?**

12   And who had won it then?

13   **Which Motherwell player set a Scottish League scoring record, with 52 goals in the season?**

14   Who were runners-up to Rangers in the Scottish FA Cup, going down 3-0 in a replay after the first match had been drawn 1-1?

15   **Name the Celtic and Scotland goalkeeper who died from head injuries after throwing himself at the feet of a Rangers player during the Old Firm match at Ibrox on September 5.**

 **Quiz 30**   Season 1932-1933

1 **Who won the English League Championship, the first of three consecutive titles?**

2 Who were the so-called Wünderteam, who played against England at Stamford Bridge?

3 **Which former Bolton Wanderers player was their national coach?**

4 What was the score in this match?

5 **Who won the FA Cup, beating Manchester City 3-0 in the Final?**

6 Who scored the goals?

7 **Who pulled off one of the great shocks of FA Cup history when they beat Arsenal 2-0 in the third round?**

8 Who scored for the Third Division club?

9 **Which Arsenal player never played for the club again after giving away a penalty in this match?**

10 Which team finished runners-up in both the Scottish League and FA Cup?

11 **Who was their leading scorer for the second season running, with 45 goals?**

12 How many times did he play for Scotland?

13 **Who won the Scottish Championship, despite winning one fewer game and scoring one fewer goal than the runners-up?**

14 Which two clubs were expelled from the Scottish League in November 1932 for inability to meet match guarantees?

15 **In which year had they both joined the League?**

 Quiz 31   **Season 1933-1934**

1   **Who took over as Arsenal manager after the untimely death of Herbert Chapman from pneumonia while watching his third team play at Guildford on January 6, 1934?**

2   What had been his previous job?

3   **Who was his first purchase?**

4   Where did he get him from?

5   **Who won the FA Cup, beating Portsmouth 2-1 in the Final?**

6   Who was the winning goalkeeper?

7   **Who scored both the winning team's goals?**

8   Which future President of FIFA refereed the Final?

9   **Who was the First Division's leading scorer for the second season running, with 35 goals for fourth-placed Derby County?**

10   Who was top scorer, with 41 goals, for Scottish double winners Rangers?

11   **Who won the home International Championship for the second year running?**

12   Who came 20th in the Second Division, the lowest league position in their distinguished history, which already included two Championships, and avoided relegation to the Third Division (North) by only one point?

13   **Who were runners-up to Arsenal in the First Division?**

14   Who was their manager, a former captain and one of their most distinguished players?

15   **Who did Rangers beat 5-0 in the Scottish FA Cup Final?**

 **Quiz 32**   **Season 1934-1935**

1   **Which future manager of Chelsea scored 42 goals in the season for Arsenal?**

2   Arsenal won the Championship for the third year in succession, a feat previously achieved by one team only. Which?

3   **Which country were the opposition in the so-called Battle of Highbury, which England won 3-2?**

4   Which Manchester City outside left missed a penalty in this match and then scored the first in open play?

5   **Which great Stoke City player scored the second on his second international appearance?**

6   The third goal was scored by Ted Drake - how many other Arsenal players were in the England side?

7   **Who scored both goals for the opposition?**

8   Who scored two goals for Sheffield Wednesday in their 4-2 Cup Final victory over West Bromwich Albion? (He also scored in every round of the competition that year.)

9   **Which Lancashire club lost to West Brom in the semi-finals but had the consolation of promotion as runners-up in Division Two?**

10 Which London club won the Second Division, thus gaining promotion to the top flight for the first time in their history?

11 **Who was their legendary manager?**

12 Which London club was relegated from the First Division after having been promoted in 1933, and coming third in Division One in 1934?

13 **Who was their manager until they were relegated?**

14 Rangers did the double for the fourth time. Who did they beat in the Scottish FA Cup Final?

15 **Which Heart of Midlothian player was Scotland's top scorer, with 38 goals?**

 **Quiz 33**   **Season 1935-1936**

1   **Sunderland won the League Championship - what was the nickname given to this team?**

2   Who was their manager?

3   **One of the stars of this team was the great inside forward known to everyone as 'Raich' Carter. What was his real Christian name?**

4   Which member of the championship-winning side was nicknamed 'The Mighty Atom'?

5   **For which two countries did he play at international level?**

6   Who was the First Division's leading scorer, with 39 goals for West Bromwich Albion?

7   **Arsenal won the FA Cup, beating Sheffield United 1-0 in the Final. Who scored the goal?**

8   Which two founder members of the Football League were relegated together from the First Division for the first time in their history?

9   **Who equalled the First Division scoring record with seven goals against Aston Villa on December 14?**

10 Who, in 1888, was the only other player to have scored seven in a First Division match?

11 **On Boxing Day, 1935, in a Third Division (North) game, who scored a record nine goals for Tranmere Rovers in their 13-4 win over Oldham Athletic?**

12 Then, on April 13, 1936, in the Third Division (South), who broke this record when he scored 10 goals in Luton Town's 12-0 defeat of Bristol Rovers?

13 **Who scored 50 goals in the season for Scottish champions Celtic?**

14 Who scored eight goals for Morton in their Division Two game against Raith Rovers on April 18?

15 **Who were runners-up to Rangers in the Scottish FA Cup?**

Lanark

1 The Bank of England 2 Johnny Cochrane 3 Horatio 4 Patsy Gallagher 5 Northern Ireland and the Republic of Ireland 6 Ginger Richardson 7 Ted Drake 8 Aston Villa and Blackburn Rovers 9 Ted Drake (Arsenal) 10 James Ross for Preston North End v Stoke City 11 Robert 'Bunny' Bell 12 Joe Payne 13 Jimmy McGrory 14 John Calder 15 Third

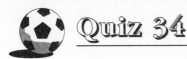 ## Quiz 34   Season 1936-1937

1 **Who were First Division Champions?**

2 What unwanted feat did they achieve the following season?

3 **Which London club became the first Third Division side to reach the semi-finals of the FA Cup?**

4 Name this team's player manager who scored both goals in their 2-0 sixth round victory over high-flying Manchester City.

5 **Who created a new First Division scoring record, with 375 goals in his career?**

6 In Division Three, two players scored 55 goals in the season. One played for Mansfield Town in the Third Division (North). Name him.

7 **The other 55-er played for Luton Town in the Third Division (South). Who was he?**

8 How many goals did this player score on his only appearance for England, an 8-0 victory over Finland during the summer tour?

9 **Who scored a hat-trick on his home ground as England beat Hungary 6-2 at Highbury?**

10 The First Division's leading scorer was Freddie Steele, with 33 goals. Which team did he play for?

11 **Who won the FA Cup for the first time, beating Preston North End 3-1 in the Final?**

12 Who was their captain?

13 **Which Scottish international centre forward scored in the Final for Preston North End?**

14 Who won the Home International championship, winning all three games?

15 **In Scotland, Rangers won the League and Celtic the FA Cup. Who were runners-up in both competitions?**

Quiz 35

Season 1937-1938

1 **Who won the League Championship?**

2 How many times had they won it before?

3 **Who was the First Division's leading scorer, with 28 goals for 14th-placed Everton?**

4 Which team scored the most goals in the First Division - 80, three more than the champions?

5 **In the FA Cup Final, in which Preston North End beat Huddersfield Town 1-0, two things happened that had never happened before in this fixture at Wembley. What?**

6 Name the Scottish international inside right who scored the Preston winner.

7 **How many times did he play for Scotland?**

8 In Scotland, Celtic won the League. Who won the FA Cup for the first time, and became the only Second Division club ever to win the trophy?

9 **Who did they beat 4-2 after extra time in the Final replay after the first match had been drawn 1-1?**

10 Which team took the Cup winners to two replays in the semi-final only two years before going out of the Scottish League for ever?

11 **The Scottish First Division's leading scorer was Andy Black, with 40 goals in the season. Which team did he play for?**

12 Which Fife team won the Scottish Second Division scoring a British record 142 goals in 34 games?

13 **What was the score in the controversial Germany v England international in Berlin at the start of which the England players gave the Nazi salute?**

14 Adolf Hitler did not attend the match. Which two leading Nazis were guests of honour?

15 **Which West Ham United player scored for England in this game with a 25-yard drive?**

Quiz 36   Season 1938-1939

1 Which Tottenham Hotspur player equalled the England scoring record with five goals against Northern Ireland at Maine Road?

2 Who was the First Division's leading scorer, with 35 goals for League Champions Everton?

3 Who won the FA Cup, beating Wolverhampton Wanderers in the Final, and held the trophy for longer than any other club, because of the outbreak of the Second World War?

4 Who was the winning manager with the lucky spats?

5 Which former Wolves player, transferred only two months previously, scored one of the goals in their 4-1 victory?

6 Which Wolves player had moved to Arsenal earlier in the season at a cost of £14,000?

7 Which Highbury legend was he bought to replace?

8 Who was the leading scorer in Scotland, with 34 goals for League Champions Rangers?

9 Who won the Scottish FA Cup for the first time?

10 Who scored with his hand to help Italy draw 2-2 with England in Turin?

11 Who scored the England goals?

12 In the Second Division, Blackburn Rovers were champions and Sheffield United were promoted as runners-up. Who did United beat into third place by one point?

13 Which game on January 2 had the highest-ever attendance - 118,567 - at a British football match?

14 Who was relegated to the Third Division (North) after suffering more defeats in a season - 31 out of 42 games played - than any other team in the history of the Second Division?

15 Who were the leaders of the First Division - played three, won three - on September 3, 1939 when the League was suspended because of the outbreak of the Second World War?

 **Quiz 37**   **Season 1946-1947**

1 Which Yorkshire team won Division Three (North) with a
   record number of points (72), a record number of wins (33),
   a record number of away wins (18) and a record number of
   away points (37)?

2 Which London club won the FA Cup for the only time in their history?

3 Who scored their winning goal in extra time in the Final?

4 Which Lancashire team were runners-up in both the Cup and Division Two,
   but had the consolation of promotion?

5 Liverpool won the League Championship, Manchester United were
   second. Which team came third and had the highest scorer -
   Dennis Westcott, with 37 goals in the season?

6 England's end of season tour began with a 1-0 defeat in Switzerland. They
   then travelled west and defeated which country 10-0?

7 Who won his first cap in this game and scored four goals?

8 Which other England player scored four goals in this match?

9 Who scored six goals on his debut for Newcastle United in their
   record 13-0 Second Division victory over Newport County?

10 From which other Second Division club had Newcastle United bought him
   for £13,000?

11 The sale of whom to Liverpool earlier that season for the same
   amount had helped Newcastle to finance the deal?

12 This player finished the season with 24 goals in the First Division. Which
   other Liverpool player was joint top scorer?

13 The four top teams in Scottish Division A were also the
   semi-finalists in the FA Cup. Name them.

14 Who went on to win the Scottish Cup for the first time in their history?

15 Top scorer in the Scottish First Division was Bobby Mitchell, with
   22 goals. Which team did he play for?

Quiz 38 Season 1947-1948

1 **Arsenal won the League Championship for the sixth time. Who was their leading scorer, with 33 goals?**

2 Runners-up in the League, Manchester United had the consolation of winning the FA Cup. Who did they beat 4-2 in the Final?

3 **Which member of the losing side scored in every round of the competition, a total of 10 goals?**

4 Which Third Division side sensationally bought England centre forward Tommy Lawton from Chelsea for £20,000 - £5,000 more than the previous highest transfer fee?

5 **Where did Manchester United play their home matches?**

6 Who did First Division Sunderland buy from Second Division Newcastle United for £20,050?

7 **Which Blackpool player made every one of England's goals in their 5-2 victory over Belgium in Brussels?**

8 And which three players scored them?

9 **Which Manchester City player - the first goalkeeper to captain England - kept a clean sheet for his country in the 4-0 defeat of Italy in Turin?**

10 And which three players scored the goals in this match?

11 **Who won the Scottish League Championship?**

12 Which Falkirk player was the First Division's leading scorer, with 20 goals?

13 **Who won the Scottish FA Cup, beating Morton 1-0 in a replay after the first game had finished 1-1?**

14 Who won the Scottish League Cup, beating Falkirk 4-1 in a replay after the first match had been drawn 0-0?

15 **What other distinction did the same team achieve this season?**

 Quiz 39   Season 1948-1949

1   **Which team became the first to rise from the Third Division and win the League Championship?**

2   Who was their manager?

3   **Who came second in the First Division for the third year in a row?**

4   Which Second Division side reached the FA Cup Final?

5   **Which future England manager missed playing for them in the Final because of illness?**

6   Who scored both goals in Wolverhampton Wanderers' 2-0 victory over them in the FA Cup Final?

7   **The First Division's leading scorer was Willie Moir, with 25 goals. For which team did he play?**

8   Which team was knocked out of the FA Cup in the 4th round in the mist on the sloping pitch of Southern League Yeovil?

9   **Which future manager of Queen's Park Rangers was the only Yeovil player in this match with League experience?**

10   Who beat Yeovil 8-0 in the FA Cup 5th round?

11   **Who scored five of their goals?**

12   Which Newcastle United legend scored on his debut for England in their 3-1 defeat against Scotland at Wembley?

13   **Rangers won the Scottish Championship, but who was the First Division's leading scorer, with 30 goals for runners-up Dundee?**

14   Rangers also won the Scottish FA Cup: who did they beat in the Final?

15   **Rangers completed the treble by winning the League Cup - who did they beat in the Final of this competition?**

Quiz 40

Season 1949-1950

1 Portsmouth won the League Championship on goal average ahead of which Midlands club?

2 Name the First Division's leading scorer, who netted 25 times for third- placed Sunderland.

3 **Who, famously, ignored the Arsenal captain's instruction to stay back, went up for a corner and headed the equaliser in their FA Cup semi-final against Chelsea?**

4 Who was the Arsenal captain and 1950 Football Writers' Player of the Year?

5 **Who scored both goals for Arsenal in their 2-0 FA Cup Final win over Liverpool?**

6 Which great England Test cricketer won a Cup winner's medal in this match?

7 **Who was manager of Liverpool?**

8 Which London team on the verge of greater things won the Second Division Championship?

9 **Who became the youngest player to win a cap for Wales when he played against Northern Ireland aged 18 years 71 days?**

10 Who was captain of the Republic of Ireland team that beat England for the first time away at Goodison Park?

11 **Which Scottish team won its first major honour, winning the League Cup, a trophy they were to retain the following year?**

12 Which Heart of Midlothian player was Scotland's leading scorer, with 30 goals?

13 **Which Chelsea player scored England's goal in their 1-0 Home International victory over Scotland at Hampden?**

14 Which of the Home nations qualified for the World Cup finals in Brazil?

15 **Which of the Home nations actually took part?**

---

*1 **Wolverhampton Wanderers** 2 Dickie Davis 3 **Leslie Compton** 4 Joe Mercer 5 **Reg Lewis** 6 Denis Compton 7 **George Kay** 8 Tottenham Hotspur 9 **John Charles** (**Leeds United**) 10 Johnny Carey (Manchester United) 11 East **Fife** 12 Willie Bauld 13 **Roy Bentley** 14 England and Scotland 15 **England only - Scotland refused to take part** if they did not win the Home International Championship*

 **Quiz 41**   Season 1950-1951

1 What was the name given to the style of play that brought Tottenham Hotspur the League Championship for the first time in their history?

2 Who was Spurs' manager?

3 **Which future Spurs manager played for them at right-half?**

4 Which future Ipswich and England manager played for them at right back?

5 **Who were runners-up in the First Division?**

6 Who became the oldest player to make his England debut, appearing in the match against Wales at the age of 38 years and 2 months?

7 **What was the surname of Alec and David, the father and son who played together for Stockport County in their 2-0 Division Three (North) defeat of Hartlepool on the last day of the season?**

8 Who won the FA Cup, beating Blackpool 2-0 in the Final?

9 **Who scored both goals in the Final (and had also scored in every previous round that season)?**

10 Which team of Oxbridge graduates won the FA Amateur Cup, beating Bishop Auckland 2-1 in the Final in front of 100,000 at Wembley?

11 **Which Lancashire team won the Second Division Championship two years after relegation from the top flight?**

12 In the match against Scotland at Wembley, which England player had to go off after a clash of heads with Billy Liddell?

13 **What was the final score in this match?**

14 Who won the Scottish Championship, finishing 10 points ahead of second placed Rangers?

15 **Who won the Scottish League Cup and were runners-up to Celtic in the FA Cup?**

 **Quiz 42**   **Season 1951-1952**

1 **Who won the Championship for the first time in 41 years after finishing second four times since the War?**

2 Which was the first English club to install floodlights? (They played their first game under them this season - a 6-1 victory over Hapeol of Tel Aviv.)

3 **In the FA Cup Final, Newcastle United beat Arsenal 1-0. What were the names of the opposing captains, who had served together in the Army during the War?**

4 Which Chilean scored the winning goal in the Cup Final, to add to the 33 which had made him the League's top scorer?

5 **Who was the Newcastle United manager who told his defeated opponents: 'We have won the Cup, but the glory is yours'?**

6 Who scored 46 goals in 32 games as Sheffield Wednesday won the Second Division title?

7 **Whose record for the number of England caps did Billy Wright of Wolverhampton Wanderers break when he made his 42nd international appearance against Austria in Vienna?**

8 How many caps did Wright eventually win altogether?

9 **Who scored two of England's goals in their 3-2 victory in this international match?**

10 Which Sheffield Wednesday player scored the other goal?

11 **What had been the score in that season's previous meeting between England and Austria at Wembley?**

12 What nickname did the press give to Austrian centre half Ernst Ocwirk?

13 **Which member of the so-called 'Famous Five' was Scotland's leading scorer, with 27 goals for champions Hibernian?**

14 Who won the Scottish FA Cup for the first time in their history?

15 **Which of the Home Nations celebrated its centenary by beating the Rest of the UK 3-2?**

1 Manchester United 2 Arsenal 3 Joe Harvey (Newcastle United) and Joe Mercer (Arsenal) 4 George Robledo 5 Stan Seymour 6 Derek Dooley 7 Bob Crompton (Blackburn Rovers) 8 105 9 Nat Lofthouse 10 J. Sewell 11 England 2 Austria 2 12 Clockwork Ocwirk 13 Lawrie Reilly 14 Motherwell 15 Wales

Quiz 43 — Season 1952-1953

1 Which manager led Arsenal to their seventh Championship (then a record)?

2 Which Lancashire team did they edge out at the last on goal average?

3 **The runners-up had the First Division's leading scorer, with 24 goals. Name him.**

4 Which goalkeeper retired at the age of 43 after serving Everton since 1929 - the longest ever career (24 years) with a single club?

5 **By what name will this season's FA Cup Final forever be known?**

6 Which teams played in it, and what was the result?

7 **In this match, who became the first man ever to score a hat-trick in the FA Cup Final?**

8 Who scored the last goal in this match and became the first South African to win an FA Cup winner's medal?

9 **Who scored in every round of the FA Cup, including the Final?**

10 Which First Division team conceded three own goals at home on Boxing Day in a 5-4 defeat by West Bromwich Albion?

11 **The career of which rising Sheffield Wednesday star was cruelly ended at the age of 23 when he had to have a leg amputated after challenging the opposition goalkeeper in a League game against Preston North End?**

12 Rangers did the double in Scotland, but won the League only on goal average. Who were runners-up?

13 **And who did Rangers beat in the FA Cup Final after a replay?**

14 Who won the Scottish League Cup, beating Kilmarnock 2-0 in the Final?

15 **The Scottish First Division had joint top scorers, both with 30 goals in the season. One was Lawrie Reilly of Hibernian. Who was the other?**

 ## Quiz 44   Season 1953-1954

1. Wolverhampton Wanderers won the League Championship for the first time. What name was given to their style of play?

2. Who was manager of Wolves?

3. The defeat of which two European clubs in friendly matches led the Wolves manager to claim that his team were 'Champions of the World'?

4. Which competition is believed to have been set up as a result of this hype?

5. Which other Midlands team were runners-up in the League?

6. Who was the League's leading scorer, with 29 goals in the season for third-placed Huddersfield Town?

7. Which Lancashire team were relegated after finishing bottom of the First Division and did not return until 1962?

8. Which Third Division (North) team created records by conceding the fewest goals ever (21) in a season, keeping the greatest number of clean sheets (30), and suffering the fewest defeats (three)?

9. Who achieved the unique feat of winning a Cup winner's medal in three countries when he played for Derry City in Northern Ireland after winning the Scottish Cup with Celtic in 1937 and the English FA Cup with Manchester United in 1948?

10. What was the score in the historic game in which Hungary inflicted the first defeat ever suffered by England against overseas opposition at Wembley?

11. Which Hungarian scored a hat-trick in this match?

12. What was the score in the return fixture in Budapest six months later?

13. Who scored two goals in both games?

14. Who did West Bromwich Albion beat 3-2 in the Final of the FA Cup?

15. In Scotland, Celtic won the League and the FA Cup. Who won the League Cup, beating Partick Thistle 3-2 in the Final?

Quiz 45

Season 1954-1955

1 Chelsea won the League Championship for the only time in their history. Who was their manager?

2 Who beat them 6-5 on their own pitch?

3 Which Chelsea amateur scored a hat-trick in this match?

4 Which West Bromwich Albion forward was the First Division's leading scorer, with 27 goals?

5 Which three teams tied on 54 points at the top of the Second Division?

6 Who set a Second Division scoring record, with seven goals in Blackburn Rovers' 8-3 victory over Bristol Rovers?

7 Which Third Division side reached the semi-final of the FA Cup?

8 Who won the FA Cup, beating Manchester City 3-1 in the Final?

9 Who scored the first goal after only 45 seconds?

10 Which future Cup-winning manager of Sunderland played a blinder in the winners' defence?

11 Who won the Scottish League Championship for the first time in their history?

12 Who won the Scottish FA Cup, beating Celtic 1-0 in a replay after the first match had been drawn 1-1?

13 Heart of Midlothian won the League Cup, beating Motherwell 4-0 in the Final. Who was their leading scorer, with 21 goals?

14 In the Home International Championship, Scotland lost to England by a record score of 7-2. Which Wolverhampton Wanderers forward scored four of the England goals?

15 In which year had Scotland beaten England by the same score?

 ## Quiz 46   Season 1955-1956

1 **Name the Manchester City goalkeeper who broke his neck in the FA Cup Final but played on and collected a winner's medal.**

2 Who were their opponents in the Final?

3 **Which future England manager played at centre forward for City?**

4 Who was the leading scorer in the First Division, with 32 goals for Bolton Wanderers?

5 **Who won the first ever European Cup, the first of five consecutive victories in this tournament?**

6 Which French team did they beat 4-3 in the Final in Paris?

7 **Who scored a hat-trick for the winning side?**

8 What was his nationality?

9 **Who were Britain's sole representatives in the competition?**

10 Who scored a hat-trick in England's 4-2 victory over Brazil at Wembley?

11 **What was historic about the First Division match between Portsmouth and Newcastle United at Fratton Park on February 22, 1956?**

12 Who won the First Division by a record margin, finishing 11 points ahead of the runners-up?

13 **Who came second and third, both with 49 points?**

14 Who beat Celtic 3-1 in the Scottish FA Cup Final?

15 **Who won the Scottish League Cup, beating St Mirren 2-1 in the Final?**

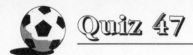 **Quiz 47**   **Season 1956-1957**

1 **Which Leeds United forward was the First Division's leading scorer, with 38 goals?**

2 Manchester United won the League Championship, but who denied them the double by beating them 2-1 in the Final of the FA Cup?

3 **Who was the winning team's manager?**

4 Name the United goalkeeper who had to go off with concussion, returning later to play on the wing.

5 **Who took his place in the Manchester goal?**

6 Who scored United's goal?

7 **Who was the Manchester United captain?**

8 Which Third Division (South) club knocked Wolverhampton Wanderers out of the FA Cup in the 4th round?

9 **Who scored the only goal of this game?**

10 Which First Division opponents did the same team knock out in the 5th round of the 1957 FA Cup?

11 **Which team won the Second Division Championship for the second time in three years?**

12 Which great Englishman became the first European Footballer of the Year?

13 **Who knocked Manchester United out of the European Cup?**

14 In Scotland, Rangers won the League Championship - who won the FA Cup, beating Kilmarnock 2-1 in a replay after the first game had been drawn 1-1?

15 **Scotland's leading scorer was Hugh Baird, with 33 goals. Which team did he play for?**

Quiz 48   Season 1957-1958

1 **Who won the English League Championship?**

2 Which team was relegated from the English First Division for the first time since 1890?

3 **Who were Champions of the Second Division?**

4 Which Tottenham Hotspur player was the First Division's leading scorer, with 36 goals?

5 **Name the eight Manchester United first team members who were killed in the Munich air crash on February 6.**

6 Manchester United were returning from a European Cup match against the Champions of Yugoslavia - who were they?

7 **Despite the tragedy, Manchester United reached the Final of the FA Cup. Which four survivors played at Wembley?**

8 They lost 2-0 to Bolton Wanderers. Who scored both the goals?

9 **Which Welsh international was the leading scorer in the Italian League, with 28 goals in 34 games for Juventus?**

10 In the last season of the Third Division North and South, who won their respective sections?

11 **Who beat Rangers 7-1 in the Final of the Scottish League Cup?**

12 Who won the Scottish League Championship for the first time in the 20th century, scoring a record number of goals (132) in the process?

13 **With 28 goals apiece, the joint top scorers both played for the Champions. What were their names?**

14 Who won the Scottish FA Cup for the third time, beating Hibernian 1-0 in the Final?

15 **Barcelona won the first Inter-Cities Fairs Cup. Who did they beat 8-2 on aggregate in the Final?**

---

1 **Wolverhampton Wanderers** 2 Sunderland 3 **West Ham United** 4 Bobby Smith 5 **Roger Byrne, Geoff Bent, Eddie Colman, Duncan Edwards, Mark Jones, David Pegg, Tommy Taylor, Billy Whelan** 6 Red Star Belgrade 7 **Bobby Charlton, Harry Gregg, Bill Foulkes and Dennis Viollet** 8 Nat Lofthouse 9 **John Charles** 10 Scunthorpe United and Brighton and Hove Albion 11 **Celtic** 12 Heart of Midlothian 13 **Jimmy Murray and Jimmy Wardhaugh** 14 Clyde 15 A combined team called London

 ## Quiz 49   Season 1958-1959

1 **Who became Scotland's youngest international, winning his first cap at the age of 18 years 236 days?**

2 Who was he then playing for?

3 **Who won the English League Championship, for the third time in five years?**

4 Which Chelsea and England star was the First Division's leading scorer, with 32 goals?

5 **Who won the English FA Cup, having won it once before in 1898?**

6 Who were the runners-up?

7 **Which future manager of Northern Ireland was on the losing side?**

8 Who scored the opening goal and then broke his leg in the 32nd minute?

9 **Which Third Division side reached the semi-final?**

10 With 42 goals, which MIddlesbrough centre forward was the Second Division's leading scorer for the second season running?

11 **In Scotland, Rangers won the League Championship. Who won the FA Cup for the second time in their history?**

12 Who did Heart of Midlothian beat 5-1 in the Scottish League Cup Final?

13 **Who, on April 11, became the first player to win 100 England caps in a match against Scotland at Wembley?**

14 England won this game 1-0. Who scored the goal?

15 **Which former Tottenham Hotspur player became the manager of the club, in succession to Jimmy Anderson?**

---

1 **Denis Law** 2 Huddersfield Town 3 **Wolverhampton Wanderers** 4 Jimmy Greaves
5 **Nottingham Forest** 6 Luton Town 7 **Billy Bingham** 8 Roy Dwight (Nottingham Forest)
9 **Norwich City** 10 Brian Clough 11 **St Mirren** 12 Partick Thistle 13 **Billy Wright**
(**Wolverhampton Wanderers**) 14 Bobby Charlton (Manchester United) 15 **Bill Nicholson**

Quiz 50 — Season 1959-1960

1 **Which player scored all the goals in the English Football League's 5-0 defeat of the Irish League in Belfast?**

2 Which Midlands First Division club became the first to score 100 goals in three consecutive seasons?

3 **Which emerging player - later a Liverpool star - scored a hat-trick in less than three minutes for Motherwell in a Scottish League Cup tie against Hibernian?**

4 Against which Cheshire club did Tottenham Hotspur record their highest-ever victory - 13-2 - in an FA Cup 4th round replay?

5 **Who were their four scorers?**

6 The European Cup Final between Real Madrid and Eintracht Frankfurt led to a record result. What was the score?

7 **And there was also a record attendance - 135,000. Where was the match played?**

8 Which Lancashire club won the League Championship for the second time in their history?

9 **When had they previously won it?**

10 Which Manchester United player was the First Division's leading scorer, with 32 goals?

11 **Who won the FA Cup, beating Blackburn Rovers 3-0 in the Final?**

12 Who won the first European Nations Cup, beating Yugoslavia 2-1 in the Final in Paris?

13 **In Scotland, which team did the League and League Cup double?**

14 Who was their leading scorer, with 42 goals?

15 **Which Real Madrid star was European Footballer of the Year?**

1 **Brian Clough** 2 Wolverhampton Wanderers 3 Ian St John 4 Crewe Alexandra 5 **Harmer, Smith (4), Allen (5), Jones (3, including one penalty)** 6 Real Madrid 7 **Eintracht Frankfurt 3 7 Hampden Park, Glasgow** 8 Burnley 9 1920-21 10 Dennis Viollet 11 **Wolverhampton Wanderers** 12 The USSR 13 **Heart of Midlothian** 14 Joe Baker 15 Alfredo di Stefano

 # Quiz 51   Season 1960-1961

1 **Tottenham Hotspur did the double for the first time this century. Which two clubs had previously done it?**

2 Jimmy Greaves was the First Division's leading scorer, with 41 goals for Chelsea. To which Italian club was he soon to move?

3 **Which Yorkshire team were runners-up to Spurs in the League?**

4 Which East Midlands team were runners-up to Spurs in the FA Cup?

5 **Which Midlands team were the first winners of the new League Cup competition?**

6 Which five leading clubs declined to take part in the inaugural League Cup?

7 **Who won the Fourth Division Championship in their first season in the League?**

8 Who became England's first £100-a-week footballer?

9 **Real Madrid - who had won the European Cup in each of the five years it had been contested - finally lost a tie. Who beat them?**

10 Who knocked English Champions Burnley out of the European Cup in the quarter-final?

11 **Who was Burnley's manager?**

12 Which Italian team beat Birmingham City 4-2 on aggregate in the Final of the Inter-Cities Fairs Cup?

13 **With 42 goals, the leading scorer in the Scottish First Division was Alex Harley, who played for a club which, by 1967, had ceased to exist. Which club?**

14 Who won the Scottish FA Cup for the first time in their history, beating Celtic 2-0 in a replay after the first game had been drawn 0-0?

15 **Meanwhile, the Scottish League and League Cup were both won by a Rangers team inspired by recent signing Jim Baxter. Where had he been bought from?**

14 Dunfermline Athletic 15 Raith Rovers

and Wolverhampton Wanderers 7 Peterborough United 8 Johnny Haynes (Fulham and
England) 9 Barcelona 10 FC Hamburg 11 Harry Potts 12 AS Roma 13 Third Lanark

1 Preston North End and Aston Villa 2 AC Milan 3 Sheffield Wednesday 4 Leicester
City 5 Aston Villa 6 Arsenal, Sheffield Wednesday, Tottenham Hotspur, West Bromwich Albion

Quiz 52   Season 1961-62

1 **Which prolific scorer and manager of the future moved from Middlesbrough to Sunderland for £45,000?**

2 Which team resigned from the Football League on March 6 because of financial problems?

3 **Which team would replace them in the Fourth Division, with effect from the start of the 1962-63 season?**

4 Who won the League Championship only a year after being promoted from the Second Division?

5 **Who was their - and the First Division's - leading scorer, with 33 goals in the season?**

6 Tottenham Hotspur only just failed to repeat their feats of the previous season - they slipped to third in the League, but had the consolation of retaining the FA Cup. Which Lancashire team did they beat 3-1 in the Final?

7 **And where had the Cup runners-up finished in the League?**

8 How far did Tottenham go in the European Cup?

9 **Who knocked them out of the competition?**

10 Which foreign-based Hungarian scored a hat-trick in the 1962 European Cup Final?

11 **Who won the European Cup Winners' Cup Final, beating Fiorentina 3-0 in a replay after the first game had been drawn 1-1?**

12 Which Fourth Division Lancashire team did Norwich City beat 4-0 on aggregate to win the League Cup?

13 **Who won the Scottish League Championship for the first time in their history?**

14 Who was their - and Scotland's - leading scorer, with 24 goals?

15 **Which member of this Championship-winning side went on to greater fame with Arsenal?**

15 Ian Ure

1 **Brian Clough** 2 Accrington Stanley 3 **Oxford United** 4 Ipswich Town 5 **Ray Crawford**
6 Burnley 7 **Second** 8 Semi-final 9 **Benfica, the holders and eventual winners** 10 Ferenc
Puskas (Real Madrid) 11 **Atletico Madrid** 12 Rochdale 13 **Dundee** 14 Alan Gilzean

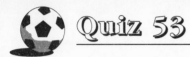

Quiz 53   Season 1962-1963

1 Who did Manchester United bring back to Britain from Torino for a record fee of £115,000?

2 Who, with 37 goals, was the First Division's leading scorer, a position he would occupy the following season and the season after that?

3 **Who won the League Championship for the sixth time but the first time since 1939?**

4 Who was their manager?

5 **Manchester United won the FA Cup. Which club were runners-up for the third time in their history?**

6 Whose legal action against Newcastle United led to the end of the fixed wage for footballers?

7 **Tottenham Hotspur became the first British side to win a European trophy when they beat Atletico Madrid 5-1 in the Cup Winners' Cup Final in Rotterdam. Name any of the three Spurs scorers.**

8 Who did Alf Ramsey succeed as England manager?

9 **Who was Ramsey's first new cap?**

10 What was the result of his first game in charge, against France in Paris in the European Nations Cup?

11 **Who won the League Cup, their first major honour, beating Aston Villa 3-1 on aggregate in the Final?**

12 The European Cup Final was held at Wembley for the first time. Who did AC Milan beat 2-1 in this match?

13 **Who won the Second Division Championship?**

14 Which 48-year-old scored his first goal of the season in the game in which they clinched the Second Division title?

15 **In Scotland, Rangers won the League Championship and the FA Cup. Who won the League Cup?**

1 Denis Law 2 Jimmy Greaves (Tottenham Hotspur) 3 Everton 4 Harry Catterick
5 Leicester City 6 George Eastham 7 Jimmy Greaves (2), John White and Terry Dyson
(2) 8 Walter Winterbottom 9 Ron Henry (Tottenham Hotspur)
10 5-2 to France 11 Birmingham City 12 Benfica 13 Stoke City 14 Stanley Matthews
15 Heart of Midlothian

 **Quiz 54**   **Season 1963-1964**

1 Who did West Ham United beat 3-2 in the Final to win the FA Cup for the first time in their history?

2 Who scored the West Ham goals?

3 Who, at 17 years 345 days, became the youngest player to appear in an FA Cup Final?

4 The previous Boxing Day, West Ham United had suffered their record defeat, 8-2 at home to which Lancashire club?

5 Apart from the score, what was unusual about the Home International in which England beat Northern Ireland 8-3?

6 Which Lancashire team won the First Division Championship?

7 Which Yorkshire team won the Second Division Championship, heralding the dawn of an era?

8 Who became the first Fourth Division side to reach the 6th round of the FA Cup?

9 Which Bradford Park Avenue player scored the fastest first class goal on record, timed at four seconds after the kick-off, against Tranmere Rovers?

10 Which Tottenham Hotspur and Northern Ireland star announced his retirement after failing to overcome a persistent knee injury?

11 Who did Spurs manager Bill Nicholson buy from Fulham for £72,500 to replace him?

12 What was unusual about the Finals of the Inter-Cities Fairs Cup in both this and the following year?

13 What was unusual about the European Cup Winners' Cup Final between Sporting Lisbon and MTK Budapest?

14 Which great goalkeeper was voted European Footballer of the Year?

15 Which future Tottenham Hotspur star was top scorer in the Scottish First Division, with 32 goals for Dundee?

---

1 **Preston North End** 2 John Sissons, Geoff Hurst and Ron Boyce 3 **Preston's Howard Kendall** 4 Blackburn Rovers 5 **It was the first game at Wembley to be played under floodlights** 6 Liverpool 7 **Leeds United** 8 Oxford United 9 **Jim Fryatt** 10 Danny Blanchflower 11 **Alan Mullery** 12 They were one-off matches, rather than two-legged affairs 13 **It was the first of these finals to go to a replay** 14 Lev Yashin (Dynamo Moscow and USSR) 15 Alan Gilzean

 **Quiz 55**   Season 1964-1965

1 Who won their first Scottish League title, beating Heart of Midlothian 2-0 in the last match of the season and thus edging the Edinburgh side into second place on goal average?

2 Name the highest British goalscorer of all time, with 434 League goals in his career, who retired this year after spending his last season as player-manager of Shrewsbury Town.

3 There were joint top scorers in the English First Division, both with 29 goals. One was Jimmy Greaves (Tottenham Hotspur); the other played for Blackburn Rovers - name him.

4 Who won the 1965 League Championship?

5 Who won the FA Cup?

6 Who scored their goals in their 2-1 Final victory?

7 Who were runners-up in both the League and the FA Cup?

8 Who became the first footballer to be knighted?

9 How old was he when he played his last match?

10 West Ham United won the European Cup Winners' Cup. Who did they beat 2-0 in the Final at Wembley?

11 Who scored both goals?

12 Which Tottenham Hotspur and Scotland international was killed at the age of 27 after being struck by lightning while playing golf?

13 Name the England international who retired this year after making a record number of League appearances - 764 - for his only club, Portsmouth.

14 Which Manchester United and Scotland star was voted European Footballer of the Year?

15 Which Rangers player was the leading goalscorer in the Scottish First Division?

Quiz 56   Season 1965-1966

1   On the opening day of the season, who became the first ever substitute in an English League match, when he came on for Charlton Athletic against Bolton Wanderers in Division Two?

2   On December 4, 1965, who became the first Tottenham Hotspur player to be sent off since October 27, 1928?

3   Liverpool won the League Championship. Who was their leading scorer - for the fifth year running - with 30 goals?

4   Everton won the FA Cup, beating Sheffield Wednesday 3-2 in the Final. Who scored the Toffeemen's goals?

5   And who scored for Wednesday?

6   Which former Wolverhampton Wanderers and England star left Arsenal, where he had been manager for four years?

7   In the last two-legged League Cup Final, which London team did West Bromwich Albion beat 5-3 on aggregate?

8   Whose record did Liverpool equal when they won their seventh English League title?

9   Who was the Liverpool captain?

10   Who beat Liverpool 2-1 after extra time in the Final of the European Cup Winners' Cup?

11   Who did Real Madrid beat 2-1 in the Final to win the European Cup for the sixth time in its 11-year history?

12   Which two Spanish teams contested the Final of the Inter-Cities Fairs Cup?

13   Which two English teams had they knocked out in the semi-finals?

14   There were joint top scorers in the Scottish First Division, both with 31 goals in the season. One played for Celtic, the other for Dunfermline Athletic. Name either.

15   Who was voted European Footballer of the Year, even before his outstanding contribution to the 1966 World Cup?

Quiz 57 — Season 1966-1967

1 **Which Third Division side won the League Cup in the first year the Final was held at Wembley?**

2 Which First Division side did they beat?

3 **Who scored the three goals that brought them victory after going 2-0 down?**

4 Who was their manager?

5 **Who sensationally knocked Rangers out of the Scottish FA Cup in the first round?**

6 Who was the manager of Celtic, who won the European Cup, the Scottish League Championship, the FA Cup, the League Cup and the Glasgow Cup?

7 **Who won the English First Division Championship?**

8 Who was the leading scorer in the First Division, with 37 goals for 19th-placed Southampton?

9 **Tottenham Hotspur beat Chelsea 2-1 in the first all-London FA Cup Final. Who scored the goals?**

10 Who were the only two survivors of Tottenham's previous Cup-winning side in 1962?

11 **Who became the first 6-figure British footballer when he moved from Blackpool to Everton for £110,000 in August 1966?**

12 Where in the First Division table did Blackpool finish the season?

13 **Which German club beat Rangers 1-0 after extra time in the Final of the European Cup Winners' Cup?**

14 Who won the Second Division Championship and promotion to the top flight for the first time in their history?

15 **Who became the first country to beat England after their World Cup triumph?**

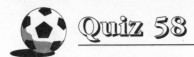 **Quiz 58**　　　　**Season 1967-1968**

1　From which club did Tottenham Hotspur buy Martin Chivers, for a British record fee of £125,000?

2　Manchester City won their second League Championship. When had they previously won it?

3　They were managed by Joe Mercer and coached by Malcolm Allison. Who was their captain?

4　Who won the FA Cup, beating Everton 1-0 in extra time in the Final?

5　The First Division had joint leading scorers, with 28 goals apiece. One was George Best of Manchester United. The other played for Southampton - name him.

6　In the semi-final of the European Championships in Italy, who became the first English player ever to be sent off in a full international?

7　Manchester United won the European Cup, beating Benfica 4-1 after extra time in the Final. Who scored United's goals?

8　And who equalised for Benfica late in the second half of normal time?

9　Who was the leading scorer in Scotland, with 32 goals for Celtic?

10. How many Celtic players were sent off in the third, play-off, match for the World Club Championship against Racing Club (Argentina) in Montevideo?

11　Leeds United won the Inter-Cities Fairs Cup - which Hungarian side did they beat 1-0 on aggregate in the Final?

12　Name the 1967 European Footballer of the Year who played for the Hungarians in this match.

13　Who overtook Jimmy Greaves as England's all-time leading scorer when he netted his 45th international goal in the 3-1 victory over Sweden at Wembley on May 22?

14　Which British team reached the semi-final of the Cup Winners' Cup, losing 4-3 on aggregate to SV Hamburg?

15　Who was their manager?

 # Quiz 59 — Season 1968-1969

1 **Which Scottish team knocked West Bromwich Albion out in the quarter-final of the European Cup Winners' Cup?**

2 They themselves lost in the semi-final to the Czech club that went on to win the competition. Who?

3 **Tommy Docherty managed three clubs in six weeks. Which three?**

4 When they were relegated from the Third Division, which team had gone full circle - from Fourth to First and back to Fourth again - in nine years?

5 **Who won the League Championship for the first time?**

6 Who was their leading scorer, with only 14 League goals?

7 **Who was the First Division's leading scorer, with 27 goals for Tottenham Hotspur?**

8 Which English team won the Inter-City Fairs Cup?

9 **Which Hungarian team did they beat 3-0 and 3-2 in the Final?**

10 Who scored the winner in Manchester City's 1-0 FA Cup Final victory over Leicester City?

11 **What other blow did Leicester suffer in the same season?**

12 Third Division Swindon Town won the League Cup, beating Arsenal 3-1 in the Final. Who scored two of the goals?

13 **Who won the Second Division Championship and went quickly on to much higher things?**

14 Who took over from Sir Matt Busby when he retired as manager of Manchester United?

15 **Who scored six goals in West Ham United's record 8-0 victory in a First Division match against Sunderland on October 19?**

Quiz 60

Season 1969-1970

1 Who scored on his 100th international appearance for England in a 3-1 Home International victory over Northern Ireland?

2 Cambridge United were elected members of the Football League. Which Yorkshire team went out to make room for them?

3 Which World Cup star - not a Briton - scored his 1000th goal in first-class football?

4 Which World Cup star did Tottenham Hotspur buy from West Ham United?

5 Which great international player went in the other direction as part of the deal?

6 On his return from a month's suspension, George Best scored six goals for Manchester United in their 8-2 FA Cup 5th round victory over who?

7 Who knocked Leeds United out in the semi-final of the 1970 European Cup?

8 Who then beat them in the Final?

9 What was historic about the FA Cup Final between Chelsea and Leeds United?

10 Who eventually scored the winner for Chelsea?

11 The two FA Cup finalists came second and third in the First Division. Who were the Champions?

12 Who scored two goals for Aberdeen in their shock 3-1 victory over Celtic in the Scottish FA Cup Final?

13 Which team won the Second Division championship, to the delight of Prime Minister Harold Wilson, their most famous fan?

14 Who was their manager?

15 Despite being the First Division's leading scorer with 25 goals, which West Bromwich Albion forward will forever be remembered for one he missed against Brazil later the same year?

 **Quiz 61**   **Season 1970-1971**

1 **Which Fourth Division side knocked First Division leaders Leeds United out of the FA Cup in the fifth round?**

2 Rangers won their first trophy for four years when they beat Celtic 1-0 in the Final of the League Cup. Who was their goalscorer - the youngest player ever to appear in a Scottish cup final?

3 **Arsenal did the League and FA Cup double. Which was the last team to have achieved this feat?**

4 Who was the Arsenal manager?

5 **Who did Arsenal beat 2-1 in the FA Cup Final?**

6 Who won the European Cup Winners' Cup, beating Real Madrid 2-1 in a replay after the first match had been drawn 1-1?

7 **Which other English club had they beaten in the semi-final?**

8 Who won the Inter-Cities Fairs Cup, beating Juventus on away goals after the two legs had finished 2-2 and 1-1, in the last year before the competition's name was changed to the UEFA Cup?

9 **Why was the first leg of the Inter-Cities Fairs Cup Final against Juventus abandoned?**

10 Which other English club had the victors beaten in the semi-final?

11 **Which other English club reached the quarter-finals of the same competition?**

12 Which two founder members of the Football League were relegated to the Third Division for the first time in their history?

13 **For the second year in succession, a West Bromwich Albion forward was the First Division's leading scorer (with 28 goals). Who was he?**

14 Who was Celtic's - and Scotland's - leading scorer, with 22 goals?

15 **Who won the European Cup, the first of three successive triumphs in this competition?**

1 **Colchester United** 2 Derek Johnstone 3 **Tottenham Hotspur in 1961** 4 Bertie Mee 5 **Liverpool** 6 Chelsea 7 **Holders Manchester City** 8 Leeds United 9 **Because of torrential rain in Turin (Italy)** 10 Liverpool 11 **Arsenal** 12 Blackburn Rovers and Bolton Wanderers 13 **Tony Brown** 14 Harry Hood 15 **Ajax (Holland)**

Quiz 62 — Season 1971-1972

1 Who won the Scottish League Cup, their first trophy since 1921?

2 Leeds United won the 100th FA Cup Final, beating Arsenal 1-0. Who scored the winner?

3 Which outfield player saved a penalty for West Ham United in the second replay of their epic League Cup semi-final with Stoke City?

4 Stoke won that game and then beat Chelsea 2-1 in the Final, to win the first major trophy in their 109-year history. Who scored for them at Wembley?

5 Who won the English League Championship for the first time in their history?

6 Which midfielder did Leeds United nearly buy from West Bromwich Albion before pulling out at the last minute when a medical revealed that he had a hole in his heart?

7 To which club did the player subsequently move?

8 Which Manchester City player was the First Division's leading scorer, with 33 goals?

9 Who scored eight goals for Chelsea in their 21-0 aggregate defeat of Jeunesse Hautcharage (Luxembourg) in the European Cup Winners' Cup?

10 Which non-League side knocked Newcastle United out of the FA Cup?

11 Who scored the goals in their 2-1 home victory after a 2-2 draw at St James' Park?

12 Later that season, the same side won election by one vote to the Football League. Who did they replace in the Fourth Division?

13 After their 1963 Cup Winners' Cup victory, Tottenham Hotspur became the first English club to win two different European competitions when they won the UEFA Cup. Which other English club did they beat in the Final?

14 Which former England star, recalled from Fulham where he had been on loan, scored Spurs' goal in the second leg of the UEFA Cup Final?

15 Which ex-Motherwell striker scored a hat trick for Celtic in their 6-1 defeat of Hibernian in the Scottish FA Cup Final?

 **Quiz 63**   **Season 1972-1973**

1 Sunderland became the first Second Division side to win the FA Cup since who?

2 Who scored the goal in their 1-0 Final victory over Leeds United?

3 **Which Leeds player was making a record fifth appearance in the FA Cup Final?**

4 Who went down to the Third Division for the first time in their distinguished history, which included three League Championships?

5 **Who was the First Division's leading scorer, with 28 goals for sixth-placed West Ham United?**

6 Which Italian team beat Leeds United 1-0 in the European Cup Winners' Cup Final in Salonika (Greece)?

7 **Celtic won the Scottish Championship but were beaten in the finals of both cups. By which two teams?**

8 Which great hero of the 1966 and 1970 World Cups lost the sight in his right eye in a road accident on October 22?

9 **Tottenham Hotspur goalkeeper Pat Jennings saved two penalties in a League match at Anfield. Who took them?**

10 Liverpool won both the League Championship and the UEFA Cup. Which German team did they beat in the Final of the latter competition?

11 **Kevin Keegan scored two goals in their 3-0 victory in the first leg. Which defender scored the other?**

12 Which star of the 1966 World Cup won the Golden Boot for being Europe's leading scorer with 40 goals?

13 **Which other '66 hero hung up his boots, finishing as his club's leading scorer for the season, albeit with only 6 goals?**

14 Who made his 100th international appearance for England in the game against Scotland at Hampden Park?

15 **Name one of the scorers in England's 5-0 victory in this match.**

1 West Bromwich Albion (1931) 2 Ian Porterfield 3 Johnny Giles 4 Huddersfield Town
5 Bryan Robson 6 AC Milan 7 Rangers (FA Cup) and Hibernian (League Cup)
8 Gordon Banks 9 Kevin Keegan and Tommy Smith 10 Borussia Moenchengladbach
11 Larry Lloyd 12 Eusebio 13 Bobby Charlton (Manchester United) 14 Bobby Moore
15 Peter Lorimer, Allan Clarke (2), Mick Channon and Martin Chivers

Quiz 64

Season 1973-1974

1 **This was the first season in which promotion and relegation became three up and three down. Which was the first First Division club to be relegated after finishing 20th?**

2 And which was the first club to be promoted to the top flight after finishing third in the Second Division?

3 **Who won the Second Division Championship by 15 points, a record margin?**

4 Who became the first Welsh player to be sent off in an international match (versus Poland)?

5 **Which Third Division team reached the semi-finals of the FA Cup?**

6 Which three First Division sides had they beaten en route?

7 **What was historic about the FA Cup 3rd round match between Cambridge United and Oldham Athletic on January 6?**

8 Which Southampton player was the First Division's leading scorer?

9 **After the dismissal of Sir Alf Ramsey, who briefly became manager of England?**

10 Which East German club won the European Cup Winners' Cup?

11 **Wolverhampton Wanderers won the League Cup, beating Manchester City 2-1 at Wembley. Name one of their goalscorers.**

12 Joao Havelange became President of FIFA. Who did he succeed?

13 **Which Dutch club beat Tottenham Hotspur in the Final of the 1974 UEFA Cup?**

14 Who won the first of four successive European Cups?

15 **Celtic were Champions for the ninth year running and also won the FA Cup. Who was their - and Scotland's - leading scorer?**

Quiz 65

Season 1974-1975

1 After a close title race in which the leadership of the First Division changed hands 21 times, who won the Championship for the second time in four seasons?

2 Who was their leading scorer, with 15 goals in the season?

3 **Who was the First Division's leading scorer, with 21 goals for 15th-placed Newcastle United?**

4 Against which country did the same player equal Willie Hall's England record of five goals in an international match?

5 **West Ham United won the FA Cup for the second time in eleven years - which Second Division side did they beat 2-0 in the Final?**

6 Who scored two goals for West Ham in the quarter-final, the semi-final and the Final?

7 **From which Lancashire club had West Ham bought him during the winter of 1974?**

8 Who beat Leeds United 2-0 in the Final of the European Cup?

9 **In which European capital was the match played?**

10 Aston Villa won the League Cup - which Second Division club did they beat 1-0 in the Final?

11 **It was third time lucky for the Villa manager, who had previously lost in the League Cup Final with Norwich City and Manchester City - name him.**

12 In Scotland, there were joint leading scorers, both with 20 goals. One was Willie Pettigrew of Motherwell. The other was a Dundee United player who later became more famous at Aston Villa, Wolverhampton Wanderers, Everton and on Sky TV - name him.

13 **Rangers won the Scottish League Championship, bringing to an end Celtic's record run of nine titles in a row. Which Rangers player was voted Scottish Footballer of the Year?**

14 Which Soviet club won the European Cup Winners' Cup, beating Ferencvaros of Hungary 3-0 in the Final?

15 **Which great player, now with Barcelona after moving from his native country, was European Footballer of the Year?**

---

1 **Derby County** 2 Bruce Rioch 3 **Malcolm Macdonald** 4 Cyprus 5 **Fulham** 6 Alan Taylor 7 **Rochdale** 8 Bayern Munich 9 Paris 10 Norwich City 11 **Ron Saunders** 12 Andy Gray 13 Sandy Jardine 14 Dynamo Kiev 15 **Johann Cruyff**

 **Quiz 66**   **Season 1975-1976**

1   Who scored the only goal of the FA Cup Final in which Southampton beat Manchester United?

2   Who won both the League Championship and the UEFA Cup?

3   Who resigned as manager of Preston North End?

4   Who knocked English champions Derby out of the European Cup, coming back from a 4-1 first leg defeat to win the return 5-1 after extra time?

5   Which striker did Derby sell to FC Bruges for £130,000?

6   Who won the European Cup Winners' Cup, beating West Ham United 4-2 in the Final?

7   Which star of the winning side later went to play for the losers?

8   When Aston Villa drew 2-2 with Leicester City on March 20, who scored all four goals?

9   Rangers won the Scottish League Championship, the FA Cup and the League Cup. Who was their captain?

10 Who won the European Cup, beating St Etienne (France) 1-0 in the Final, and the World Club Championship, beating Cruzeiro (Brazil) 2-0 on aggregate?

11 Name the goalkeeper who was the star of Czechoslovakia's victory over West Germany in the Final of the 1976 European Championship in Yugoslavia.

12 Which Norwich City striker was the First Division's leading scorer?

13 Name three of the seven other clubs he played for in a career that lasted from 1966 to 1980.

14 Which Celtic striker was top scorer in the Scottish First Division, with 24 goals?

15 Who became only the third Fourth Division club to reach the semi-finals of the English FA Cup?

 **Quiz 67**   **Season 1976-1977**

1   **What new accessories did referees show for the first time?**

2   Who joined Second Division Fulham and scored within two minutes of making his debut?

3   **Who played his 1000th League game and then retired on May 14?**

4   Which Southampton, Hereford United and England winger retired after a record 824 League appearances?

5   **Which Southern League team was elected to the Football League?**

6   Who did they replace in the Fourth Division?

7   **What did Wales do on May 31 for the first time in their history?**

8   Who awarded himself his 48th Republic of Ireland cap on March 30?

9   **League Champions Liverpool won the European Cup for the first time. Who did they beat in the Final in Rome?**

10   The final score in this match was 3-1 - who netted for Liverpool?

11   **The English First Division had joint top scorers, both with 25 goals. One played for Arsenal, the other for Aston Villa - name them.**

12   Aston Villa eventually won the League Cup after extra time in the second replay. Who were the runners-up?

13   **Who did the double in Scotland?**

14   Who denied them a clean sweep by beating them 2-1 after extra time in the Scottish League Cup Final?

15   **Who became the first player ever to win Cup medals with both Celtic and Rangers?**

Quiz 68

Season 1977-1978

1 How much did Liverpool pay Celtic when they bought Kenny Dalglish on August 10?

2 Don Revie quit as England manager to coach which Middle Eastern country?

3 Scotland qualified for the World Cup finals in Argentina by beating Wales 2-0 in the last group match. The game was played on neutral territory - where?

4 Scotland's first goal in this match was scored by Don Masson from the penalty spot after the referee thought he saw a Welsh player handle the ball, but television replays revealed that it was really a Scot - who?

5 Nottingham Forest won the English Championship in their first season back in the First Division. Which of their players - ex-Birmingham City and widely regarded as a wild man - was voted PFA Player of the Year?

6 Which club finished in the bottom four of the Fourth Division, thus having to apply for re-election only two seasons after having been in the Second Division?

7 How many Liverpool players were in the England team that faced Switzerland in Ron Greenwood's first match in charge of the national side?

8 Which non-league club reached the 5th round of the FA Cup?

9 Ipswich Town won the FA Cup, beating hot favourites Arsenal 1-0 in the Final. Who scored the goal?

10 Liverpool retained the European Cup, beating FC Bruges 1-0. Who scored the winner?

11 Nottingham Forest also won the League Cup, beating Liverpool 1-0 in the replayed Final after the first match had been drawn 0-0. Which future England international kept goal for Forest?

12 Which established international goalkeeper did he replace, and why?

13 European Footballer of the Year was Allan Simonsen, of Borussia Moenchengladbach and Denmark. For which English team did he subsequently play?

14 Which Everton player, formerly with Birmingham City, was the First Division's leading scorer?

15 In Scotland, Rangers did the treble (League, FA Cup and League Cup). Who was their leading scorer, with 25 goals?

Johnstone

1 £400,000 2 The United Arab Emirates 3 Anfield, Liverpool 4 Joe Jordan 5 Kenny Burns 6 York City 7 Six 8 Blyth Spartans 9 Roger Osborne 10 Kenny Dalglish 11 Chris Woods 12 Peter Shilton, who was Cup-tied 13 Charlton Athletic 14 Bob Latchford 15 Derek

 **Quiz 69**   **Season 1978-1979**

1 Which two members of Argentina's World Cup-winning squad did Tottenham Hotspur manager Steve Burkinshaw buy only 15 days after the Final?

2 Which other member of the Argentina team later went to Birmingham City?

3 Who became Britain's first £1 million player, when he went from Birmingham City to Nottingham Forest?

4 The First Division's leading scorer was Frank Worthington. For which of his 11 League clubs was he then playing?

5 Who was banned from football for 10 years for bringing the game into disrepute in 1977?

6 Who scored Arsenal's winner in their 3-2 FA Cup Final victory over Manchester United?

7 Who knocked Liverpool out of the 1979 European Cup in the second round?

8 Who scored Nottingham Forest's winner in their 1-0 European Cup Final victory over Malmo?

9 Who was the Forest captain?

10 On November 29, which Forest player became the first black footballer to win a full England cap in the game against Czechoslovakia at Wembley?

11 Which team began their rise to prominence by winning promotion from the Fourth Division for the first time in their history?

12 Who was their manager at this time?

13 For which team did the Scottish First Division's leading scorer, Andy Ritchie, play?

14 Who won the 1979 Scottish FA Cup in a second replay after two 0-0 draws?

15 Who were the runners-up?

12 Dario Gradi 13 Morton 14 Rangers 15 Hibernian

Forest 8 Million-pound Trevor Francis 9 John McGovern 10 Viv Anderson 11 Wimbledon
Wanderers 5 Former England manager Don Revie 6 Alan Sunderland 7 Nottingham
1 Osvaldo Ardiles and Ricardo Villa 2 Alberto Tarantini 3 Trevor Francis 4 Bolton

THE ULTIMATE FOOTBALL FACT AND QUIZ BOOK

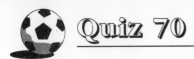 **Quiz 70**   **Season 1979-1980**

1 **Who became the first Israeli to play in the English First Division when he made his debut for Liverpool at home to Aston Villa?**

2 How did he mark the occasion?

3 **Second Division West Ham United won the FA Cup, beating Arsenal 1-0 in the Final. How many times had they won it before?**

4 Who scored the only goal of the match?

5 **Nottingham Forest retained the European Cup when they beat SV Hamburg 1-0 in the Final in Madrid. Who scored the goal?**

6 Which England striker was on the losing side?

7 **Which English First Division team had he already contracted to join the following season?**

8 This same English team already had the First Division's leading scorer, with 23 goals in 1979-80 - what was his name?

9 **Northern Ireland won the Home International Championship outright - when had they last achieved this feat?**

10 What was unprecedented about the European Cup Winners' Cup Final in which Arsenal lost to Valencia?

11 **Who briefly became Britain's most expensive footballer when Manchester City manager Malcolm Allison bought him for £1,437,500 from Wolverhampton Wanderers?**

12 Who shortly afterwards broke this record when Wolverhampton Wanderers bought him from Aston Villa for £1,469,000, and then scored the winning goal in the League Cup Final?

13 **Who was the wheeler-dealer manager of Wolves?**

14 Name the Ipswich Town goalkeeper who saved a League record of eight penalties in the season, including two in the same match, out of 10 faced?

15 **What unusual distinction was achieved by Colin Garwood, who played 24 matches for Portsmouth before being transferred to Aldershot, for whom he appeared in 16 games?**

13 **John Barnwell** 14 Paul Cooper 15 He was the season's leading scorer for both clubs
10 It was the first major cup final to be decided on penalties 11 **Steve Daley** 12 Andy Gray
Brooking 5 **John Robertson** 6 Kevin Keegan 7 **Southampton** 8 Phil Boyer 9 1914
1 **Avi Cohen** 2 By scoring an own goal and then a goal for his own side 3 **Twice** 4 Trevor

Quiz 71

Season 1980-1981

1 **Which club won their seventh League Championship, their first for 71 years?**

2 Who was their captain?

3 **Who was their manager?**

4 Who won the League Cup for the first time in their history, beating West Ham United 2-1 in a replay?

5 **After the first game had been drawn 1-1, West Ham manager John Lyall was quoted as saying 'We have been cheated', to which the match referee responded angrily 'No one calls me a cheat'. Who was the referee?**

6 In British soccer's biggest ever transfer swap, Arsenal gave striker Clive Allen - who had been on their books for only 62 days - and goalkeeper Paul Barron to Crystal Palace in return for whom?

7 **Who broke the record for the number of League appearances by a player at a single club when he played his 765th game for Swindon Town on October 18?**

8 Name the Scotsman, the Dutchman and the Englishman - all from Ipswich Town - who took the first three places in the PFA Player of the Year poll.

9 **Ipswich won the UEFA Cup Final 5-4 on aggregate (won 3-0 at home; lost 4-2 away). Which Dutch team did they beat?**

10 Who scored a goal and an own goal in the 100th English FA Cup Final between Tottenham Hotspur and Manchester City?

11 **Which West Country Third Division side reached the FA Cup 6th round despite having been drawn away in all but one of their ties?**

12 Who beat Liverpool on January 31, thus becoming the first team to win away at Anfield for three years, 10 days - an all-time record run that included a total of 85 matches?

13 **Who scored the goal in Liverpool's 1-0 defeat of Real Madrid in the European Cup Final?**

14 Which England international played for the Spanish side in this match?

15 **In Scotland, who won the FA Cup and finished runners-up in the League Cup?**

---

13 Alan Kennedy 14 Laurie Cunningham **15 Dundee United**

9 AZ 67 Alkmaar (Holland) 10 City's Tommy Hutchison 11 **Exeter City** 12 Leicester City

6 Kenny Sansom **7 John Trollope** 8 John Wark (winner), Frans Thijssen and Paul Mariner

1 Aston Villa 2 Dennis Mortimer **3 Ron Saunders** 4 Liverpool **5 Clive Thomas**

 **Quiz 72**   **Season 1981-1982**

1 **Which former Liverpool manager died on September 29, 1981, at the age of 67?**

2 Who was manager of the current Liverpool side which won its fifth League title in seven seasons, its 13th in all, and the League Cup for the second year in succession?

3 **Which Southampton player was the First Division's leading scorer, with 26 goals?**

4 Who became the first paid director of a Football League club when appointed by Fulham on November 19?

5 **Who became the first club apart from Celtic and Rangers to win the Scottish FA Cup since 1970?**

6 Who did Manchester United manager Ron Atkinson buy from West Bromwich Albion?

7 **The fee was a British transfer record. How much was it?**

8 Tottenham Hotspur retained the English FA Cup, beating Queens Park Rangers 1-0 in a replay after the Wembley Final had been drawn 1-1. Who scored the winning goal?

9 **This goal was scored from the penalty spot. How many previous spot kicks had there been in FA Cup Finals?**

10 How many had been scored from?

11 **Which Spurs player was PFA Footballer of the Year?**

12 Which German team did Aston Villa beat 1-0 in the European Cup Final?

13 **Who scored the winning goal in the Final in Rotterdam?**

14 Which member of the winning team was playing in only his second competitive first class match?

15 **Name the European Footballer of the Year who played on the losing side.**

 **Quiz 73**   **Season 1982-1983**

1   In the dying moments of extra time in the FA Cup Final, with the score at 2-2, which Brighton and Hove Albion player hesitated in front of goal, allowing Manchester United's keeper to make a crucial save?

2   Brighton's sad season ended with them being relegated from the League's top flight. When had they been promoted to it?

3   Swansea City also went down, after a stay of only two seasons. By the last day of the season, the third relegation spot was a straight fight between Manchester City and Luton Town, who played each other at Maine Road. Who scored the only goal of the game?

4   Liverpool won their 14th League Championship by an 11-point margin. Who were the runners-up?

5   In winning the Scottish FA Cup, how did Aberdeen join a club of which only Celtic and Rangers were members?

6   Which other major trophy did Aberdeen win?

7   Who did they beat in the Final in Gothenburg?

8   Who won the Scottish Championship for the first time in their history?

9   Which team were runners-up in both the Scottish FA Cup and the Scottish League Cup?

10 Whose report recommended - among other things - a reduction in the size of the English First Division from 22 to 20 clubs?

11 On July 7, the FA appointed Bobby Robson England manager in succession to Ron Greenwood. Which League club had Robson run until then?

12 Who took over as manager of Robson's old club?

13 Which French international, playing for Juventus (Italy) won the first of three consecutive European Footballer of the Year awards?

14 Who lifted the Milk Cup for Liverpool after their 2-1 victory over Manchester United in the Final?

15 Which future Chelsea star gained the extraordinary distinction of scoring four goals in a match and yet finishing on the losing side, as Reading went down 7-5 to Doncaster Rovers in the Third Division?

 **Quiz 74**　　　　　**Season 1983-1984**

1　Which businessman made an unsuccessful £10 million takeover bid for Manchester United?

2　Who won the Scottish FA Cup?

3　**What happened in this Final for the third year running?**

4　Who scored a famous goal for England when they beat Brazil for the first time ever in a friendly at the Maracana Stadium, Rio de Janeiro?

5　**This season marked the end of the Home International Championship. Who were the last winners?**

6　Which Third Division side from Staffordshire reached the semi-finals of the Milk Cup?

7　**Which West Country Third Division side reached the semi-finals of the FA Cup?**

8　Who became only the third player to score 100 League goals in both Scotland and England?

9　**Who came second in the Scottish First Division and were runners-up in both the Scottish FA Cup and the League Cup?**

10　Which Italian team did Liverpool beat in the Final of the European Cup?

11　**Where was the match played?**

12　The score was 1-1 after extra time, and then Liverpool won 4-2 on penalties. This was the famous occasion when Bruce Grobelaar did his knocking-knees routine to put the penalty taker off. Who missed?

13　**Tottenham Hotspur won the UEFA Cup, beating Anderlecht of Belgium in the Final on penalties. Who was Spurs' heroic goalkeeper in this match?**

14　Whose last game as Spurs' manager was the UEFA Cup Final?

15　**Who was the manager France when they won the European Championship for the first time?**

Quiz 75

Season 1984-1985

1 After crowd trouble at Parkhead, where were Celtic forced to play the home leg of their Cup Winners' Cup tie against Rapid Vienna?

2 Which team won the Second Division Championship, thus gaining promotion to the First Division for the first time in their history?

3 **Which ex-Chelsea player returned to Stamford Bridge with Sunderland and scored two goals which helped to knock his old team out of the Milk Cup in the semi-final?**

4 Which goalkeeper completed 472 League appearances, a record?

5 **Which Manchester United defender became the first player ever to be sent off in an English FA Cup Final?**

6 Who scored the winner in the Final against Everton?

7 **Which English team won the home leg of their UEFA Cup tie with Partizan Belgrade 6-2 and then lost 4-0 in Yugoslavia, thus going out on away goals?**

8 Which two great tragedies cast a shadow over the world of football?

9 **English clubs were banned from European competitions: when were they readmitted?**

10 What unprecedented - and partly unwanted - double did Norwich City achieve in 1985?

11 **Who won the League Championship and the European Cup Winners' Cup?**

12 Where was the European Cup Winners' Cup Final played?

13 **Which Austrian team were the Cup Winners' Cup runners-up?**

14 Who scored the winning team's three goals in the Final?

15 **Which great Austrian international scored a consolation goal for the losers?**

1 **Old Trafford, Manchester** 2 Oxford United 3 **Clive Walker** 4 Pat Jennings (Tottenham Hotspur and Arsenal) 5 **Kevin Moran** 6 Norman Whiteside 7 **Queen's Park Rangers** 8 The Bradford fire and the Heysel Stadium riot 9 **1990 for all clubs except Liverpool, who were readmitted in 1991** 10 They won the Milk Cup and were relegated from the First Division in the same season 11 **Everton** 12 The Feyenoord Stadium, Rotterdam 13 **Rapid Vienna** 14 Andy Gray, Trevor Steven and Kevin Sheedy 15 **Franz Krankl**

 ## Quiz 76 — Season 1985-1986

1 Which great manager suffered a fatal heart attack during Scotland's World Cup qualifying match with Wales at Ninian Park?

2 Who won the Milk Cup?

3 Which club announced plans to ban away fans from its stadium?

4 Who won the Double?

5 What was unique about the season's Merseyside FA Cup Final?

6 Who was the only member of the Liverpool Cup Final team to have been born in England?

7 Who became the first Australian to score in an FA Cup Final?

8 Which Third Division team created a League record by winning their first 13 games of the season?

9 Who became the first Scotsman to win 100 international caps?

10 Which London club came third in the First Division, the highest League position in their history?

11 Who became the first Iron Curtain winners of the European Cup?

12 Spain had clubs in the finals of all three main European club competitions - the European Cup, the Cup Winners' Cup and the UEFA Cup. Name them.

13 Which was the only one of the three to win their competition?

14 Who became manager of Rangers?

15 Which Scottish team suffered a double disappointment, finishing runners-up to Celtic in the First Division on goal difference, and losing 3-0 to Aberdeen in the Final of the Scottish FA Cup?

Quiz 77   Season 1986-1987

1   What happened to Graeme Souness in his first match as player manager of Rangers, away to Hibernian?

2   Which four-times winner of the FA Cup, now languishing in the Fourth Division, was knocked out in the First Round by non-league Chorley?

3   **Which two London teams attempted to merge?**

4   Which team became the first champions of the GM Vauxhall Conference to win promotion to the Fourth Division of the Football League?

5   **Which Fourth Division team did they replace?**

6   Which Portuguese team won both the European Cup and the World Club Championship?

7   **Which team were runners-up in both the UEFA Cup and the Scottish FA Cup?**

8   What happened to English Divisions One and Two at the end of the season?

9   **The bottom two clubs in the First Division were Manchester City and Aston Villa. Which was the extra team relegated from the First Division to accommodate this change?**

10 Which Tottenham striker was both the First Division's leading scorer, with 33 goals, and the players' Player of the Year?

11 **Apart from Spurs, this player was on the books of seven other clubs in a career that ran from 1978 to 1994. Name the clubs, all but one of which were in London.**

12 Which one of these did he never actually play a match for?

13 **Who won the League Championship for the ninth time in their history and the second time in three years?**

14 Which team were runners-up in both the League and the League Cup?

15 **Who won the FA Cup for the first time in their history?**

Quiz 78   **Season 1987-1988**

1 **Which company became the sponsors of the Football League in its centenary year?**

2 Who, on April 9, became - at 17 years and 240 days - the youngest player ever to score a First Division hat trick?

3 **Who won the FA Cup after being in the League for only 10 years?**

4 Who did they beat 1-0 in the Final?

5 **Who scored the winning goal?**

6 Who missed a penalty for the opposition?

7 **For the first time, four teams were relegated from the First Division - Portsmouth, Watford, Oxford and which London club?**

8 What was unique about the circumstances of their relegation?

9 **Which team took their place?**

10 Which Welsh club lost its status as a member of the Football League?

11 **Which re-elected team filled the gap created by their demise?**

12 Who won the Littlewoods (League) Cup?

13 **They beat the holders 3-2 in the Final. Who were they?**

14 Who took a penalty in this match for the eventual losers?

15 **Who saved it?**

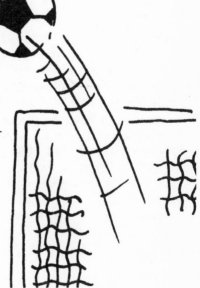

15 Andy Dibble
10 Newport County **11 Lincoln City** 12 Luton Town 14 Nigel Winterburn
Division after a play-off against the team that finished third in Division Two **9 Middlesbrough**
Division. **8 They are the only team ever to be relegated from the First**
6 John Aldridge **7 Chelsea** **13 Arsenal**
1 Barclays Bank 2 Alan Shearer **3 Wimbledon** 4 Liverpool **5 Lawrie Sanchez**

Quiz 79

Season 1988-1989

1 Who, on July 7, became Britain's first £2 million footballer?

2 Which club sold him?

3 Which club bought him?

4 Whose transfer from Newcastle United to Liverpool had been the previous British record?

5 On August 18, Liverpool bought Ian Rush for a reported £2.8 million from the European club to which they had sold him only 12 months previously for £3.2 million. Which club?

6 Rush had not enjoyed himself abroad. What, according to reports, did he say Italy was like?

7 By the end of the season, the Championship rested on the result of the final match between Liverpool and Arsenal at Anfield. If Liverpool won, drew or lost 1-0, they would retain the title. Any worse defeat, and Arsenal themselves would win. What was the final score?

8 Who scored the goals?

9 Who took the indirect free kick from which the first goal was headed in?

10 The scorer of the first goal was the First Division's leading scorer for the whole season. How many goals did he score: 23, 33 or 43?

11 The leading scorer in European football, Dorin Mateut of Dinamo Bucharest, scored how many - 33, 43 or 53?

12 Which former England manager died on May 26?

13 On October 22, three brothers appeared on the same side in a First Division match, the first time this had happened since the Carrs of Middlesbrough in 1920. What were their names?

14 How was the format of the play-offs changed?

15 Which London club was promoted from the Second Division through the play-offs?

 **Quiz 80**   **Season 1989-1990**

1   Who tried, unsuccessfully, to buy Manchester United in a £20 million takeover deal?

2   Who beat Sunderland 1-0 on May 28 to win the Second Division play-off Final?

3   What happened to the victors 10 days later?

4   What was unprecedented about the Scottish FA Cup Final in which Aberdeen beat Celtic?

5   Aberdeen also won the Scottish League Cup. Which team had last performed this Cup double, and in which year?

6   In the English FA Cup Final, Manchester United drew 3-3 with Crystal Palace. When was the last time six or more goals had been scored in this fixture?

7   Which game-changing 104-page document was published on January 29, 1990?

8   Who were the English Second Division champions?

9   When had they last been in the First Division?

10   What were they destined to achieve two years later?

11   Bobby Robson announced his intention to resign as manager of England after the 1990 World Cup finals to take up the same position with which club?

12   Which three Italian clubs made a clean sweep of the European cups?

13   Which English Second Division team reached their first FA Cup semi-final since 1913 and their first ever League Cup Final?

14   Who became the Republic of Ireland's all-time leading scored when he netted twice in the 3-0 win in Malta on June 2?

15   Which team was promoted to the Fourth Division of the English Football League only a year after having been relegated from it?

---

1 Ken Knighton 2 Swindon Town 3 They were relegated to Division Three because of financial irregularities dating from 1985, although they played the following season in the Second Division 4 It was the first Scottish Cup Final to be decided on penalties 5 Aberdeen themselves, in 1986 6 1953 7 The Taylor Report 8 Leeds United 9 1981-82 10 They were to win the First Division Championship 11 PSV Eindhoven (Holland) 12 AC Milan (European Cup), Sampdoria (Cup Winners' Cup) Juventus (UEFA Cup) 13 Oldham Athletic 14 Frank Stapleton (Arsenal) 15 Darlington

 **Quiz 81**   **Season 1990-1991**

1 **Who won the First Division Championship?**

2 Who resigned unexpectedly as manager of Liverpool after his team had drawn 4-4 with Everton in an FA Cup fifth round replay on February 22?

3 **Who became manager of Liverpool on April 16, 1991?**

4 Who had been caretaker manager during the intervening period?

5 **Who won the Scottish FA Cup, beating Dundee United 4-3 after extra time in the Final?**

6 When had they last won it?

7 **What was unusual about the relationship between the managers of the two Scottish FA Cup finalists?**

8 Which Dundee United player was voted Scottish Footballer of the Year?

9 **In the English FA Cup Final, into whom did Paul Gascoigne launch the infamous tackle which led to him (Gascoigne) being stretchered off?**

10 Which club became the first to win promotion on a shoot-out, when they beat Blackpool 5-4 on penalties after their Fourth Division play-off Final had ended 2-2 after extra time?

11 **Which group of islands entered its first ever European Championship qualifiers?**

12 They were not allowed to play home games at home because UEFA banned them from using artificial pitches. Where in Sweden did they play their first home match?

13 **Who were their opponents in this match?**

14 What was the score?

15 **On June 5, Wales beat West Germany 1-0 in their European Championship qualifying match at Cardiff Arms Park. Who scored?**

 **Quiz 82**   **Season 1991-1992**

1 Which Arsenal striker scored the goal when England beat Turkey 1-0 at Wembley in the European Championship qualifier?

2 Which was the first Division One team ever to be knocked out of the FA Cup on penalties?

3 **Who did they lose to?**

4 This was the final season of the old Football League before the new Premiership. Who were the last First Division Champions?

5 **One member of this team was winning his second Champion's medal, having won one with Arsenal the previous year. Name him.**

6 What was this player's connection with the 1958 Munich air disaster in which eight members of the Manchester United team were killed?

7 **Which Rangers player won the Golden Boot as the leading scorer in European club football?**

8 Who won the European Championship without having qualified for it in the first place?

9 **Which country did they replace?**

10 In which country were the European Championship finals held?

11 **Which Everton and former Manchester United Northern Ireland international was forced to retire at the age of 26?**

12 In the FA Cup Final, what was unusual about the awards ceremony?

13 **And why did this not work?**

14 Which two teams contested this Final?

15 **Which team was expelled from the Football League?**

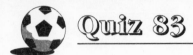 Quiz 83   Season 1992-1993

1   Who was sent off for the first time in his career in his 971st League game while player manager of Plymouth Argyle?

2   After starting the season with 11 wins off the reel, Premiership Newcastle United suffered their first defeat at home to which First Division club?

3   Who was paid £1,500 by a film company but fined £20,000 by the FA for his starring role in the notorious video 'Soccer's Hard Men'?

4   Which former England captain and all-time great died on February 24, 1993?

5   Brian Clough retired. Which two clubs had he led to the League Championship?

6   Which other two clubs had he also managed?

7   Ian Rush became Liverpool's all-time leading scorer. Whose record did he beat with his 287th goal for the club?

8   Which team resigned from the Football League?

9   Which team achieved an unprecedented double by winning both the Coca-Cola Cup and the FA Cup?

10 Who did they beat in both the Coca-Cola Cup Final and the FA Cup Final?

11 Who broke his arm during the team's Coca-Cola victory celebrations when he fell off Tony Adams?

12 The FA Cup Final went to a replay: when was the last time this had happened?

13 This was the first season in which the old First Division became the FA Premier League, and the first champions were Manchester United. Who was the team captain?

14 Who was the club captain?

15 In their previous Championship year, 1967, Manchester United had been managed by Matt Busby. Now they were managed by Alex Ferguson. How many managers had they had in the intervening period, and what were their names?

---

1 Peter Shilton 2 Grimsby Town 3 Vinnie Jones (Wimbledon) 4 Bobby Moore 5 Derby County and Nottingham Forest 6 Leeds United and Brighton and Hove Albion 7 Roger Hunt 8 Maidstone United 9 Arsenal 10 Sheffield Wednesday 11 Steve Morrow 12 1990. Manchester United v Crystal Palace 13 Steve Bruce 14 Bryan Robson 15 Five - Wilf McGuinness, Frank O'Farrell, Tommy Docherty, Dave Sexton, Ron Atkinson

 **Quiz 84**   **Season 1992-1993**

1 **Which team won promotion to the Football League from the GM Vauxhall Conference?**

2 Which team came bottom of the Third Division and were therefore relegated to the GM Vauxhall Conference?

3 **Which country had a team in the Final of each of the three main cup tournaments - the European Cup, the Cup-Winners' Cup and the UEFA Cup?**

4 Name the clubs.

5 **Two of the three won - which lost?**

6 The losers had the consolation of having one of their players voted European Footballer of the Year for the third time in his career. He was a Dutch international. Name him.

7 **Who had been the last Dutchman to win the award?**

8 Which three teams were the first to be relegated from the Premiership?

9 **Which three teams were the first to be promoted to it?**

10 Which team came third in the First Division but missed out in the play-offs?

11 **Who was sacked as chief executive of Tottenham Hotspur on May 14, 1993?**

12 Which strangely tonsured one-hit wonder was voted the Football Writers' English Footballer of the Year?

13 **Which team did he then play for?**

14 Which Aston Villa and Republic of Ireland defender was the PFA Footballer of the Year?

15 **The season ended with Manchester United qualifying for the European Cup and Arsenal for the Cup Winners' Cup. But as Arsenal had done the Cup double, which English team took the Coca-Cola Cup winner's place in the UEFA Cup?**

 **Quiz 85**   **Season 1993-1994**

1   In the Third Division on October 16, 1993, which team became the first to have both their original and their substitute goalkeepers sent off in the same match?

2   Who were their opponents in that game?

3   In July 1993, who did Rangers buy from Dundee United for a then British record fee of £4 million?

4   In 1993-4, Kidderminster Harriers of the GM Vauxhall Conference reached the fifth round of the FA Cup. Which League teams did they beat in the third and fourth rounds?

5   Who eventually knocked Kidderminster out, 1-0 in the fifth round?

6   In 1993, who won the Welsh Cup and qualified for Europe with a Final victory over Cardiff City, 22-times winners of the trophy?

7   What was the score in this historic match?

8   Who did Blackburn Rovers sign from Southampton for £2 million, then a British record for a goalkeeper?

9   In the second year of the Premiership, Manchester United became the fourth team in the 20th century to win the Championship and FA Cup in the same season. Who were the other three double winners, and when?

10 Who won the GM Vauxhall Conference?

11 Why were they not promoted to the Third Division?

12 Who thus escaped relegation from the Football league, despite having come bottom of the Third Division?

13 Which Newcastle striker was the Premiership's leading scorer?

14 Which Blackburn Rover was the PFA Footballer of the Year?

15 Rangers won the Scottish League Championship. When was the last time they had not done so?

 **Quiz 86**   **Season 1993-1994**

1 Who scored the goal with which Arsenal beat Parma 1-0 in the European Cup Winners' Cup Final in Copenhagen?

2 Arsenal's Ian Wright and John Jensen were awarded Winners' medals. Why was this odd?

3 Who scored the goals when England lost 2-0 to the USA in Foxboro, Massachusetts?

4 Who scored Holland's goals in their 2-0 victory over England in the World Cup qualifying game in Rotterdam?

5 When Ronald Koeman committed his famous foul on the edge of the Dutch penalty area, which England player was through on goal?

6 In which Italian city was the San Marino v England World Cup qualifying match played?

7 Who scored the first goal after 10 seconds' play?

8 Who scored four goals in England's 7-1 victory?

9 Which three teams were relegated from the Premiership?

10 Who were promoted to the Premiership as champions of Division One?

11 Which other team won automatic promotion to the Premiership by finishing second in Division One?

12 Although Millwall came third in the First Division, which team was promoted to the Premiership in their place through the play-offs?

13 Which team did Manchester United beat 4-0 in the FA Cup Final?

14 Who scored two penalties in this match?

15 When was the last time the FA Cup Final had been won by the same score?

Quiz 87　　　　　Season 1994-1995

1　Who was the manager of FA Premier League Champions Blackburn Rovers?

2　Which other team had he previously managed to a League title?

3　Which other two managers had previously won the English League with two different clubs?

4　When had Blackburn Rovers last been English League Champions?

5　Who was the great benefactor who financed Blackburn's transformation from Second Division obscurity to title-winners?

6　To which club did Blackburn Rovers pay £5 million for Chris Sutton?

7　Which World Cup star scored seven goals in his first six games for Tottenham Hotspur?

8　Which was his last club before moving to White Hart Lane?

9　Which star of the 1992 European Championship scored his first goal for Arsenal after 98 appearances?

10　What was the record Premiership victory achieved by Manchester United on March 4 in their home game against Ipswich Town?

11　Which Canadian international was the hapless Ipswich Town goalkeeper that day?

12　Which former Aston Villa full back was sent off on his debut for Everton?

13　Liverpool won the Coca-Cola Cup, beating Middlesbrough 2-1 in the Final. Who scored both their goals?

14　Who won the FA Cup, beating Manchester United in the Final?

15　Who scored the only goal of the game?

Quiz 88

Season 1994-1995

1. **Who was the leading scorer in the FA Premiership, with 34 goals in 42 games?**

2. Which London club were beaten semi-finalists in both the Coca-Cola and the FA Cups?

3. **Name the four teams relegated from the top flight as the Premiership began to reduce itself in size.**

4. Middlesbrough were Champions of the First Division - who were the runners-up?

5. **But which club was promoted with Middlesbrough in their stead after beating the League's second-placed team in the play-off final at Wembley?**

6. Who won the GM Vauxhall Conference but were not promoted to the Third Division because their ground was not up to the standard now required by the Football League?

7. **Which team were thus saved from relegation despite finishing bottom of the Third Division?**

8. Which Turkish team knocked Aston Villa out of the UEFA Cup?

9. **Which Newcastle United and former Charlton Athletic midfielder scored on his international debut for England against Romania?**

10. In Scotland, Rangers won their seventh Premier title in a row and Celtic finished fourth - who were runners-up?

11. **Who beat Celtic 6-5 on penalties in the Final of the Scottish League Cup?**

12. Celtic won the Scottish FA Cup, beating Airdrieonians 1-0 in the Final. Which Dutchman scored the goal?

13. **For which Dutch club had this striker played immediately before moving to Glasgow?**

14. Which two clubs came into the new Scottish Third Division?

15. **Who won the first ever Scottish Third Division Championship?**

1 Alan Shearer (Blackburn Rovers) 2 Crystal Palace 3 Norwich City, Leicester City, Ipswich Town and Crystal Palace 4 Reading 5 Bolton Wanderers 6 Macclesfield Town 7 Exeter City 8 Trabzonspor 9 Robert Lee 10 Motherwell 11 Raith Rovers 12 Pierre van Hooijdonk 13 NAC Breda 14 Caledonian Thistle and Ross County 15 Forfar Athletic

Quiz 89

Season 1995-1996

1 **Manchester United did the double, winning the FA Carling Premiership for the third time in the four years of its existence and the FA Cup. Who were runners-up in the Premiership?**

2 Who were the beaten finalists in the FA Cup?

3 **Who scored the only goal of the Final?**

4 On New Year's Day 1996, who became the youngest player to appear in the Premiership when he kept goal for West Ham United against Manchester City at the age of 17 years 3 days?

5 **Dutch international striker Dennis Bergkamp went to Arsenal. From which Italian club was he transferred?**

6 Who scored on his Middlesbrough debut after a close season transfer from Tottenham Hotspur?

7 **Which three clubs were relegated from the Premiership?**

8 Who won the First Division Championship?

9 **Which other club was promoted automatically after finishing second in the First Division?**

10 Who came third in the First Division but failed to win promotion after losing in the play-offs?

11 **Which was the third promoted team?**

12 Who became the first Italian to play in the Premiership when he joined Nottingham Forest from Torino?

13 **Who made his Premiership debut at the age of 34 when he played for Queen's Park Rangers in December?**

14 Which Geordie defender did Southampton buy from Galatasaray in Turkey?

15 **Aston Villa beat Leeds United 3-0 in the Coca-Cola Cup Final. Who scored their goals?**

 **Quiz 90**   Season 1995-1996

1 **Which Dutch team knocked Everton out of the European Cup Winners' Cup?**

2 Which English team did best in Europe, reaching the quarter finals of the UEFA Cup?

3 **Who won the GM Vauxhall Conference, but were not promoted to the Third Division because their ground facilities were held to be sub-standard by the Football League?**

4 Which club were thus spared relegation despite finishing bottom of the Third Division?

5 **This is the year in which Manchester United changed out of their grey away strip at half time because their players complained they couldn't see each other. Who were they playing?**

6 In this season, Wimbledon officials started talking about the possibility of a move to Dublin. Who is their Chairman?

7 **Which UEFA restriction on the composition of teams was outlawed as a result of the so-called 'Bosman Ruling' by the European Court of Justice?**

8 Which goalkeeper scored in a UEFA Cup match in September?

9 **At which English Premiership ground did Holland beat the Republic of Ireland in a play-off for Euro '96?**

10 Name the visiting goalkeeper who saved with a 'scorpion kick' during the England v Colombia international in September.

11 **Which 1996 film starring Sean Bean told the story of a Sheffield United trainee hopeful?**

12 Rangers made it eight Premiership titles in a row and also won the Scottish FA Cup. Which two players scored the goals in their 5-1 Final defeat of Heart of Midlothian?

13 **Who scored a hat trick against Aberdeen in the match in which Rangers clinched the title and was voted Player of the Year by both the Scottish PFA and the Scottish Football Writers' Association?**

14 Who won the Scottish League Cup, beating Dundee 2-0 in the Final?

15 **Which new club replaced Meadowbank Thistle in the Scottish League and won the Third Division in their first season?**

 ## Quiz 91   Season 1996-1997

1 Manchester United won the FA Carling Premiership for the fourth time in five years. Who was their leading scorer, with 19 goals?

2 For the second year running, the Premiership's leading scorer was Alan Shearer, with 25 goals for his new club, Newcastle United. Who ran him a close second, with 23 goals in the League, and outscored him 30 to 28 in all competitions?

3 Which team were runners-up in both the FA and Coca-Cola Cups and were relegated from the Premiership?

4 Which other two teams went down with them?

5 Which two teams won automatic promotion to the Premiership from the First Division?

6 The third team promoted was Crystal Palace, who won the play-off final - which club had finished third in the Second Division League table?

7 Who won the Coca-Cola Cup, beating Middlesbrough 1-0 in a replay after the first match had been drawn 1-1?

8 Who scored the winning goal?

9 Where was the replay held?

10 Which Second Division club reached the FA Cup semi-final?

11 After only 43 seconds, who scored the fastest ever goal in an FA Cup Final as Chelsea beat Middlesbrough 2-0?

12 Whose record - a goal after 45 seconds for Newcastle United against Manchester City in 1955 - did he beat?

13 Who scored Chelsea's second goal in that match?

14 Who did former Dutch international Ruud Gullit succeed in May 1996 as player-manager of Chelsea?

15 Which two February signings scored 13 goals between them in the remainder of the season and lifted West Ham United to Premiership safety?

---

1 Ole Gunnar Solskjaer 2 Ian Wright (Arsenal) 3 Middlesbrough 4 Sunderland and Nottingham Forest 5 Bolton Wanderers and Barnsley 6 Wolverhampton Wanderers 7 Leicester City 8 Steve Claridge 9 Hillsborough 10 Chesterfield 11 Roberto di Matteo 12 Jackie Milburn 13 Eddie Newton 14 Glenn Hoddle 15 John Hartson and Paul Kitson

 **Quiz 92**   **Season 1996-1997**

1 Who left his job as manager of Newcastle United in mid-season when his team were second in the Premiership?

2 Which French club knocked Newcastle United out of the UEFA Cup in the quarter final?

3 **Which French club knocked Liverpool out of the Cup Winners' Cup in the semi-final?**

4 Middlesbrough had three points deducted for cancelling a Premiership fixture without sufficient notice - which club were they due to have played?

5 **Macclesfield Town won the GM Vauxhall Conference to gain entry to the Football League for the first time. Which former Manchester United and Northern Ireland star was their manager?**

6 Which team did they replace in the Third Division of the Football League?

7 **Which club retained its League status only by drawing 1-1 with Hereford United on the last day of the season?**

8 Which London team reached the semi-finals of the Coca-Cola and FA Cups?

9 **In Scotland, Rangers won the Premier League for the ninth year in succession, thus equalling Celtic's record of 1966-1974. They also won the League Cup - which two internationals scored twice in their 4-3 Final victory over Heart of Midlothian?**

10 Who won the 1997 Scottish FA Cup, beating Falkirk 1-0 in the Final?

11 **In which year had these two teams previously faced each other in the Final?**

12 Who knocked Celtic out of the UEFA Cup in the first round?

13 **Which Welsh club did Aberdeen beat in the first round of the UEFA Cup?**

14 Which Danish club knocked Aberdeen out in the second round of the UEFA Cup?

15 **Which clubs contested the relegation/promotion play-off between the Scottish Premiership and the First Division?**

---

1 **Kevin Keegan** 2 AS Monaco 3 **Paris St Germain** 4 Blackburn Rovers 5 **Sammy McIlroy** 6 Hereford United 7 **Brighton and Hove Albion** 8 Wimbledon 9 **Ally McCoist and Paul Gascoigne** 10 Kilmarnock 11 1957 12 Hamburg 13 **Barry Town** 14 Brøndby 15 **Hibernian and Airdrieonians**

 **Quiz 93**   **Season 1996-1997**

1   Which Czech star of Euro '96 did Liverpool sign for £3.25 million from Borussia Dortmund?

2   At the start of the season, what serious illness kept Andy Cole out of contention for a Manchester United first team place?

3   Which entrepreneur from the music business bought Queen's Park Rangers for £10 million?

4   Which Celtic player was sent off during their UEFA Cup qualifying match against KC Kosice in Slovakia?

5   Which controversial goalkeeper signed a one-year contract with Plymouth Argyle?

6   Which Liverpool defender was fined £2000 by the FA for exceeding 45 disciplinary points in the previous season?

7   Who did Manchester United sell to Leeds United for £4.5 million?

8   Who became Director of Football at Portsmouth?

9   Who was sacked after 61 weeks as manager of Arsenal?

10 Of which club had his successor, Arsene Wenger, previously been the coach?

11 Wenger's first signings were fellow Frenchmen Remi Garde on a free transfer from Strasbourg and Patrick Viera for £3.5 million - from where?

12 Who resigned as manager of Barnet to become England goalkeeping coach?

13 Which club bought striker Niall Quinn from Manchester City for £1.3 million?

14 Who scored the first goal of the season in a 1-0 win for Manchester City over Ipswich Town in the Nationwide First Division?

15 Who scored a hat-trick on his debut for Middlesbrough?

1 **Patrik Berger** 2 Pneumonia 3 **Chris Wright** 4 Simon Donnelly 5 **Bruce Grobbelaar** 6 Neil Ruddock 7 **Lee Sharpe** 8 Terry Venables 9 **Bruce Rioch** 10 Grampus Eight (Japan) 11 **AC Milan** 12 Ray Clemence 13 **Sunderland** 14 Steve Lomas 15 **Fabrizio Ravanelli**

 **Quiz 94** **Season 1996-1997**

1 Which former Gunner scored a hat-trick for Nottingham Forest in their opening game, a 3-0 victory at Coventry City?

2 Still on the opening day of the season, who scored for Manchester United against Wimbledon with a shot from inside his own half?

3 Which Tottenham Hotspur player broke his leg in their 2-0 victory at Blackburn Rovers?

4 Which former Liverpool star was now player manager of Swansea City?

5 Who did Barry Town beat in the UEFA Cup to become the first League of Wales side to reach the first round proper of a European competition?

6 Who left Blackburn Rovers on August 21, 1996?

7 Which Yorkshire club were the early leaders in the FA Carling Premiership, with three wins out of three?

8 Who resigned on August 26 as manager of Manchester City?

9 Who took over from Tony Adams as captain of England?

10 What was the score in England's opening World Cup qualifying match, away to Moldova?

11 Who resigned as player-manager of Queen's Park Rangers and then played for Wycombe Wanderers the following week?

12 Who was sent off for the 12th time in his career as Wimbledon beat Tottenham Hotspur 1-0?

13 Who robbed Sheffield Wednesday of their hundred per cent record, with a 2-0 victory at Hillsborough on September 7?

14 Who was sacked after eight years in charge of Leeds United?

15 Who took over as manager of Queen's Park Rangers?

1 Kevin Campbell 2 David Beckham 3 Gary Mabbutt 4 Jan Molby 5 Budapest Vasutas 6 Kenny Dalglish 7 Sheffield Wednesday 8 Alan Ball 9 Alan Shearer (Newcastle United) 10 Moldova 0 England 3 11 Ray Wilkins 12 Vinnie Jones 13 Chelsea 14 Howard Wilkinson 15 Stewart Houston

Quiz 95   Season 1996-1997

1 Which former England international signed for Falkirk?

2 Who took over as manager of Leeds after 19 months out of the game?

3 Which Yorkshire First Division club was the last team in England to lose its hundred per cent League record, with a 3-1 home defeat by Queen's Park Rangers?

4 Who had four men sent off in their 3-0 defeat at Ibrox Park?

5 In which country was new Rotherham United manager Danny Bergara born?

6 Which former Arsenal No 1 became No 2 at Queen's Park Rangers?

7 Which Swedish club knocked Aston Villa out of the UEFA Cup?

8 Which Arsenal midfielder was recalled to the England squad two years after confessing to alcoholism and drug dependence?

9 Which Arsenal and England defender now admitted alcoholism?

10 Who was sacked as manager of Wycombe Wanderers, after only 15 months in charge?

11 Which club had he previously managed?

12 Which Nationwide Third Division club knocked First Division Manchester City out of the Coca-Cola Cup, with a 5-1 aggregate victory?

13 Which German club knocked Arsenal out of the UEFA Cup?

14 Who resigned as manager of Hibernian after 10 years in charge?

15 The life, love and drinking habits of which England player were the subject of a controversial television documentary?

1 Chris Waddle 2 George Graham 3 Barnsley 4 Heart of Midlothian 5 Uruguay
6 Bruce Rioch 7 Helsingborg 8 Paul Merson 9 Tony Adams 10 Alan Smith
11 Crystal Palace 12 Lincoln City 13 Borussia Moenchengladbach 14 Alex Miller
15 Paul Gascoigne

Quiz 96

Season 1996-1997

1   At which Nationwide Third Division club were there three pitch invasions during October?

2   Which Celtic striker scored two goals for Holland in their 3-1 defeat of Wales in the World Cup qualifiers?

3   **Which Manchester United striker broke his ankle in a collision with Liverpool's Neil Ruddock?**

4   Who took over as manager of Manchester City, six weeks after they sacked the previous incumbent?

5   **Which nation didn't turn up for their World Cup qualifying match against Scotland?**

6   A year after fouling Tottenham's Jurgen Klinsmann, whose arm movements got him into even hotter water at White Hart Lane?

7   **From which Italian club did Sheffield Wednesday buy Benito Carbone for £3 million?**

8   Which striker - then with Arsenal - was the first Premiership player to be suspended this season after accumulating 21 disciplinary points?

9   **Which Dutchman did Southampton buy for £1.3 million from Galatasaray (Turkey)?**

10 In which Cental American country were 80 people killed at a football match due to overcrowding?

11 **Which Rangers player was sent off as his team lost 4-1 to Ajax?**

12 Who beat Manchester United 5-0 in the Premiership?

13 **Which Aston Villa coach took over as manager of Nationwide Second Division Wycombe Wanderers?**

14 Which Chelsea director was killed in a helicopter crash on the way back from his team's Coca-Cola Cup match at Bolton Wanderers?

15 **Who resigned as manager of Blackburn Rovers?**

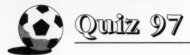

Quiz 97 — Season 1996-1997

1 **Who beat Manchester United 6-3 in the Premiership?**

2 Which Red Devil was shown a red card in this match?

3 **Who inflicted Manchester United's first ever home defeat in European competition?**

4 Who took over as manager of Coventry City as Ron Atkinson was moved upstairs?

5 **Ex-West Ham United defender Tommy Taylor took over as manager of Leyton Orient. At which club had he previously been in charge?**

6 Who was fined by Liverpool for refusing to play in the Reserves?

7 **Who became captain of Wales?**

8 What was the score in England's World Cup victory away to Georgia?

9 **Who scored a hat-trick in Holland's 7-1 defeat of Wales?**

10 Who missed a penalty for Rangers in their Premier League match at Celtic Park?

11 **And who missed a penalty for Celtic in the same match?**

12 Who became part-time manager of the Australian national soccer team?

13 **Which Scotland international did Queen's Park Rangers buy from Chelsea for £2.5 million?**

14 Which other Chelsea player did Queen's Park Rangers take on loan?

15 **Which Sheffield Wednesday player was banned by FIFA until December 6 because of claims by Udinese, one of his previous clubs, that they had prior claims on his services?**

 **Quiz 98**   **Season 1996-1997**

1 Which former Chelsea star scored the goal for non-League Woking that knocked First Division Millwall out of the FA Cup?

2 Which Dutch winger who cost Arsenal £2.3 million joined Benfica on loan?

3 **For what was Faustino Asprilla booked during Newcastle United's UEFA Cup quarter-final against Metz?**

4 Which former Liverpool and Southampton star was sacked as manager of Brighton and Hove Albion?

5 **From which Norwegian club did Tottenham Hotspur buy Steffen Iversen for £2.7 million?**

6 After thinking seriously about a move to Leeds United, to which club did Liverpool and former Wimbledon defender John Scales actually transfer for £2.6 million?

7 **Which Portuguese international retired while at West Ham?**

8 Who did Blackburn Rovers announce would be their next manager, with effect from the following June?

9 **Which Nationwide Second Division team knocked West Ham United out of the Coca-Cola Cup?**

10 Who resigned as manager of Nottingham Forest?

11 **Who took over as caretaker manager?**

12 For which team did Peter Shilton make his 1000th League appearance on December 22?

13 **Which club sacked two managers - Colin Murphy and Steve Thompson - and then appointed two more - Gary Strodder and Tony Agana?**

14 Which Premiership club announced plans to become a public company?

15 **Who took over as Manchester City manager, the previous occupant having resigned after only 33 days 'for health reasons'?**

 *Quiz 99*   **Season 1996-1997**

1   Who scored his 200th League goal in Arsenal's 2-0 victory over Middlesbrough on New Year's Day 1997?

2   Which Nationwide First Division side knocked Southampton out of the FA Cup in a third round match on an icy pitch?

3   For which club was Ian Culverhouse playing when he achieved the unwanted distinction of being sent off after only 52 seconds - sooner than anyone else in the history of the FA Cup?

4   Which of the season's sacked managers became the first Technical Director of the FA?

5   From which Italian club did Tottenham Hotspur sign Swiss international defender Ramon Vega for £3.7 million?

6   Onto which club did West Ham United manage to offload Romanian midfielder Ilie Dumitrescu for £1 million?

7   Which other Romanian did West Ham United return to sender - Espanol (Spain)?

8   From which club did Leeds United sign Robert Molenaar for £1 million?

9   Which former England captain - a star with West Bromwich Albion, Manchester United and Middlesbrough - finally gave up playing on his 40th birthday?

10 Who, on January 14, became manager of Newcastle United?

11 And, six days later, which Portuguese defender became his first signing for his new club?

12 Who did Middlesbrough buy for £2.7 million from Inter Milan?

13 Who announced his intention to play for Arsenal next season in the morning and got dropped in the evening by his present club, Paris St Germain?

14 From which Nationwide First Division club did Leicester City sign Matt Elliott for £1.6 million?

15 Which Scottish manager was banned from the touchline for a year after making remarks to officials after a local derby?

---

15 **Tommy Burns** (Celtic)
10 Kenny Dalglish 11 **Raul** 12 Gianluca Festa 13 Nicolas Anelka 14 Oxford United
Futbol (Mexico) 7 **Florin Raducioiu** (Holland) 8 FC Volendam (Holland) 9 **Bryan Robson**
1 **Ian Wright** 2 Reading 3 **Swindon Town** 4 Howard Wilkinson 5 **Cagliari** 6 Clube de

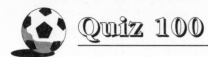

Quiz 100   Season 1996-1997

1   Name the owner of the Pizza Express restaurant chain who bought a 97% stake in Peterborough United for about £1 million.

2   Who bought twenty-five per cent of Rangers for £40 million?

3   Who bought fifty-one per cent of Portsmouth for one pound?

4   Which Portuguese scored for West Ham United in their FA Cup third round match on a frozen pitch at Second Division Wrexham?

5   And who scored a last minute winner for Wrexham in the replay at Upton Park?

6   Which former England international scored the winner for Bradford City as they beat Everton 3-2 at Goodison Park in the FA Cup third round?

7   Recovering rapidly from his illness while at Maine Road, who became part-time assistant to Dave Bassett at Crystal Palace?

8   To which Italian club did unsettled Andrei Kanchelskis move from Everton?

9   Who was sacked as manager of Plymouth Argyle after leading them to promotion in the previous season?

10   Who took over as manager of West Bromwich Albion?

11   Who was sacked as manager of First Division Millwall as part of a cost-cutting exercise?

12   Which former Everton player resigned as manager of Oldham Athletic?

13   Whose goal for Italy inflicted England's first ever World Cup defeat at Wembley?

14   Who was the England goalkeeper beaten at the near post?

15   Who did Blackburn Rovers buy from Odense for £2.5 million?

 Quiz 101 **Season 1996-1997**

1 **Which referee awarded Chelsea a controversial penalty in extra time in their FA Cup fifth round replay with Leicester City?**

2 Who took over as general manager of Nottingham Forest?

3 **Who did Manchester United beat 4-0 at Old Trafford in the Champions' Cup quarter-final?**

4 Who did Nottingham Forest buy from Celtic to get them out of trouble?

5 **Who did Blackburn Rovers announce would be their next manager after the last appointment said he was very sorry but he wouldn't be coming after all?**

6 Of which team was he previously manager?

7 **For which Italian club did Queen's Park Rangers striker Daniele Dichio sign?**

8 Who refereed the Premiership clash at Highbury in which Liverpool were awarded a penalty despite the protestations of Robbie Fowler that he had not been fouled?

9 **Which former Leeds United and Scotland forward left his job as manager of Bristol City by mutual consent?**

10 Which former England forward left his job as manager of his old club, Everton, by mutual consent?

11 **Who took over as caretaker player-manager at Goodison?**

12 Which Liverpool season ticket holder is chairman of Everton?

13 **Who did Celtic buy from Aston Villa for £2.4 million?**

14 Which Swiss World Cup referee was banned for life for attempted bribery, partly through the evidence of Eric Cantona?

15 **Who announced his retirement from international football after winning 99 caps for Wales?**

1 **Mike Reed** 2 Dave Bassett 3 **FC Porto** 4 Pierre van Hooijdonk 5 **Roy Hodgson** 6 Inter Milan 7 **Sampdoria** 8 Gerald Ashby 9 **Joe Jordan** 10 Joe Royle 11 **Dave Watson** 12 Peter Johnson 13 **Tommy Johnson** 14 Kurt Rothlisburger 15 **Neville Southall**

 # Quiz 102 — Season 1996-1997

1 Faced with the prospect of playing their last four matches in nine days, which Premiership club applied to have the season extended?

2 The manager of which club - then second in the Premiership - described the idea as ridiculous?

3 For the second leg of their Cup Winners' Cup semi-final against Paris St Germain, who did Liverpool drop for the first time in his long and distinguished career?

4 Which Chesterfield player had what looked like a good goal disallowed in their FA Cup semi-final against Middlesbrough?

5 Why did UEFA warn that, after 1997-98, they would let no more English Coca-Cola Cup winners into the UEFA Cup?

6 Who returned as chairman of Watford after a seven-year absence?

7 Who was PFA Footballer of the Year?

8 Who was the Football Writers' Footballer of the Year?

9 Who was sacked as manager of Celtic?

10 Who were Sunderland's opponents in the last ever match at Roker Park, and what was the result?

11 Who was the captain of the Luton Town youth team signed by Arsenal for £1 million?

12 How much did Aston Villa pay Liverpool for Stan Collymore?

13 Whose move from West Ham United to Everton for £4.25 million created a new Premiership transfer record?

14 Who became the first player in the 20th century to win four FA Cup winner's medals?

15 Which player announced his retirement on May 18, six days before his 31st birthday?

Quiz 103   **Season 1997-1998**

1 **Why was Scotland's international scheduled for Saturday September 6 postponed?**

2 Which Blackburn player scored two goals for Scotland in their 4-1 defeat of Belarus in a World Cup qualifier?

3 **Which Chelsea player scored the winner for Norway against Azerbaijan in a World Cup qualifier?**

4 Which Arsenal player scored two goals for England in their 4-0 World Cup victory over Moldova?

5 **Which Arsenal player captained England in their World Cup qualifier away to Italy?**

6 Who was the captain of Italy?

7 **Who was the manager of Italy?**

8 Who had he replaced after Euro '96?

9 **Which Italian was sent off during the 0-0 draw with England?**

10 Which club chairman said 'I have never believed in managers' after sacking Mervyn Day?

11 **Who were Chelsea's opponents in the first round of the European Cup Winners' Cup?**

12 Who scored off his backside for Chelsea in the second leg of this tie?

13 **In the Premiership in September, which teams drew 3-3, three of the goals coming controversially in time added on at the end of the match?**

14 Which former Chelsea central defender did West Ham United buy from Blackburn Rovers for £2.3 million?

15 **Which Danish central defender did West Ham United sell to Celtic for £1.4 million?**

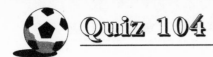 **Quiz 104**   Season 1997-1998

1 Why was West Ham United's Rio Ferdinand dropped from the England squad for the game against Moldova?

2 Who bought Fulham of the Nationwide Second Division?

3 Which other going concern in West London did he already own?

4 To which French club was Fabrizio Ravanelli eventually transferred from Middlesbrough for £5 million?

5 Who did Liverpool meet in the first round of the UEFA Cup?

6 Which defender scored both goals for Newcastle United in their 2-2 draw away to Dynamo Kiev in the Champions' League?

7 Who did Sheffield Wednesday buy from Molde in his native Norway for £800,000?

8 Who did Bolton Wanderers buy for a club record £3.5 million?

9 Which Arsenal player missed an away match in Greece because of his fear of flying?

10 Which Nationwide First Division team knocked Manchester United out of the Coca-Cola Cup in the third round?

11 In September, which chairman said of which recently deceased fellow director: 'He left bitterness and wounds'?

12 Who scored for PSV Eindhoven as they beat Newcastle United 1-0 in the Champions' League?

13 With which Spanish team did Aston Villa draw 0-0 in the UEFA Cup second round first leg?

14 Who beat Liverpool 3-0 in the UEFA Cup second round first leg?

15 Who resigned as manager of Swansea City only 13 days after taking over?

Quiz 105   Season 1997-1998

1 **Which three other clubs were in Manchester United's Champions' League group?**

2 Which three other clubs were in Newcastle's Champions' League group?

3 **Who was sacked in October as manager of Northern Ireland?**

4 Name the Northern Ireland assistant manager, who also got the boot.

5 **Name the player bought by Liverpool from Columbus Crew.**

6 What was the score in the snowy first leg of Chelsea's Cup Winners' Cup second round tie in Tromso (Norway)?

7 **Which Villa striker accused one of his team-mates of being, not 'Stan the man' but 'the wrong man'?**

8 Which Arsenal defender was sent off in the Premiership match against Aston Villa for handling the ref?

9 **Who scored a hat trick in Manchester United's 7-0 Premiership defeat of Barnsley?**

10 Which Bolton Wanderers defender was sent off in their match at West Ham United on October 18?

11 **Why, according to John Hartson of West Ham United, is referee Mike Reed like an ancient Greek poet?**

12 Who announced in October his intention to leave Rangers at the end of the 1997-98 season?

13 **Which Manchester United player scored the Republic of Ireland's goal in their 1-1 draw with Belgium in the first leg of the World Cup qualifying play-off?**

14 And which six other nations were paired in the other three play-offs?

15 **Who were Derby County's Premiership visitors on the night the floodlights went out during the match?**

Quiz 106   Season 1997-1998

1. **Which was the second Premiership match of the season to be abandoned through floodlight failure?**

2. Who scored the goals that took Aston Villa through 2-1 in the second leg of their second round UEFA Cup tie with Athletic Bilbao?

3. **Who hit a Champions' League hat-trick for Manchester United in their 3-1 win at Feyenoord?**

4. In November, who was appointed manager of Brentford in succession to David Webb?

5. **What was the score in the second leg of Chelsea's Cup Winners' Cup second round tie with Tromso?**

6. Who hit whom during the Chelsea v West Ham United Premiership match at Stamford Bridge?

7. **Who was given a vote of confidence by the board of Manchester City?**

8. Who was sacked as manager of Queen's Park Rangers?

9. **Who did Crystal Palace buy from Juventus for £1.7 million?**

10. Ron Atkinson took over as manager of Sheffield Wednesday - who had just been sacked?

11. **Where had Atkinson first been a manager, between December 1971 and November 1974?**

12. Where was Atkinson's first League manager's job, from November 1974 to January 1978?

13. **Which Scot took over as manager of Benfica?**

14. Who scored for the Republic of Ireland in their 2-1 defeat in the second leg of the World Cup qualifying play-off against Belgium in Brussels?

15. **Who was the manager of Belgium?**

Quiz 107   Season 1997-1998

1   Who scored the only goal of the World Cup qualifying play-off second leg that enabled Italy to go through to the finals at the expense of Russia?

2   For which Italian Serie A club was he playing at the time?

3   In November, it was widely reported that the world's richest man was interested in buying Everton - who was he?

4   Which Nationwide First Division team knocked Leeds United out of the Coca-Cola Cup at Elland Road?

5   Who took over as coach of Tottenham Hotspur after the departure of Gerry Francis?

6   With which Swiss club had he previously held the same position?

7   What was the name of the fitness coach he tried but failed to bring with him to England?

8   Who scored Barnsley's goal in their Premiership win at Anfield?

9   Which Romanian team beat Aston Villa 2-1 in the first leg of their third round UEFA Cup tie?

10 Who scored Villa's valuable away goal?

11 In an Internet poll of half a million people in 110 countries, who was voted the best footballer of all time?

12 Which British player was runner-up?

13 Which Englishman came third?

14 Which Dutchman came fourth?

15 Which former England captain was fifth?

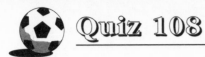

Quiz 108   Season 1997-1998

1 In December, which manager left West Bromwich Albion to take over the reins at Queen's Park Rangers?

2 By winning 6-1 at White Hart Lane, which team inflicted Tottenham Hotspur's worst home defeat since 1935?

3 **Who scored Aston Villa's goals in their 2-0 UEFA Cup third round second leg victory against Steua Bucharest to take them through 3-2 on aggregate?**

4 Who scored the goal for Juventus that beat Manchester United in their Champions League game in Turin?

5 **Name the former Leeds United and Scotland star who died on December 7.**

6 In December, Coventry City fans may have been surprised to see someone other than Steve Ogrizovic in their goal - who was his replacement?

7 **Who scored his first goal for Southampton after 10 years as a regular (against Leicester City)?**

8 Who missed his third penalty in succession for Manchester United during their 1-0 Premiership victory over Aston Villa?

9 **Which Unibond League team knocked Lincoln City out of the FA Cup to earn a crack at Premiership opposition in the third round?**

10 Which former Newcastle player scored the winning goal for Manchester United on his return to St James's Park?

11 **Which Premiership match was the scene of the season's third floodlight failure?**

12 Which Romanian international did Coventry City buy for £3.25 from Grasshopper Zurich?

13 **Who came back to Spurs after having left in 1994?**

14 In which Scottish Third Division match was the referee hit by a coin thrown from the crowd?

15 **Which ailing Yorkshire team did Leyton Orient beat 8-0 in a Third Division match, thus equalling their highest ever score?**

1 **Ray Harford** 2 Chelsea 3 **Ian Taylor and Dwight Yorke** 4 Filippo Inzaghi 5 **Billy Bremner** 6 Magnus Hedman 7 **Francis Benali** 8 Teddy Sheringham 9 **Emley** 10 Andy Cole 11 **Wimbledon v Arsenal** 12 Viorel Moldovan 13 **Jürgen Klinsmann** 14 Montrose v Arbroath 15 **Doncaster Rovers**

Quiz 109

Season 1997-1998

1 **Which old Preston North End hero was the only sporting knight in the New Year's Honours List?**

2 From which Spanish club did Everton acquire French international striker Mickael Medar?

3 **Which BBC radio programme celebrated its 50th anniversary on Saturday January 3, 1998?**

4 Now on Radio Five Live, which station had it previously been on?

5 **Who scored for Emley at West Ham in the FA Cup third round?**

6 Who missed a penalty for West Ham United in their Coca-Cola Cup quarter-final against Arsenal?

7 **Name the four Coca-Cola Cup semi-finalists.**

8 Which Rangers star announced in March that he would be joining Chelsea at the end of the season?

9 **Who finally moved from Middlesbrough to Tenerife?**

10 Which former England striker moved from Sheffield United to Benfica?

11 **When the draw for the qualifying matches of Euro 2000 was announced, who came out in England's group?**

12 Who was drawn in Northern Ireland's group?

13 **Who was drawn in the Republic of Ireland's group?**

14 Who was drawn in Scotland's group?

15 **Who was drawn in the same group as Wales?**

Quiz 110   Season 1997-1998

1   Which goalkeeper scored in the penalty shoot-out in which his team knocked Watford out of the FA Cup?

2   Which club announced plans for a permanent move to Wembley?

3   Which Liverpool player was widely reported in January to be on the brink of a move to Barcelona?

4   In a Carling Net website poll, who was voted the most popular British football commentator?

5   Uwe Rosler missed a penalty for Manchester City in their FA Cup fourth round tie at home to West Ham United. Which club in the former East Germany did he come from?

6   Which club sacked manager Chris Kamara?

7   To which club did he go two weeks later?

8   Who did he replace there?

9   In the FA Cup fourth round, Newcastle United drew 1-1 at Stevenage Borough. Who scored for the Premiership club?

10   Who equalised for the underdogs from the Vauxhall Conference?

11   Which Aston Villa player allegedly spat at his own club's fans?

12   Which Queen's Park Rangers striker moved to West Ham United?

13   A couple of weeks later, which two Northern Ireland internationals made the same journey across London in the opposite direction?

14   Who bought Andy Hinchcliffe from Everton for £3 million?

15   How did Marco Negri sustain the eye injury that left him unfit to play for Rangers?

 **Quiz 111**   Season 1997-1998

1 During which **Nationwide First Division** match on February 2 was a linesman attacked and knocked unconscious by a spectator?

2 Who was named as the English referee for the forthcoming World Cup?

3 **Who was named as the Scottish referee for the forthcoming World Cup?**

4 What is the name of Derby County's new stadium?

5 **What was the name of their old stadium?**

6 Which Englishman was appointed manager of Northern Ireland?

7 **Which former Scotland international is his assistant?**

8 Who became the youngest England international this century when he won his first cap against Chile at the age of 18 years and 59 days?

9 **Who scored both goals in Chile's 2-0 victory in this match?**

10 Who was the manager of Chile?

11 **In the fifth round of the FA Cup, who won at Villa Park for the first time ever?**

12 Who was appointed the new manager of Rangers?

13 **Which was his previous club?**

14 From which Italian club did Middlesbrough buy Marco Branca?

15 **Who scored Middlesbrough's first goal in the second leg of their Coca-Cola Cup semi-final against Liverpool?**

---

1 Portsmouth v Sheffield United 2 Paul Durkin 3 Hugh Dallas 4 Pride Park 5 The Baseball Ground 6 Lawrie McMenemy 7 Joe Jordan 8 Michael Owen (Liverpool) 9 Marcelo Salas 10 Nelson Acosta 11 Coventry City 12 Dick Advocaat 13 PSV Eindhoven 14 Internazionale 15 Paul Merson

Quiz 112   Season 1997-1998

1   After a 2-1 Arsenal victory over Chelsea in the first game, what was the score in the Coca-Cola Cup semi-final second leg at Stamford Bridge?

2   Which Arsenal player was sent off in the second game?

3   What upheaval had Chelsea suffered in the fortnight between the two legs?

4   What is the name of the Aston Villa chairman?

5   Who took over from Brian Little as manager of Aston Villa?

6   Of which Nationwide Second Division club had he previously been manager?

7   What is his unusual method of attracting his players' attention during the course of a match?

8   At about the same time, which sponsor announced its intention not to take up an option to continue having its name on the front of Villa's shirts?

9   Of which electronics company are they a subsidiary?

10   Who scored two goals for Barnsley in their FA Cup fifth round replay victory over Manchester United?

11   Frank Clark's November vote of confidence was followed in February by the sack. Who took his place as manager of Manchester City?

12   Which millionaire businessman announced plans to buy Crystal Palace?

13   Which leading Italian club was said to be a major part of this deal?

14   Who was sacked as manager of Brighton and Hove Albion?

15   Who was appointed to replace him?

15 Brian Horton
9 Samsung 10 Scott Jones 11 Joe Royle 12 Mark Goldberg 13 Juventus 14 Steve Gritt
4 Doug Ellis 5 John Gregory 6 Wycombe Wanderers 7 He whistles at them 8 AST
1 Chelsea 3 Arsenal 1 2 Patrick Viera 3 The departure of player-manager Ruud Gullit

Quiz 113   Season 1997-1998

1   **In March, who won the African Cup of Nations?**

2   Who were the runners-up?

3   **Where was the tournament played?**

4   Who scored the only goal of the UEFA Cup quarter-final first leg match in which Atletico Madrid beat Aston Villa?

5   **Which former Brighton and Liverpool forward was one of Spanish television's top commentators at the game?**

6   What injury prevented Juninho from playing in this match for Atletico?

7   **Who left his job as manager of Sheffield United four days before their FA Cup sixth round tie against Coventry City?**

8   Who scored the only goal in Arsenal's Premiership victory at Old Trafford?

9   **Who scored both goals in Chelsea's 2-1 Cup Winners' Cup quarter final win over Real Betis?**

10   Who scored a goal and gave a way a penalty in the FA Cup sixth round match between Arsenal and West Ham United?

11   **Which two German-speakers had a public row in the Tottenham tunnel?**

12   Who walked out on Birmingham City but came back to them a couple of days later?

13   **Who did Newcastle United buy for £2 million from Olympiakos?**

14   Which Liverpool player did Stan Collymore accuse of making racist remarks to him during Aston Villa's visit to Anfield?

15   **Which two Chelsea players scored twice in their 6-2 defeat of Crystal Palace at Stamford Bridge in the Premiership?**

1 **Egypt** 2 South Africa 3 **Ouagadougu, Burkina Faso** 4 Christian Vieri (penalty)
5 **Michael Robinson** 6 A broken leg 7 **Nigel Spackman** 8 Marc Overmars 9 **Tore Andre
Flo** 10 Ian Pearce (West Ham United) 11 **Christian Gross and Jurgen Klinsmann** 12 Trevor
Francis 13 **Nicos Dabizas** 14 Steve Harkness 15 **Gianluca Vialli and Tore Andre Flo**

Quiz 114   Season 1997-1998

1   Who stepped down as chairman of Manchester City?

2   In their FA Cup sixth round replay against Arsenal, which three West Ham players failed to score in the penalty shoot-out?

3   **Who scored for Aston Villa's two goals in the second leg of their UEFA Cup quarter-final against Atletico Madrid?**

4   Who scored Atletico's goal to send the Spanish club through on away goals?

5   **Who knocked Manchester United out of the European Cup?**

6   After a 0-0 draw in the away leg, United drew 1-1 at home - which French international scored after four minutes for the visitors?

7   **And who equalised for United early in the second half?**

8   What was the score in the second leg of Chelsea's Cup Winners' Cup quarter-final against Real Betis?

9   **Which Nationwide Third Division club was served with a winding-up order by the Inland Revenue?**

10 Which two directors of Newcastle United resigned after tabloid press revelations about their behaviour in Marbella?

11 **Who moved from Rangers to Middlesbrough?**

12 Which Tottenham Hotspur player scored in the Switzerland v England friendly international?

13 **Where was this match played?**

14 Name the two Blackburn Rovers players who took part in this match.

15 **How many Barnsley players remained on the pitch at the end of their Premiership match at home to Liverpool?**

 Quiz 115   Season 1997-1998

1   Chelsea won the Coca-Cola Cup, beating Middlesbrough 2-0 in the Final at Wembley. Who scored the goals?

2   Dennis Wise was captain, but who collected the Cup for Chelsea?

3   Which government minister handed him the Cup?

4   Who made his Middlesbrough debut when he came on as a substitute in the Coca-Cola Cup Final?

5   With which airline did Leeds United fly home from their Premiership match at Upton Park?

6   From which airport did they take off?

7   Who kept Arsenal's title hopes alive by scoring the only goal in their Premiership victory at the Reebok Stadium, Bolton?

8   In the European Cup semi-final first leg, who scored a hat-trick - including two penalties - for Juventus against AS Monaco?

9   Who replaced Tim Flowers in goal during Blackburn Rovers' 2-1 Premiership victory over Barnsley?

10   In the other European Cup semi-final first leg, who scored the goals that gave Real Madrid a 2-0 victory over Borussia Dortmund?

11   Why was the kick-off in this match delayed for 75 minutes?

12   Who scored for Vicenza when they beat Chelsea 1-0 in the first leg of the Cup Winners' Cup semi-final?

13   In the other Cup Winners' Cup semi-final, who scored in the last minute to give Stuttgart a 2-1 victory over Lokomotiv Moscow?

14   Which Third Division club became the first side to guarantee promotion in March since Middlesbrough went up from Division Two in 1974?

15   Which former Scotland international and Cup-winner with Newcastle United in 1955 died on March 19, 1998 at the age of 73?

1 Frank Sinclair and Roberto di Matteo 2 Player-manager Gianluca Vialli 3 Home Secretary Jack Straw 4 Paul Gascoigne 5 Emerald Airways 6 Stansted 7 Christopher Wreh 8 Allesandro del Piero 9 Alan Fettis 10 Fernando Morientes and Christian Karembeu 11 Because a broken goalpost had to be replaced 12 Lamberto Zauli 13 Bobic 14 Notts County 15 Jimmy Scoular

Quiz 116 Season 1997-1998

1 **Outside which Second Division ground was a fan stabbed to death after the game against Fulham?**

2 Who scored two goals for Heart of Midlothian in their 3-1 defeat of Falkirk in the semi-final of the Scottish FA Cup?

3 **Who scored for Falkirk?**

4 Who scored the killer blow for Hearts in the 90th minute?

5 **Who was manager of Falkirk?**

6 Which defender headed spectacularly into his own net as Barnsley went down 2-1 at Leeds in the Premiership?

7 **Who scored for Barnsley and was then sent off for two bookable cases of dissent in less than a minute?**

8 Who scored for Arsenal in their 1-0 FA Cup semi-final victory over Wolverhampton Wanderers?

9 **Who was the Littlewoods Man of the Arsenal v Wolves FA Cup semi-final, nominated by Ron Atkinson?**

10 Where was the match played?

11 **Who scored for Newcastle United as they beat Sheffield United 1-0 in the other FA Cup semi-final?**

12 Who was the manager of Sheffield United?

13 **At which neutral venue was this match played?**

14 Who scored the goals for Rangers that knocked Celtic out of the Scottish FA Cup at the semi-final stage?

15 **Hampden Park was under reconstruction, so the two teams drew lots to decide at which of their grounds the semi-final would be played. Who won the draw?**

1 **Gillingham** 2 Stephane Adam 3 **Kevin McAllister** 4 Neil McCann 5 **Alex Totten** 6 Adrian Moses 7 **Georgi Hristov** 8 Christopher Wreh 9 **Patrick Viera** 10 Villa Park 11 **Alan Shearer** 12 Alan Thompson 13 **Old Trafford** 14 Ally McCoist and Jorg Albertz 15 Celtic - the match was played at Parkhead

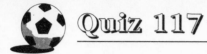 **Quiz 117**   Season 1997-1998

1 Which of Arsenal's foreign legion was PFA Player of the Year?

2 Name the Irish international who was the last Arsenal player to win this award in 1979.

3 **Which Manchester United striker was runner-up in the 1998 poll?**

4 Who was PFA Young Player of the Year, ahead of Kevin Davies (Southampton) and Rio Ferdinand (West Ham United)?

5 **Which folk hero (or villain, depending on your view) moved from Wimbledon to Queen's Park Rangers?**

6 On Good Friday, April 10, which Second Division side became the second team in England to clinch promotion this season after their closest rivals, Grimsby Town, failed to win at Wycombe Wanderers?

7 **Who scored and was then sent off in the Good Friday Premiership match between Manchester United and Liverpool?**

8 Which PSV Eindhoven centre back - the Dutch Player of the Year - was linked in early April with a £9 million move to Manchester United?

9 **Bob Taylor - the scorer of Bolton Wanderers' winning goal against Blackburn Rovers - was on loan from which Midlands club?**

10 A week after their semi-final victories, the FA Cup finalists met in the Premiership, Arsenal beating Newcastle United 3-1 at Highbury. Who scored two goals in this match?

11 **Martin Keown missed this match because of an injury to his eye socket - who took his place in the Arsenal defence?**

12 Who scored Newcastle's goal - the first Arsenal had conceded in nearly 14 hours of Premiership football?

13 **Which club learned on April 11 that they had lost their Football League status?**

14 Which two players - one from each side - were sent off in West Ham United's 0-0 draw with Derby County in the Premiership?

15 **Which Italian scored a hat-trick for Middlesbrough as they beat Bury 4-0 in the First Division?**

1 **Dennis Bergkamp** 2 Liam Brady 3 **Andy Cole** 4 Michael Owen (Liverpool) 5 **Vinnie Jones** 6 Bristol City 7 **Michael Owen** 8 Jaap Stam 9 **West Bromwich Albion** 10 Nicholas Anelka 11 **Steve Bould** 12 Warren Barton 13 **Doncaster Rovers** 14 John Hartson and Stefano Eranio 15 **Marco Branca**

 **Quiz 118**   Season 1997-1998

1 **Who scored two goals for Arsenal in their 4-1 defeat of Blackburn Rovers at Ewood Park on Easter Monday?**

2 Which former Nottingham Forest striker scored for Watford in the 1-1 draw with Bristol City that assured them of promotion from the Second Division?

3 **Which Brazilian scored both goals for Internazionale as they beat Spartak Moscow 2-1 in the second leg of the UEFA Cup semi-final, winning 4-2 on aggregate?**

4 Who knocked Atletico Madrid, conquerors of Aston Villa, out of the UEFA Cup in the semi-final?

5 **Who came on as substitute and scored the killer goal for Chelsea in their 3-1 victory over Vicenza in the second leg of the Cup Winners' Cup semi-final?**

6 In this match, which Uruguayan made his first appearance for Chelsea in six months after sustaining a career-threatening knee injury?

7 **Who did VfB Stuttgart beat in the other semi-final of the Cup Winners' Cup?**

8 Name the three 'H's who scored for Leeds United in their 3-2 win at Bolton Wanderers in the Premiership on April 18.

9 **Which Manchester United player was sent off during their 1-1 home draw with Newcastle United?**

10 Who notched up their first home win of the season with a 3-1 victory over Derby County on April 18?

11 **Halifax Town assured themselves of the GM Vauxhall Conference title and thus booked their return to the Football League. In which year had they dropped out of it?**

12 Which Tottenham Hotspur player was sent off in their Premiership match at Barnsley on April 18?

13 **Who scored his 23rd and 24th goals of the season for West Ham United in their Premiership victory over Blackburn Rovers?**

14 What was the name of the faith healer summoned to help England in their preparations for their friendly with Portugal?

15 **Who won their first trophy for 18 years when they beat Bournemouth 2-1 after extra time in the Final of the Auto Windscreens Trophy?**

214

THE ULTIMATE FOOTBALL FACT AND QUIZ BOOK

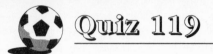 **Quiz 119** **Season 1997-1998**

1 Who scored for Aberdeen in the 1-0 defeat of Rangers which left the losers three points behind Celtic with three matches to play?

2 In April, for which Juventus and Italy striker were Manchester United reported to have made an £18 million bid?

3 Which Southampton player staked a claim for a place in the full England World Cup squad with a hat-trick in the 'B' international against Russia at Loftus Road?

4 Which Reading striker, formerly with West Ham United and Manchester City, announced that he was retiring at the end of the season to go and live with his Norwegian wife and child in Bergen?

5 Which was the only Premiership club to take six points off West Ham United in 1997-98?

6 Who came on as a substitute in the second half for Newcastle United at Tottenham, only to leave the field with a ligament injury four minutes later?

7 What was unusual about the ball used in the Premiership match between Everton and Sheffield Wednesday on April 25?

8 Who scored his first goal for Chelsea in six years as they beat Liverpool 4-1?

9 Who scored a hat-trick for Coventry City in their 3-3 draw at Leeds United?

10 Who scored twice for Leeds in the same match?

11 Which team won promotion to the Nationwide Second Division in their first year as a member of the Football League?

12 Which seaside team completed a drop from First to Third Divisions in successive seasons?

13 Manchester City announced that Uwe Rosler would be returning to Germany at the end of the season. For which Bundesliga club had he signed?

14 Who was made full-time manager of Wycombe Wanderers after doing the job on a temporary basis since the departure of John Gregory?

15 Name the club which was the last to have been promoted from last season's First Division and the first to be relegated from this year's Premiership.

1 Stephen Glass 2 Alessandro del Piero 3 Matthew Le Tissier 4 Trevor Morley 5 Southampton 6 Keith Gillespie 7 It was an experimental fluorescent yellow colour 8 Steve Clarke 9 Darren Huckerby 10 Jimmy Floyd Hasselbaink 11 Macclesfield Town 12 Southend United 13 Kaiserslautern 14 Neil Smillie 15 Crystal Palace

Quiz 120

Season 1997-1998

1 **As Arsenal edged towards their first Premiership title, which Frenchman scored the only goal - his second for the club - in their victory over Derby County?**

2 Which Blackburn Rovers player was shown the red card while on the bench during his team's 2-0 defeat at Coventry?

3 **Who scored four of Tottenham Hotspur's goals in their 6-2 victory at Wimbledon?**

4 Which Wimbledon defender was sent off in this match for the second time this season?

5 **Which team was relegated from the top division for the first time since the Scottish League was founded in 1890?**

6 When Attilio Lombardo stood down as acting player-coach of Crystal Palace, who first took over the day-to-day running of team affairs?

7 **And who took over from him?**

8 Who beat Rangers in their last home match of the season?

9 **Dennis Bergkamp was voted the Football Writers' Footballer of the Year. Who, in 1971, was the last Arsenal player to have won this award?**

10 Name the Greek international who scored the goal for Leicester City that condemned Barnsley to relegation?

WELCOME TO THE NEW GROUND!

11 **Reading played their last match at Elm Park, their home since 1896. What is the name of their new ground?**

12 Why is it so called?

13 **Which clubs clinched the two automatic promotion places from Division One?**

14 Who scored for Tranmere Rovers against Wolverhampton Wanderers in his last match before retirement?

15 **Which three clubs were relegated from Division One?**

---

1 **Emmanuel Petit** 2 Tim Flowers 3 **Jurgen Klinsmann** 4 Ben Thatcher 5 **Hibernian**
6 Chairman Ron Noades 7 **Brian Sparrow** 8 Kilmarnock 9 **Frank McLintock**
10 Theo Zagorakis 11 **The Madejski Stadium** 12 After club chairman John Madejski
13 **Nottingham Forest and Middlesbrough** 14 John Aldridge 15 **Manchester City,**
Reading and Stoke City

Quiz 121   Season 1997-1998

1 Which former Norwich and Nottingham Forest forward was found dead in a garage in Shoreditch, East London, at the age of 37?

2 Arsenal clinched the Premiership title by beating Everton in their last home match of the season. Which Arsenal player made his 500th appearance for the club in this game?

3 **Who scored two goals in Arsenal's 4-0 victory over Everton?**

4 Which Nigerian-born 20-year-old scored his first two goals for West Ham United in their 3-3 draw with relegated Crystal Palace?

5 **Who scored twice for Liverpool in their 4-0 Premiership victory over new Champions Arsenal?**

6 Which forward scored for Liverpool in this match and also missed a penalty?

7 **In the UEFA Cup Final, Inter Milan beat Lazio 3-0. Where was the match played?**

8 One player from each side was sent off - name either.

9 **What was the name of Inter Milan's coach?**

10 In Newcastle United's Premiership match against Leicester City, who did England captain Alan Shearer allegedly kick when he was down?

11 **Who was sacked as manager of Fulham shortly after leading them to a place in the Second Division play-offs?**

12 Who parted company with First Division Millwall 'by mutual consent' after managing the club since June 1997?

13 **Who scored a penalty for Fulham as they drew 1-1 with Grimsby Town in the first leg of their Second Division play-off?**

14 Who scored for Celtic as they beat St Johnstone 2-0 in their final League match of the season to clinch their first Scottish title since 1988?

15 **Who was Celtic's Dutch coach?**

Quiz 122   **Season 1997-1998**

1 Who was the first captain of Celtic to lift the Premier League trophy for 10 years?

2 Who scored a penalty and was sent off in Rangers' last League match of the season at Dundee United?

3 **Who scored for Everton in the 1-1 home draw with Coventry City that guaranteed their safety in the Premiership?**

4 Which Everton player had a penalty saved in the same match?

5 **And who saved it?**

6 Which was the only Premiership team beaten at home and away by Crystal Palace in 1997-98?

7 **Which Newcastle United player was sent off at Ewood Park in the last match of the season against his previous club?**

8 Which Chelsea player scored his first Premiership goal in their 2-0 defeat of Bolton Wanderers at Stamford Bridge?

9 **Who scored a penalty in Aston Villa's home win over new Champions Arsenal?**

10 Who was the FA Carling Premiership's leading scorer in the 1997-98, with 25 goals in all competitions?

11 **A month before the start of the World Cup squad, which member of the England squad was outed as a cigarette smoker?**

12 Which former Manchester United and Leeds United striker was appointed manager of Oldham Athletic in place of Neil Warnock?

13 **To which Spanish club did Aston Villa sell Yugoslav international Savo Milosevic for £3.5 million?**

14 Who was sacked as manager of Second Division Burnley?

15 **Who took over as manager of Stoke City?**

Quiz 123   Season 1997-1998

1   Where was the European Cup Winners' Cup Final played?

2   Graeme Le Saux had a calf injury - who took his place at left back for Chelsea in the Cup Winners' Cup Final?

3   Gianfranco Zola came on as substitute in the 71st minute and scored the winner with his first touch. Which Chelsea forward did he replace?

4   Which Chelsea player was sent off?

5   Which VfB Stuttgart player was dismissed in the dying seconds of the match?

6   To which Chelsea player was the Cup Winners' Cup presented?

7   This victory made England the country with the greatest number of victories in the history of the Cup Winners' Cup - how many?

8   Who did Sunderland beat in their First Division play-off semi-final?

9   Who did Charlton Athletic beat in their First Division play-off semi-final?

10   Which Fulham player was sent off in the second leg of their Second Division play-off semi-final against Grimsby Town?

11   Who scored the first goal for Arsenal in the FA Cup Final against Newcastle United?

12   Who scored the second goal for Arsenal in the same match?

13   Who was Littlewoods Man of the Match in the 1998 FA Cup Final?

14   When was the last time Arsenal won the League and Cup double?

15   Frank McLintock was their captain then - who was their victorious captain now?

1 Stockholm 2 Daniel Granville 3 Tore Andre Flo 4 Dan Petrescu 5 Gerhard Poschner
6 Dennis Wise 7 Eight 8 Sheffield United 9 Ipswich Town 10 Paul Peschisolido
11 Marc Overmars 12 Nicolas Anelka 13 Ray Parlour (Arsenal) 14 1971 15 Tony Adams

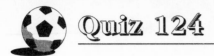 **Quiz 124**   **Season 1997-1998**

1   **Who scored from the penalty spot for Heart of Midlothian against Rangers after two minutes of the Scottish FA Cup Final?**

2   Who had been fouled in the area?

3   **Who scored the second Hearts goal after 52 minutes?**

4   Who came on as substitute and pulled a goal back for Rangers nine minutes from time?

5   **Who was manager of Hearts?**

6   When had Hearts last won the Scottish FA Cup?

7   **When had Hearts last won anything, and what was it?**

8   In which year had Rangers last failed to win a trophy?

9   **Which Scottish Third Division team played their last home game at Boghead and start the 1998-99 season at a new stadium in Castle Road?**

10   Which former Italian national coach took over from Raddy Antic as coach of Atletico Madrid?

11   **Who was appointed the new manager of Millwall?**

12   Who bought Georgi Kinkladze from Manchester City?

13   **Who offered all the England and Scotland players a week on his private island (Necker - normal price £13,000 a night) if they won the World Cup?**

14   When his name did not appear in the England World Cup squad, who said:'I realise that it will probably need Hoddle to go before I get a chance and that might be a long time'?

15   **Who took over as manager of Walsall?**

 ## Quiz 125   Season 1997-1998

1. **Who did Real Madrid beat in the Final of the European Cup?**

2. Where was the Final played?

3. **What nationality is Predrag Mijatovic, who scored the only goal of the game?**

4. Who was the German manager of Real Madrid?

5. **How many times had Real previously won the European Cup?**

6. In which year had they last won it?

7. **Which Premiership club's season tickets became the first to break the £1000 mark?**

8. Which Premiership club has the cheapest top-price season ticket in 1998-99, a comparative snip at £295?

9. **Who did Colchester United beat in the Third Division Play-Off Final at Wembley?**

10. Who scored the only goal of the match, from the penalty spot?

11. **When was the last time Colchester United had been out of the lowest division?**

12. With which country did England draw 0-0 in their last home game before the World Cup finals?

13. **Who did Grimsby Town beat 1-0 in the Second Division play-off Final to secure a return to the First Division only a year after they had been relegated?**

14. Who scored the Grimsby winner?

15. **Who is the manager of Grimsby Town?**

 # Quiz 1 **Shields**

Which clubs feature the following legends or mottoes on their shields?

1 **Arte et Labore ('Through skill and labour')**

2 Audere Est Facere ('To dare is to do')

3 **Consectatio Excellentiae ('The eager pursuit of excellence')**

4 Crede Signo ('Believe in this sign')

5 **Europe's Food Town**

6 Ich Dien ('I serve' - the motto of the Prince of Wales)

7 **Iron**

8 Nil Satis Nisi Optimum ('Nothing but the best is good enough')

9 **No Battle No Victory**

10 The Friendly Football Club

11 **The Town's Club**

12 Upon This Rock

13 **Vincit Omnia Industria ('Work conquers everything')**

14 Vis Unita Fortior ('United power is stronger')

15 **Which English League club has three lions on a shirt?**

 **Quiz 1**   **Songs and Chants**

1 **Fill in the missing name in the chant of Nottingham Forest, Sheffield Wednesday and England supporters:**
   You'll never beat — ———!

2 Which team is associated with the song 'I'm Forever Blowing Bubbles'?

3 **Which team's signature tune is 'When The Saints Go Marching In'?**

4 On whose terraces might you hear the following lyric, sung to a tune from the film 'Mary Poppins':
   'Chim-chiminee, chim-chiminee, chim-chim cheroo,
   We've got a kit that's more yellow than blue'?

5 **Supporters of which team have adopted - and adapted - the song 'When The Red, Red Robin Comes Bob, Bob, Bobbin' Along'?**

6 Although widely used by many supporters, especially those of Manchester United, which club has been linked most closely since their great days of the 1960s with the hymn 'Glory, Glory Hallelujah'?

7 **Complete the following couplet:**
   'My name is Edward Ebenezer Jeremiah Brown
   I'm a football supporter of ——— ——'.

8 'On the ball, City - never mind the danger' - which City?

9 **If the football isn't up to much, what do Leicester City fans sing to keep themselves happy?**

10 Where might you hear the song 'Swing Low, Sweet Wheelbarrow'?

11 **Fans of which team sing a version of John Denver's 'Annie's Song' which begins:**
   'You light up my senses
   Like a gallon of Magnet
   Like a packet of Woodbines
   Like a good pinch of snuff'?

12 What is the title of the Newcastle United song with the chorus that begins:
   'Oh, me lads, you shoulda seen us gannin''?

13 **Which fans sing the following lyric, to the tune of Neil Diamond's 'Daydream Believer' (a '60s hit for The Monkees):**
   'We once thought of you as a Scouser dressed in blue
   Now you're red and white through and through'?

14 And who are they singing about?

15 **The Liverpool anthem 'You'll Never Walk Alone' is best known as a '60s hit for Gerry and the Pacemakers. But from which musical does it originally come?**

 # Quiz 2

Songs and Chants

1 **Which team's supporters sing 'Blue Moon'?**

2 Which hit by Oasis has more recently been adopted by the same set of fans?

3 **Which Tom Jones hit is popular on the terraces at Stoke City?**

4 And which other Tom Jones hit then became popular at Port Vale?

5 **Which team's anthem is 'Keep Right On To The End Of The Road'?**

6 At which ground might you hear the following sung:
   'Irene, goodnight, Irene goodnight,
   Goodnight, Irene, goodnight Irene
   I'll see you in my dreams'?

7 **Which team does this describe:**
   'Here they come, our mighty champions,
   Raise your voices to the anthem,
   Marching like a mighty army...'?
   (Clue: it is sung to the tune 'Men of Harlech'.)

8 Whose fans made up the following words to the tune of 'The Internationale':
   'Flying high, up in the sky, we'll keep the blue flag flying high'?

9 **Whose fans sing The Dave Clark Five's '60s hit 'Glad All Over'?**

10 Where would you be most likely to hear a community singing 'You've Lost
    That Loving Feeling', originally a hit for The Righteous Brothers?

11 **Which fans sing these lyrics, to the tune of 'John Brown's Body' or**
    'Glory, Glory Hallelujah':
    'Come on the Quaker men, the boys in black and white,
    We cheer them every morning, every afternoon and night'?

12 When they play away at grounds with fewer amenities than their own,
    whose fans sing this, to the tune of 'When The Saints Go Marching In':
    'My garden shed is bigger than this
    My garden shed is bigger than this,
    It's got a door and a window,
    My garden shed is bigger than this'?

13 **'I can't help falling in love with you' - who took over this Elvis**
    Presley song, adding only their team's name at the end?

14 Who did Southampton fans hail as 'The King of Israel' - to the tune of 'The
    First Nowel' - until he upped and took himself off to West Ham in 1997?

15 **Whose fans sing this, to the tune of 'Yellow Submarine':**
    'We all follow a black and amber team
    A black and amber team
    That sometimes play in green'?

 **Quiz 1**   **Transfers**

1 Bristol City's record transfers in and out both involved the same player. They bought him for £500,000 from Arsenal in July 1992 and sold him to Newcastle United for £1.75 million eight months later. Who is he?

2 Crewe Alexandra is a nursery of talent. For which full back did they receive their highest transfer fee - £600,000 - from Liverpool in October 1991?

3 **For which Brazilian club did Romario play until June 1996, when Valencia (Spain) bought him for £8 million?**

4 For which forward did Blackpool receive their record transfer fee (£750,000) when they sold him to Queen's Park Rangers in August 1993?

5 **For which forward did Nottingham Forest pay Arsenal £2.8 million in July 1995?**

6 For which player did Leeds United pay Charlton Athletic £2.8 million in July 1996?

7 **For which player did Liverpool under Graeme Souness pay Coventry City £3.75 million in September 1994?**

8 For which Portsmouth player did Tottenham Hotspur pay £2 million in May 1992?

9 **For which Wolverhampton Wanderer did Manchester City under Malcolm Allison surprisingly pay £1.15 million in September 1979?**

10 From which club did Derby County buy Craig Short in September 1992?

11 **From which club did Internazionale buy Dennis Bergkamp for £8 million in June 1993?**

12 From which club did Manchester City buy Michael Robinson for £765,000 in June 1979?

13 **From which club did Manchester United buy Lee Sharpe for £180,000 in May 1988?**

14 From which club did Notts County make their record signing - Tony Agana for £685,000 in November 1991?

15 **From which club did Swansea City make their record signing - Colin Irwin for £340,000 in August 1981?**

 **Quiz 2** **Transfers**

1 From which club did Swansea City receive £375,000 for Des Lyttle in July 1993?

2 From which club did Wimbledon buy Dean Holdsworth for £720,000 in August 1992?

3 From which Danish club did Luton Town make their record purchase - £850,000 for Lars Elstrup in August 1989?

4 From which Dutch club did Barcelona buy Brazilian star Ronaldo for £13.25 million in June 1996?

5 From which Lancashire club did Aston Villa buy Earl Barrett for £1.7 million in February 1992?

6 How much did Everton receive for Andrei Kanchelskis when they sold him to sold him to Fiorentina in in February 1997?

7 How much did Manchester United receive for Paul Ince when they sold him to Internazionale in June 1995?

8 How much did Newcastle United pay Blackburn Rovers for Alan Shearer in July 1996?

9 How much did Newcastle United pay Queen's Park Rangers for Les Ferdinand in June 1995?

10 How much less than that did they receive from Tottenham Hotspur when they sold him in June 1995?

11 Impressed by his showing in the 1996-97 FA Cup, which forward did Southampton buy from Chesterfield?

12 In January 1996, which Dutch club broke the world record for money spent on a Rotherham United player when they bought Mike Jeffrey for £255,000?

13 In July 1995, which club was paid £3.25 million by Aston Villa for Mark Draper?

14 In June 1992, who did AC Milan buy from Torino for £13 million?

15 In June 1995, how much did Liverpool pay Nottingham Forest for Stan Collymore?

 ## Quiz 3

Transfers

1   In May 1980, Liverpool paid Chester City £300,000 - more money than they have received in a transfer deal before or since. But it was still a snip for the purchaser - who was the player?

2   In May 1980, which club learned that £333,333 was the value of Money?

3   **In October 1993, Alen Boksic became the record transfer when he was sold by Marseille for £8.4 million - to which Italian club?**

4   Ipswich Town's record sale and purchase have both involved Tottenham. Who did they sell to the London club for £1.9 million in August 1993?

5   **Who did they buy from Spurs for £1 million in June 1994?**

6   Name the Welsh international striker sold by Derby County to Liverpool for £2.9 million in July 1991.

7   **To which Belgian club did Colchester United pay their record transfer fee - £400,000 - for Dale Tempest in August 1987?**

8   To which club did Manchester City pay £1.5 million for Kevin Horlock in January 1997?

9   **To which club did Stoke City sell Mark Stein in October 1993 for a club record £1.5 million?**

10 To which London club did Newcastle United pay £4 million in June 1995 for Warren Barton?

11 **To which London club did Walsall sell David Kelly in July 1988 for £600,000?**

12 To which Nationwide club did Southampton pay £750,000 for Mickey Evans in March 1997?

13 **To which other Yorkshire club did Sheffield Wednesday pay £2.7 million for Andy Booth in July 1996?**

14 And a month later, who became the seller's record purchase - £1.2 million from Bristol Rovers?

15 **From which club did Wimbledon buy record £1.7 million signing Ben Thatcher?**

 Quiz 4   Transfers

1   **Which club's record sale was Darren Peacock to Queen's Park Rangers in December 1990?**

2   Which current Aston Villa star moved from Port Vale to Sheffield Wednesday for £1 million in August 1994?

3   **Which current Coventry City star was sold by Lincoln City to Newcastle United in November 1995?**

4   Which former Colchester United player became Wycombe Wanderers' record signing when they bought him from Birmingham City for £140,000 in March 1995?

5   **Which former Queen's Park Rangers and West Ham United striker was transferred from Derby County to Millwall for £800,000 in December 1989?**

6   Which French star moved from Olympique Marseille to AC Milan for £10 million in June 1992?

7   **Which future Bolton Wanderers star was Cardiff City's record sale when he moved in February 1994 to Sheffield United for £300,000?**

8   Which future captain of Sheffield Wednesday was sold by Wigan Athletic to Coventry City for £329,000 in August 1991?

9   **Which future Chelsea manager moved from Sampdoria to Juventus in June 1992 for a then record £12 million?**

10 Which homesick Oxford boy was Swindon Town's record purchase from West Ham United in August 1994?

11 **Which Italian World Cup star moved from Juventus to AC Milan for £8.5 million in June 1995?**

12 Who did Bolton Wanderers sell for £4.5 million in September 1995?

13 **Which player did Sheffield Wednesday sell to Blackburn Rovers in September 1993 for £2.65 million - a club record?**

14 Who - at £3 million from Internazionale - is Sheffield Wednesday's most expensive purchase?

15 **Which Welsh international full back became Wrexham's record signing when they bought him from Liverpool for £210,000 in October 1978?**

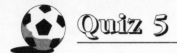 ## Quiz 5   **Transfers**

1 Which striker did Sunderland sell to Crystal Palace in September 1991 for £1.5 million?

2 Who did Sunderland buy from Newcastle for £2.5 million in June 1997?

3 Who - at £4 million - is Chelsea's most expensive signing to date?

4 Who - at £2.2 million - is Chelsea's most lucrative sale?

5 Who became the world's most expensive goalkeeper when he moved from Sampdoria to Internazionale for £7.5 million in August 1994?

6 Name the player bought by Barnsley from Nottingham Forest for £1.5 million in May 1991.

7 Who did Leyton Orient sell to Notts County for £600,000 in August 1981?

8 Who is Brighton and Hove Albion's record purchase - £500,000 from Manchester United in October 1980?

9 Who is Brighton and Hove Albion's record sale - £900,000 to Liverpool in August 1981?

10 Who is Cambridge United's record sale - £1 million to Manchester United in August 1992?

11 Who, three months later, became Cambridge United's record purchase - £190,000 from Luton Town?

12 Who is Coventry City's record signing - £3 million from Leeds United in July 1996?

13 Who is Crystal Palace's record sale - £4.5 million to Tottenham Hotspur in June 1995?

14 Who, a month later, became Crystal Palace's record signing - £2.25 million from Millwall?

15 Who is Millwall's record sale - £2.3 million to Liverpool in March 1995?

 ## Quiz 6 — Transfers

1 Who is Norwich City's most expensive signing - £1 million from Leeds United in June 1994?

2 Who is Oldham Athletic's record signing - £750,000 from Aston Villa in June 1992?

3 Who is Sheffield United's record purchase - £1.2 million from West Ham United in January 1996?

4 Who is Sheffield United's record sale - £2.7 million to Leeds United in July 1993?

5 Who is Tranmere Rovers' record sale - £1.5 million to Sheffield Wednesday in August 1994?

6 Who is Tranmere Rovers' record purchase - £450,000 from Aston Villa in August 1995?

7 Who is West Bromwich Albion's record signing - £1.25 million from Preston North End in June 1997?

8 Who moved from Sampdoria to Parma for £11 million in June 1996?

9 Who moved from Southampton to Grimsby Town for £300,000 in July 1996, a record for the Nationwide club?

10 Who paid Aston Villa £5.5 million for David Platt in July 1991?

11 Who was Luton Town's record sale - £2.5 million to Arsenal in January 1995?

12 Who, in October 1981, became West Bromwich Albion's most lucrative sale?

13 Who, in 1957, became the first British player ever to transfer to a foreign club?

14 Who, in 1961, became Britain's first £100,000 player when he moved from Manchester City to Torino?

15 Who had previously been transferred from Chelsea to AC Milan for £99,999, because, it was said, 'no one could be worth £100,000?'

Greaves

1 Jon Newsome 2 Ian Olney 3 Don Hutchison 4 Brian Deane 5 Ian Nolan 6 Shaun Teale
7 Kevin Kilbane 8 Enrico Chiesa 9 Tommy Widdrington 10 Bari (Italy) 11 John Hartson
12 Bryan Robson 13 John Charles (Leeds United to Juventus) 14 Denis Law 15 Jimmy

 **Quiz 1**   UEFA Cup

1 Originally known as the Inter-Cities Fairs Cup, when was the UEFA Cup given its present name?

2 What was the special significance of the tie between Dunfermline Athletic and Dinamo Zagreb in the 1966-67 Fairs Cup?

3 Who, in 1968, became the first English winners of the Fairs Cup?

4 Which English team won the trophy in the year it was renamed the UEFA Cup?

5 Who scored twice for Liverpool in two UEFA Cup finals?

6 Who, in 1976 and 1977, became the only team ever to win the European Cup the year after winning the UEFA Cup?

7 In 1979-80, all four UEFA Cup semi-finalists came from the same country. Which?

8 And which two contested the Final?

9 Who won this Final on the away goals rule, after the two legs finished level at 3-3?

10 Which two English clubs won the Cup during the 1980s?

11 Name the Scot who scored 14 goals for an English club in the 1980-81 UEFA Cup.

12 Who, in 1985 and 1986, became the last team to retain the UEFA Cup?

13 Who, in 1987, became the only Scottish club to reach the UEFA Cup Final?

14 Who beat them in the Final of the competition?

15 Which two Italian teams contested the 1990 Final?

 # Quiz 2

UEFA Cup

1 Which German international scored 10 goals for Roma in their 1990-91 UEFA Cup campaign?

2 Whose six goals helped Inter Milan win the 1990-91 UEFA Cup?

3 Name the Englishman who scored against Liverpool for Kuusysi Lahti of Finland in the 1991-92 UEFA Cup.

4 Who scored in both legs of Norwich City's victory over Bayern Munich in the 1993-94 UEFA Cup?

5 In 1994, who became the first Austrian team to reach the UEFA Cup Final?

6 Who scored all five goals for Juventus in one leg of their 1994-95 match against CSKA Sofia?

7 Who scored for winners Parma in both legs of the 1994-95 Final against Juventus?

8 Who scored a hat-trick for Leeds United in their 1995 UEFA Cup match against Monaco?

9 Which English team reached the quarter-finals of the competition in 1995-96?

10 Who, in 1996, became the first French club to reach the UEFA Cup Final?

11 Which German team beat them 5-1 on aggregate to win the competition for the first time in their distinguished history?

12 In the 1996-97 UEFA Cup, which German team did Brondby of Denmark beat 8-1 on aggregate after losing the home leg 3-1?

13 Who won the UEFA Cup in 1997?

14 Who did they beat 4-1 on penalties in the Final after the match had finished 1-1 at the end of extra time?

15 Name the six English clubs that have won the Inter-Cities Fairs or UEFA Cup a total of nine times to the end of 1997.

1 Rüdiger Völler 2 Lothar Matthaus 3 Mike Belfield 4 Jeremy Goss 5 Salzburg 6 Fabrizio Ravanelli 7 Dino Baggio 8 Tony Yeboah 9 Nottingham Forest 10 Bordeaux 11 Bayern Munich 12 Karlsruhe 13 FC Schalke '04 14 Inter Milan 15 Leeds United (twice), Newcastle United, Arsenal, Tottenham Hotspur (twice), Liverpool (twice), and Ipswich Town

Quiz 1 Where Did They Get Him?

1   Name the Croatian international defender bought by West Ham United from Karlsruhe in 1995 for £1.65 million.

2   Name the Australian team from which Aston Villa signed international goalkeeper Mark Bosnich on a free transfer.

3   From which team did both Sasa Curcic and Savo Milosevic come into the English Premiership?

4   To which English Premiership team did Curcic first move?

5   From which club did Middlesbrough buy Juninho?

6   To whom did they sell him?

7   From where did Aston Villa sign Dwight Yorke for a mere £120,000?

8   For whom did Derby County pay Flora £500,000, and where is Flora?

9   Where did Newcastle buy Colombian international Faustino Asprilla for £7.5 million?

10 And to who did they sell him?

11 From which club in his native Coast Rica did Derby County sign Paulo Wanchope for £600,000?

12 Name the Swiss international with the Spanish name whom Tottenham Hotspur bought from Cagliari (Italy) for £3.75 million.

13 Which two players did Derby County buy from Hajduk Split?

14 From which Moscow club did Chelsea buy goalkeeper Dmitri Kharine for £200,000?

15 Name the one Belorussian playing in the English Football League in 1997-98, who was bought by Sheffield United for £650,000 from Dinamo Minsk.

1 Slaven Bilic 2 Croatia Sydney 3 Partizan Belgrade (Yugoslavia) 4 Bolton Wanderers 5 Sao Paulo (Brazil) 6 Atletico Madrid 7 Signal Hill (Trinidad) 8 Mart Poom, Estonia 9 Parma (Italy) 10 The same club - Parma (Italy) 11 Herdiano 12 Ramon Vega 13 Alijosa Asanovic and Igor Stimac 14 CSKA 15 Petr Katchuro

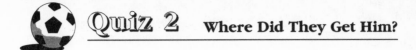

Quiz 2 — Where Did They Get Him?

1 **From which club in his native country did Newcastle United buy Belgian international defender Philippe Albert for £2.65 million?**

2 To whom did Chelsea pay £2.5 million for the services of Frank Leboeuf?

3 **Where did Manchester City find Georgi Kinkladze?**

4 What nationality is Middlesbrough defender Vladimir Kinder?

5 **Which was Kinder's previous club?**

6 Name the four Czech internationals playing in the Premiership in 1997-98.

7 **In 1996-97, which three Danish internationals came into the Premiership from Brondby?**

8 Which of the trio was the most expensive?

9 **At the start of 1997-98, who was the only Israeli international playing in the English Premiership?**

10 Which club in his native country did he come from?

11 **Which Israeli international, formerly with Liverpool and Tottenham Hotspur, played for Watford in 1997-98?**

12 Who were West Ham United's two notorious Romanians?

13 **Which country is captained by Leeds United's Lucas Radebe?**

14 From which club did Leeds buy him for £250,000?

15 **From where did Middlesbrough pick up Danish international Mikkel Beck for nothing?**

1 **Anderlecht** 2 Strasbourg (France) 3 **Dynamo Tbilisi** 4 Slovakian 5 **Slovan Bratislava** (Slovakia) 6 Patrik Berger (Liverpool), Ludek Miklosko (West Ham United), Karel Poborsky (Manchester United), Pavel Srnicek (Newcastle United) 7 **Allan Nielsen (Tottenham Hotspur), Marc Rieper (West Ham United), Peter Schmeichel (Manchester United)** 8 Allan Nielsen (£1.65 million) 9 **Eyal Berkovic (West Ham United)** 10 Maccabi Haifa 11 **Ronnie Rosenthal** 12 Ilie Dumitrescu and Florin Raducioiu 13 **South Africa** 14 Kaiser Chiefs 15 **Fortuna Cologne (Germany)**

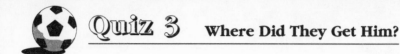

Quiz 3   Where Did They Get Him?

1   From which Dutch club did Arsenal buy Marc Overmars?

2   Which was the previous club of Tottenham Hotspur's Portuguese international Jose Dominguez?

3   **Which 1997-98 Arsenal signing played for Sporting Lisbon?**

4   Which Premiership club signed Stig Inge Johansen from FK Boda (Norway)?

5   **Where did Sheffield Wednesday pick up Patrick Blondeau?**

6   Which two Frenchmen did Arsenal buy in 1997 from AS Monaco?

7   **From which Greek club did Newcastle United buy Georgian international Temur Ketsbaia?**

8   Which was former West Ham United and Everton striker Tony Cottee's last club before joining Leicester City?

9   **Where did Leeds United find Jimmy Floyd Hasselbaink?**

10   Hasselbaink and Ruud Gullit are both Dutch nationals - in which country were they born?

11   **From which club in Austria did Arsenal get David Seaman's goalkeeping understudy, Alex Manninger?**

12   Which two internationals came into the Premiership in 1997 from the IA club in their native Iceland?

13   **What nationality is Chelsea's Gustavo Poyet?**

14   Which was his former club?

15   **And from where did Chelsea acquire Nigerian international Celestine Babayaro?**

1 **Ajax (Amsterdam)** 2 Sporting Lisbon 3 Luis **Boa Morte** 4 Southampton 5 **AS Monaco** 6 Gilles Grimandi and Emmanuel Petit 7 **AEK Athens** 8 Selangor (Malaysia) 9 **Boavista (Portugal)** 10 Surinam 11 **Graz** 12 Arnar Gunnlaugsson (Bolton Wanderers) and Bjarni Gudjonsson (Newcastle United) 13 **Uruguayan** 14 Real Zaragoza (Spain) 15 **Anderlecht (Belgium)**

Quiz 4 — Where Did They Get Him?

1   Premiership debutants Barnsley bought Georgi Hristov from Partizan Belgrade. Which country does he represent at international level?

2   From which Italian club did the Barnsley buy South African international Eric Tinkler?

3   **What nationality is Leeds United forward Harry Kewell?**

4   In 1997, David Ginola moved from Newcastle United to Tottenham Hotspur. Which club had he last played for in his native France?

5   **Which was the previous club of Liverpool's German international Karl-Heinz Riedle?**

6   Another of Liverpool's new acquisitions, Oyvind Leonhardson went to Merseyside from Wimbledon. Which was the last club he played for in his native Norway?

7   **Which Tottenham Hotspur defender used to play for the same Norwegian club?**

8   From which French club did Crystal Palace buy Scotsman Jamie Fullarton?

9   **Who did Blackburn Rovers buy from the French club Bastia?**

10   For which Italian club did South African international Mark Fish play before his move to Bolton Wanderers?

11   **Tomas Brolin ended the season at Crystal Palace, having started it with Leeds United, who had bought him from Parma. From which club in his native Sweden had he moved to Italy?**

12   Which four clubs has Paul Ince played for?

13   **Crystal Palace bought Itzhali Zohar from Royal Antwerp (Belgium). What is his nationality?**

14   Who were the previous employers of Derby County's Stefano Eranio?

15   **And for which Italian team did the same club's Francesco Baiano formerly play?**

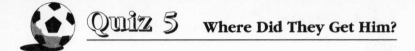

Quiz 5 Where Did They Get Him?

1 Who sold Mustafa ('Muzzy') Izzet to Leicester City for £650,000 in July 1996?

2 To whom did Chelsea sell Paul Furlong for £1.5 million in July 1996?

3 Where did Charlton Athletic find Clive Mendonca, for whom they paid £700,000 in May 1997?

4 To which club did Queen's Park Rangers sell Sieb Dykstra for £100,000 in December 1996?

5 In 1997-98, Paolo (Paul) Peschisolido went to Fulham from West Bromwich Albion. For which country has he played?

6 Torquay United have a St Vincent international, who they got on a free transfer from Lambada. What is his name?

7 To which English League club did Queen's Park Rangers pay £600,000 for Jurgen Sommer?

8 What nationality is Sommer?

9 From which Italian club did Nottingham Forest buy Dutch international Bryan Roy for £2.5 million in 1996-97?

10 From which club was Portuguese forward Hugo Porfirio on loan to West Ham United until the end of the 1996-97 season?

11 Which Polish international did Reading pick up from Celtic on a free transfer?

12 From which German club did Leeds United sign Ghanaian Tony Yeboah?

13 From which Yorkshire club did Middlesbrough sign Mark Schwarzer for £1.5 million?

14 What nationality is Schwarzer?

15 Who, in 1997-98, was the only Finn playing in the FA Carling Premiership?

1 Chelsea 2 Birmingham City 3 Grimsby Town 4 Dundee United 5 Canada 6 Rodney Jack
7 Luton Town 8 Canadian 9 Foggia 10 Sporting Lisbon 11 Dariusz Wdowczyk
12 Eintracht Frankfurt 13 Bradford City 14 Australian 15 Mixu Paatelainen (Bolton Wanderers)

Quiz 1   **Where in the World Is...?**

Teams not named after the places they're in:

1 **Admira Wacker**
2 Ajax
3 **Albion Rovers**
4 Anderlecht
5 **Benfica**
6 Boca Juniors
7 **Castilla**
8 East Fife
9 **East Stirlingshire**
10 Espanol
11 **Vasco da Gama**
12 Feyenoord
13 **Fisher Athletic**
14 Heart of Midlothian
15 **Hibernian**

 ## Quiz 2   Where in the World Is...?

Teams not named after the places they're in:

1 **Juventus**

2 Marine

3 **Partick Thistle**

4 Port Vale

5 **Queen of the South**

6 Queen's Park

7 **Queen's Park Rangers**

8 Raith Rovers

9 **Real Sociedad**

10 Ross County

11 **Sampdoria**

12 St Johnstone

13 **St Mirren**

14 Cruzeiro

15 **Tranmere Rovers**

 ## Quiz 1

The World Cup

1 **By the end of the 20th century, how many World Cups will have been held altogether?**

2 Before the start of the 1998 tournament, how many different countries had won it?

3 **How many times has the host nation won the World Cup?**

4 Which country had won it four times before the start of the 1998 finals?

5 **Which two countries had won it three times?**

6 Which two countries had won it twice?

7 **Which country had won it once?**

8 Which is the only country to have competed in all the 20th century's World Cup finals tournaments?

9 **In which year did the holders not defend the trophy?**

10 Which team has held the World Cup for longest (1934-50)?

11 **In which year did England first take part in the World Cup?**

12 In which World Cup did all four British nations - England, Northern Ireland, Scotland and Wales - make the finals?

13 **In how many World Cup finals have Scotland failed to progress past the first round?**

14 Which is the only country to have won the World Cup outside their own continent?

15 **Which countries will co-host the World Cup in 2002?**

1 **Sixteen** 2 Six 3 **Six** 4 Brazil 5 **Italy and West Germany** 6 Argentina and Uruguay
7 **England** 8 Brazil 9 1934 (Uruguay in Italy) 10 Italy 11 **1950** 12 1958 13 **Eight**
14 Brazil in Sweden (1958) and the USA (1994) 15 **South Korea and Japan**

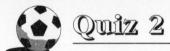 ## Quiz 2

The World Cup

1. Two pairs of brothers have played together in World Cup winning teams. One was the Charltons in 1966 - who was the other?

2. Who are the only two players to have scored in the Final of two World Cups?

3. Who is England's leading scorer in World Cup matches?

4. Who are the only men to have both played for and managed a World Cup winning side?

5. Who is the oldest player to score in the finals of the World Cup?

6. Who, in 1970, became the first player to score in every round of the World Cup finals?

7. Who scored 13 goals in the 1958 finals, the highest total ever?

8. In which year was the number of teams in the World Cup finals increased from 16 to 24?

9. What was the name of the Chilean goalkeeper who - in an attempt to have the qualifying match against Brazil abandoned - pretended to have been hurt by an object thrown from the crowd and was subsequently banned for life?

10. In which World Cup finals were substitutes first allowed?

11. Which two countries have hosted the World Cup finals twice?

12. Where were the 1986 finals originally scheduled to have taken place?

13. Which four European countries have reached a World Cup Final but never won the tournament?

14. Who is the only man to have played in World Cup Finals for different countries?

15. Which country was eliminated on goal difference from three World Cup finals in succession?

---

1 **Fritz and Ottmar Walter (West Germany 1954)** 2 Pele (Brazil) in 1958 and 1970 and Paul Breitner (West Germany) in 1974 and 1982 3 **Gary Lineker** 4 Franz Beckenbauer (West Germany) and Mario Zagalo (Brazil) 5 **Roger Milla (Cameroon) in 1990** 6 Jairzinho (Brazil) 7 **Just Fontaine (France)** 8 1982 9 **Roberto Rojas** 10 1970 11 **Mexico in 1970 and 1986 and France in 1938 and 1998** 12 Colombia 13 **Czechoslovakia, Holland, Hungary and Sweden** 14 Luis Monti (Argentina) in 1930 and Italy in 1934) 15 **Scotland in 1974, 1978 and 1982**

 **Quiz 3**   The 1930 World Cup

1   **Which international body organised this and all subsequent World Cups?**

2   In which year was this international body formed?

3   **Of the 13 participants in the first World Cup finals, which were the only four European nations?**

4   Name the seven South American countries that took part.

5   **Which two other nations played in the 1930 tournament?**

6   Which two teams met in the first ever World Cup match, on July 13, 1930?

7   **In the group match between Argentina and Mexico, a record number of penalties were awarded - how many?**

8   Who were the four semi-finalists?

9   **Who did the hosts meet in the Final on July 30, 1930?**

10 How did the Finalists resolve a disagreement over which ball to play with?

11 **Who was the captain of Uruguay?**

12 Name the Uruguayan centre forward who had the lower part of an arm missing.

13 **Who presented the World Cup to Uruguay at the end of the Final, which they won 4-2?**

14 Who was the tournament's leading scorer, with eight goals for Argentina?

15 **Where were all 18 matches in the 1930 World Cup finals played?**

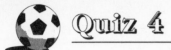 ## Quiz 4   ### The 1934 World Cup

1   Who was the manager of victorious host nation Italy?

2   Often described in newspapers as 'The Father of Italian Football', on which pre-First World War English club did the Italian manager try to model his team's style of play?

3   Who did Italy beat by the record score of 7-1 in the first round?

4   Who scored the first goal for Czechoslovakia in the Final?

5   Which Argentine-born left winger then equalised for Italy?

6   For which Italian club had he played since 1929?

7   Who then scored the winner for Italy in extra time?

8   Who was the goalkeeper captain of Italy?

9   Who was the goalkeeper captain of Czechoslovakia?

10   Which European nations had been beaten in the semi-finals?

11   In which two Italian cities were the semi-finals played?

12   Which were the only two South American nations to appear in the 1934 World Cup finals?

13   In 1934, who became the first African nation to appear in the World Cup finals?

14   What was the nationality of John Langenus, the 1930 World Cup Final referee, who officiated in one match in 1934 and famously described the tournament as 'a sporting fiasco'?

15   At the end of the 1934 World Cup Final in Rome, who presented the Jules Rimet trophy to the winners?

 **Quiz 5**   **The 1938 World Cup**

1   Which South American country wanted to host the 1938 tournament and refused to take part when they were turned down in favour of France?

2   Which country qualified in 1937 but by the time of the finals had ceased to exist as a separate national entity?

3   The withdrawal of which Asian country left the way open for the Dutch East Indies to appear in the finals?

4   What was the name of the manager of Germany?

5   Who was the tournament's leading scorer - a Brazilian, with eight goals in the tournament, including four in against Poland?

6   Which Pole also scored four goals in this match?

7   Which Swede then scored another four goals in the quarter-finals?

8   Which Hungarian was the second highest scorer, with seven goals in the tournament?

9   The players of which nation refused to give the Nazi salute during the national anthems before their first round match with Germany?

10 To which country had Germany lost 6-3 in Berlin only a few weeks before the start of the World Cup finals?

11 What was the name of the Brazilian coach who decided to rest his star players in the semi-final, which they lost to Italy?

12 Who did Italy beat 4-2 in the World Cup Final in Paris on June 19, 1938?

13 Which two Italians scored twice in this match?

14 Giuseppe Meazza was one of only two survivors of Italy's previous World Cup triumph in 1934. On his death in 1979, which famous Italian football stadium was renamed in his honour?

15 Which Caribbean island reached the quarter finals after beating Romania in the first round?

 ## Quiz 6 — The 1950 World Cup

1 **Where were the 1950 World Cup finals held?**

2 How many countries took part in the finals?

3 **Who won the tournament?**

4 Which future England manager played for his country in the match versus the USA?

5 **Who scored the USA's goal in their shock victory over England?**

6 Who was the England manager?

7 **Where was the match played?**

8 Who scored England's goals in their 2-0 victory over Chile?

9 **Who beat England 1-0 in their third group match?**

10 Which team of amateurs beat the holders, Italy, 3-2 and finished above them in their group?

11 **What tragic event in 1949 had seriously weakened the Italian challenge?**

12 Which teams contested the deciding match in the Final Pool?

13 **Which Brazilian was the leading scorer in the 1950 tournament, with nine goals?**

14 For which Rio de Janeiro club did he play?

15 **Who was the World Cup winning captain?**

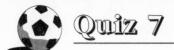 **Quiz 7**   The 1954 World Cup

1   **Where were the 1954 World Cup finals held?**

2   Ante-post favourites Hungary began their finals campaign with a 9-0 defeat of which Asian country?

3   **What was the name of Scotland's first World Cup manager, who resigned during the course of the tournament after his team lost 1-0 to Austria?**

4   Who then trounced Scotland 7-0?

5   **With which European nation did England draw 4-4 at the group stage of the tournament?**

6   What was the final score in the quarter-final between Brazil and Hungary, the so-called 'Battle of Berne'?

7   **Who knocked out the hosts, beating them 7-5 in the quarter finals?**

8   Who beat England 4-2 in the quarter finals?

9   **Which country inflicted Uruguay's first ever World Cup defeat?**

10   Which great Hungarian made his first appearance of the tournament in the Final and scored the opening goal?

11   **Where was the Final played?**

12   Who was the tournament's leading scorer, with 11 goals for Hungary?

13   **Who scored the goals in the Final that brought West Germany back from 2-0 down and made them World champions?**

14   Who was captain of the winning team?

15   **Which German club did he play for?**

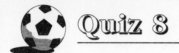

Quiz 8   The 1958 World Cup

1   **Which Englishman was manager of 1958 hosts and beaten finalists Sweden?**

2   Who knocked Wales out in the quarter finals?

3   **Which 17-year-old scored the only goal of this game, his first in World Cup finals?**

4   For which English League club did Wales' World Cup goalkeeper Jack Kelsey play?

5   **Which Arsenal left half was captain of Wales?**

6   Which Frenchman scored 13 goals in the finals, a record?

7   **Who was captain of Northern Ireland?**

8   Who was manager of Northern Ireland?

9   **Which future manager of Northern Ireland played for them on the wing in this tournament?**

10   Who knocked Northern Ireland out in the quarter finals?

11   **Which two players scored twice for Brazil in their 5-2 victory over Sweden in the Final?**

12   Which future manager of Brazil scored the other goal?

13   **To which Spanish club did Brazil midfield star Didi transfer in the year after he had made his name in the World Cup?**

14   Which nation did Didi subsequently manage in the 1970 World Cup finals?

15   **Which nation finished equal second with England at the group stage and then beat them 1-0 in the play-off for a place in the quarter finals?**

1 George Raynor 2 Brazil 3 Pele 4 Arsenal 5 Dave Bowen 6 Just Fontaine 7 Danny Blanchflower 8 Peter Doherty 9 Billy Bingham 10 France 11 Vava and Pele 12 Mario Zagalo 13 Real Madrid 14 Peru 15 The USSR

Quiz 9

The 1962 World Cup

1 In which country were the 1962 World Cup finals held?

2 Who was the tournament's leading scorer, with five goals for beaten semi-finalists Yugoslavia?

3 **Who was England's captain in the 1962 World Cup?**

4 Who scored for England in their 3-1 victory over Argentina in the group stage of the finals?

5 **Immediately before the first goal, which England debutant's shot had been handled on the line?**

6 For which English club was he playing at the time?

7 **Who scored two goals for Brazil in their 3-1 quarter final victory over England?**

8 England's consolation goal was scored by Gerry Hitchens. For which European team was he playing club football?

9 **At which English club had he started his career?**

10 Who was the English referee who sent off two Italians during their 2-0 defeat by Chile in the so-called 'Battle of Santiago'?

11 **Which Chilean - a striker in more than one sense - broke the nose of Italy's Humberto Maschio and finished the tournament as his country's leading scorer with four goals?**

12 What was the name of the so-called 'White Pele' who came on as a substitute for the black one after he pulled a muscle in the group match against Czechoslovakia?

13 **Which Brazilian scored two goals and was then sent off in his country's 4-2 semi-final victory over Chile?**

14 Who did Brazil beat in the Final to retain the trophy?

15 **Which three players scored for Brazil in this match?**

Quiz 10 — The 1966 World Cup

1 **Who scored the first goal of the tournament in the group match between Brazil and Bulgaria?**

2 Who scored England's first goal of the tournament in their second group match against Mexico?

3 **Name the captain of Argentina who was sent off in the quarter final against England.**

4 Who scored both goals for England in their 2-1 victory over Portugal in the semi-final?

5 **Which England defender punched the ball off the goal line to give away a penalty in the match against Portugal?**

6 Who did West Germany defeat in the other semi-final?

7 **Who scored West Germany's goals in the Final against England?**

8 Who was Tofik Bakhramov?

9 **Who was the tournament's top scorer, with nine goals?**

10 Who was the youngest member of England's World Cup winning team?

11 **Name the captain of West Germany in 1966 who won 72 caps but never a World Cup?**

12 At home in Germany, which Bundesliga club did he play for?

13 **What sort of animal was 1966 mascot World Cup Willie?**

14 How many matches did Jimmy Greaves play for England in the 1966 World Cup finals?

15 **Three of Geoff Hurst's four goals in the competition were scored in the Final. Against which other country did he score?**

---

1 **Pele** 2 Bobby Charlton 3 **Antonio Rattin** 4 Bobby Charlton 5 **Jack Charlton** 6 The USSR 7 **Haller and Weber** 8 The Russian linesman who ruled that Hurst's disputed goal for England had crossed the line 9 **Eusebio (Portugal)** 10 Alan Ball 11 **Uwe Seeler** 12 Hamburg 13 **A lion** 14 Three 15 **Argentina**

Quiz 11 — The 1970 World Cup

1 **Which Leeds United striker made his England debut in the group match against Czechoslovakia?**

2 Who scored Brazil's goal in their group game against England?

3 **Who was captain of Brazil in the 1970 World Cup?**

4 Who was leading scorer in the 1970 World Cup?

5 **Which European country topped its group with the following match statistics:**
Played 3 Won 1 Drawn 2 Lost 0 Goals For 1 Goals Against 0?

6 In which Mexican city did England play their group matches?

7 **In which city did England play their quarter final match against West Germany?**

8 Who scored for England to put them 2-0 up in this match?

9 **Name the England right back who supplied the crosses for both these goals.**

10 Who scored for West Germany to make it 2-1?

11 **England manager Sir Alf Ramsey then took off Bobby Charlton and Martin Peters. Who took their places?**

12 Who equalised for West Germany?

13 **Who scored the winner in extra time?**

14 Apart from West Germany, who were the other three semi-finalists?

15 **Which Brazilian star was almost blind in one eye?**

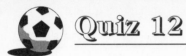

Quiz 12 — The 1974 World Cup

1 Which European nation was edged out of a place in the 1974 World Cup finals by Holland, despite being undefeated in the qualifying matches and conceding not a single goal?

2 Who supplanted Sir Stanley Rous as President of FIFA three days before the World Cup finals opening ceremony?

3 **Which Englishman refereed the 1974 World Cup Final in Munich?**

4 Which West German gave away a penalty in the Final by tripping Johan Cruyff of Holland?

5 **Who became the first player to score from the penalty spot in a World Cup Final?**

6 And who became the second, when West Germany equalised later in the first half?

7 **Who scored the winner for West Germany?**

8 Who was the Dutch captain in the 1974 World Cup Finals?

9 **Who was the manager of Holland?**

10 Who was manager of World Cup winners West Germany?

11 **Who was their captain?**

12 Who was the leading scorer in the 1974 World Cup finals, with seven goals for third-placed Poland?

13 **Who was manager of Scotland, the only British nation to qualify for the finals?**

14 Who was Scotland's World Cup captain?

15 **Who won the first meeting between East and West Germany?**

1 **Belgium** 2 Joao Havelange 3 **Jack Taylor** 4 Uli Hoeness 5 **Johan Neeskens** 6 Paul Breitner 7 **Gerd Muller** 8 Johan Cruyff 9 **Rinus Michels** 10 Helmut Schoen 11 **Franz Beckenbauer** 12 Grzegorz Lato 13 **Willie Ormond** 14 Billy Bremner 15 **East Germany, 1-0**

Quiz 13   The 1978 World Cup

1 **Which Scotland player failed a drugs test after the opening match against Peru and was sent home in disgrace?**

2 For which English League club was he then playing?

3 **Who was Scotland's manager?**

4 Who was Scotland's first-choice goalkeeper?

5 **For which Scottish League club was he then playing?**

6 Which Scotsman had a penalty saved in their match against Peru?

7 **For which English League club was he then playing?**

8 Which Argentine player scored two goals in the Final?

9 **Name the substitute who scored Holland's goal to take the Final into extra time.**

10 Who was Argentina's manager?

11 **Which two countries - one Asian, the other African - made their first appearances in the World Cup finals in 1978?**

12 Who was the tournament's leading scorer, with six goals for World Cup winners Argentina?

13 **Which great veteran - a star of the 1970 World Cup - scored five goals in the tournament for quarter finalists Peru?**

14 Which winger scored five goals in the tournament for Holland?

15 **To which Dutchman's protective arm shield did the Argentine players object at the start of the Final?**

1 Willie Johnston 2 West Bromwich Albion 3 Ally MacLeod 4 Alan Rough 5 Partick
Thistle 6 Don Masson 7 Queen's Park Rangers 8 Mario Kempes 9 Dirk Nanninga
10 Cesar Luis Menotti 11 Iran and Tunisia 12 Mario Kempes 13 Teofilo Cubillas 14 Rob
Rensenbrink 15 Rene van der Kerkhof

 **Quiz 14**   **The 1982 World Cup**

1   How many teams beat England in the 1982 World Cup finals?

2   Name the German goalkeeper involved in the infamous incident in the 1982 semi-final which left a French forward unconscious.

3   And who was the French forward?

4   Which Hungarian became the first ever substitute to score a hat trick in the World Cup finals?

5   Who scored Italy's three goals in the Final against West Germany?

6   Who scored West Germany's goal in the Final?

7   Who scored Northern Ireland's goal when they beat the hosts Spain in the 1982 World Cup?

8   For which English League club was he playing at the time?

9   Which Italian was leading scorer in the 1982 World Cup?

10   Who was manager of Italy?

11   Who was the captain of Brazil?

12   Who, in 1982, became the oldest player to win the World Cup?

13   Which Northern Ireland forward was the youngest player in the 1982 World Cup finals?

14   Which side became the first ever to be eliminated from the World Cup finals on penalties?

15   Who scored the fastest ever goal in World Cup finals after 27 seconds of the England versus France group match?

1 None 2 Harald Schumacher 3 **Patrick Battiston** 4 Laszlo Kiss v El Salvador 5 **Paolo Rossi, Allesandro Altobelli and Marco Tardelli** 6 Paul Breitner 7 **Gerry Armstrong** 8 Watford 9 **Paolo Rossi** 10 Enzo Bearzot 11 **Socrates** 12 Dino Zoff (Italy) 13 **Norman Whiteside** 14 France 15 **Bryan Robson (England)**

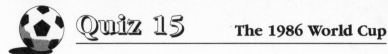

Quiz 15 — The 1986 World Cup

1 **All but one of England's seven goals in the 1986 tournament were scored by Gary Lineker. Who scored the other?**

2 Which England player was sent off in the group game against Morocco?

3 **Name the two Manchester United players in the England squad.**

4 Who were the two Manchester United players in the Scotland squad?

5 **Name the Manchester United player in the Northern Ireland World Cup squad.**

6 Who were the two Manchester United players in the Denmark squad?

7 **Which Uruguayan player was sent off after less than a minute of the match against Scotland?**

8 Who scored Portugal's goal in their 1-0 group victory over England?

9 **Who played for Northern Ireland v Brazil on his 41st birthday?**

10 Who scored four goals in Spain's 5-1 demolition of Denmark?

11 **Which neighbouring European countries were the losing semi-finalists in the 1986 World Cup?**

12 The World Cup Final reached 2-2 - Brown and Valdano scored first for Argentina; Rummenigge and Voller equalised for West Germany. Who scored Argentina's winning goal?

13 **For which French club side was he then playing?**

14 Who was the manager of England?

15 **In which city did England play their matches in the so-called Group of Sleep?**

 **Quiz 16**   ### The 1990 World Cup

1   **From which Puccini opera did the Italia 90 theme song Nessun Dorma come?**

2   For which team did Roger Milla play in the 1990 World Cup?

3   **Which two players were sent off in the West Germany v Holland second round match?**

4   Which was the first African nation to reach the World Cup quarter-finals?

5   **Who scored for the Republic of Ireland in their 1-1 draw with England in the group stage?**

6   Who scored for England in their 1-1 draw with the Republic of Ireland in the group stage?

7   **Who did the Republic of Ireland beat in a penalty shoot-out to clinch their place in the quarter-finals?**

8   Who scored for England against Belgium in the last minute of extra time to take them through to the quarter finals?

9   **Who scored West Germany's goal in their 1-1 semi-final draw with England?**

10 Off which England defender was the shot cruelly and crucially deflected?

11 **Who scored England's goal in their 1-1 semi-final draw with West Germany?**

12 Who missed England's last penalty in the semi-final shoot-out?

13 **Who scored West Germany's goal in their 1-0 victory over Argentina in the 1990 World Cup Final?**

14 Who was captain of West Germany?

15 **Who was leading goalscorer in the 1990 World Cup, with six goals for Italy?**

1 Turandot 2 Cameroon 3 **Rudi Voller and Frank Rijkaard** 4 Cameroon 5 **Kevin Sheedy** 6 Gary Lineker 7 **Romania** 8 David Platt 9 **Andreas Brehme** 10 Paul Parker 11 **Gary Lineker** 12 Chris Waddle 13 **Andreas Brehme** 14 Lothar Matthaus 15 Toto Schillachi

Quiz 17

The 1994 World Cup

1   **Name the Colombian captain who scored an own goal in the 1994 World Cup and was shot dead on his return home.**

2   Which Argentine player was sent home after failing a random drugs test?

3   **What was historic about the USA v Switzerland match at the Silverdome, Detroit?**

4   Who scored for the Republic of Ireland in their 1-0 victory over Italy?

5   **Which country won its first World Cup finals match in its sixth appearance in this stage of the tournament?**

6   Name the Russian and the Bulgarian who were the tournament's joint top scorers, with six goals each.

7   **Who knocked Romania out of the World Cup on penalties in the quarter-final?**

8   Who knocked out the holders, West Germany, in the quarter finals?

9   **Which three Italians missed penalties in the Final shoot-out?**

10 What were the names of the two goalkeepers in the Final?

11 **What relation are Roberto and Dino Baggio of Italy?**

12 Where was the 1994 World Cup Final held?

13 **Which Brazilian was awarded the Golden Ball as the outstanding player of the tournament?**

14 What was the name of Brazil's World Cup-winning captain?

15 **What was the nationality of referee Kurt Rothlisberger, who mistakenly denied Belgium a penalty against Germany?**

Quiz 18   The 1998 World Cup

1   **Where was the opening match of the 1998 World Cup finals played?**

2   Which Brazilian scored the first goal of the tournament?

3   **Which Scot was the first player to be booked in the tournament?**

4   Who gave away the penalty from which Scotland equalised against Brazil?

5   **Who scored for Scotland from the spot kick?**

6   Which Scot scored an own goal to give Brazil a 2-1 victory in the opening match?

7   **How many of members of the Norwegian starting line-up in the game against Morocco had played in the English Premiership in 1997-98?**

8   Who scored both goals for Chile in their 2-2 draw with Italy in the opening match of Group B?

9   **Who opened the scoring in this match for Italy?**

10   Who then equalised for Italy from the penalty spot with five minutes remaining?

11   **In which city did the hosts, France, play their opening match?**

12   Danish captain Michael Laudrup won his 100th international cap against Saudi Arabia. Which of his teammates was winning his 101st?

13   **Who was the first player to be sent off in the 1998 World Cup finals?**

14   During Mexico's 3-1 victory over South Korea, which Mexican stunned the world by gripping the ball between both feet and jumping over a tackle?

15   **Which Dutchman was sent off for elbowing Lorenzo Staelens in the chest during Holland's 0-0 draw with Belgium in Group E?**

---

1 **The Stade de France, St Denis, Paris** 2 Cesar Sampaio 3 **Darren Jackson** 4 Cesar Sampaio 5 **John Collins** 6 Tom Boyd 7 **Seven (Grodas, T Flo, Solskjaer, Bjornebye, Johnsen, Leonhardsen, Berg)** 8 Marcelo Salas 9 **Christian Vieri** 10 Roberto Baggio 11 **Marseille** 12 Peter Schmeichel 13 **Anatoli Nankov (Bulgaria)** 14 Cuauhtemoc Blanco 15 **Patrick Kluivert**

Quiz 19 — The 1998 World Cup

1 **Who was the manager of Argentina at the 1998 World Cup finals?**

2 Who scored for Argentina in their 1-0 win over Japan in the opening match of Group H?

3 **Who scored Jamaica's first ever goal in the World Cup finals?**

4 Who took the free kick from which Alan Shearer scored England's first goal in their 2-0 victory over Tunisia in Group G?

5 **Who was standing in an offside position when Paul Scholes scored England's second goal against Tunisia?**

6 Who scored for Scotland in their 1-1 draw with Norway?

7 **Which English-based Norwegian fouled Gordon Durie right on the edge of the penalty area, an offence which some thought was committed inside the box?**

8 Who walked out of the Colombia squad after less than a week of the tournament?

9 **Which French player was sent off in their 4-0 defeat of Saudi Arabia?**

10 Which referee sent off two players in the Belgium v Mexico group match?

11 **Who scored both goals for Belgium in their 2-2 draw with Mexico?**

12 Who did Holland beat 5-0 in Group E?

13 **Who scored a ten-minute hat trick in Argentina's 5-0 defeat of Jamaica?**

14 How many players were sent off altogether in the two matches played on 'Red Thursday', June 18, 1998?

15 **During the course of the 1998 tournament, which German broke the record for the number of minutes played in the World Cup?**

1 **Daniel Passarella** 2 Gabriel Batistuta 3 **Robbie Earle** 4 Graeme Le Saux 5 **Paul Ince**
6 Craig Burley 7 **Stig Inge Bjornebye** 8 Faustino Asprilla 9 **Zinedine Zidane**
10 Hugh Dallas 11 **Marc Wilmots** 12 South Korea 13 **Gabriel Batistuta** 14 Five
15 Lothar Matthaus

Quiz 20   The 1998 World Cup

1 Who became the first team to go out of the World Cup finals on the golden goal?

2 Who scored twice for Brazil as they beat Chile 4-1 in the round of 16?

3 Which Dane scored against Nigeria 16 seconds after coming on as substitute?

4 Who missed a penalty for Yugoslavia against Holland?

5 Whose twice-taken penalty was enough to take Croatia past Romania in the second round?

6 Name the Danish referee of the Argentina v England match.

7 Who moved to right back after David Beckham had been sent off?

8 Which England player had a goal disallowed in the dying seconds of normal time against Argentina?

9 Where was the Argentina v England match played?

10 Which German was sent off in their quarter final match against Croatia?

11 Who scored Holland's last-minute quarter final winner against Argentina, thus becoming the leading scorer in his country's history?

12 Which Italian missed the last kick in their quarter-final penalty shoot-out against France?

13 Who scored two goals for Brazil in their quarter final against Denmark?

14 Who scored for Holland in both the quarter final and the semi-final?

15 What was the name of the Paraguay goalkeeper who took long-range shots from free kicks?

Quiz 21   The 1998 World Cup

1 **Who scored straight after half-time to give Brazil the lead in their semi-final against Holland?**

2 Who scored both goals for France in their semi-final victory over Croatia?

3 **Which Frenchman was sent off in the semi-final against Croatia?**

4 Which Croatian defender did the French player appear to hit?

5 **What was the score in the third place play-off between Holland and Croatia?**

6 Who was passed fit to play only 45 minutes before kick-off in the World Cup Final?

7 **For which club does French goalkeeper Fabien Barthez play football?**

8 Who was the captain of France?

9 **Who was the captain of Brazil?**

10 Who was the manager of Brazil?

11 **Who was the manager of France?**

12 Which Frenchman was sent off in the World Cup Final?

13 **Who scored twice for France in the World Cup Final?**

14 Who won the Golden Boot as the competition's leading scorer, with six goals in the tournament?

15 **Where will the 2002 World Cup finals be held?**

1 **Ronaldo** 2 Lilian Thuram 3 **Laurent Blanc** 4 Slaven Bilic 5 **Holland** 1 **Croatia** 2
6 Ronaldo 7 **AS Monaco** 8 Didier Deschamps 9 **Dunga** 10 Mario Zagalo
11 **Aimé Jacquet** 12 Marcel Desailly 13 **Zinedine Zidane** 14 Davor Suker (Croatia)
15 **Japan and South Korea**

FOOTBALL
Fact Book

FACTS CONTENTS

THE DAWN OF TIME

The Dawn of Time

Facts

The first England versus Scotland match was played at The Oval, Kennington, London on March 5, 1870. The two teams drew 1-1.

The first FA Cup was won by The Wanderers, who beat The Royal Engineers 1-0 in the Final at the Kennington Oval on March 16, 1872.

The winning goal in the first FA Cup Final was scored by M.P. Betts.

The Cup-winning Wanderers captain, C.W. Alcock, was also Secretary of the Football Association.

The first FA Cup had 15 entrants.

 **Facts**

The Dawn of Time

The FA Cup itself was known throughout the game as The Little Tin Idol. It was 18 inches high, had two curved handles and was crowned with a figure of a footballer on the lid.

The Cup had been made by Martin, Hall & Co and cost £20.

Queen's Park of Glasgow - Scotland's first football club - took part in the first English FA Cup, and received byes to the semi-final.

In the semi-final, Queen's Park drew with The Wanderers but could not afford to stay in London for the replay, so had to scratch from the tournament.

The first Scotland versus England match was played at the West of Scotland Cricket Ground, Partick on November 30, 1872. The final score was 0-0.

The first official international between England and Scotland was played at The Oval, Kennington, London on March 8, 1873. The score was England 4 Scotland 2.

The Dawn of Time

Facts

The scorer of England's first ever international goal was Alexander Bonsor of Old Etonians and The Wanderers.

In March 1873, the Scots founded a Football Association and inaugurated their own FA Cup.

The first Scottish FA Cup trophy and badges cost £56.12s. 11d (about £56.64p).

In 1876, the Welsh FA was formed and Wales played their first international football match - they lost 4-0 to Scotland in Glasgow.

The first recorded match under electric lights was played on October 14, 1878, at Bramall Lane, Sheffield, between sides captained by the brothers J.C. and W.E. Clegg, both England internationals. 20,000 people are thought to have been present.

The first official football match in Northern Ireland was an exhibition game between the Scottish clubs Queen's Park and Caledonians on October 24, 1878.

 **Facts**   The Dawn of Time

1878 was also the year in which referees used whistles for the first time.

FA Cup Finals of the 1870s

1872	The Wanderers	1	Royal Engineers	0
1873	The Wanderers	2	Oxford University	0
1874	Oxford University	2	Royal Engineers	0
1875	Royal Engineers	1	Old Etonians	1
	Replay			
	Royal Engineers	2	Old Etonians	0
1876	The Wanderers	1	Old Etonians	1
	Replay			
	The Wanderers	3	Old Etonians	0
1877	The Wanderers	2	Oxford University	1 (aet)
1878	The Wanderers	3	Royal Engineers	1
1879	Old Etonians	1	Clapham Rovers	0

The Dawn of Time

Scottish FA Cup Finals of the 1870s

1874	Queen's Park	2	Clydesdale	0
1875	Queen's Park	3	Renton	0
1876	Queen's Park	1	Third Lanark	1
Replay				
	Queen's Park	2	Third Lanark	0
1877	Vale of Leven	0	Rangers	0
Replays				
	Vale of Leven	1	Rangers	1
	Vale of Leven	3	Rangers	2
1878	Vale of Leven	1	Third Lanark	0
1879	Vale of Leven	1	Rangers	1

(Vale of Leven then won the Cup by default when Rangers refused to take part in a replay because they had had a goal disallowed in the first match.)

In 1879, at the age of 17 years 245 days, James Prinsep of Clapham Rovers became the youngest man ever to appear in an FA Cup Final.

In 1883, the FA Cup went north for the first time, when Blackburn Olympic beat the Old Etonians 2-1 after extra time.

Blackburn Olympic retained the Cup the following year, 1884, but in 1885 the trophy was won by their neighbours, Blackburn Rovers, who beat Queen's Park 2-1 in the Final.

Blackburn Rovers then won the FA Cup three years running - they beat Queen's Park again 2-0 in the 1885 Final, then West Bromwich Albion 2-0 in a replay at the Racecourse Ground, Derby, after the first match at the Oval had been drawn 0-0.

The first Home International Championship was contested in 1884. Scotland won it with a clean sweep, beating Wales 4-1 in Glasgow, Ireland 5-0 in Belfast and England 1-0 at Cathkin Park, Glasgow.

 **Facts**   The Dawn of Time

The record score in any British first-class football match was Arbroath's 36-0 victory over Bon Accord in the Scottish FA Cup on September 5, 1885.

Arbroath winger John Petrie scored 13 goals in this match - a scoring record that still stands.

England's first professional footballer was James Forrest, who was paid to play against Scotland in 1885.

Scotland dominated the Home International Championship until 1886, when they shared the title with England.

In the first all-Midlands FA Cup Final in 1887, Aston Villa beat West Bromwich Albion 2-0 at Kennington Oval.

On their way to the trophy, Aston Villa had beaten Glasgow Rangers 3-1 in the semi-final.

In 1888, the winners of the English and Scottish FA Cups played each other for what was billed as 'The Championship of the World'. Renton beat West Bromwich Albion 2-1.

England won the Home International Championship outright for the first time in 1888, beating Ireland 5-1, Wales 5-1 and Scotland 5-0.

On April 17, 1888, the Football League was founded after a meeting at the Royal Hotel, Manchester. The mastermind - often known as The Father of League Football - was William McGregor, a director of Aston Villa.

The twelve founder members of the English Football League were Accrington, Aston Villa, Blackburn Rovers, Bolton Wanderers, Burnley, Derby County, Everton, Notts County, Preston North End, Stoke, West Bromwich Albion and Wolverhampton Wanderers.

The Dawn of Time

 Facts

The first English League Champions were Preston North End, who went through the whole 1888-89 season undefeated. They also won the FA Cup in that year, thus completing the first ever double.

The First English Football League Final Table, Season 1888-89

		P	W	D	L	F	A	Pts
1	Preston North End	22	18	4	0	74	15	40
2	Aston Villa	22	12	5	5	61	43	29
3	Wolverhampton Wanderers	22	12	4	6	50	37	28
4	Blackburn Rovers	22	10	6	6	66	45	26
5	Bolton Wanderers	22	10	2	10	63	59	22
6	West Bromwich Albion	22	10	2	10	40	46	22
7	Accrington	22	6	8	8	48	48	20
8	Everton	22	9	2	11	35	46	20
9	Burnley	22	7	3	12	42	62	17
10	Derby County	22	7	2	13	41	61	16
11	Notts County	22	5	2	15	40	73	12
12	Stoke	22	4	4	14	26	51	12

Preston North End retained the Championship in 1889-90; the runners-up this time were Everton.

Blackburn Rovers beat The Wednesday 6-1 in the 1890 FA Cup Final and William Townley became the first man to score a hat-trick in this fixture.

In 1891-92, the First Division was enlarged to 14 clubs - the two new entrants were Darwen and Stoke.

 **Facts**   The Dawn of Time

FA Cup Finals of the 1880s

1880	Clapham Rovers	1	Oxford University	0
1881	Old Carthusians	3	Old Etonians	0
1882	Old Etonians	1	Blackburn Rovers	0
1883	Blackburn Olympic	2	Old Etonians	1 (aet)
1884	Blackburn Rovers	2	Queen's Park	1
1885	Blackburn Rovers	2	Queen's Park	0
1886	Blackburn Rovers	0	West Bromwich Albion	0
	Replay			
	Blackburn Rovers	2	West Bromwich Albion	0
1887	Aston Villa	2	West Bromwich Albion	0
1888	West Bromwich Albion	2	Preston North End	1
1889	Preston North End	3	Wolverhampton Wdrs	0

Scottish FA Cup Finals of the 1880s

1880	Queen's Park	3	Thornliebank	0
1881	Queen's Park	3	Dumbarton	0
1882	Queen's Park	4	Dumbarton	2
1883	Dumbarton	2	Vale of Leven	2
	Replay			
	Dumbarton	2	Vale of Leven	1
1884	Queen's Park beat Vale of Leven by default			
1885	Renton	0	Vale of Leven	0
	Replay			
	Renton	3	Vale of Leven	1
1886	Queen's Park	3	Renton	1
1887	Hibernian	2	Dumbarton	1
1888	Renton	6	Cambuslang	1
1889	Third Lanark	2	Celtic	1

The Dawn of Time

 Facts

On March 15, 1890, England fielded two international sides on the same day - one beat Wales 3-1 at Wrexham, the other beat Ireland 9-1 in Belfast.

In 1890, the Scots followed the English lead and formed their own Football League. The eleven inaugural members were Abercorn, Celtic, Cowlair, Cambuslang, Dumbarton, Heart of Midlothian, Rangers, St Mirren, Renton, Third Lanark and Vale of Leven.

Renton were expelled from the Scottish League after only five matches, for professionalism.

At the end of the season in Spring 1891, there was a tie at the top between Dumbarton and Rangers. In an effort to break the deadlock, a play-off was arranged, but when this ended 2-2 it was decided to share the Championship - the only time this has ever happened.

There was not a single 0-0 draw throughout the whole of the first Scottish League season; 409 goals were scored in 90 matches, an average of 4.5 goals per game.

The First Scottish Football League Final Table, Season 1890-91

		P	W	D	L	F	A	Pts
1=	Dumbarton	18	13	3	2	61	21	29
1=	Rangers	18	13	3	2	58	25	29
3	Celtic	18	11	3	4	48	21	21
4	Cambuslang	18	8	4	6	47	42	20
5	Third Lanark	18	8	3	7	38	39	15
6	Heart of Midlothian	18	6	2	10	31	37	14
7	Abercorn	18	5	2	11	36	47	12
8	St Mirren	18	5	1	2	39	62	11
9	Vale of Leven	18	5	1	12	27	65	11
10	Cowlairs	18	3	4	11	24	50	6

 Facts   The Dawn of Time

In 1891, the Scots expanded their First Division to 12 clubs. Cowlairs went out of the League after finishing last in 1891; the three newcomers were Clyde, Leith Athletic and a re-formed Renton.

In 1892, the English Second Division was inaugurated. At the end of the season, there were 'test matches' between the bottom three in Division One and the top three in Division Two to decide promotion and relegation.

The twelve founder members of the Second Division were Ardwick, Bootle, Burton Swifts, Burslem Port Vale, Crewe Alexandra, Darwen, Grimsby Town, Lincoln City, Northwich Victoria, Sheffield United, Small Heath and Walsall Town Swifts.

The English First Division was increased in size again, from 14 clubs to 16. The two new additions were Nottingham Forest and The Wednesday.

At the end of the 1892-93 season, Notts County and Accrington became the first clubs to be relegated from the English First Division.

The Dawn of Time

 **Facts**

At the end of the 1892-93 season, Darwen and Sheffield United became the first clubs to be promoted from the English Second Division.

The top team in Division Two, Small Heath, lost their test match with Newton Heath, the third-from-bottom club in Division One, so neither of these clubs changed divisions the following season.

In 1893, the Scots again followed the English example by recognising professionalism and introducing their own Second Division. The ten clubs that played in it were Abercorn, Clyde, Cowlairs, Greenock Morton, Hibernian, Motherwell, Northern, Partick Thistle, Port Glasgow Athletic and Thistle.

At the end of the 1893-94 season, the English League was expanded from 28 clubs to 31, taking three more clubs into the Second Division.

The three new League members in 1894 were Bury, Leicester Fosse and Manchester City.

The British Ladies' Football Club was formed in 1895 and played its first match at Crouch End, London.

On the night of September 11, 1895, the FA Cup was stolen from the window of football outfitters William Shillcock in Newton Row, Birmingham while it was held by Aston Villa. It was never recovered.

The replacement FA Cup cost Villa £25, and the club were fined as much again by the FA for their negligence in allowing it to be stolen. For several years to come, the winners of the trophy were presented with a replica of the original until a newly designed Cup was specially commissioned in time for the 1911 Final.

 **Facts**   The Dawn of Time

English Football League Champions 1888-99

1888-89 Preston North End
1889-90 Preston North End
1890-91 Everton
1891-92 Sunderland
1892-93 Sunderland
1893-94 Aston Villa
1894-95 Sunderland
1895-96 Aston Villa
1896-97 Aston Villa
1897-98 Sheffield United
1898-99 Aston Villa

FA Cup Finals of the 1890s

1890	Blackburn Rovers	6	The Wednesday	1
1891	Blackburn Rovers	3	Notts County	1
1892	West Bromwich Albion	3	Aston Villa	0
1893	Wolverhampton Wdrs	1	Everton	0
1894	Notts County	4	Bolton Wanderers	1
1895	Aston Villa	1	West Bromwich Albion	0
1896	Sheffield Wednesday	2	Wolverhampton Wdrs	1
1897	Aston Villa	3	Everton	2
1898	Nottingham Forest	3	Derby County	1
1899	Sheffield United	4	Derby County	1

Scottish Football League Champions 1891-99

1890-91 Dumbarton and Rangers
1891-92 Dumbarton
1892-93 Celtic
1893-94 Celtic
1894-95 Heart of Midlothian
1895-96 Celtic
1896-97 Heart of Midlothian
1897-98 Celtic
1898-99 Rangers

The Dawn of Time

Scottish FA Cup Finals of the 1890s

1890	Queen's Park	1	Vale of Leven	1
	Replay			
	Queen's Park	2	Vale of Leven	1
1891	Heart of Midlothian	1	Dumbarton	0
1892	Celtic	5	Queen's Park	1
1893	Queen's Park	2	Celtic	1
1894	Rangers	3	Celtic	1
1895	St Bernard's	2	Renton	1
1896	Heart of Midlothian	3	Hibernian	1
1897	Rangers	5	Dumbarton	1
1898	Rangers	2	Kilmarnock	0
1899	Celtic	2	Rangers	0

In 1898-99, the English Football League was enlarged to 36 clubs by increasing both divisions to 18 clubs. The four new members were **Barnsley, Burslem Port Vale, Glossop** and **New Brighton Tower**.

THE EARLY
20TH CENTURY

The Early 20th Century

Facts

**The first League Champions of the 20th century were Aston Villa -
with 77 goals, they were the First Division's leading scorers for the
sixth season running.**

The first FA Cup winners of the 20th century were Bury - they won it again
in 1903, but had no other major honours before the millennium. The
attendance at the 1900 Cup Final was 68,945.

**The first Scottish League Champions of the 20th century were
Rangers.**

The first Scottish FA Cup winners of the 20th century were Celtic.

**The 1901 Cup Final between Tottenham Hotspur and Sheffield
United drew a record crowd of 114,815.**

The Sheffield United goalkeeper in the 1900 Final was Willie Foulke, who
weighed at least 20 stones throughout his career.

**There were numerous
legends about Foulke.
He was said to have
been able to carry a
man under each arm
and to punch the ball as
far as the halfway line.
One match in which he
played had to be
stopped when the
crossbar snapped after
he swung on it.**

 **Facts**   The Early 20th Century

Of the bottom five clubs in the First Division at the end of the 1900-01 season, four - Sheffield United, Aston Villa, Preston North End and West Bromwich Albion - had won the Championship, the FA Cup or both.

In 1900-01, Linthous dropped out of the Scottish League but its total membership increased to 21 clubs with the addition of East Stirlingshire and St Bernard's.

Scotland beat England 4-1 in the 1900 Home International Championship match. Three of their goals were scored by R.S. McColl of Queen's Park, the last remaining Scottish amateur.

On February 23, 1901, Scotland notched up their highest score in an international, beating Ireland 11-0.

For the 1901-02 season, the Scottish League was expanded again, this time to 22 clubs, with the addition of Arthurlie.

On April 5, 1902, 26 people were killed and 500 were injured when a new stand collapsed at Ibrox Park, Glasgow during the Scotland v England match.

The match was replayed at Villa Park, Birmingham. This was the first international in which all the players were professionals. The final score was England 2 Scotland 2.

In 1901-02, the maximum wage for professional footballers in England was £4 a week.

In 1901-02, goalscoring in the First Division reached a record low, averaging only 2.75 goals a game.

Pitch markings were changed for the 1902-03 season - henceforth, the goal area would be 20 yards wide and 6 yards deep; there would be a penalty area at 18 yards and a penalty spot 12 yards from the goal line.

The Early 20th Century  Facts

The 1902-03 Home International Championship was a three-way tie between England, Scotland and Ireland.

In 1903-04, the Scottish League grew again - this time to 26 clubs, with the addition of Albion Rovers and Ayr Parkhouse.

On May 21, 1904, the world governing body of football was formed at a meeting in Paris between representatives of the football associations of Belgium, Denmark, France, Holland, Spain, Sweden and Switzerland. It was called FIFA (Fédération Internationale de Football Association).

England became a member of FIFA in 1905 and thereafter rapidly took a leading role in its affairs.

The first international in South America, between Argentina and Uruguay for the Lipton Cup, ended in a draw.

In 1906, Daniel Burley Woolfall of the English FA was elected President of FIFA.

On December 5, 1904, Woolwich Arsenal beat a team of French internationals 26-1.

 **Facts**   The Early 20th Century

England international Alf Common became the first £1000 transfer when he moved from Sunderland to Middlesbrough.

In 1904, Sheffield FC - the oldest football club then in existence, founded in 1857 - won their first major honour, the FA Amateur Cup.

In 1904-05, Wales notched up their first international victory over Scotland at the 30th attempt, winning 3-1 at Wrexham.

In 1904-05, Rangers and Celtic finished level on points at the top of the Scottish First Division.

Celtic won the title in a play-off, but if either goal average or goal difference had been used, Rangers would have been Champions - they had scored 83 and conceded 28, which was superior by either method of reckoning to Celtic's 68 for and 31 against.

At the start of the 1905-06 season, the English Football League was enlarged to 40 clubs by increasing the two divisions to 20 clubs each. Because of the reorganisation, there was no relegation from Division One this year. The two clubs to benefit from this were Bury and Notts County, who finished in 17th and 18th place respectively in 1905.

Doncaster Rovers failed to gain re-election after finishing bottom of Division Two in 1904-05.

The five new clubs elected for 1905-06 were Chelsea, Hull City, Leeds City, Stockport County and Clapton Orient.

Also in 1905-06, the FA Cup was increased from five rounds to six.

Liverpool won the First Division in 1906, the first time a newly promoted club had gone on to take the title the following season.

The Early 20th Century

Facts

In 1905-06, the Scottish League was altered for the fifth time this century. The League was enlarged to 28 clubs - a 16-club First Division and a 12-club Second Division.

The two new clubs admitted to the Scottish Second Division were Cowdenbeath and Vale of Leven.

In 1906-07, the Scottish League was enlarged to 30 clubs - a First Division of 18 clubs and a Second Division of 12. The newcomers were Dumbarton and - back after a two-year absence - Ayr Parkhouse.

In 1907, Celtic became the first Scottish club to win the League and FA Cup double.

Wales won the 1907 Home International Championship - it was their first victory in this competition and the first time it had been won outright by anyone but England or Scotland.

Newcastle United dropped only one point at home in their Championship-winning 1906-07 season.

 **Facts**   The Early 20th Century

When Bristol City finished second in the First Division at the end of the 1906-07 season, this was the highest position ever achieved by a southern club.

A crowd of between 110,000 and 130,000 watched the 1-1 draw between Scotland and England on April 4, 1908.

Falkirk became the first club to score more that 100 goals in a League season - but their total of 103 was not enough to bring them the 1908 Championship, which went to Celtic.

In 1908, the first Charity Shield was played in England between League Champions Manchester United and Southern League winners Queen's Park Rangers.

The 1909 Scottish FA Cup was withheld after riots between groups of rival supporters during the final replay between Celtic and Rangers. The second match had finished 1-1 after a 2-2 draw in the first Final, and many fans were disgruntled because they suspected that the results had been rigged so that the two clubs might gain extra revenue.

On December 11, 1909, Vivian Woodward of Tottenham Hotspur became the first player to score a double hat-trick twice when he slotted six for England in an amateur international against Holland. His previous double hat-trick had been for England against France in 1906 - a match in which he had scored eight!

In 1911, a new FA Cup was commissioned at a cost of 50 guineas (£52.50).

The new trophy was made in Bradford and first presented to one of the local teams - Bradford City - when they won the Cup in 1911.

The Early 20th Century

Facts

The Final against Newcastle United featured twelve Scotsmen, eight of whom played for Bradford City.

The second FA Cup - a replica of the one that had been stolen in 1895 and never recovered - was presented to Lord Kinnaird to mark his 21st year as President of the FA.

In his playing career, Kinnaird (1847-1923) had played in nine FA Cup Finals and won five winners' medals with The Wanderers and The Old Etonians.

When the 1912 Cup Final became the third in a row to be drawn, the FA decided that, henceforth, there would be extra time in the first Final if it was needed.

After keeping an unaltered format since 1907, Scotland again increased the size of its League. Instead of 30 clubs, there would henceforth be 32, with a First Division of 18 and a Second Division of 14.

The two new clubs that came into the Scottish League as a result of this reorganisation were Dunfermline Athletic and St Johnstone.

In the 1912-13 season, every player who appeared for Morton in the Scottish First Division scored a goal for the club.

In 1913, England lost to Ireland for the first time, suffering a 2-1 defeat in Belfast. Three minutes before full-time, the crowd mistook a free kick for the final whistle and invaded the pitch. The match could not be restarted, but the result stood.

After this historic victory, Ireland went from strength to strength, and the following year (1914) won the Home International Championship outright for the first time.

 **Facts**　　　　　The Early 20th Century

The 1914 FA Cup Final between Burnley and Liverpool was the first to be watched by a reigning monarch, King George V.

The 1914 FA Cup Final was the last to be played at Crystal Palace - the following year, it was held at Old Trafford, then the Great War intervened. After the end of hostilities, the 1920, 1921 and 1922 Finals were held at Stamford Bridge. And then in 1923 the fixture moved to Wembley.

The Great War began in August 1914. By the next FA Cup Final on April 24, 1915, most of the spectators were in uniform.

The Khaki Cup Final - as the 1915 fixture became known - was a muted affair played at Old Trafford in front of 49,557 spectators.

The Cup was won by Sheffield United, who beat Chelsea 3-0 in the Final. The trophy was presented to the Blades' captain by Lord Derby, who took the opportunity to make a recruiting speech: 'It is now the duty of everyone to join with each other and play a sterner game for England'.

On Easter Monday 1915, in a First Division match at Middlesbrough, Oldham Athletic full-back Billy Cook refused to leave the field when ordered off by referee Mr H. Smith. So the referee himself went off, ending the game 30 minutes early.

The Early 20th Century

Facts

After an FA inquiry into this incident, Oldham were fined £350 and Cook was suspended for a year. But the result - a 4-1 Middlesbrough victory - was allowed to stand.

In the Scottish League Division Two, there was a tie at the top between Cowdenbeath, Leith Athletic and St Bernard's, necessitating a three-way play-off. Cowdenbeath won it - beating both the other teams - but none was promoted because only the Scottish First Division went on playing throughout the rest of the First World War.

The Football League and FA Cup programmes in England and Scotland continued after the outbreak of the First World War on August 4, 1914.

This was a matter of great controversy - the Church of England was particularly strong in its condemnation of those who watched football while others were serving their country.

 **Facts** The Early 20th Century

Nevertheless, the decision had been taken in consultation with the War Office, who thought that maintaining a vestige of normality would be good for morale. Football clubs helped the recruitment drive - there was no conscription at first - and it is thought that eventually perhaps as many as half a million new soldiers were enlisted at football grounds.

At first, though, recruiting drives at football grounds were almost farcically unsuccessful. Only one person enlisted at a 1915 Arsenal game, while at a Nottingham Forest match there was no one at all ready to fight.

Yet although few spectators were keen to join up, many of those who earned their living from football were among the first to enlist. The game produced 100,000 recruits in the first four months of the War and FA statistics revealed that only 600 men who worked in football had not volunteered by August 1915.

The willingness of players to join up was used by the War Office in its recruitment drive. Outside Stamford Bridge, advertisement hoardings bore the legend: 'Do you want to be a Chelsea diehard? … Follow the lead given by your favourite football players'.

Many professionals who enlisted went into the 17th Service Batallion of the Middlesex Regiment based at the Richmond Athletic Ground.

The Footballers' Batallion, as it became known, went into action in France in the summer of 1915. Their second-in-command, Major Frank Buckley, was wounded in the shoulder and lung in 1916. He was later manager of Wolverhampton Wanderers during the interwar years.

By the summer of 1915, gates had dwindled because so many men had gone to fight in France. It was decided to suspend the English League and carry on with regional leagues. Matches would be played only on Saturdays and holidays - there were to be no midweek games and no internationals.

The Early 20th Century

 Facts

In Scotland, the FA Cup was suspended, but the First Division of the League continued throughout the War.

During the First World War, Scottish First Division players were not allowed to make their whole living from football and their earnings from the game were restricted to no more than £2 a week. The remainder of their income had to be from work that helped the war effort.

With no midweek matches, Scottish clubs sometimes had to play two matches a day. On April 15, 1915, Celtic beat Raith Rovers 6-0 in the afternoon. In the evening, they went to Motherwell - who had lost 3-0 to Ayr that afternoon - and won 3-1.

The First World War was a particularly successful period for Celtic, who went 62 matches without defeat from November 13, 1915 to April 21, 1917.

In 1918, Rangers broke Celtic's domination, winning the League Championship by a single point. Controversially, the Gers took full advantage of the temporary transfers that enabled footballing servicemen who found themselves in a new billet to play for the local side if picked. Their 1918 team had guest players from as far away as Sheffield.

In 1915 there was a match fixing scandal. A Football League committee of enquiry discovered that players in the Manchester United v Liverpool match at Easter had bet large sums on a 2-1 win for United at odds of 7-1. Four players from each side were suspended for life.

The players found guilty of match-fixing were Tom Fairfoul, Tommy Miller, Bob Purcell and Jackie Sheldon of Liverpool, Laurence Cook, Sandy Turnbull, Enoch West and Arthur Whalley of Manchester United.

 **Facts**   The Early 20th Century

Of the United players found guilty, only West had actually played in the fixed match. He was the only one of the eight who did not have his ban lifted at the end of the First World War.

In 1918 and 1919, the winners of the Lancashire regional league met the winners of the Midlands regional league in a play-off for the Championship Cup, the wartime equivalent of the League Championship.

In 1918, Midlands league winners Leeds City beat Lancashire league winners Stoke 2-1 on aggregate over the two-legged tie.

In the 1919 Championship Cup play-off - after the end of the War, but before normal fixtures could be resumed - Nottingham Forest (Midlands) beat Everton (Lancashire) 1-0 at Goodison Park after a goalless draw at the City Ground.

In the Nottingham Forest goal in that final was Sam Hardy, the England keeper who normally played for Aston Villa but who was permitted under wartime regulations to guest for a club closer to his billet.

Outstanding among the footballers honoured for their bravery in the First World War was Donald Bell, the Bradford full back, who won the Victoria Cross posthumously at the Battle of the Somme.

Steve Bloomer, the Derby and England forward, retired early in 1914 and was unlucky enough to take a coaching job in Berlin. Instead of taking up his post on arrival in the German capital, he was interned for the duration of the War.

The Early 20th Century

Title Winners of the First World War

London Combination

1915-16 Chelsea
1916-17 West Ham United
1917-18 Chelsea
1918-19 Brentford

Lancashire Regional Tournament

1915-16 Manchester City
1916-17 Liverpool
1917-18 Stoke
1918-19 Everton

Midland Regional Tournament

1915-16 Nottingham Forest
1916-17 Leeds City
1917-18 Leeds City
1918-19 Nottingham Forest

Wartime League Championship

1917-18 Leeds City
1918-19 Nottingham Forest

Scottish League Champions

1915-16 Celtic
1916-17 Celtic
1917-18 Rangers
1918-19 Celtic

BETWEEN THE WARS

Between the Wars

Facts

The First World War ended on November 11, 1918, but it was not until the following season that football got back to normal and the League programme resumed.

The Home Nations - England, Ireland, Scotland and Wales - withdrew from FIFA because they refused to play against Germany. They remained outside the organisation until 1922.

For the 1919-20 season, the English Football League was increased from 40 to 44 clubs in two divisions of 22.

Glossop had dropped out of the League in 1915, while Leeds City were expelled from it in 1919 because of irregularities in payments to players during the First World War.

During the First World War, 35 guests had played for Leeds, including seven internationals. This was not a problem in itself, because it was permitted under wartime rules, but when the club refused to render accounts for the 1917-18 and 1918-19 seasons, the League threw them out.

In the aftermath of the Leeds scandal, four of its directors and two of its former managers were banned for life from involvement in football and were even forbidden to attend matches.

One of Leeds City's former managers was George Cripps; the other was Herbert Chapman.

Thus there were six vacancies in the new postwar English Second Division. These were taken up by Coventry City, Port Vale, Rotherham County, Stoke City, South Shields and West Ham United.

 **Facts**   **Between the Wars**

Coventry City had been formed in 1883 by workers at a bicycle factory and originally played under the name Singer's FC.

Port Vale - who replaced Leeds City in mid-season and took their points - had been a League club before. Founded in 1876, from 1884 to 1911 they were known as Burslem Port Vale. They had been founder members of the Second Division in 1892 but failed to win re-election in 1896. Re-elected in 1898, they resigned from the League in 1907 because of financial difficulties.

Port Vale took their name from that of the house in Burslem, Stoke-on-Trent, where the founders first met.

Rotherham County grew out of a previous club called Thornhill United which had been founded in 1878. Neighbouring Rotherham Town had been a member of the League from 1893 to 1896, when they failed to win re-election. After joining the Second Division, Rotherham County amalgamated with Rotherham Town in 1925 to form Rotherham United.

Stoke were founder members of the League in 1888 but went bankrupt in 1908 and had to resign. They reformed as Stoke City in 1919 to fill one of the new vacancies.

Between the Wars

Facts

West Ham United started as Thames Ironworks FC, a club formed by workers at a shipyard owned by Arnold F. Hills. Renamed in 1900, the club won election to the Football League in 1919 under the management of Syd King.

The reorganisation of the League was not good news for everyone. Tottenham Hotspur were relegated to the Second Division. This might not have upset them, since they finished bottom of the First Division in 1915, had it not been for the fact that Arsenal took their place in Division One despite having finished only fifth in Division Two in 1915.

With 42 matches instead of 38, there were new records aplenty in the 1919-20 League season. West Bromwich Albion scored a record 104 goals in their Championship year, while Tottenham scored 102 goals to win the Second Division.

On March 15, 1920, at the age of 45 years 229 days, Billy Meredith of Manchester City became the oldest player to appear in an international match - for Wales against England.

 **Facts**   **Between the Wars**

For the 1919-20 season, the two divisions of the Scottish Football League were amalgamated into one division of 22 clubs.

Rangers won the Scottish Championship, with a record 71 points from their 42 matches. They scored 106 goals.

At the start of the 1920-21 season, there was another reorganisation of the English Football League. The total number of clubs was increased from 44 to 66 clubs by accepting the en bloc application of every member of the Southern League Division One.

All but one of the new clubs went into the newly formed Third Division. The exception was Cardiff City, who went straight into Division Two; to accommodate this, Grimsby Town, last season's bottom League club, were relegated to the Third.

Cardiff City went from strength to strength, winning promotion to the First Division in their first season in the League.

Lincoln City, who finished next to bottom of the Second Division in 1919-20, were not re-elected. Their place in Division Two was taken by Leeds United, a new club with the same ground and infrastructure as Leeds City.

The 21 Founder Members of the Third Division were as follows: Brentford, Brighton and Hove Albion, Bristol Rovers, Crystal Palace, Exeter City, Gillingham, Luton Town, Merthyr Town, Millwall Athletic, Newport County, Northampton Town, Norwich City, Plymouth Argyle, Portsmouth, Queen's Park Rangers, Reading, Southampton, Southend United, Swansea Town, Swindon Town and Watford.

Between the Wars

The new formation was immediately popular - Millwall's first gate was over 25,000, Portsmouth and Queen's Park Rangers had attendances of over 20,000.

At the other end of the scale, the Second Division match between Stockport County and Leicester City on May 7, 1921, was watched by fewer paying spectators than any other game in League history. Stockport were already doomed to relegation; their Edgeley Park ground was closed, so the match was played at Old Trafford, Manchester.

Only 13 people paid to watch the game, which was a 0-0 draw. Nevertheless, this statistic is not as impressive as it is sometimes made to sound - another 2000 fans stayed on after watching Manchester United earlier the same day.

Dumbarton goalkeeper James Williamson died on the night of November 12, 1921, from injuries sustained in a collision with a member of the opposition during his team's match with Rangers.

The 1921-22 season saw a further expansion of the English League from 66 clubs to 86. The 20 newcomers entered a new Third Division which was regionalised into Third Division (North) and Third Division (South).

The 20 clubs that joined the Football League in 1921 were as follows: Aberdare Athletic, Accrington Stanley, Ashington, Barrow, Charlton Athletic, Chesterfield, Crewe Alexandra, Darlington, Durham City, Halifax Town, Hartlepools United, Lincoln City, Nelson, Rochdale, Southport, Stalybridge Celtic, Tranmere Rovers, Walsall, Wigan Borough and Wrexham.

Lincoln City were making a return to League football after having failed to gain re-election in 1920.

 **Facts**   **Between the Wars**

Stockport County were relegated from Division Two at the end of the 1920-21 season but went straight back up again the following year as the first Champions of Division Three (North).

The inaugural winners of Division Three (South) were Southampton. They had come second in the year of the old Third Division but, because of the impending reorganisation, only champions Crystal Palace had been promoted.

In Scotland, the experiment with a single division was abandoned and the League re-formed with 42 clubs - a top division of 22 and a second division of 20.

Because of this reorganisation, there was no relegation from the Scottish First Division at the end of the 1920-21 season, thus saving the bottom two clubs, Dumbarton and St Mirren, from the drop.

Some of the 20 clubs in the new Scottish Division Two had previously been members of the League before the disruptions caused by the First World War.

The full list of clubs in Scottish League Division Two (1921-22) was as follows: Alloa Athletic, Arbroath, Armadale, Bathgate, Bo'ness, Broxburn United, Clackmannan, Cowdenbeath, Dundee Hibernians, Dunfermline Athletic, East Fife, East Stirlingshire, Forfar Athletic, Johnstone, King's Park, Lochgelly United, St Bernard's, St Johnstone, Stenhousemuir and Vale of Leven.

At the end of the 1921-22 season, Alloa Athletic were promoted to the First Division as Champions of the Second.

However, during the course of the season the Scottish League had announced plans to alter its formation yet again - the two divisions were to be reduced to 20 teams each.

Between the Wars

This meant that three clubs - Dumbarton, Queen's Park and Clydebank - were relegated from the First Division in 1922.

The bottom two clubs in Division Two at the end of 1921-22 had to drop out of the League - the unlucky sides were Dundee Hibernians and Clackmannan.

On April 28, 1923, the English FA Cup Final was held for the first time at Wembley Stadium.

The finalists were Bolton Wanderers, who finished 13th in the First Division, and West Ham United, who were vying for promotion from Division Two.

Bolton won 2-0, but the day is best remembered for the near disaster in the crowd. The official attendance is given as 126,047, but many thousands of others scaled the walls and broke down flimsy barriers to watch the match.

Unofficially, there are thought to have been at least 200,000 and possibly a quarter of a million people in the stadium.

The masses flowed onto the pitch, making play impossible. They were eventually pushed back by the police, notably by PC George Scorey and his white horse, Billy.

 **Facts** Between the Wars

Constable Scorey later said: 'We arrived at kick-off time and were given orders to clear the pitch. Clear the pitch indeed! You couldn't see it'.

The match eventually got under way 45 minutes late. The crowd lined the edge of the playing area, making throw-ins and corners unusually hazardous - on several occasions, the ball stayed in play after bouncing off spectators on the line.

The Cup was presented to the winning captain by King George V.

This near disaster was an early warning of the need to control football crowds more closely. The FA acknowledged this by making all subsequent Finals strictly all ticket.

Two days after their Wembley disappointment, West Ham United had the consolation of winning promotion for the first time after only four years in the League.

Between the Wars

Facts

On Monday, April 30, West Ham went to Hillsborough and beat Sheffield Wednesday 2-0, a win which took them to the top of the Second Division, ahead of both Notts County and Leicester City on goal difference.

On May 5, the last Saturday of the 1922-23 season, West Ham's final game was at home to second-placed County. Leicester, meanwhile, were away to mid-table Bury.

Notts County beat West Ham 1-0 and went up as Second Division Champions, but the Hammers were still promoted as runners-up on goal difference because Bury beat Leicester.

The leading lights of West Ham's promotion campaign were centre forward Vic Watson, goalkeeper Ted Hufton and winger Jimmy Ruffell.

On January 30, 1923, Lord Kinnaird died. A Scottish international and the winner of five English FA Cup-winner's medals with Old Etonians, Kinnaird had been President of the FA for 33 years.

Since the end of the First World War, amateur football clubs had been increasing the frequency with which they used substitutes. This was frowned upon by the game's governing bodies.

In order to resist this trend and ensure that it did not spill over into the professional game, the International Board redrafted the rules specifically to emphasise that only 11 players were permitted in any game unless the match was a friendly and unless the use of substitutes had been agreed by the two captains in advance.

The growth of English football continued into the 1923-24 season. The League was enlarged again to 88 clubs by increasing the Third Division (North) from 20 to 22 clubs - this created four divisions, each of 22 teams.

 **Facts**   **Between the Wars**

At the end of 1922-23, both clubs relegated from Division Two went into the Third Division (North) - these were Rotherham County and Wolverhampton Wanderers.

One club - Nelson - was promoted to the Second Division from Division Three (North), which had previously been composed of 20 clubs.

One club - Bristol City - was promoted to the Second Division from Division Three (South).

This might have created a numerical imbalance, but the symmetry was maintained when Stalybridge Celtic dropped out of the Third Division (North) at the end of 1922-23 after only two seasons in the League.

There were consequently three vacancies in the League, which were filled by Bournemouth, Doncaster Rovers and New Brighton.

Bournemouth went into the Third Division (South), filling the vacancy created when Bristol City were promoted and no club was relegated to this division from Division Two.

Bournemouth were destined to remain in the Third Division (South) throughout its existence, until 1958.

Doncaster Rovers and New Brighton went into the Third Division (North). Their arrival, together with the fact that Rotherham County and Wolverhampton Wanderers were relegated from Division Two, maintained the total number of teams in Division Three (North) at 22, despite the demise of Stalybridge Celtic.

Doncaster Rovers had first joined the League as members of the Second Division in 1901. They lost their place in 1903, returned in 1904, then dropped out again in 1905. Their re-entry coincided with their move to a new, permanent home at Belle Vue.

Between the Wars

New Brighton lasted in the League until 1951, when they failed to gain re-election; their place was taken by Workington.

The English League Championship of 1923-24 was the closest ever, with Huddersfield Town beating Cardiff City into second place on goal average. (Goal average was calculated by dividing the number of goals scored by the number of goals conceded.)

At the end of the 1923-24 season, the top of the First Division table read as follows:

	P	W	D	L	F	A	Pts
Huddersfield Town	42	23	11	8	60	33	57
Cardiff City	42	22	13	7	61	34	57

This gave Huddersfield a goal average of 1.8181, which was 0.024 superior to that of Cardiff, who finished with a goal average of 1.7941.

 **Facts**   Between the Wars

At the age of 41 years and 8 months, Walter Hampson became the oldest player ever to appear in an FA Cup Final, helping Newcastle United to a 2-0 victory over Aston Villa.

Earlier in the season, Billy Meredith of Manchester City had become the oldest player to appear in any round of the FA Cup when he played against Newcastle United at the age of 49 years and 8 months.

The manager of Huddersfield Town was Herbert Chapman, the man who had been banned for life after the Leeds City debacle in 1919.

Between the Wars

Facts

In winning the 1924 Home International Championship, Wales defeated all three other nations in the same season for the first time. They beat Scotland 2-0 in Cardiff, England 2-1 at Blackburn, and Ireland 1-0 in Belfast.

In their one home match, both captains - Fred Keenor of Wales and Jimmy Blair of Scotland - played for the club at whose ground the game was played, Cardiff City.

In the same tournament, England played their first international match at Wembley - they drew 1-1 with Scotland.

At the start of the 1923-24 season, the Scottish League was expanded again. A 16-club Third Division was introduced, and there was to be a two-up, two-down system of promotion and relegation.

The 16 new clubs in Scottish League Division Three were as follows: Arthurlie, Beith, Brechin City, Clackmannan, Dumbarton Harp, Dykehead, East Stirlingshire, Galston, Helensburgh, Mid-Annandale, Montrose, Nithsdale Wanderers, Peebles Rovers, Queen of the South, Royal Albert and Solway Star.

One of the 16, Clackmannan, was making a return to the League after having been forced to drop out at the end of the 1921 season.

At the start of the 1924-25 season, the FA made two important changes to the rules of football. One concerned corners - before now, the ball was not in play until it had been touched by a player other than the one who took the corner kick. But henceforth it would be in play from the moment it left the corner semi-circle and, as a result, it was now for the first time legal to score direct from a corner.

The other change the FA made was to the offside rule (Law 6), which since 1866 had read as follows:

 **Facts**   Between the Wars

'When a player plays the ball, any player of the same side who at such moment of playing is nearer to his opponents' goal line is out of play and may not touch the ball himself nor in any way interfere with an opponent, or with the play, until the ball has again been played, unless there are at such moment of playing at least three of his opponents nearer their own goal-line'.

The FA's alteration to this rule was simply: 'From the first sentence of Law 6 delete the word "three" and substitute the word "two"'.

The above 16 words changed football for ever. The effects were apparent immediately - in the last season under the old rule, 4700 goals had been scored in the English Football League; in the first season under the new rule, that total increased to 6373.

The first English League player to score directly from a corner was Billy Smith, for Huddersfield Town against Arsenal on October 11, 1924.

In 1925-26, so many clubs in the Scottish Third Division got into financial difficulties that the League was suspended before the completion of the programme. The bottom club, Galston, played only 15 of their 30 scheduled matches and dropped out of the League for ever only two years after having joined it.

After leading Huddersfield Town to two League Championships in 1924 and 1925, Herbert Chapman moved south to manage Arsenal. His legacy to the Yorkshire team was still powerful, however, and they won the League again in 1926 under the managership of Cecil Potter.

Just before he left Huddersfield, Chapman bought outside right Alex Jackson from Aberdeen for £2500. He scored 16 goals in his first season in England, and made many more for centre forward George Brown, who finished the season with 35, a club record.

Between the Wars  Facts

Chapman quickly laid the foundations of Arsenal's future greatness. He persuaded club chairman Sir Henry Norris to buy inside forward Charlie Buchan from Sunderland.

Although Norris baulked at the asking price for Buchan of £4000, the two clubs made a deal in which the player moved for £2000 plus £100 per goal.

In his first season with Arsenal, Buchan scored exactly 20 goals - 19 in the League and one in the FA Cup, so Sunderland eventually got the amount they had originally asked for.

Norris was a property developer who first became involved with Arsenal in 1910 when they had gone into liquidation. One of his earliest plans for the club was a proposed merger with Fulham. When this failed to happen, he was influential in the club's move from Woolwich to their present home in Islington.

In 1919, when the Football League was expanded, Sir Henry Norris used his money to secure the Arsenal a place in the First Division which strictly they should not have had because they had finished only fifth in the Second Division in 1915.

Sir Henry Norris moved out of football in 1925 after being found guilty of financial irregularities, including the unauthorised use of a chauffeur. His team, by contrast, have never since been out of the First Division or the Premiership - a record.

In 1926, Manchester City became the first club to reach the FA Cup Final and be relegated in the same season.

In 1927, the FA Cup left England for the only time in its history when the trophy was won by Cardiff City. They beat Herbert Chapman's Arsenal 1-0 in the Final.

 **Facts**   **Between the Wars**

The year was a Cup double for Cardiff, who also won the Welsh Cup for the fifth time in their history.

On January 22, 1927, the League match between Arsenal and Sheffield United became the first to be broadcast live on radio.

While the BBC commentator described the action, another voice in the background called out numbers which referred to squares in a diagram of a football pitch printed in that week's *Radio Times*. After a goal was scored, the ball would be returned to the centre circle: this was square No 1 on the diagram, and this popularised the expression 'Back to square one'.

In the Home International Championship, England won at Hampden Park for the first time since 1904. Both England's goals were scored by Everton centre forward William Ralph Dean.

Dean was born in Birkenhead in 1907 and joined local club Tranmere Rovers in 1924. He moved to Everton in 1925, but his career was threatened when he fractured his skull in a motorbike accident.

Dean was almost universally known as Dixie because of his dark complexion (Dixieland - the American Deep South - was famous for its black slaves). The player himself hated the name.

In 1927-28, Dean scored 60 goals in 39 games for Everton in their Championship-winning season, a First Division record that has never been beaten.

One of the all-time greats, Dean scored 18 goals in only 16 appearances for England. In his League career, he scored 379 goals in 437 games.

As the table overleaf shows, Dean is the only England international ever to have scored more than a goal a game.

Between the Wars

Facts

England's Most Prolific Scorers

	Caps	Goals	Ratio
Dixie Dean	16	18	1.12
Tommy Lawton	23	22	0.96
Stan Mortensen	25	23	0.92
Nat Lofthouse	33	30	0.91
Jimmy Greaves	57	44	0.77
Gary Lineker	80	48	0.60
Geoff Hurst	49	24	0.49
Alan Shearer	38	18	0.47
Bobby Charlton	106	49	0.46
David Platt	62	27	0.43
Tom Finney	76	30	0.39

William Ralph Dean died in 1980 at Goodison Park after watching Everton play Liverpool.

On September 14, 1928, Jimmy McGrory set a Scottish First Division individual scoring record when he netted eight goals in Celtic's 9-0 victory over Dunfermline Athletic.

In 1927-28, Jim Smith of Ayr United in the Scottish Second Division set a British record of 66 goals in a season. This magnificent tally was run up in 38 matches.

Bathgate dropped out of the Scottish Second Division during the 1928-29 season and were not replaced, thus reducing the Scottish League from 40 clubs to 39.

Arthurlie, another Scottish Second Division club, resigned from the League with four matches unplayed. These were against Bo'ness, East Fife, Forfar Athletic and Stenhousemuir.

 **Facts** Between the Wars

Despite these troubles in the lower reaches of the League, top-grade Scottish football had never been healthier on the field. In March, the national side came to Wembley and beat England 5-1. Three of their goals were scored by Alex Jackson of Huddersfield Town. At 5 feet 7 inches in height, Jackson was the tallest of a Scottish forward line that also featured 'The Wee Blue Devil', Rangers' Alan Morton.

When Arsenal's Charlie Buchan retired at the end of the 1927-28 season, manager Herbert Chapman moved swiftly and replaced him with David Jack, an inside right whom he bought from Bolton Wanderers for a then British record transfer fee of £10,890.

On August 25, 1928, Arsenal and Chelsea became the first League clubs to wear numbered shirts.

On April 6, 1929, Jock Buchanan of Rangers became the first player to be sent off in a Cup Final as the Gers went down 2-0 to Kilmarnock.

On May 15, England suffered their first ever defeat on foreign soil, losing 4-3 to Spain in Madrid.

Bradford City won Division Three (North), scoring 128 goals in the process, a League record.

The Scottish League was reorganised again, for the 16th time since 1900, this time into two Divisions of 20 clubs each. As there had previously been 19 in the Second Division and Bathgate had resigned during the previous season, this created two vacancies. These were filled by Brechin City and Montrose.

Brechin City had been formed in 1906 through the amalgamation of the Angus clubs Hearts and Harp. Despite the new team's grand name, the town in which it played was - and remains - the smallest place in the British Isles with its own League football team.

Between the Wars

The British Isles were not represented at the inaugural World Cup because of a dispute over payments to amateur players to compensate them for the regular earnings they would have lost by playing football for their countries. FIFA demanded that players be paid for what was known as broken time. The home countries claimed that to make such payments would damage the game and in 1928 all four of them withdrew from both FIFA and from the Olympic football competition.

The first World Cup was staged in Uruguay in 1930. Thirteen nations took part: Argentina, Belgium, Bolivia, Brazil, Chile, France, Mexico, Paraguay, Peru, Romania, Uruguay, the USA and Yugoslavia.

Montrose, the other newcomers, were founded in 1879 and later merged with Montrose United. Nicknamed The Gable Endies, Montrose play their home matches at a ground called Links Park.

 **Facts**   **Between the Wars**

The first World Cup Final was played in front of 90,000 people at the Centenary Stadium, Montevideo on July 30, 1930. The match was between the hosts, Uruguay, and neighbouring Argentina.

1930 World Cup Final

Uruguay	4	Argentina	2
Dorado, Cea, Iriarte, Castro		*Peucelle, Stabile*	

Uruguay: Ballesteros, Nasazzi, Mascheroni, Andrade, Fernandez, Gestido, Dorado, Scarone, Castro, Cea, Iriarte
Argentina: Botasso, Della Torre, Paternoster, J. Evaristo, Monti, Suarez, Peucelle, Varallo, Stabile, Ferreyra, M. Evaristo

At the end of the match, the World Cup was presented to Jose Nasazzi, the captain of Uruguay, by Jules Rimet, a French lawyer who had become President of FIFA in 1921.

Between the Wars

Six years after taking over as manager, Herbert Chapman led Arsenal to the League Championship in 1931.

This was Arsenal's first Championship since joining the Football League in 1893.

Arsenal were the first club from south of the River Trent to win the English League Championship.

Herbert Chapman was the first man to manage two different Championship-winning sides.

Jack Lambert set a club scoring record with 38 goals in the season. Arsenal's other big guns were 28-goal Cliff Bastin, Joe Hulme (14 goals), David Jack (31 goals) and Alex James.

Arsenal won the League with a record number of points - 66.

Arsenal scored 127 goals in the 42-game season - a huge number, but one fewer than runners-up Aston Villa.

In the 1930-31 season, Arsenal failed to score in only one match - a 0-0 draw with Huddersfield Town at Highbury on March 7.

Third-placed Sheffield Wednesday also scored over a hundred goals; at the bottom of the table, relegated Manchester United conceded 115.

West Bromwich Albion became the first club to win the FA Cup and gain promotion in the same season. They were runners-up in the Second Division, seven points behind Everton, whom they beat in the semi-final of the Cup. In the Final, they beat Birmingham City 2-1.

 **Facts**　　　　　　　　　**Between the Wars**

On September 5, 1931, Celtic's Scotland international goalkeeper, John ('Jock') Thompson, aged 23, was killed after sustaining a kick in the head when he dived at the feet of Rangers' forward Sam English during the Old Firm clash at Ibrox.

In 1931, Wigan Borough of the Third Division (North) became the first team to resign from the English Football League during the course of a season. They had played only six games, and their record was expunged.

Wigan Athletic were founded in 1932 to replace Borough, but the new club did not gain a place in the Football League until 1978. Their most famous supporter is believed to be former Russian leader Mikhail Gorbachev - this sounds as if it must be apocryphal, but may not be.

Between the Wars

Facts

Reigning Champions Arsenal strove to go one better in 1931-32, reaching the Final of the FA Cup and pushing hard near the top of the First Division throughout the season. But they finished the season empty-handed - they were runners-up to Everton in the League and lost the FA Cup Final 2-0 to Newcastle United.

In 1931-32, the Champions of all four divisions of the English Football League - Everton, Wolverhampton Wanderers, Lincoln City and Fulham - all scored more than 100 goals in the season.

The outcome of the 1932 FA Cup Final turned on a controversial refereeing decision. Newcastle's Jimmy Richardson chased the ball to the byline and then centred for Jack Allen to score. But many people - especially the Arsenal defenders - thought the ball had gone out of play before Richardson reached it, and newsreel footage of the match tends to support this view. The match is sometimes known as The Over-the-Line Goal Final.

Everton's Championship victory came in their first season back in the top flight of English football.

The last club to have won the First Division in their first season back was Liverpool in 1906.

In 1932, Motherwell became the first team other than Celtic or Rangers to win the Scottish League Championship since Third Lanark in 1904. They finished five points ahead of second-placed Rangers and scored a record 119 goals in the 38-game season.

Motherwell's leading scorer was centre forward Bill McFadyean, with 52 goals in 34 games.

 **Facts**   **Between the Wars**

Sam Weaver of Newcastle United and England became the game's first acknowledged long-throw expert - he could throw the ball a distance of some 30 yards, from the touchline to the middle of the penalty area.

In November 1932, Armadale and Bo'ness were expelled from the Scottish League after being unable to meet match guarantees. They were not replaced, thus reducing the Scottish League to 38 clubs.

On December 7, 1932, Ted Parris of Bradford City became the first black player to be capped by Wales in their 4-1 victory over Northern Ireland at Wrexham. The second was George Berry of Wolverhampton Wanderers, who made his debut against West Germany in 1979.

How are the mighty fallen. Arsenal were beaten 2-0 in the third round of the 1932-33 FA Cup by Third Division Walsall. Although every leading club has suffered a Cup upset at some time in its history, this is the classic case.

The First Division leaders were weakened by a flu epidemic which robbed them of Eddie Hapgood, Bob John and Jack Lambert. In addition, manager Herbert Chapman dropped Joe Hulme.

Walsall's first goal against Arsenal was scored after an hour's play by centre forward Gilbert Alsop, who headed home from a corner. Five minutes later, Bill Sheppard scored the second from the penalty spot. Tommy Black, the defender who committed the foul in the area, was immediately transfer-listed and never played for Arsenal again.

Arsenal did have the consolation of winning the League for the second time in three seasons and the third time since 1931.

Between the Wars

Facts

The Gunners began the 1934-35 season where they had left off the previous spring, and went on to their fourth Championship. But their season was overshadowed by the untimely death of manager Herbert Chapman, who succumbed to pneumonia on January 6, 1935, after watching the Arsenal Third XI play at Guildford.

The first manager to win the League Championship with two different clubs, Herbert Chapman was perhaps the greatest tactician and shrewdest transfer market dealer in the history of the game. The only other managers whose achievements even stand comparison with his are Brian Clough (Derby County and Nottingham Forest), Kenny Dalglish (Liverpool and Blackburn Rovers), and Alex Ferguson (Aberdeen and Manchester United), who all won League titles with two different British clubs.

Tactically, Chapman is best remembered for his development of the stopper, or centre back, at the heart of the defence as a response to the challenge of the new offside rule. It seems, however, that the ploy was not his idea but that of one of his players, Charlie Buchan, who forcefully suggested that Arsenal's centre half, Jack Butler, should undertake that role. It was first tried out against West Ham United in 1925-26, and Arsenal won the match 4-0.

The son of a Yorkshire coal miner, Herbert Chapman was born in 1875, eight years before Arsenal itself was founded. Although he studied mining engineering at Sheffield Technical College, he did not follow in his father's footsteps. Instead, he played football for Stalybridge Rovers, Rochdale, Grimsby, Swindon, Sheppey United, Worksop, Northampton, Sheffield United, Notts County and Tottenham Hotspur. After two years at White Hart Lane, he moved back to Northampton as player manager before moving to Leeds City and then Huddersfield. His life was not without controversy, but the histories of great men seldom are.

 **Facts** Between the Wars

Herbert Chapman's influence was not confined to the pitch. He lobbied tirelessly in other areas, being responsible for (among other things) the name of the local tube station being changed from Gillespie Road to Arsenal; the use of numbers on the players' shirts, rubber studs, all-weather pitches and floodlighting.

The referee of the 1934 FA Cup Final was Hertfordshire schoolteacher Stanley Rous. Later that year, Rous was appointed FA Secretary and from 1961 to 1974 was President of FIFA. The author of the simplified set of 17 Laws under which football is played today, Rous was knighted in 1949.

The 1934 FA Cup was won by Manchester City, who beat Portsmouth 2-1 in the Final through goals from Freddy Tilson.

Between the Wars

Facts

The other star of the City team was goalkeeper Frank Swift, then aged 19, who was so overcome at the final whistle that he collapsed in his goal as he bent to pick up his gloves and had to be helped up to the Royal Box to receive his medal.

Frank Swift was famous for his agility and his huge hands, which were known as 'the frying pans'. After the Second World War, he went on to become the first goalkeeper to captain England.

When Frank Swift retired, he became a newspaper sports writer. He travelled with Manchester United to watch them play Red Star Belgrade in the quarter finals of the 1958 European Cup and was killed in the Munich air crash on the return journey.

 **Facts**

Between the Wars

The second World Cup was held in Italy in 1934. The tournament was hijacked by the ruling Fascists, who sought to use it as an instrument of propaganda and a showcase of extreme nationalism. As the Italian delegate to FIFA said, with evident satisfaction: 'Our guests felt the pulsating of the masculine energies of a bursting vitality in this our Mussolini's Italy'.

Sixteen nations took part in the 1934 World Cup finals - Argentina, Austria, Belgium, Brazil, Czechoslovakia, Egypt, France, Germany, Holland, Hungary, Italy, Romania, Spain, Sweden, Switzerland and the USA.

Pressure on officials was intense, and home advantage was more than usually favourable to the host nation. It was therefore no surprise when Italy reached the Final in Rome on June 10, 1934. Their opponents were Czechoslovakia.

The captains of both Italy and Czechoslovakia were goalkeepers.

1934 World Cup Final

Italy	2	Czechoslovakia	1
Orsi, Schiavio		Puc	

(after extra time: score after 90 minutes 1-1)

ITALY: Combi, Monzeglio, Allemandi, Ferraris, Monti, Bertolini, Guaita, Meazza, Schiavio, Ferrari, Orsi
CZECHOSLOVAKIA: Planicka, Zenizek, Ctyroky, Kostalek, Cambal, Krcil, Junek, Svoboda, Sobotka, Nejedly, Puc

The Jules Rimet trophy was presented to Italian captain Combi by Benito Mussolini, the Fascist leader of Italy.

Between the Wars

 **Facts**

The international between England and new World Champions Italy on November 14, 1934, was a notoriously bruising encounter which became known as The Battle of Highbury.

After a quiet opening, the Battle of Highbury exploded into aggressive life after Italian captain Lusito Monti - a former Argentine citizen - was forced to leave the field with a broken foot after going into a tackle with Arsenal's Ted Drake.

Monti's teammates thought that this injury had been caused by foul play, and thereafter their challenges became very physical.

Captain Eddie Hapgood was among the wounded Englishmen - his nose was broken by an elbow in the face. The Italians had enormous incentives to win - money, cars and, perhaps most attractive of all, exemption from military service.

Yet, despite missing a penalty, England went three up in 15 minutes, with two goals from Eric Brook - the man who had missed from the spot - and another from Drake. In the second half, Italy came back strongly with two goals from Guiseppe Meazza, who also hit the bar. But there was no further scoring, and England won 3-2.

Hapgood said after the match: 'It was difficult to play like a gentleman when somebody closely resembling an enthusiastic member of the Mafia is wiping his studs down your legs'.

The Battle of Highbury featured seven Arsenal players - a record number of players from one club in an international match.

In the League, Arsenal went from strength to strength despite the death of Herbert Chapman. Under new manager George Allison, they won the Championship in 1935, their third consecutive League title, scoring 115 goals in the process, 42 of them through Ted Drake.

 **Facts**   **Between the Wars**

Ellis Rimmer scored in every round of the 1935 FA Cup as his team, Sheffield Wednesday, carried off the trophy, beating West Bromwich Albion 4-2 in the Final.

At the end of the 1935-36 season, Aston Villa and Blackburn Rovers, founder members of the Football League, were relegated from the First Division for the first time in their history.

In 1937, Millwall became the first Third Division club to reach the semi-finals of the English FA Cup. They lost 2-1 to the eventual winners, Sunderland.

On April 24, 1937, the Scottish Cup Final at Hampden Park was watched by a British record crowd of 146,433. Celtic beat Aberdeen 2-1.

A week earlier, 149,547 people had paid to see Scotland lose 3-1 to England at Hampden Park. This remained the record attendance for an international match until the 1950, when 199,854 people attended the World Cup Final between Brazil and Uruguay at the Maracana Stadium, Rio de Janeiro.

At Wembley on May 1, 1937, a relatively sparse crowd of 93,495 saw Sunderland win the FA Cup for the first time in their great history after a 3-1 Final victory over Preston North End.

The scorer of Sunderland's second goal in the 1937 Final was their captain, England international Horatio Stratton ('Raich') Carter (1913-94), thought by many to have been the greatest inside forward of the inter-War years.

The third World Cup was held in France in 1938. FIFA hoped to attract 16 finalists, and although 36 of the 57 FIFA member nations originally entered the competition, only fifteen nations eventually took part - Belgium, Brazil, Cuba, Czechoslovakia, Dutch East Indies, France, Germany, Holland, Hungary, Italy, Norway, Poland, Romania, Sweden and Switzerland.

Between the Wars

Facts

Of the rest, Argentina withdrew in something like pique after being turned down as hosts. With war in central Europe now imminent, Mexico and the USA withdrew from the competition; Spain, already consumed by civil war, pulled out before the start of the qualifying tournament; Austria qualified and would have taken part in the tournament had it not been for the fact that, by the start of the finals, they had ceased to exist as a nation after Anschluss with Germany. The FAs of England, Ireland, Scotland and Wales were still in dispute with FIFA, so none of the British nations took part.

Because there were only 15 nations participating, Sweden were given a bye in the first round of matches.

The 1938 World Cup Final was played at the Parc des Princes, Paris on June 19 in front of 55,000 people.

The 1938 World Cup Final

Italy	4	Hungary	2
Coulassi (2), Piola (2)		*Titkos, Sarosi*	

ITALY: Olivieri, Foni, Rava, Serantoni, Andreolo, Locatelli, Biavati, Meazza, Piola, Ferrari, Coulassi
HUNGARY: Szabo, Polgar, Biro, Szalay, Lazar, Sas, Vincze, Sarosi, Zsengeller, Titkos

Italy became the first nation to retain the World Cup. They also retained it for longer than anyone else, because the Second World War broke out in September 1939 and the next World Cup was not held until 1950.

 **Facts**   Between the Wars

Another attendance record was set on January 2, 1939, when 118,567 people gathered at Ibrox to watch Rangers' traditional New Year match against Celtic.

Portsmouth won the 1939 FA Cup, beating bookies' favourites Wolverhampton Wanderers 4-1 in the Final. Although Portsmouth have never won the trophy before or since, they hold the unique distinction of holding it for longer than any other club - the next Cup Final was not played until 1946.

At the start of the 1938-39 season, Arsenal manager George Allison spent a record £14,000 on Wolverhampton Wanderers' Welsh international Bryn Jones.

On November 16, 1938, Willie Hall equalled the England scoring record with five goals in the Home International match against Northern Ireland at Maine Road, Manchester. The final score was England 7 Northern Ireland 0.

On May 13, 1939, England played World Champions Italy in Milan. Although many people feared a repeat of the 1934 Battle of Highbury, this match was relatively pacific, and the teams drew 2-2. Tommy Lawton of Everton scored first for England; Biavati equalised early in the second half. Then centre forward Piola put the Italians ahead when he diverted the ball into the net with his fist - the offence went unnoticed by the referee. After a long period of England pressure, they finally equalised with a goal by Willie Hall of Tottenham Hotspur.

When Britain declared war on Germany on September 3, 1939, Blackpool were top of Division One and Arsenal were in second place. Football was suspended for the duration of the hostilities, and the League did not recommence until the start of the 1946-47 season.

Between the Wars

Facts

In 1941, an English-language propaganda broadcast by Rome Radio claimed that the Italians had captured Arsenal forward Cliff Bastin and were holding him as a prisoner of war. This attempt to undermine British morale was unsuccessful because it was common knowledge in this country that Bastin had failed his army medical on the grounds of deafness and had never left the country.

Many footballers became army fitness trainers. Some people objected that this was favouritism, and demanded to know why more professional players were not sent into action in the front line. But most ordinary people were delighted to play training matches under the supervision of - and sometimes on the same side as - the great stars they had watched from the terraces before the War.

Among the leading players who became drill instructors during the Second World War were Ted Drake of Arsenal, Sam Bartram of Charlton Athletic and Tommy Lawton of Everton.

POSTWAR FOOTBALL

Postwar Football

Facts

The Second World War ended in August 1945. Although the Football League was not ready to restart in full until the 1946-47 season, the FA recommenced the Cup for 1945-46 on a two-leg, home-and-away basis.

The 1946 Cup campaign was marred by the Burnden Park disaster on March 9, when 33 people were crushed to death and more than 500 injured at Bolton Wanderers' sixth round match with Stoke City. The ground was full to its 65,000 capacity, but more than 20,000 other people were milling around outside. Many had turned up in the hope of catching a glimpse of Stoke star Stanley Matthews. They forced their way into the stadium shortly before kick-off, and the weight of the extra people caused a crash barrier to collapse.

In the aftermath of the tragedy, the Moelwyn Hughes Report recommended limitations on the size of crowds and the licensing of football grounds.

The FA Cup semi-final replay at Maine Road, Manchester, between Derby County and Birmingham City was watched by a crowd of 80,407, which remains the record attendance for a British midweek match at any venue other than Wembley.

This match was held in the afternoon, and the huge crowd it attracted alarmed the government who were concerned about the popularity of football leading to absenteeism from work. They quickly passed legislation to ensure that henceforth matches on working days should be evening kick-offs only.

After six years of War, many people were keen to make the best use of their leisure time and football became more popular than ever before. The greatly increased sums that League clubs were taking on the turnstiles were not, however, lead to an increase in the players' wages. This caused discontent and threats of strikes unless pay was increased from its pre-War ceiling of £8 a week. The threat of industrial action got a result of sorts - the players won an increase to £9 a week.

 **Facts**   Postwar Football

Bolton Wanderers eventually reached the semi-final of the 1946 FA Cup competition, in which they lost 2-0 to Charlton Athletic. The other semi-final was won by Derby County, who beat Birmingham City 5-1 on aggregate.

The 1946 FA Cup Final was held on April 27 at its now traditional Wembley venue. Derby County were favourites, not least because they had been greatly strengthened by the recent purchase of Raich Carter from Sunderland and Peter Doherty from Manchester City. Although they won - handsomely, in the end - they needed extra time and an own goal from Charlton's Herbert Turner to set them on their way.

A minute later, Turner equalised with a deflected goal for Charlton, thus becoming the first man to score for both teams in a Wembley Cup Final.

During the summer, Dynamo Moscow toured Britain. The Russians led a cloistered existence while they were abroad, eating all their meals at the Soviet Embassy in London and insisting that at least one of their matches be refereed by a Russian.

A the start of their first match, against Chelsea at Stamford Bridge, they presented their opponents with bunches of flowers. Then they drew 3-3 with the Londoners in front of 82,000 people.

In their next match, Dynamo Moscow beat Cardiff City 10-1, then returned to the capital for a game against Arsenal, who fielded Stanley Matthews and Stan Mortensen as guests. The match was played at White Hart Lane because Highbury was being rebuilt. In thick fog, the Russians won 4-3.

In their next game, the Russians drew 2-2 with Rangers. They were then slated to play an FA XI at Villa Park but flew home without notice before the kick off.

Postwar Football

Facts

Jack Stamps might have won the Cup for Derby in normal time, but his goal-bound effort was thwarted when the ball burst after he had kicked it and it was gathered easily by Charlton keeper Sam Bartram.

In extra time, Derby pulled away, with a goal from Doherty and two from Stamps - final score Derby County 4 Charlton Athletic 1.

The 1946 FA Cup was Derby County's first major honour since joining the Football League in 1888.

In Scotland, a new competition was launched in the 1945-46 season to herald the postwar era. However, the League Cup failed at first to attract a great deal of public interest.

The inaugural Scottish League Cup was won by Aberdeen, who beat Rangers 3-2 in the Final at Hampden. Aberdeen also won the FA Cup in the same year, thus becoming the first British club to do the so-called 'new double'.

At the start of the 1946-47 season, the Scottish League was re-formed again, now with 30 teams divided into Division 'A' of 16 and Division 'B' of 14. This was eight fewer teams than had competed in the Scottish League in 1939 - the clubs that had dropped out in the meantime were Brechin City, East Stirlingshire, Edinburgh City, Forfar Athletic, King's Park, Leith Athletic, Montrose and St Bernard's.

The first English Football League Champions of the postwar era were Liverpool - the 1947 title was the fifth in their history.

 **Facts**   Postwar Football

On October 3, 1946, Len Shackleton scored six goals on his debut for
Second Division Newcastle United after his £13,000 transfer from Bradford
Park Avenue. Newcastle went on to beat Newport County 13-0, despite
missing a penalty in the second minute.

**Newport County eventually conceded a total of 133 goals in the
42-match season and were relegated to the Third Division (South).**

Charlton Athletic put last year's disappointment behind them by beating
Burnley 1-0 in the 1947 FA Cup Final.

**The winning goal was scored in extra time by Chris Duffy. The
other incident of note in the match was that - for the second year
running - the ball burst.**

Doncaster Rovers had a record-breaking season as they won the Third
Division (North) - the most wins (33), the most away wins (18), the most
away points (37) and the highest points total (72) while there were two
points for a win. They also had the League's leading scorer - Clarrie Jordan,
with 42 goals in the season.

**In 1946, the FAs of England, Northern Ireland, Scotland and Wales
finally rejoined FIFA, from which they had withdrawn in 1928
because of a dispute over broken time. To celebrate their re-entry,
the Home Nations played a Rest of Europe XI in an exhibition
match in front of a crowd of 135,000 at Hampden Park, Glasgow.**

Great Britain won the match 6-1, with three goals from Wilf Mannion, two
from Tommy Lawton and one from Billy Steel.

**The only player in the Rest of Europe XI with English as his native
language was Johnny Carey of Manchester United and Eire.**

Postwar Football

Facts

England centre forward Tommy Lawton moved from Everton to Chelsea after the War but never settled at the London club because of a contractual dispute. In 1947, he was sensationally transferred to Third Division Notts County for a record fee of £20,000 plus wing half Bill Dickson.

At the start of the 1947-48 season, the Scottish League was increased from 30 clubs to 32. The two teams added to Division 'B' were Leith Athletic - returning after a season's absence - and newcomers Stirling Albion.

Stirling Albion were founded in 1945 after the demise of King's Park, another club from the same town. King's Park had dropped out of the Scottish League in 1939; thereafter, they had been plagued by accusations of financial mismanagement and had their ground at Forthbank Park destroyed by German bombs during the War. Stirling Albion had a new ground at Annfield Park.

On January 17, 1948, a record First Division crowd of 83,260 watched Manchester United draw 1-1 with Arsenal. The match was played at United's temporary home, Maine Road.

Old Trafford had suffered greater bomb damage in the War than any other Football League ground - the Main Stand and some of the terraces had been destroyed in 1941 by two German bombs and the pitch itself had been scorched by the resulting inferno. The refurbished stadium did not open again until 1949.

On March 27, 1948, a crowd of 143,570 attended the Scottish FA Cup semi-final between Rangers and Hibernian at Hampden Park, Glasgow - this is a British attendance record for a match other than a cup final.

 **Facts**   **Postwar Football**

Arsenal won the 1948 Championship, leading the table from start to finish. They conceded only 32 goals (a First Division record) and more than 2,000,000 watched their games. This was their sixth title, bringing them level with Aston Villa and Sunderland.

The 1948 FA Cup was won by Manchester United, who beat Blackpool 4-2 in a classic Wembley Final.

Blackpool's Stan Mortensen scored in every round of the 1947-48 FA Cup, a total of 10 goals.

On May 4, 1949, a plane carrying the Torino team back from a testimonial game in Portugal against Benfica hit the Basilica of Superga, a village outside Turin. Among the 31 people killed in the crash were 18 footballers, including the entire Torino first team who made up most of the Italian national side.

Torino had been the dominant club in Italy throughout the 1940s, with five successive Championships and victory in the 1943 Italian Cup. In 1948, they had beaten Alessandria 10-0, the highest margin of victory in the history of Serie A.

The victims included Leslie Lievesely, their English manager, captain Valentino Mazzola and Ezio Loik.

After the crash, Torino fielded their youth team in the remaining four matches of the season and, as a mark of respect, their opponents fielded their youth teams against them. Torino won all these games and, with them, the Italian Championship.

Postwar Football

 **Facts**

In 1948-49, the English League Championship was won for the first time by Portsmouth. Although they had not a single international player, Pompey were a formidable side with an unbeaten home record - in the 1948-49 season, they won 18 and drew three of their 21 matches at Fratton Park.

Portsmouth also had a good Cup run, but lost in the semi-final to unfancied Leicester City of the Second Division.

The 1948 FA Cup went to Wolverhampton Wanderers. They won the Final 3-1 against a Leicester side suffering from the absence through illness of their promising inside right Don Revie.

Wolverhampton Wanderers captain Billy Wright received the FA Cup from Princess Elizabeth.

 **Facts**   **Postwar Football**

The architect of the great Wolves sides of the period was their former centre half Stan Cullis, who had taken over as secretary manager in 1948 from Ted Vizard. The 1949 FA Cup was the start of the most successful period in the club's history, other highlights of which included three League Championships in 1954, 1958 and 1959, and a second FA Cup in 1960.

In 1948-49, Rangers became the first Scottish club to do the domestic treble of League Championship, FA Cup and League Cup.

On March 8, 1950, John Charles of Leeds United became Wales' youngest international when he played for them against Northern Ireland at Wrexham at the age of 18 years 71 days.

Portsmouth retained the League title in 1950, but only just. In 1949, they had romped home, five points ahead of runners-up Manchester United. This year, they needed to beat Aston Villa on the last day of the season to make sure. They won 5-1, making Wolverhampton Wanderers only the second team in League history to be denied the title by goal difference (1.95 against 1.55). The other was Cardiff City, who had been edged out by Huddersfield Town in 1924.

Postwar Football

Facts

1949-50 Top of the First Division Final Table

	P	W	D	L	F	A	Pts
Portsmouth	42	22	9	11	74	38	53
Wolverhampton Wanderers	42	20	13	9	76	49	53

Arsenal won the FA Cup without leaving London - even their semi-final was played at White Hart Lane because their opponents were fellow Londoners Chelsea.

Losing finalists Liverpool also had a local derby in the semi-finals, beating Everton 2-0.

Arsenal won the FA Cup Final 2-0, both goals being scored by Reg Lewis.

In Scotland, Rangers did the double and completed their second hat-trick of FA Cup wins. The only shadow over their season was defeat in the semi-finals of the League Cup by East Fife, the eventual winners of the trophy.

On September 21, 1949, the Republic of Ireland played their first international on British soil, beating England 2-0 at Goodison Park. They were captained by Johnny Carey of Manchester United, and their goals were scored by Con Martin of Leeds United from a penalty and Peter Farrell of Everton, who was playing for the visiting team on his home ground.

 **Facts**   **Postwar Football**

After a 12-year gap because of the Second World War, the fourth World Cup was staged in Brazil in June and July 1950. Twelve nations took part - Bolivia, Brazil, Chile, England, Italy, Mexico, Paraguay, Spain, Sweden, Switzerland, Uruguay, the USA and Yugoslavia.

Scotland could have gone to the 1950 World Cup finals, too, but declined to take part after losing to England in the Home International in Glasgow. FIFA had promised the Home Nations two places in the finals, but the Scottish FA announced that they would go only as British Champions. They needed just a draw to win the tournament, but lost 1-0 to England, whose goal was scored by Roy Bentley of Chelsea.

After the match, England captain Billy Wright and Scotland captain George Young pleaded with the Scottish FA to reverse their decision, but to no avail.

West Germany were ineligible for the 1950 World Cup because they were not yet members of FIFA.

Scotland's place in the 1950 World Cup finals was offered to Portugal, but they turned it down.

Turkey qualified for the 1950 World Cup finals but then withdrew - their place was offered to France, who accepted and then changed their minds when they learned the proposed itinerary.

India also withdrew from the 1950 World Cup finals because they refused to wear boots.

Because of these withdrawals, the four South American qualifiers - Bolivia, Brazil, Chile and Uruguay - made it through to the finals without playing a match.

Postwar Football

It had originally been thought that the finalists would be divided into four groups of four, but it was so late in the day when it became apparent that only 13 countries would be taking part that other arrangements could not be made - this created a lop-sided tournament with two groups of four, one group of three and one group of only two.

The finals began satisfactorily for England, who beat Chile 2-0 in their opening match with goals by Stan Mortensen and Wilf Mannion. There was little warning of the disaster to come.

The next match was one of the great humiliations in England's footballing history - they lost 1-0 to the USA. The winning goal was scored by Haitian-born Larry Gaetjens. Then they lost 1-0 to Spain and failed to progress beyond the group stage.

Instead of a dramatic knockout, the later stages of the 1950 World Cup were a pool of four countries - Brazil, Spain, Sweden and Uruguay. Brazil and Uruguay beat Sweden and Spain and then faced each other in the deciding match - effectively the Final. This was played at the Maracana Stadium, Rio de Janeiro, on July 16, 1950, in front of the largest crowd in football history - 173,830 people paid, but history books record a total attendance of 199,854.

1950 World Cup 'Final'

Brazil	1	Uruguay	2
Friaca		*Schiaffino, Ghiggia*	

BRAZIL: Barbosa, Augusto, Juvenal, Bauer, Danilo, Bogode, Friaca, Zizinho, Ademir, Jair, Chico
URUGUAY: Maspoli, Gonzales, Tejera, Gambetta, Varela, Andrade, Ghiggia, Perez, Miguez, Schiaffino, Moran

 **Facts**   **Postwar Football**

At the end of the match, the football World Cup - which had newly been named The Jules Rimet Trophy in honour of the French President of FIFA - was awarded to Obdullo Varela, the captain of champions Uruguay.

For the 1950-51 season, the English League was enlarged to 92 clubs by increasing both the Third Division (North) and the Third Division (South) from 22 to 24 clubs.

The four new clubs thus admitted to the League for the first time were Scunthorpe United and Shrewsbury Town to the Third Division (North) and Colchester United and Gillingham to the Third Division (South).

Scunthorpe United had been founded in 1899. After entering the League, they won the Third Division Championship in 1958. Their best season in the Second Division was 1961-62, when they finished fourth.

Shrewsbury Town had been founded in 1886 and had twice won the Welsh Cup (1891 and 1938). After election to the English League, they went on to win the Third Division Championship in 1979 and 1994, and have since added a further four Welsh Cup victories - 1977, 1979, 1984 and 1985. In the FA Cup, they reached the sixth round in 1979 and 1982.

Colchester United were founded in 1937 as successors to amateur Colchester Town. They lost their League status in 1990, after finishing bottom of the Fourth Division, but returned in 1992 after winning the GM Vauxhall Conference. The greatest moment in the club's history is probably their victory over Leeds United in the fifth round of the FA Cup in 1971. Colchester won 3-2, and had been 3-0 ahead. Seven members of the team that achieved this great result were over 30 years of age, and it was thus that they acquired the nickname 'Grandad's Army'. In the Football League, Colchester United's best position was third in the Third Division (South) in 1956-57.

Postwar Football

Facts

Gillingham were founded in 1893 in the wake of the success of another local club, the Royal Engineers. They started life as Excelsior, but in 1894 turned professional and changed their name to New Brompton. They took their present name in 1913. They first joined the Third Division in 1920, but dropped out in 1938 before returning in 1950. Their major League honour has been the Fourth Division Championship in 1964 - their run of 52 home matches without defeat was a record which was not broken until 1981, when Liverpool completed a run of 85 home games without defeat. Gillingham's best **FA Cup** performance came in 1970, when they reached the fifth round.

On November 15, 1950, Leslie Compton of Arsenal became the oldest British player in history to make his international debut when he played for England against Wales at the age of 38 years 2 months.

On December 13, 1950, Scotland lost for the first time at home to foreign opposition when they went down 1-0 to Austria.

On May 27, 1950, Billy Steel of Derby County became the first Scot to be sent off in an international. Scotland lost 4-0 to Austria in Vienna.

A father and son - Alec (39) and David Herd (17) - played in the same Stockport County team as they beat Hartlepool 2-0 on the last day of the 1950-51 season.

Tottenham Hotspur won the League Championship for the first time in the season after they were promoted from Division Two. Among the stars of their team were two great managers of the future - Alf Ramsey at right back and Bill Nicholson at right half.

 **Facts**   Postwar Football

Newcastle United won the FA Cup, beating Blackpool 2-0 in the Final. Both goals were scored by Jackie Milburn, and the match is often known simply as 'Milburn's Final'. Many commentators believed that the Seasiders lost this match because they were over-reliant on Stan Mortensen, who was the First Division's leading scorer with 30 goals. Other Blackpool stars of the period were Footballer of the Year Harry Johnson and the incomparable Stanley Matthews on the wing.

George Robledo, the maker of Milburn's first goal, had come to England as a refugee following the revolution in his native Chile. He made his name with Barnsley just after the Second World War and then Newcastle bought him and his brother Ted for £26,500. In his career at St James' Park, George scored 91 goals in 164 matches. When they retired, the pair returned to South America.

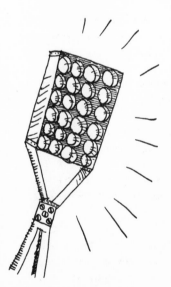

On September 19, 1951, Arsenal beat Hapoel Tel Aviv (Israel) 6-1 in the first official match under floodlighting since 1878. Floodlights had been built into the West Stand at Highbury in the 1930s on the orders of their great manager Herbert Chapman, but clubs had been banned from using them by the FA, which feared too much money might be spent.

Newcastle United won the FA Cup again in 1952, thus becoming the first club to retain the trophy in the 20th century.

The last club to win the FA Cup for two years in succession had been Blackburn Rovers (1890 and 1891).

Newcastle beat Arsenal 1-0 in the 1952 Final - the winning goal was scored by George Robledo.

Postwar Football

Facts

George Robledo was also the First Division's leading scorer, with 33 goals in the 1951-52 season.

Arsenal were desperately unfortunate in this match - Ray Daniel played with a plaster cast on his broken wrist, Doug Lishman had a septic cut and Jimmy Logie an internal haemorrhage. During the game, Walley Barnes had to go off with a knee injury after half an hour, reducing the Londoners to 10 men.

Manchester United won the 1952 Championship after finishing second in four seasons out of the five since the end of the Second World War. It was the third League title in their history, but their first since 1911.

England and Austria drew 2-2 at Wembley on November 28, 1951. The visitors scored first through Melchior, who had been set up by Ernst Ocwirk, their great ball-playing centre half who was nicknamed 'Clockwork' by the British press. England equalised through a penalty by Alf Ramsey and took the lead seven minutes from time through Nat Lofthouse. Two minutes later, however, Stojaspal brought the Austrians back level with another penalty for handball.

 # Facts

Postwar Football

On May 25, 1952, England beat Austria 3-2, thanks mainly to Nat Lofthouse, the Bolton Wanderers centre forward. He scored the first goal after 20 minutes, but Huber equalised almost immediately from a penalty after Froggatt had fouled Dienst. England regained their lead through Sewell of Sheffield Wednesday, then Dienst levelled again just before half time. Lofthouse scored the winner at the end of a 50-yard run, then went off injured but returned to help England hang on to their lead. Henceforth, Lofthouse was always popularly known as The Lion of Vienna.

The 1953 English Champions were Arsenal, winning their seventh League title - a record at the time. The race was very tight, and the Gunners only pipped Preston North End on the very last day of the season, when they beat Burnley 3-2 at home.

1952-53 Top of the First Division Final Table

	P	W	D	L	F	A	Pts
Arsenal	42	21	12	9	97	64	54
Preston North End	42	21	12	9	85	60	54

Arsenal and Preston North End were separated only by goal average - 1.51 against 1.41.

On September 24, 1952, Nat Lofthouse scored six goals for the Football League against the League of Ireland at Molineux - a record for this fixture.

Postwar Football

Facts

On Boxing Day, 1952, Sheffield Wednesday lost 5-4 at home to West Bromwich Albion and three of their players scored own goals. The unlucky trio were Vince Kenny, Norman Curtis and Eddie Gannon.

Sheffield Wednesday centre forward Derek Dooley broke a leg while challenging the Preston North End goalkeeper in a game on St Valentine's Day, 1953. The fracture turned gangrenous and had to be amputated. Dooley had scored 16 goals in 29 matches that season.

In the Scottish FA Cup on February 28, 1953, Celtic's Charlie Tully put the ball into the net direct from a corner against Falkirk. When the referee disallowed the goal because there had been spectators on the pitch, Tully put the ball in almost exactly the same spot - this time, the goal stood.

The great highlight of the 1952-53 season was the FA Cup Final between Blackpool and Bolton Wanderers. In the year of the accession of Queen Elizabeth II, it would probably be remembered as the Coronation Cup Final, but it is known as the Matthews Final because of the extraordinary performance of - and the nation's sentimental attachment to - one great man: Stanley Matthews.

Stanley Matthews had twice finished on the losing side in classic Cup Finals - in 1948, when Manchester United won and 1951, the year of Jackie Milburn.

 **Facts**   **Postwar Football**

Bolton went 3-1 up after 55 minutes and it looked as if history was about to repeat itself. At the age of 38, it was almost certainly Matthews' last appearance at Wembley. But after 68 minutes Stan Mortensen scored his own and Blackpool's second as Matthews began to show the world why he was called the Wizard of Dribble.

Bolton held on until the last minute of normal time, when Mortensen became the only man to score a hat trick in the Cup Final, equalising from a free kick just outside the area.

In extra time, Matthews went on another run and set up the winner for Perry, who became the only South African to score in the English FA Cup Final. Final score: Blackpool 4 Bolton Wanderers 3.

Postwar Football

Facts

Stanley Matthews played until 1965, retiring at the age of 50. He played 54 times for England. He was knighted in 1965.

Rangers did the double in Scotland, but it was a close run thing in both competitions. In the FA Cup, they needed a replay to overcome Aberdeen. Three days after securing the Cup, they beat Dundee 3-1 in their penultimate League match - this left them needing at least a draw in their last game at Queen of the South. The Dumfries team led for much of the game, but thanks to a 75th minute equaliser by Willie Waddell, they finished level on points with Hibernian but took the title because of a greatly superior goal average - 2.05 against 1.82. (If the Championship had been decided on goal difference, the Edinburgh team would have won it.)

1953-54 Top of the Scottish Division 'A' Final Table

	P	W	D	L	F	A	Pts
Rangers	30	18	7	5	80	39	43
Hibernian	30	19	5	6	93	51	43

Since Willie Struth took over as manager in 1920, Rangers had won 18 Championships, 10 FA Cups and three League Cups.

In 1953-54, a new force emerged in English football as Wolverhampton Wanderers won the Championship for the first time in their history. Founder members of the Football League and twice winners of the FA Cup in 1893 and 1908, their history had been otherwise unremarkable. The arrival of Stan Cullis as manager in 1948 and the development of the new so-called 'kick and rush' style led Wolves to the pinnacle of achievement. They were English champions again in 1958 and 1959.

 Facts   Postwar Football

Cullis claimed that Wolves were champions of the world, a boast which led, only slightly indirectly, to the inception of the European Cup in 1955-56.

Runners-up in the League were local rivals West Bromwich Albion, who did have the consolation of winning the FA Cup - they beat Preston North End 3-2 in the Final.

On November 25, 1953, England suffered their first ever home defeat by foreign opposition when they lost 6-3 to Hungary at Wembley Stadium.

Hungary were unbeaten in international football since 1950, with 20 wins in 23 games during that period.

The stars of their glorious victory were centre forward Sandor Kocsis, inside left Ferenc Puskas, Nandor Hidegkuti, who played 'in the gap', right half Jozsef Bozsik and goalkeeper Gyula Groscis.

Hidegkuti scored the opening goal for Hungary in the first minute. England equalised after 13 minutes through Sewell of Sheffield Wednesday, but then Hidegkuti scored again and Puskas added two more before Mortensen brought it back to 4-2 at half time. After the break, Bozsik scored and then Hidegkuti completed his hat trick. England's third goal came from an Alf Ramsey penalty.

Puskas was nicknamed The Galloping Major. At club level, he played centre forward for the Budapest club Kispest, which changed its name in 1949 to Honved and won four consecutive League titles. He retired in 1966, after scoring 83 goals in 84 internationals, a record surpassed only by Pele of Brazil.

Kocsis - nicknamed Golden Head - played at home for Ferencvaros and then for Honved. He was masterful in the air and scored 75 goals in 68 international appearances for his country.

Postwar Football

Hidegkuti played club football for MTK Budapest. Despite his Wembley hat trick, he was, overall, the least prolific of the trio. Nevertheless, he scored 39 goals in his 68 internationals.

The visit of the so-called Magic Magyars was a watershed in English international football. An even worse defeat was to follow in the return match, when England went to Budapest and were beaten 7-1 on May 23, 1954.

In Scotland, Celtic won the double. Rangers fell back from their pinnacle in 1953 - they were knocked of both the Scottish FA Cup and the League Cup at the semi-final stage and finished fourth in Division 'A'.

Jimmy Delaney became the only man ever to win the FA Cup in England, Scotland and Ireland. He won the 1954 FAI trophy with Derry City, and put the medal in his collection alongside those he had already won with Celtic in 1937 and Manchester United in 1948.

The 1954 World Cup finals were held in Switzerland. The format was changed yet again - this time there were four groups of four, each group containing two seeded countries who would not play each other.

The 16 finalists in the 1954 World Cup were Austria, Belgium, Brazil, Czechoslovakia, England, France, Hungary, Italy, Mexico, Scotland, South Korea, Switzerland, Turkey, Uruguay, West Germany and Yugoslavia.

Hungary were the clearest favourites in the history of the competition - most observers already thought of them as world champions in all but name. And they started off like winners, with beating South Korea 9-0 and West Germany 8-3.

 **Facts**   **Postwar Football**

England qualified for the finals by winning the Home International Championship. As in 1950, FIFA again offered a place to the runners-up in this competition and, in a change of their earlier policy, the Scots' FA this time accepted it.

After an unlucky 1-0 defeat by Austria, Scotland were demoralised by the resignation of manager Andy Beattie and proceeded to lose 7-0 to Uruguay.

England qualified from the group stage by drawing 4-4 with Belgium and beating Switzerland 2-0. The other seeds in their group were Italy.

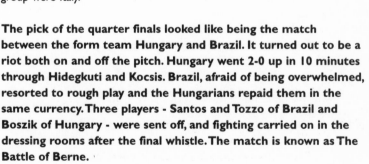

The pick of the quarter finals looked like being the match between the form team Hungary and Brazil. It turned out to be a riot both on and off the pitch. Hungary went 2-0 up in 10 minutes through Hidegkuti and Kocsis. Brazil, afraid of being overwhelmed, resorted to rough play and the Hungarians repaid them in the same currency. Three players - Santos and Tozzo of Brazil and Boszik of Hungary - were sent off, and fighting carried on in the dressing rooms after the final whistle. The match is known as The Battle of Berne.

Postwar Football

England lost in the quarter finals, 4-2 to Uruguay. In the other two quarter-finals, Austria beat hosts Switzerland 7-5, after having gone from 3-0 down to 5-3 up in only 10 minutes. West Germany - entering the World Cup for the first time after recognition by FIFA - beat Yugoslavia 2-0.

In the semi-finals, West Germany thrashed Austria 6-1, while Hungary beat Uruguay 4-2 in a classic.

The 1954 World Cup Final was held in front of 60,000 spectators at the Wankdorf Stadium, Berne on July 4, 1954.

Ferenc Puskas - the captain of Hungary - had missed the Battle of Berne and the semi-final through injury, but insisted on playing in the Final. The decision seemed vindicated when he opened the scoring after six minutes. Two minutes later, Czibor made the score Hungary 2 West Germany 0.

But the resilient Germans - under the guidance of Sepp Herberger, their manager since 1936 - hit back with a goal from Morlock and two more from Rahn. Final score: West Germany 3 Hungary 2

The 1954 World Cup Final teams were as follows:
West Germany: Turek, Posipal, Kohlmeyer, Eckel, Liebrich, Mai, Rahn, Morlock, O. Walter, F. Walter, Schaefer
Hungary: Grosics, Buzansky, Lantos, Bozsik, Lorant, Zakarias, Czibor, Kocsis, Hidegkuti, Puskas, Toth.

Although the Hungarian national side had twice humiliated England, at club level the tables were turned when Wolverhampton Wanderers beat Honved of Budapest 3-2 in an exhibition match under floodlights at Molineux in 1954-55. The visitors, orchestrated by Puskas, went two up with goals by Kocsis and Machos, but Wolves hit back after half time through a Hancocks penalty and two from Swinbourne.

 **Facts**   Postwar Football

It was after this match that Wolves manager Stan Cullis claimed his team were champions of the world and was thus instrumental in the creation of the European Cup the following season.

In 1955, Chelsea won the League Championship for the only time in their history. They were managed by former Arsenal star Ted Drake and are thus sometimes nicknamed Drake's Ducklings.

The inaugural European Cup was held during the 1955-56 season. Although entry into this competition eventually became through winning the domestic League Championship, it was at first by invitation. Chelsea were drawn to play Djurgarden of Sweden but withdrew on the advice of the English Football League, who opposed the European Cup because they feared it would cause fixture congestion.

In the FA Cup Final, Newcastle United beat Manchester City 3-1 with goals from Milburn, Mitchell and Hannah. City were hampered by the loss of right back Jimmy Meadows, who had to go off after 20 minutes with a knee injury. This was the second time a Magpies Cup victory had been aided by their opponents' loss of a player - the 1952 defeat of Arsenal had swung on the departure of Walley Barnes with the same kind of injury.

Postwar Football

Facts

On February 5, 1955, Tommy Briggs of Blackburn Rovers scored seven goals in the 8-3 defeat of Bristol Rovers - an English Second Division record.

On April 20, 1955, two pairs of brothers played for Wales in the Home International against Northern Ireland in Belfast - John and Mel Charles and Ivor and Len Allchurch. John Charles scored a hat trick in a 3-2 Welsh win.

In the Home International decider on April 2, 1955, England beat Scotland 7-2 at Wembley. This was the Scots' record defeat in this fixture, and mirrored their own record victory by the same score in 1878.

This was England's first win against the old enemy at Wembley since 1934. Dennis Wilshaw of Wolves scored four of their goals, Nat Lofthouse of Bolton another two. The seventh was scored by Manchester City inside right Don Revie.

Another landmark of this match was the debut of Duncan Edwards - at the age of 18 years 183 days, he was the youngest England international of the 20th century.

 **Facts**   **Postwar Football**

England's Youngest Full Internationals

James Prinsep	v Scotland	1879	aged 17 years 252 days
Tot Rostron	v Scotland	1881	aged 17 years 311 days
Clem Mitchell	v Wales	1880	aged 18 years 23 days
Duncan Edwards	v Scotland	1955	aged 18 years 183 days
Jimmy Brown	v Wales	1881	aged 18 years 210 days
Arthur Brown	v Wales	1904	aged 18 years 328 days
Rio Ferdinand	v Cameroon	1997	aged 19 years 10 days
Michael Owen	v Chile	1998	aged 18 years 59 days

There were two other England debuts in this match - Ken Armstrong of Chelsea and Jimmy Meadows of Manchester City. Neither player won another cap for his country.

In Scotland, for once the Old Firm won nothing. The League Championship went to Aberdeen, with Celtic three points behind in second place and Rangers in third. Clyde beat Celtic in the Scottish FA Cup in a replay after the first match had been drawn 1-1. The Scottish League Cup was won by Heart of Midlothian, who beat Motherwell 4-2 in the Final.

The Scottish League was reorganised yet again for the 1955-56 season and enlarged from 32 clubs to 37 - 18 in Division 'A' and 19 in Division 'B'.

The five newcomers and returnees were Berwick Rangers, Dumbarton, East Stirlingshire, Montrose and Stranraer.

1956 was Manchester's year. Manchester United won the Championship by a record margin under the two points for a win system, with 11 points more than runners-up Blackpool.

Manchester City won the FA Cup, beating Birmingham City 3-1 in a Final that will always be remembered as the one in which City keeper Bert Trautmann broke his neck but played on.

Postwar Football

Facts

German-born Trautmann had been held captive in England during the Second World War but settled here afterwards and, despite general anti-German feeling, became one of the country's most popular players. Even before his Cup Final heroics, he had been voted the Football Writers' Player of the Year for 1956.

City were 2-0 up at Wembley and cruising to victory when Trautmann was kicked as he dived at the feet of Birmingham's Peter Murphy. Dazed and reeling, he opted to carry on in goal, and the crowd sang 'For He's A Jolly Good Fellow'. Only after he had collected his winner's medal did he go for an x-ray which revealed an injury that could well have been fatal.

 **Facts**   **Postwar Football**

Manchester City's goals were scored by Joe Hayes, Jack Dyson and
Bobby Johnstone. Although he did not appear on the scoresheet,
another star was Don Revie, who returned to play at centre
forward after having been dropped by both club and country .

The first European Cup was won by Real Madrid, who beat Reims 4-3 in the
Final in Paris. That the Spanish champions were able to come back from 2-0
down is largely to the credit of their great Argentine-born front man
Alfredo di Stefano.

Although Di Stefano was a goalscoring No 9, he was not a centre
forward in the accepted sense of the term - he ran the play from
area to area. Born in Buenos Aires in 1926, he joined Real in 1953
and won 31 international caps for his adopted country, Spain.

In the absence of English champions Chelsea, Britain's sole representatives in
the European Cup were Hibernian. The Scots reached the semi-finals of the
competition, where they were knocked out by Reims.

In September 1955, Harold Bell missed a match for Tranmere
Rovers after 401 consecutive League appearances for the club -
a record.

On September 3, Wolverhampton Wanderers equalled Sunderland's record
for the number of goals scored away from home in the First Division when
they beat Cardiff City 9-1.

For the only time in its history, the Home International
Championship was a four-way tie between England, Northern
Ireland, Scotland and Wales. The man who made it happen was
Johnny Haynes of Fulham and England, who scored a last-minute
equaliser for his country in the final match against Scotland at
Hampden Park.

Postwar Football

Facts

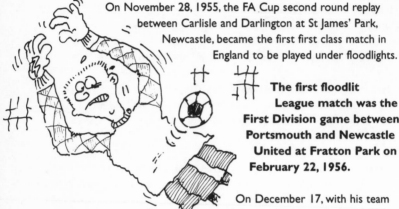

On November 28, 1955, the FA Cup second round replay between Carlisle and Darlington at St James' Park, Newcastle, became the first first class match in England to be played under floodlights.

The first floodlit League match was the First Division game between Portsmouth and Newcastle United at Fratton Park on February 22, 1956.

On December 17, with his team 4-0 up at Highbury, Arsenal left back Dennis Evans mistook a whistle in the crowd for the referee signalling the end of the match. He lashed the ball into his own net to give a final score Arsenal 4 Blackpool 1.

In Scotland, Rangers were the 1956 League Champions, Heart of Midlothian won the FA Cup and Aberdeen the League Cup.

At the start of the 1956-57 season, the Scottish League changed the name of Divisions 'A' and 'B' to the First and Second Divisions, respectively.

The English Football League dropped their opposition to the European Cup, and in 1956-57 Manchester United became England's first entrants into the competition.

Manchester United started well in European competition, defeating Belgian champions Anderlecht 2-0 in the first leg in Brussels and then 10-0 in the second leg, which was played at Maine Road because the floodlights at Old Trafford were not yet ready.

 **Facts**   **Postwar Football**

United went on to beat Athletic Bilbao and then reached the semi-final, the first leg of which was their first game under floodlights. They lost this 2-0 and went out 5-3 on aggregate to Real Madrid, the holders, who went on to retain the trophy.

Within less than a week of their elimination, Manchester United clinched the Championship and thus had the consolation of knowing that they would be back in the European Cup the following season. They finished eight points ahead of their nearest challengers, Tottenham Hotspur.

United's 13-man championship-winning squad featured the following: Johnny Berry, Jackie Blanchflower, Roger Byrne (captain), Bobby Charlton, Eddie Colman, Duncan Edwards, Bill Foulkes, Mark Jones, David Pegg, Tommy Taylor, Dennis Viollet , Liam 'Billy' Whelan and Ray Wood (goalkeeper).

Manchester United were close to the double, but fell at the last to Aston Villa, who beat them 2-1 in the FA Cup Final. United lost their goalkeeper, Ray Wood, had to go off after only six minutes after sustaining a fractured cheekbone when challenged by Villa's Peter McParland. He was replaced in goal by centre half Jackie Blanchflower. Wood returned to play on the wing.

Both Villa's goals were scored by Irish international McParland; United's reply came from Tommy Taylor.

The champions of each of the four divisions of the English League - Manchester United, Leicester City, Derby County and Ipswich Town - all scored over 100 goals, the first time this had happened since 1931-32.

Postwar Football

Facts

1957's FA Cup giantkillers par excellence were Bournemouth and Boscombe Athletic. The Third Division (South) side beat Wolverhampton Wanderers 1-0 at Molineux in the fourth round, courtesy of a goal by Reg Cutler, who had earlier collided with a goalpost - play had to be stopped while the post was mended. In the fifth round they beat Tottenham Hotspur 3-1 and led Manchester United 1-0 in the sixth round before two goals by Johnny Berry put paid to the Cherries' dreams of Wembley.

In Scotland, Rangers won the League Championship for the 29th time outright and the 30th time altogether in their history (the 1890-91 title had been shared with Dumbarton).

The Scottish FA Cup was won by Falkirk for the second time in their history (the other occasion had been in 1913). They had been brought round from the brink of relegation by new manager Reggie Smith.

Celtic won the Scottish League Cup, beating Partick Thistle 3-0 in a replay after the first Final had been drawn 0-0 after extra time.

At four minutes past three on the afternoon of February 6, 1958, the season was overshadowed by the terrible Munich air disaster, in which the cream of the so-called Busby Babes of Manchester United were killed.

United were returning from Yugoslavia, where they had just drawn 3-3 in their European Cup quarter final against Red Star Belgrade. After a refuelling stop en route, the Elizabethan airliner of British European Airways (BEA) made two attempts to take off from Munich airport but each time aborted the attempt at the last minute because of snow.

 **Facts**   **Postwar Football**

The pilot made a third effort to take off, reached the point of no return, but failed to get the airborne, probably because of the slush on the runway, although some people have attributed the crash to ice on the wings. The plane ploughed through the airport perimeter fence and split in half; the port wing and part of the tail section hit a house.

Of the 43 passengers, 23 lost their lives. Among the dead were eight Manchester United players - captain Roger Byrne, reserve left back Geoff Bent, right half Eddie Colman, left half Duncan Edwards, centre half Mark Jones, outside left David Pegg, centre forward Tommy Taylor and inside right Billy Whelan.

Another of those killed was the former Manchester City and England goalkeeper Frank Swift, who had been there in his new capacity as a newspaper sports reporter.

Among those seriously injured were manager Matt Busby together with Johnny Berry and Jackie Blanchflower, who never played again. Of those who escaped with relatively minor injuries were Bobby Charlton, Bill Foulkes, Harry Gregg, Ken Morgans and Dennis Viollet.

Despite the tragedy, Manchester United fulfilled their fixture commitments. Although - not surprisingly - they lost the second leg of their match with Red Star, UEFA offered the team a place in Europe the following season. The English FA and Football League, however, banned them from participating on this basis.

Three months later, on May 3, 1958, Manchester United played in the Final of the FA Cup. Four of the Busby Babes had recovered sufficiently to play - Bobby Charlton, Harry Gregg, Bill Foulkes and Dennis Viollet.

Bolton Wanderers beat Manchester United 2-0 at Wembley with goals by Nat Lofthouse. The second was controversial because he charged Harry Gregg into the net after the United goalkeeper had parried a shot.

Postwar Football

Facts

The 1958 League Championship was won by Wolverhampton Wanderers. This was their second title, the first having come in 1954.

John Charles, the Wales and former Leeds United forward, had an outstanding first season in Italy, where he helped Juventus to the Serie A title and was the leading scorer in the top flight with 28 goals in 34 matches.

In England, the leading scorer in 1957-58 was Bobby Smith of Tottenham Hotspur, with 36 in 42 matches.

In Scotland, Jimmy Murray and Jimmy Wardhaugh, two Heart of Midlothian forwards, were joint top scorers with 28 goals apiece.

On October 19, 1957, Celtic recorded the highest score in any major British final when they beat Rangers 7-1 in the Final of the Scottish League Cup. Their scorers that day were Neil Mochan (2), Sammy Wilson, Billy McPhail (3) and Willie Fernie (penalty).

Clyde won the Scottish FA Cup for the third time in their history - the other Bully Wee years had been 1939 and 1955.

In the Final of the first Inter-Cities Fairs Cup, Barcelona beat London 8-2 on aggregate (2-2 away, 6-0 at home).
The 1958 World Cup finals were held in Sweden. It was the first - and, to date, the only - such tournament for which all four British home nations - England, Northern Ireland, Scotland and Wales - have qualified together.

Wales went to Sweden despite failing to win their qualifying group. This was because so many African and Asian countries had withdrawn rather than face Israel that there had to be a ballot of countries that had come second in their groups. Wales won the poll and then beat Israel at home and away in a play-off.

 **Facts**   **Postwar Football**

The 16 countries that took part in the 1958 World Cup finals were as follows: Argentina, Austria, Brazil, Czechoslovakia, England, France, Hungary, Mexico, Northern Ireland, Paraguay, Scotland, Sweden, the USSR, Wales, West Germany and Yugoslavia.

At the end of the group stages, Scotland were eliminated after finishing bottom of their group. The other three home countries had to play off for a place in the quarter finals - England lost 1-0 to the USSR, but Northern Ireland beat Czechoslovakia 2-1 and Wales defeated Hungary by the same score.

Both Northern Ireland's goals in the play-off were scored by Peter McParland of Aston Villa.

Wales won thanks to goals by Ivor Allchurch of Swansea Town and Terry Medwin of Tottenham Hotspur.

In the quarter finals, Wales lost 1-0 to Brazil, whose goal was Pele's first in the competition.

Northern Ireland lost 4-0 to France, for whom leading scorer Just Fontaine scored two of his record 13 goals in the World Cup finals.

Postwar Football

Facts

In the semi-finals, Brazil beat France 5-2 - Pele scored a hat trick. In the other semi-final, hosts Sweden upset highly fancied West Germany 3-1.

The 1958 World Cup Final between Sweden and Brazil was held in front of 49,737 spectators at the Rasunda Stadium, Stockholm on June 29, 1958.

The 1958 World Cup Final teams were as follows:
SWEDEN: Svensson, Bergmark, Axborn, Borjesson, Gustavsson, Parling, Hamrin, Gren, Simonsson, Liedholm, Skoglund
BRAZIL: Gylmar, D. Santos, N. Santos, Zito, Bellini, Orlando, Garrincha, Didi, Vava, Pele, Zagalo

The final score in the 1958 World Cup Final was Sweden 2 Brazil 5.

Vava and Pele both scored twice for Brazil, and the fifth was added by Mario Zagalo. Sweden scored through Liedholm and Simonsson.

In 1958-59, the English Football League was restructured by deregionalising the old Third Divisions North and South. The top teams in each of the old divisions (Scunthorpe United and Brighton and Hove Albion) were promoted to Division Two, while the bottom two teams in the Second Division (Doncaster Rovers and Notts County) were relegated to the new Third Division. The teams that finished between second and eleventh in the old Third Divisions went into the new Division Three, while the 12 teams that finished between 13th and 23rd in the Third Divisions North and South made up the new Division Four.

Wolverhampton Wanderers won their third League title, finishing five points ahead of Manchester United.

 **Facts**

Postwar Football

Manchester United had begun the long, hard road back to their previous pinnacles after the Munich tragedy. Manager Matt Busby had splashed out in the transfer market, buying England international inside forward Albert Quixall from Second Division Sheffield Wednesday for a British record fee of £45,000.

Nottingham Forest won the FA Cup for the first time in the 20th century - their one previous success had been in 1898.

In the Final, Forest beat Luton Town 2-1 despite being reduced to 10 men after 32 minutes when right winger Roy Dwight - who had previously put his team ahead - was carried off with a broken leg.

Middlesbrough centre forward Brian Clough became the Second Division's leading scorer for the second year running, with 42 goals in the season. It was the third consecutive season in which he averaged a goal a game, and he reached 100 goals in his career quicker than any other player in the history of the game.

Denis Law of Huddersfield Town became Scotland's youngest full international when he played for his country against Wales at the age of 18 years 236 days. He scored in Scotland's 3-0 victory.

Jimmy Greaves was the leading scorer in the English First Division, with 32 goals in the season for Chelsea.

Tottenham Hotspur appointed their former player Bill Nicholson as manager in succession to Jimmy Anderson.

Postwar Football

Facts

Nicholson's appointment was announced just before Spurs' home game against Everton. As if to celebrate, the team went out and beat Everton 10-4 in the highest-scoring First Division match of the 20th century. Captain and centre forward Bobby Smith scored four, Alf Stokes got two, and there were also contributions from Terry Medwin, George Robb and Tommy Harmer and John Ryden. Jimmy Harris scored a hat-trick for the visitors and Bobby Collins hit their other goal.

In Scotland, the honours were shared by three clubs - Rangers won the League, St Mirren the FA Cup and Heart of Midlothian the League Cup. The leading scorer was Joe Baker of Hibernian, with 25.

Burnley won the 1960 League Championship. They had not led the table until the final whistle on the last day of the campaign. This was their second title, their other success having come in 1921.

Burnley's manager was Harry Potts and among their star players were right half Jimmy Adamson, England right winger John Connelly (20 goals in the season), inside forward Jimmy McIlroy, centre forward Ray Pointer (19 goals), inside forward Jim Robson (18 goals) and 18-year-old left back Alex Elder.

Wolverhampton Wanderers, who finished third, became the first English First Division team to score over 100 goals in three consecutive seasons.

The 1960 FA Cup was won by Wolverhampton Wanderers, who beat Blackburn Rovers 3-0 in the Final through an own goal by Mick McGrath and two from their winger Norman Deeley.

 **Facts**   Postwar Football

The match is remembered for the abuse and rubbish poured by Blackburn supporters onto the Wolves team when they tried to parade the Cup and for objects thrown at the referee. Ewood Park had been a hotbed of discontent and rumour for some weeks before the Final, and Rovers' Northern Ireland star Derek Dougan had put in a transfer request.

To make the Blackburn fans' humour even worse, their left back Dave Whelan went off after he broke a leg in a tackle early in the match.

Brian Clough scored another 39 times in the League for Second Division Middlesbrough and all the goals in the Football League's 5-0 defeat of the League of Ireland in Belfast.

On Good Friday and Easter Saturday (April 15 and 16) 1960, Cliff Holton of Fourth Division Watford became the first player to score hat-tricks on two successive days - one in the 4-2 defeat of Chester, the other in a 5-0 win over Gateshead.

In Scotland, Heart of Midlothian won both the League and the League Cup, while Rangers won the FA Cup.

For the second season running, Scotland's leading scorer was Joe Baker, with 42 goals for Hibernian.

On August 15, 1959, Ian St John scored a hat-trick in two and a half minutes for Motherwell against Hibernian in the League Cup.

Real Madrid retained the European Cup in 1960, beating Eintracht Frankfurt 7-3 in the Final. This was their fifth victory in the five years of the competition. The match at Hampden Park, Glasgow was watched by a crowd of 127,621.

Postwar Football

Facts

Real Madrid went on to win the first World Club Championship between the winners of the European Cup and the South American Copa Libertadores, beating Penarol of Uruguay 5-1 over two legs.

Barcelona retained the Inter-Cities Fairs Cup, beating Birmingham City 4-1 on aggregate over two legs in the Final.

On July 10, 1960, the USSR became the first winners of the European Nations Cup, beating Yugoslavia 2-1 in the Final in Paris. Among the countries that did not take part in this competition were the Home Nations (England, Northern Ireland, Scotland and Wales) Italy and West Germany. Spain pulled out when drawn against the USSR because of the vehement anti-communism of General Franco's government.

THE SIXTIES

The Sixties

The Sixties began with the launch of a new competition in England - the League Cup. Originally, both the semi-finals and the Final of this competition were on a two-legged basis.

The League Cup took a long time to establish itself, and in the first year five leading clubs - Arsenal, Sheffield Wednesday, Tottenham Hotspur, West Bromwich Albion and Wolverhampton Wanderers - all turned down invitations to take part.

The first winners of the League Cup were Aston Villa, who beat Second Division Rotherham United 3-2 on aggregate in the Final.

Tottenham Hotspur became the first team in the 20th century to win the League and FA Cup double. The feat had previously been achieved only twice - by Preston North End in 1889 and Aston Villa in 1897 - and the consensus had long been that the feat could never be repeated because of the higher level of competition and the greater number of fixtures - in 1897, there had been only 16 teams in the First Division; now there were 22.

But Spurs announced their intention of confounding the sceptics by kicking off the with 11 straight wins in the League. By the end of the season, they had scored 115 goals - the highest total since since Arsenal scored the same number in 1934-35 - and clocked up more wins (31) and more away wins (16) than any other team in First Division history. Spurs also equalled Arsenal's 1931 record number of points (66) under the two-points-for-a-win system.

 **Facts**   The Sixties

In the modern age of huge squads, it is remarkable to note how few players Tottenham called on throughout their greatest season. The 12 main contributors to their great triumphs were Bill Brown, Peter Baker, Ron Henry, Danny Blanchflower, Morris Norman, Dave Mackay, Cliff Jones, John White, Bobby Smith, Les Allen, Terry Dyson and Terry Medwin.

Spurs' leading scorers in their double year were Bobby Smith, with 28, and Les Allen with 23.

The First Division's leading scorer was Jimmy Greaves, with 41 goals for 12th-placed Chelsea. At 21, Greaves also became the youngest player to score 100 goals in English League football.

In the FA Cup Final, Spurs' opponents, Leicester City, were reduced to 10 men when their right back Len Chalmers had to go off injured after only 18 minutes. The rest of the team hung on grimly, however - outstanding in goal was a young keeper called Gordon Banks. The deadlock was not broken until midway through the second half when Bobby Smith scored for Spurs. Their second goal was scored by Terry Dyson.

After 12 previous unsuccessful applications, Peterborough United were finally elected to the Football League as replacements for Gateshead. They then won the Fourth Division at a canter, scoring 134 goals - a League record. An amazing 52 of them were scored by centre forward Terry Bly.

A threatened strike by members of the Professional Footballers' Association was called off at the last minute in January 1961 when the Football League abolished the £20-a-week maximum wage and agreed to scrap the standard contract which bound players to a club for life.

The Sixties

 Facts

The PFA's spokesman and one of the main agitators for fairer terms of employment was Jimmy Hill, then an inside forward at Fulham, who later became chairman of Coventry City and afterwards took over his former club. Today, Hill is best known as a football pundit on BBC Television.

The agreement reached between the League and the PFA also headed off the threat of litigation by George Eastham, now of Arsenal, against his former club, Newcastle United, which he accused of restraint of trade when they refused to sell him. This case eventually dragged on until July 4, 1963.

After the abolition of the maximum wage, footballers' pay rose rapidly. The same season, Johnny Haynes of Fulham and England became the country's first £100-a-week player.

 **Facts**   The Sixties

Other players had moved to Italy in search of better wages. Among the most prominent were Joe Baker, who moved from Hibernian to Torino for £73,000; Denis Law, who had gone from Manchester City to Torino for £100,000; and Jimmy Greaves, sold by Chelsea to AC Milan for £80,000.

England won the 1961 Home International Championship with a hundred per cent record, beating Northern Ireland 5-2, Wales 5-1 and then Scotland 9-3 at Wembley on April 15. England's goals in this match were scored by Jimmy Greaves (3), Johnny Haynes (2), Bobby Smith (2), Bobby Robson of West Bromwich Albion and Bryan Douglas of Blackburn Rovers.

In Scotland, Rangers took the League and the League Cup, while Dunfermline Athletic won the FA Cup for the first time.

In the European Cup, Real Madrid finally lost a match after winning the trophy every year since the competition started in 1956. They were knocked put in the first round of the 1960-61 competition by fierce national rivals Barcelona.

Barcelona themselves were eventually beaten in the Final, 3-2 by Benfica, the Champions of Portugal.

English Champions Burnley reached the third round of the European Cup, where they took a 3-1 lead against Hamburg in the home leg at Turf Moor but lost the return in Germany 4-1.

The new competition in Europe was the Cup Winners' Cup. Britain's representatives met in the semi-final, where Rangers beat Wolverhampton Wanderers.

Rangers thus became the first British club to play in a major European final. In the only Cup Winners' Cup Final to be played over two legs, Rangers lost 4-1 on aggregate to Fiorentina of Italy.

The Sixties

Facts

Rangers had been greatly strengthened by the purchase from Raith Rovers in 1960 of Jim Baxter, who went on to play 34 times for Scotland.

In the third year of the Inter-Cities Fairs Cup, Birmingham City lost for the second time in the Final, beaten 4-2 on aggregate by Roma.

The 1961 Second Division Championship was won by Ipswich Town, managed by Alf Ramsey. Ramsey had taken over from Scott Duncan in 1955 and guided Ipswich to the Third Division (South) Championship in 1957.

In 1961-62, newly-promoted Ipswich Town won the League Championship in their first ever season in the First Division.

Their leading scorer - and the First Division's - was Ray Crawford, with 33 goals. Ted Phillips chipped in with another 28.

Ray Crawford played twice for England that season, against Northern Ireland and Austria.

Burnley were runners-up in both the League and the FA Cup, losing 3-1 in the Final to the holders, Tottenham Hotspur.

Burnley's leading players were Jimmy Adamson - voted Footballer of the Year 1962 - and Northern Ireland international inside forward Jimmy McIlroy, who had come second in the same Football Writers' poll.

Spurs were bolstered by the signing of Jimmy Greaves from AC Milan, after the former Chelsea forward had spent only a year in Italy. The fee was set at £99,999 because Spurs' manager Bill Nicholson did not want to saddle the player with the tag of 'the world's first £100,000 player'. Greaves started to repay the investment - a British transfer record - with a goal in the FA Cup Final.

 **Facts**   **The Sixties**

Burnley's equaliser in this match - scored by Jimmy Robson - was the 100th goal in a Wembley Cup Final.

Spurs won the 1962 FA Cup Final 3-1. Bobby Smith scored their second and Danny Blanchflower clinched it with a late penalty.

Brian Clough - who had scored 197 goals in his 213 League games for Middlesbrough - moved to Sunderland for £45,000. He scored 29 goals in 34 matches for his new club, who missed promotion from the Second Division by a single point.

At the age of 46, Stanley Matthews left First Division Blackpool and went back to Second Division Stoke City for £2500. The local hero's return to the Potteries trebled home gate receipts.

On November 1, the Italian League beat the Scottish League 2-0 at Hampden Park. Outstanding for the visitors were a Welshman, an Englishman and a Scotsman - John Charles, Gerry Hitchens and Denis Law.

In the second League Cup Final, Second Division Norwich City beat Fourth Division Rochdale 4-0 on aggregate over two legs.

The 1962 Second Division Championship was won by Liverpool, who returned to the top flight for the first time since 1954.

Also promoted at the end of 1961-62 were Leyton Orient, for whom the following season would be their first taste of First Division football.

On March 6, 1962, financially beleaguered Accrington Stanley resigned from the Football League with debts of £60,000 and insufficient assets to continue trading. Their results to date that season were expunged from the Fourth Division record and their place in the League was taken the following season by Oxford United.

The Sixties   Facts

Accrington Stanley's record at the time of their demise was as follows:

P	W	D	L	F	A	Pts
33	5	8	20	19	60	18

Accrington were founder members of the League, but they had had a chequered history. They had resigned from the League once before, in 1893, in the wake of accusations that they had paid one of their players. In 1896, they disbanded altogether. They pulled themselves together in the early years of the 20th century, however, and regained League status in 1921. Between the Wars, they regularly attracted crowds of about 20,000 and, in 1955, became one of the first clubs to have a match televised. Also in the 1950s, Accrington Stanley became the first English League club to field a side composed entirely of Scots.

Accrington Stanley's last ever match in the Football League was at Crewe Alexandra, where they lost 4-0.

Peel Park - Accrington Stanley's ground from 1919-1962 - is no more. In 1968, a new Accrington Stanley was founded - their home ground is at Livingstone Road and they play in the Northern Premier League.

In the Fourth Division, Wrexham (who won promotion this year) beat Hartlepools United (who had to apply for re-election) 10-1. Three of the Welsh side's players scored hat-tricks - Ron Barnes, Roy Ambler and Wyn Davies.

Reigning English Champions Tottenham Hotspur reached the semi-final of the 1962 European Cup, going down heroically to the Cup holders Benfica, 4-3 on aggregate.

Benfica went on to retain the European Cup, beating Real Madrid 5-3 in the 1962 Final. Hungarian star Ferenc Puskas scored a first-half hat-trick for the Spaniards, but the Portuguese Champions hit back with two goals from their emerging star, 20-year-old Eusebio.

 **Facts**   **The Sixties**

The 1962 European Cup Winners' Cup Final was held in Glasgow - Atletico Madrid drew 1-1 with Fiorentina. The replay in Stuttgart was won by the Spaniards 3-0.

The 1962 Final of the Inter-Cities Fairs Cup was an all-Spanish affair in which Valencia beat Barcelona 7-3 on aggregate.

Dundee won the Scottish League Championship for the first - and, to date, the only - time in their history. Their team included forward Alan Gilzean and defender Ian Ure, two players destined to go on to greater fame south of the border.

Gilzean was the season's leading scorer in the Scottish First Division, with 24 goals.

Rangers did a Cup double. Their 2-0 FA Cup Final victory over St Mirren was the 16th time they had won the trophy. The League Cup Final went to a replay when they drew 1-1 with Heart of Midlothian. But Rangers won the replay 3-1 to take the new Cup for the fourth time in its history.

Scotland recovered well from the fiasco of the previous year and won the Home International Championship handsomely with maximum points, beating Northern Ireland 6-1, Wales 2-0 and England 2-0. This was England's first defeat at Hampden Park for 25 years.

The 1962 World Cup finals were held in Chile, a country that had not recovered after having been severely damaged by a series of devastating earthquakes in 1960. In fact, Chile was preferred to the other main candidates, Argentina, not despite the natural disasters that had befallen it, but because of them. As Chilean FA President Carlos Dittborn put it: 'We have nothing - that is why we must have the World Cup'.

The Sixties

Facts

Sixteen countries took part in the 1962 World Cup finals: Argentina, Brazil, Bulgaria, Chile, Colombia, Czechoslovakia, England, Hungary, Italy, Mexico, Spain, Switzerland, Uruguay, the USSR, West Germany and Yugoslavia.

The 1962 tournament is remembered for all the wrong reasons - four players were sent off and four more broke limbs in the first eight matches.

The World Cup organising committee called the 16 national managers together and warned them not to let things degenerate. But the next group stage match - between Chile and Italy - was already charged with enormous ill-feeling, not least because of disparaging remarks made about conditions in the host country by Italian pressmen.

The match had only just begun when Chilean players began spitting at their Italian opponents. Chile's Leonel Sanchez punched Italy's Humberto Maschio and broke his nose, an assault seen clearly by most people in the stadium and millions on television, but missed by the linesman who was standing right next to the incident.

 **Facts**   **The Sixties**

Just before half time, Mario David of Italy was sent off by English referee Ken Aston for trying to kick Sanchez. This reduced Italy to nine men, and they duly lost the match 2-0. The game is often known as The Battle of Santiago.

The eight teams to qualify for the 1962 World Cup quarter finals were Brazil, Chile, Czechoslovakia, England, Hungary, Uruguay, West Germany and Yugoslavia.

England lost 3-1 to Brazil. The scorers were Garrincha (2) and Vava for Brazil, Gerry Hitchens for England.

In the semi-finals, Brazil beat Chile 4-2 in front of the biggest crowd of the tournament - 76,594 - while Czechoslovakia beat Yugoslavia 3-1 in front of the smallest - 6000.

The star of Brazil's defeat of the host country was again Garrincha, who made one of Vava's two goals and scored twice himself before being sent off for retaliation against kicking, spitting and virtually incessant verbal abuse.

Despite his dismissal, however, FIFA ruled that Garrincha would be permitted to play in the Final, which was held in the National Stadium, Santiago, on June 17, 1962 in front of a crowd of 68,679.

BRAZIL: **Gylmar, D. Santos, N. Santos, Zito, Mauro, Zozimo, Garrincha, Didi, Vava, Amarildo, Zagalo**
CZECHOSLOVAKIA: **Schroif, Tichy, Novak, Pluskal, Popluhar, Masopust, Pospichal, Scherer, Kadraba, Kvasnak, Jelinek**

Czechoslovakia went ahead with a goal by left half Masopust; Amarildo equalised for Brazil, then went ahead in the second half through Zito. In the 77th minute, Vava scored the killer goal after the Czech keeper had dropped an innocuous lob from D. Santos.

The Sixties

Facts

There were six leading scorers in the 1962 World Cup finals, each with four goals - Albert (Hungary), Garrincha (Brazil), Ivanov (USSR), Jerkovic (Yugoslavia), Sanchez (Chile) and Vava (Brazil).

This was Brazil's second World Cup triumph, putting them level with Italy and Uruguay on number of trophies won.

At the end of the 1962 World Cup, England manager Walter Winterbottom announced his retirement. He was replaced on May 1, 1963, by the first ever full time manager - Alf Ramsey, who had led Ipswich to the League Championship earlier that year.

During the close season, Denis Law returned to England from Italy, purchased by Manchester United from Torino for £115,000.

Torino also sold Joe Baker, their acquisition from Hibernian, to Arsenal for £70,000.

On August 23, 1962, Fulham's England international Johnny Haynes suffered a serious knee injury in a car accident which caused him to miss the greater part of the following season and brought an end to his England career. Haynes played 56 times for his country between 1955 and 1962 and had been captain since 1960.

Everton won the 1962-63 Championship - their sixth league title altogether, but their first since 1939 - under the management of Harry Catterick.

Everton's leading scorers were captain Roy Vernon, with 24 goals, and centre forward Alex Young, with 22.

Their other outstanding player was Brian Labone. This strong and skilful centre half went on to play 26 times for England between 1963 and 1970, and would almost certainly have won many more caps had he not had Jack Charlton to compete with for his international place.

 **Facts**   **The Sixties**

Everton made two big signings in the early months of 1963 - right winger Alex Scott for £40,000 from Rangers and left half Tony Kay for £60,000 from Sheffield Wednesday. On June 5, Kay won his first England cap in their 8-1 defeat of Switzerland in Basel - he had the world at his feet, but two years later he was in jail.

The First Division's leading scorer was again Jimmy Greaves, who scored 37 goals for second-placed Tottenham Hotspur.

The winter of 1962-63 caused the worst disruption ever to the British football programme. Between December 22 and March 16, there was not one Saturday on which it was possible to play the complete programme of fixtures. On FA Cup third round day, only three of the scheduled 32 fixtures were played, and 14 of them were subsequently postponed at least 10 times. This led to an immense log-jam of fixtures - the third round was not completed until March 11.

Bolton Wanderers went the longest period without a match in the history of the English Football League - 70 days from December 8, 1962 to February 16, 1963.

It was during this big freeze that the pools companies first used the pools panel to predict results.

Tottenham Hotspur became the first British club to win a major European trophy when they beat Atletico Madrid 5-1 in the Cup Winners' Cup Final in Rotterdam. Their scorers on that great night were Jimmy Greaves (2), John White and Terry Dyson (2).

For his first match in charge of England - against France in the away leg of the European Nations' Cup first round - Alf Ramsey brought in only one new face, Ron Henry of Tottenham Hotspur. England lost 5-2 in Paris on February 27.

The Sixties

Facts

Manchester United won the FA Cup, beating Leicester City 3-1 in the Final with a goal from Denis Law and two from Alex Herd. This was Leicester City's third disappointment in the FA Cup at Wembley.

Stoke City were Champions of Division Two. Their inspiration throughout the season was Stanley Matthews, still the Wizard of Dribble despite his 48 years.

Birmingham City won the League Cup, beating Aston Villa 3-1 on aggregate in the Final. To date, this is the only major trophy in their history.

In Scotland, Rangers did the double. They finished nine points ahead of second-placed Kilmarnock in the League and beat Celtic 3-0 in the replayed FA Cup Final after the first match had been drawn 1-1.

Rangers' - and Scotland's - leading scorer was Jimmy Millar, with 27 goals.

The Scottish League Cup was won by Heart of Midlothian, who beat Kilmarnock 1-0 in the Final.

AC Milan won the 1963 European Cup, beating the holders, Benfica, 2-1 in the Final at Wembley.

AC Milan then went on to make a bid for the World Club Championship against the holders, Santos of Brazil, whose star player was the great Pele. Both legs were won 4-2 by the home team. This necessitated a play-off, which the Brazilians won 1-0.

Valencia became the second club to retain the Inter-Cities Fairs Cup, beating Dynamo Zagreb 4-1 on aggregate in the Final.

 **Facts**

The Sixties

On July 4, 1963, in the High Court of England, sitting in judgment in the case of George Eastham v Newcastle United, Mr Justice Wilberforce ruled that Football League regulations concerning the retention and transfer of professional footballers were 'in unreasonable restraint of trade'.

1963-64 was the hundredth anniversary of the founding of the Football Association. To mark the centenary, an exhibition match was held at Wembley in which England defeated a Rest of the World XI featuring Eusebio, Denis Law, Ferenc Puskas, Alfredo di Stefano and Lev Yashin.

The celebrations were overshadowed by allegations in the Sunday newspaper, *The People*, that three Sheffield Wednesday players - Tony Kay, David 'Bronco' Layne and Peter Swan - had conspired to fix the result of their game at Ipswich Town in December 1962. The case eventually came to trial in January 1965.

Liverpool won the 1964 Championship, two years after being promoted from Division Two. This was their sixth League title and their first under the management of Bill Shankly.

Bill Shankly was born in 1919. His playing career started at Carlisle United and he then moved to Preston North End, where he won an FA Cup winner's medal in 1938, the same year as that in which he won all his five caps for Scotland.

The Sixties

Shankly became manager of his old club, Carlisle United, in 1949. He then had spells at Grimsby Town (1951-53), Workington (1953-56) and Huddersfield Town (1956-59) before taking over from Phil Taylor at Liverpool in 1959.

When Shankly arrived at Anfield, Liverpool were a Second Division club, having been relegated in 1954. The new manager built a new-style team around the nucleus of three outstanding players - Roger Hunt, Ian St John and Ron Yeats.

Roger Hunt was a goalscorer, with 245 goals in 401 professional matches. He was especially prolific in Liverpool's promotion year (1961-62), when he scored 42 goals in the season. He went on to win 34 England caps and a World Cup winner's medal.

Ian St John was a centre forward bought by Shankly for £37,500 from Motherwell in 1961. Highlights of his distinguished playing career included the winning goal for Liverpool in the 1965 FA Cup Final and 21 caps for Scotland. He is now a television soccer pundit.

Defender Ron Yeats was bought by Liverpool for £22,000 from Dundee United in 1961. Shankly was especially proud of this purchase, reportedly introducing him to the press with the words: 'He's a colossus - come outside and I'll give you a walk round him'. Yeats played twice for Scotland in 1965-66.

 **Facts**   The Sixties

With 35 goals in the season for fourth-placed Tottenham Hotspur, Jimmy Greaves was the First Division's leading scorer for the fourth year out of five.

West Ham United won the FA Cup for the first time in their history, beating Preston North End 3-2 in a thrilling Final at Wembley. The London club were twice behind to goals by Holden and Dawson but they came back through John Sissons and Geoff Hurst and eventually won with a headed goal by Ron Boyce in injury time.

Sissons was only 18 at the time, but even younger was Howard Kendall of Preston who - at 17 years 345 days - became the youngest FA Cup finalist this century (in fact, since 1879).

The Hammers' Final victory came shortly after they had suffered their record defeat - 8-2 at home to Blackburn Rovers.

Leicester City won their first major honour, beating Stoke City 4-3 on aggregate in the League Cup Final.

In only their second season in the Football League, Oxford United became the first Fourth Division club to reach the sixth round of the FA Cup.

On November 20, 1963, England v Northern Ireland was the first match at Wembley to be played under floodlights. Although England won the game 8-3, the Home International title ended up as a three-way tie between both these countries and Scotland.

On April 25, 1964, Jim Fryatt of Bradford Park Avenue scored the fastest goal on record after only four seconds of the game against Tranmere Rovers.

The Sixties

Facts

In Scotland, Rangers won the League, the FA Cup and the League Cup. Already the only club to have done the treble (in 1949), Rangers had now done it twice.

Kilmarnock were runners-up in the Scottish First Division for the second year running.

The European Cup stayed in Milan, but moved across town from AC to Inter, who beat Real Madrid 3-1 in the Final in Vienna.

The 1964 Cup-Winners' Cup Final went to a replay for the second time in its four-year history. Sporting Lisbon and MTK Budapest drew 3-3 after extra time in the first match in Brussels, so they reconvened in Antwerp, where the Portuguese side won 1-0.

The Inter-Cities Fairs Cup stayed in Spain, but moved from Valencia to Zaragoza, who beat the holders 2-1 in the Final in Barcelona. In a departure from established tradition, this Final was a one-off match.

On May 24, 1964, more than 318 people were killed and 500 seriously injured in Lima when riots broke out after Peru had an equalising goal disallowed in their Olympic qualifying match against Argentina. Police responded to the initial disturbance by firing into the air above the heads of the spectators, who panicked and caused a stampede.

Stanley Matthews was knighted in the Queen's 1965 New Year's list, the first footballer to be so honoured. Sir Stanley retired on February 6, five days after his 50th birthday. He went out on a winning note - in his final League match, Stoke City beat Fulham 3-1.

 **Facts**   The Sixties

Manchester United won the 1965 League Championship on goal average from Leeds United.

1964-65 Top of The First Division Final table							
	P	W	D	L	F	A	Pts
Manchester United	42	26	9	7	89	39	61
Leeds United	42	26	9	7	83	39	61

Manchester United's goal average was 2.28; Leeds' was 2.12.

Leeds were also runners-up in the FA Cup, losing 2-1 to Liverpool after extra time in the Final. This was Liverpool's first FA Cup triumph.

The 1964 Final was goalless at full time. Liverpool then scored through Roger Hunt, but Billy Bremner equalised for Leeds. Then, with nine minutes left, Ian St John headed the Liverpool winner.

Following the match-fixing allegations made in *The People* newspaper the previous year, on January 26, 1965, at Nottingham Assizes, 10 professional footballers were sent to prison for periods of between four years and four months.

In April, all 10 men were banned from football for life by the FA.

The most prominent of those convicted were Dick Beattie, Jimmy Gauld, Tony Kay and Peter Swan.

Dick Beattie was a former Celtic and Scotland Under-23 goalkeeper who later played for Portsmouth and Peterborough United.

Jimmy Gauld played inside forward for Charlton Athletic, Everton, Plymouth Argyle, Swindon Town and Mansfield Town. It was he who had 'come clean' to the Sunday newspapers the previous April for £7000. He was sentenced to four years' imprisonment and ordered to pay £5000 costs.

The Sixties

Facts

**Tony Kay and Peter Swan were England internationals. Their
account of what had happened sounded more like naivete than
conspiracy - they had simply put a small bet on Ipswich Town, to
win at home against their own club, Sheffield Wednesday. They had
in no way sought to throw the game - it was just that their
opponents were the reigning League Champions and might have
been expected to win an end-of-season game against visitors with
little to play for.**

At the end of the 1964-65 season, Jimmy Dickinson retired after playing 764
games at wing half for Portsmouth - his only club - in a career that began in
1946. He won two Championship medals, in 1949 and 1950, and played 48
times for England. Dickinson died in 1982 at the age of 57.

**On July 21, 1965, John White, the Tottenham Hotspur inside
forward, was killed at the age of 27 when he was struck by
lightning while playing golf in Enfield, Middlesex. White was a
member of the great Spurs double-winning side of 19612 and
played 22 times for Scotland.**

Arthur Rowley retired at the end of the season as player-manager of
Shrewsbury Town. Rowley was the most prolific League scorer of all time,
with 434 goals in a 619-match career. He scored four goals in 24 games for
West Bromwich Albion, 27 goals in 56 games for Fulham, 251 goals in 303
games for Leicester City and 152 goals in 236 games for Shrewsbury Town.

**1964 FA Cup winners West Ham United returned to Wembley a
year later to beat Munich 1860 in the Final of the European Cup
Winners' Cup. Both goals in their 2-0 victory were scored by
newcomer Alan Sealey. This was the second time an English club
had claimed a major European trophy.**

 **Facts**   The Sixties

In the 1965 League Cup Final, Chelsea beat the holders, Leicester City, 3-2 on aggregate.

Jimmy Greaves was yet again the First Division's leading scorer, but this time he shared the accolade with Andy McEvoy of Blackburn Rovers, both players finishing with 29 goals.

In Scotland, it was third time lucky for Kilmarnock. After finishing in second place in 1962 and 1963, they finally took their first title by a whisker from Heart of Midlothian.

Scottish First Division 1964-65 Top of the Final Table

	P	W	D	L	F	A	Pts
Kilmarnock	34	22	6	6	62	33	50
Heart of Midlothian	34	22	6	6	90	49	50

The margin of Kilmarnock's dramatic last-day victory was one of the narrowest ever recorded: they needed to win their final game of the season by two clear goals away to Hearts themselves. And that is exactly what they did, edging out the Edinburgh club on goal average - 1.88 to 1.84 - a difference of 0.04.

The leading scorer in the Scottish First Division was Jim Forrest, with 30 goals for fifth-placed Rangers.

Celtic won the Scottish FA Cup, beating Dunfermline Athletic 3-2 in the Final.

Rangers won the Scottish League Cup, beating Celtic 2-1 in the Final.

Internazionale retained the European Cup, beating Benfica 1-0 in the Final in their home city, Milan.

The Sixties

Facts

For the second and last time to date, the Final of the Inter Cities Fairs Cup was played as a one-off, rather than over two legs, home and away. In it, Ferencvaros of Hungary beat Juventus of Italy 1-0 in the latter's home city, Turin.

In a change to the rules at the start of 1965-66, every League club was henceforth to be allowed one substitute, who could come on for an injured player. On the first day of the new season, Keith Peacock of Charlton Athletic became the first player to come on in this role.

Liverpool won the 1966 League Championship - their second title in three years and the seventh in their history, the same number as Arsenal.

The First Division's leading scorer was Liverpool's Roger Hunt, with 30 in the season.

On December 4, 1965, at Burnley, Frank Saul became the first Tottenham Hotspur player to be sent off in a League match since October 27, 1928.

Everton won the FA Cup for the third time, beating Sheffield Wednesday 3-2 in the 1966 Final. Wednesday went two up through Jim McCalliog and Dave Ford, but Everton hit back with two goals from 21-year-old Mike Trebilcock. Derek Temple scored the winner.

West Bromwich Albion won the 1966 League Cup, beating West Ham United 5-3 on aggregate in the Final.

 **Facts**   The Sixties

On 20 March, 1966, the World Cup was stolen from a glass-fronted cabinet in Central Hall, Westminster, London, where it was being displayed in advance of the summer's finals in England. Shortly after the theft, the lid of the Jules Rimet trophy was sent to FA headquarters with a ransom demand. At the subsequent 'drop' a 47-year-old dock labourer was arrested, but the police failed to recapture the Cup itself. Then, a week after the robbery, David Corbett was walking his dog, Pickles, in Beulah Hill, Norwood, South London, when the black-and-white mongrel stopped to dig up a paper parcel that had been hidden under a bush. When the package was opened, it was found to contain the World Cup.

The Scottish Championship went back into the hands of the Old Firm, with Celtic winning their 21st League title.

Celtic also won the Scottish League Cup, beating Rangers 2-1 in the Final. Rangers' consolation was the FA Cup, which they won with a 1-0 win over Celtic in the Final replay after the first match had ended goalless.

The Sixties

Joint leading scorers in the Scottish First Division were Joe McBride of Celtic and Alex Ferguson of Dunfermline Athletic, both with 31 goals. (This Alex Ferguson is not the future manager of Aberdeen and Manchester United.)

After a six-year gap, Real Madrid recaptured the European Cup, beating Partizan Belgrade 2-1 in the Final in Brussels.

Borussia Dortmund won the Cup Winners' Cup, beating Liverpool 2-1 in the Final in Glasgow.

The Inter-Cities Fairs Cup stayed in Spain in 1966, as Barcelona beat Real Zaragoza 4-3 on aggregate in the Final.

The early rounds of the Inter-Cities Fairs Cup were overshadowed by foul play and controversy. In the first leg of the first round tie between Chelsea and Roma, Eddie McCreadie was sent off for retaliation. In the second leg, the English players were pelted with missiles outside the stadium.

Even worse, in the first round match between Leeds United and Torino, Bobby Collins had his thigh broken when tackled crudely by Poletti.

When Leeds United met Valencia in the third round, police were called onto the pitch to deal with fighting between the players, who were taken off by the referee for a 10-minute cooling-off period.

The 1966 World Cup finals were held in England. The main stadium was, of course, Wembley; other matches were held at Ayresome Park (Middlesbrough's ground), Goodison Park (Everton) and Hillsborough (Sheffield Wednesday).

The 16 countries that took part were as follows: Argentina, Brazil, Bulgaria, Chile, England, France, Hungary, Italy, Mexico, North Korea, Portugal, Spain, Switzerland, Uruguay, the USSR and West Germany.

 **Facts**

The Sixties

The opening match of the tournament on July 11 between the hosts, England, and Uruguay, was a goalless draw.

The first goal of the tournament was scored by Pele in the group match between Brazil and Bulgaria. He played little further part in the World Cup, however - he was treated so roughly by the Bulgarian defence that he was not fit for the next game against Hungary. Brazil lost this match 3-1, their first defeat in the World Cup since the so-called Battle of Berne against Hungary in 1954.

Pele returned for the final group match against Portugal. Brazil needed to win to remain in the competition, but Eusebio played brilliantly and the Portuguese defence chopped Pele at every opportunity. Result: Portugal 3 Brazil 1, and the holders were out.

England's first goal of the tournament was scored by Bobby Charlton in their second group match, a 2-0 victory over Mexico.

During England's third group match - a 2-0 victory over France - Manchester United half back Nobby Stiles committed an ugly-looking challenge which, despite not being considered a foul by the match referee, moved the FA council to request the withdrawal of the player from the following match. Manager Alf Ramsey replied that he would pick the team he wanted or resign at once. Stiles kept his place in the side.

The Sixties

Facts

The surprise package of the 1966 World Cup finals group stages were North Korea, who eliminated Italy with a 1-0 victory at Ayresome Park. The winning goal was scored by Pak Doo Ik.

The eight teams in the 1966 World Cup quarter final line-up were Argentina, England, Hungary, North Korea, Portugal, Uruguay, the USSR and West Germany.

In their quarter final match, North Korea went 3-0 up against Portugal before four goals from Eusebio - two of them penalties - enabled the European nation to come through 5-3.

Meanwhile, the workmanlike USSR edged past Hungary 2-1.

In England's quarter final match against Argentina, the visiting captain, Antonio Rattin, became the first player to be sent off in a World Cup finals tournament. He carried on arguing for eight minutes after the referee had pointed to the tunnel. England won the match 1-0, thanks to a Hurst header after 77 minutes.

West Germany won their quarter final 4-0 against Uruguay, who had two men sent off.

Both England's goals in their 2-1 semi-final victory over Portugal were scored by Bobby Charlton.

In the other semi-final, West Germany defeated the USSR 2-1.

The 1966 World Cup Final was held at Wembley on July 30, 1966 in front of a crowd of 93,000.

ENGLAND: Banks, Cohen, Wilson, Stiles, J. Charlton, Moore, Ball, Hurst, Hunt, R. Charlton, Peters
WEST GERMANY: Tilkowski, Hottges, Schnellinger, Beckenbauer, Schulz, Weber, Held, Haller, Seeler, Overath, Emmerich

 **Facts**   **The Sixties**

West Germany opened the scoring after 13 minutes through Haller, but Hurst equalised on 19 minutes with a header from Moore's free kick. After 78 minutes, England went took the lead through Peters. The Cup looked like England's, but Weber equalised in the dying seconds of normal time.

In extra time, Ball pulled the ball back to the edge of the six-yard box, where Hurst kicked the ball past the West German keeper and onto the crossbar. Almost everyone has an opinion about what happened next, but no one is sure whether the ball then crossed the line or bounced slightly in front of it. Nevertheless, there were only two people in the world whose opinions on the subject mattered - the Russian linesman, Tofik Bakhramov, and the Swiss referee Gottfried Dienst. The former gave a goal and the latter upheld his decision - 3-2 to England.

In the last minute of extra time, Moore sent a long clearance through to Hurst, who ran alone from the half way line to score a conclusive final goal moments before the final whistle.

The Sixties

Facts

Leading scorer in the 1966 World Cup finals was Eusebio, with nine goals for Portugal.

In 1966-67, Manchester United won the League Championship for the seventh time in their history, thus equalling the record jointly held at the time by Arsenal and Liverpool.

The First Division's leading scorer was Ron Davies, with 37 goals for 19th-placed Southampton.

The first all-London FA Cup Final was between Tottenham Hotspur and Chelsea. Spurs won 2-1, with goals from Jimmy Robertson and Frank Saul. Chelsea replied through Bobby Tambling four minutes from the end.

It was Spurs' third FA Cup of the 1960s. None of the 1961 double-winning side remained, and there were only two players from their previous Cup victory in 1962 - Jimmy Greaves and Dave Mackay.

The format of the League Cup Final was changed from a two-legged, home and away affair to a one-off showcase match at Wembley.

On March 4, 1967, a crowd of 97,952 saw Third Division Queen's Park Rangers win the League Cup at Wembley by coming back from two goals down to beat First Division West Bromwich Albion 3-2.

Both West Brom's goals were scored in the first half by ex-QPR winger Clive Clark. Then, after 63 minutes, Roger Morgan put Rangers back into contention and after 75 minutes the Londoners equalised through a solo effort by the mercurial Rodney Marsh. The winner - scored by Mark Lazarus - was controversial because the chance came after QPR centre half Ron Hunt had bundled into West Brom keeper Dick Sheppard.

Despite their League Cup triumph, QPR were not allowed to enter the Inter Cities Fairs Cup because the European competition was open only to members of the First Division.

 **Facts** The Sixties

In the first ever six-figure transfer between British clubs, World Cup winner Alan Ball was transferred from Blackpool to Everton for £110,000.

World Cup winning manager Alf Ramsey was knighted in the 1967 New Year's Honours List.

In addition to winning the 1967 Home International Championship, on April 15, Scotland had the extra thrill of becoming the first team to beat the new world champions England, winning 3-2 at Wembley.

In 1967, the club side that stood head and shoulders above everyone else in the northern hemisphere was Celtic, who made a clean sweep of the European Cup, the Scottish League Championship, the Scottish FA Cup, the Scottish League Cup and the Glasgow Cup.

Celtic became the first British team to win the European Cup, with a 2-1 victory over Inter Milan in the Final in Lisbon.

Inter Milan went a goal up after eight minutes from a Mazzola penalty. Thereafter they sat back and soaked up everything the Scots could throw at them.

Inter Milan were the world's leading exponents of a defensive formation known as *catenaccio* (the Italian for 'door bolt').

The rest of the match was wave after wave of Celtic pressure which was all absorbed by the Inter defence until their attacking left back Tommy Gemmell hit the equaliser from 25 yards out after 63 minutes.

Eight minutes from time, Gemmell again advanced down the left, pushed the ball inside to Bobby Murdoch who drove the ball into the area where Steve Chalmers deflected it into the Italian goal for the winner.

The Sixties

Facts

Club chairman Robert Kelly acclaimed the European Cup winners as the greatest Celtic team of all time. They are popularly known as The Lions of Lisbon.

Bobby Murdoch's 1967 European Cup Final winner was Celtic's 200th goal of the season.

Of Celtic's other goals, 111 had come in the Scottish League, which they won finishing three points ahead of second-placed Rangers. Twenty-one of these goals were scored by Scotland's leading marksman, Steve Chalmers.

Scottish Footballer of the Year was Ronnie Simpson, the veteran Celtic goalkeeper.

Rangers were also runners-up to Celtic in the Scottish League Cup Final. The two sides were separated on this occasion by a single goal from Bobby Lennox.

In the Scottish FA Cup, Celtic beat Aberdeen 2-0 in the Final, with two goals from Wallace.

In one of the greatest upsets in Cup history, Rangers had been knocked out of the Scottish FA Cup in the first round by Berwick Rangers. Berwick's goal was scored by Sammy Reid after 32 minutes - thereafter, the Glasgow Rangers were held at bay by Berwick's goalkeeper-manager Jock Wallace.

Although Rangers reached the Final of the Cup Winners' Cup, they lost 1-0 in extra time to Bayern Munich.

In the Final of the Inter Cities Fairs Cup, Dynamo Zagreb beat Leeds United 2-0 on aggregate over two legs.

A new rule was introduced at the start of the 1967-68 season - goalkeepers were restricted to four steps before they had to release the ball.

 **Facts**   **The Sixties**

**The season began spectacularly on August 12, when Tottenham
Hotspur goalkeeper Pat Jennings scored in the Charity Shield
against Manchester United with a punt that bounced on the edge
of the opposition penalty area and over the head of United keeper
Alex Stepney. The match ended 3-3.**

The existing British transfer record - Alan Ball's £110,000 move from
Blackpool to Everton the previous year - was broken twice this season. First
in January, when Martin Chivers went from Southampton to Tottenham
Hotspur for £125,000, and again in June, when Leicester City bough Allan
Clarke from Fulham for £150,000.

**The League Championship stayed in Manchester, but moved
across town from United to City. This was City's second title - they
had previously won it in 1937.**

Much of the credit for Manchester City's achievement went to manager Joe
Mercer, the former Everton, Arsenal and England player who had been lured
out of retirement to take the helm at Maine Road in 1965, when the club
languished in the wrong half of Division Two.

**Within a week of taking over, Mercer signed as coach and assistant
manager the former Charlton and West Ham player Malcolm
Allison. Under the pair of them City won promotion back to the
First Division in 1966.**

Among the great Mercer-Allison signings were Colin Bell from Bury for
£45,000, Francis Lee from Bolton Wanderers for £60,000 and Mike
Summerbee from Swindon Town for £35,000.

**Tony Book, the Championship-winning Manchester City captain
and right back, had been signed at the age of 29 for £13,500 from
Plymouth Argyle.**

The joint top scorers in the First Division were George Best of Manchester
United and Ron Davies of Southampton, both with 28 goals.

The Sixties

Facts

Fulham finished bottom of the First Division and were relegated. Since winning promotion in 1959, they had become the League's perennial escapologists - they never finished higher than 10th in the First Division, and were 20th - one place above the drop - three times, in 1962, 1965 and 1966.

Peterborough United were relegated from the Third Division after having had 19 points deducted for offering illegal bonuses to their players.

West Bromwich Albion won their fifth FA Cup on their record-breaking 10th appearance in the Final, beating Everton 1-0 after extra time through a goal by Jeff Astle, who had scored in every round of that season's competition.

Leeds United won the 1968 League Cup, beating Arsenal 1-0 in the Final at Wembley.

In Scotland, Celtic retained the Championship - indeed, they lost only once in the League all season, a 1-0 defeat by Rangers.

Celtic also kept the League Cup, beating Dundee 5-3 in the Final.

The Scottish FA Cup went to Dunfermline Athletic for the second time in their history. They beat Heart of Midlothian 3-1 in the Final.

At the start of the 1967-68 season, the Scottish League was enlarged from 37 to 38 clubs by the admission of Clydebank.

On entry into the Scottish Second Division, Clydebank took the unusual decision not to have a manager, making do with a coach.

Facts

The Sixties

Celtic's bid to win the World Club Championship against Racing Club of Argentina ended in failure and some of the most disgraceful scenes imaginable. The teams had drawn 2-2 over two legs - Celtic winning 1-0 in Glasgow and Racing Club winning 2-1 in Buenos Aires - and so a play-off was held in Montevideo, the capital of Uruguay. Six players - four Scots and two Argentines - were sent off and Racing Club 1-0 with a goal after 57 minutes by Cardenas.

Cardiff City of Division Two had a wonderful run in Europe, to which they gained entry through their 12th victory in the Welsh Cup. They reached the semi-final of the Cup Winners' Cup, beating NAC Breda and Torpedo Moscow on the way. Drawn against SV Hamburg in the semi-final, they drew 1-1 in the away leg but went down 3-2 at home.

Bobby Charlton's 45th international goal in a 3-1 victory over Sweden took him ahead of Jimmy Greaves as England's all-time leading goalscorer.

Ten years after the Munich air crash had destroyed the greater part of a great team, Manchester United emerged at the summit of the game when they became the first English club to win the European Cup. They beat Benfica 4-1 after extra time in the Final at Wembley with two goals by Bobby Charlton and one each from George Best and Brian Kidd, the last named playing on his 19th birthday.

The Sixties

Facts

Manchester United manager Matt Busby was knighted in the New Year's Honours List.

AC Milan won the 1968 Cup Winners' Cup, beating SV Hamburg 2-0 in the Final in Rotterdam.

Leeds United won another European trophy for England, beating Ferencvaros 1-0 on aggregate in the Final of the Inter Cities Fairs Cup.

The semi-finals and Final of the 1968 European Nations' Cup were held in Italy.

Italy won the tournament, beating Yugoslavia 2-0 in the Final in Rome. The hosts had been lucky to get this far - they had drawn their semi-final against the USSR 0-0 and had gone through on the toss of a coin.

Earlier in the tournament, Alan Mullery had become the first England player to be sent off in an international match during the 1-0 semi-final defeat by Yugoslavia. The winning goal in this match was scored by Dragan Dzajic.

Leeds United won the English Championship in 1969 for the first time in their history. During the season, they were beaten only twice in the League - a record for any English 22-club division. Their points total - 67- was also a record, surpassing Arsenal's 66 points in 1931.

One record Leeds United did not even threaten to break was for the highest number of goals scored - they netted only 66 times in the entire season.

Most of the Leeds Championship-winning side were home-grown or had been brought to Elland Road by the enviably efficient scouting system set up by manager Don Revie. Among the discoveries were goalkeeper Gary Sprake, the wingers Eddie Gray and Peter Lorimer and the play-anywhere defender Paul Madeley.

 **Facts**   The Sixties

The exceptions were Johnny Giles, Mick Jones and Mike O'Grady.

Midfielder Giles had been bought from Manchester United for £35,000 to replace Bobby Collins, who was out with a long-term injury after the previous season's Inter Cities Fairs Cup tie with Torino. Already capped 11 times by the Republic of Ireland, Giles went on to play a total of 59 full international matches.

Mick Jones was an England international centre forward bought from Sheffield United for £100,000.

Mike O'Grady was an England international winger who came from Huddersfield Town for £30,000.

Other great names of the Leeds side were World Cup winning centre half Jack Charlton, Scottish international Billy Bremner and Norman Hunter, who went on to play 28 times for England.

Mick Jones was the Champions' leading scorer, with 14 League goals. Overall top scorer was Jimmy Greaves, with 27 goals for Tottenham Hotspur. This was the sixth time since 1959 that Greaves had been either the leading or joint-leading scorer in the First Division.

Once they had won the title, in June 1969 Leeds sought to consolidate their position by buying striker Allan Clarke from Leicester City for £165,000.

In 1969, Manchester City won the FA Cup for the fourth time, beating Leicester City 1-0 in the Final through a goal by Neil Young. Leicester were also relegated from the First Division.

1968 was the year which started the legend of Tommy Docherty, the man who, by his own account, has 'had more clubs than Jack Nicklaus'. In six weeks between November 6 and December 18, he managed Rotherham, Queen's Park Rangers and Aston Villa.

The Sixties

Facts

Fulham were relegated for the second year running after finishing bottom of Division Two.

The rise and fall of Northampton Town was the most spectacular in League history. Promoted from Division Four in 1960, they won the Third Division Championship in 1963. They finished second in Division Two in 1965, and spent the 1965-66 season in the First Division, but they finished in 21st place and were relegated. In 1967, they were next to bottom of Division Two. At the end of 1969, they were relegated back to the Fourth Division - a full tour of the English Football League in less than a decade.

A Third Division team won the League Cup for the second time as Swindon Town beat First Division Arsenal 3-1 after extra time at Wembley. Swindon went ahead after 35 minutes with a goal by Roger Smart. There was then an extended period of Arsenal pressure - resisted heroically by the Swindon defence, especially keeper Peter Downsborough before Arsenal equalised after 86 minutes through Bobby Gould. In extra time, Swindon winger Don Rogers tore Arsenal apart almost singlehandedly and scored two more goals that took the Cup to Wiltshire.

1966 World Cup hat-trick hero Geoff Hurst scored six for his club in West Ham United's record victory - 8-0 against Sunderland in the First Division. The other two goals were also scored by famous international names - Bobby Moore and Trevor Brooking.

In 1969, Matt Busby - Munich air crash survivor and European Cup-winning manager - announced that he would stand down at the end of the season after 23 years as Manchester United manager.

In Scotland, Celtic completed the treble for the second time in three years, winning the League Championship, the FA Cup and the League Cup.

In the FA Cup Final, they beat Rangers 4-0 with goals by Billy McNeill, Bobby Lennox, John Connelly and Steve Chalmers.

 **Facts**   **The Sixties**

By the end of the 1960s, the celebrity of leading footballers was on a par with that of pop stars. In 1969, Manchester United's George Best - who was sometimes described in the press as a fifth Beatle - felt emboldened to go in to the office of his manager Matt Busby and demand that Pat Crerand, Denis Law and - most amazingly - Bobby Charlton be moved on. His request was noted but not acted on.

Back in Scotland, Celtic's margin of victory in the League Cup Final was even more emphatic - 6-2 against Hibernian. Lennox scored a hat-trick and there were further goals from Wallace, Auld and Craig.

The European Cup went to AC Milan, who beat Ajax Amsterdam 4-1 in the Final in Madrid.

The Cup Winners' Cup was won by Slovan Bratislava, who beat Barcelona 3-2 in the Final in Basel.

In the Cup Winners' Cup semi-final, Slovan Bratislava had eliminated Dunfermline Athletic, who had knocked out England's representatives, West Bromwich Albion, in the quarter-final.

Newcastle United won the 1969 Inter-Cities Fairs Cup, beating Ujpest Dozsa 6-2 on aggregate in the two-legged Final.

The Sixties

Facts

Despite having finished only 10th in the First Division in 1968, Newcastle qualified for the Fairs Cup because the 'one city, one club' rule then in operation meant that Arsenal, Everton and Tottenham Hotspur - who had all come above them in the League - were barred from entering.

Everton won the First Division Championship in 1970 for the seventh time in their history. They scored 66 points - one fewer than Leeds United's record total the previous season.

The leading scorer in the English First Division was Jeff Astle, with 25 goals for West Bromwich Albion.

In 1970, the FA Cup went to Chelsea for the first time.

Leeds United were runners-up in both the League and the FA Cup in the 1969-70 season.

The FA Cup Final went to a replay for the first time in its Wembley history and the first time ever since 1912.

The first 1970 FA Cup Final was a 2-2 draw - Leeds led twice with goals by Jack Charlton and Mick Jones; Chelsea equalised twice through Peter Houseman and Ian Hutchinson.

In the Cup Final replay at Old Trafford, Leeds again took the lead with another goal by Mick Jones, but Chelsea levelled the match after 78 minutes through a Peter Osgood header. Chelsea's winner came just before half-time in extra time, when a long throw by Hutchinson into the Leeds penalty area was headed in. The scorer was defender David Webb, who had been roasted by Eddie Gray in the first match at Wembley.

In the fifth round of the FA Cup, George Best equalled what was then the competition scoring record with six goals for Manchester United as they beat Fourth Division Northampton Town 8-2.

 **Facts** The Sixties

The League Cup was won by Manchester City, who beat West Bromwich Albion 2-1 in the Final.

1970 was a great double year for the blue half of Manchester as City also won the Cup Winners' Cup, beating Gornik Zabrze of Poland 2-1 in the Final in Vienna.

Celtic beat Leeds United 3-1 on aggregate in the semi-final of the European Cup. The Scots won the first leg at Elland Road with a single goal scored after only a minute and a half by George Connelly. Leeds' captain Billy Bremner opened the scoring in the return at Hampden Park to level the tie, but in the second half a goal from John 'Yogi' Hughes restored Celtic's lead. Then Leeds' goalkeeper Gary Sprake had to go off injured; the first time his replacement, David Harvey, touched the ball was to pick it out of the net after a third goal by Bobby Murdoch.

In the European Cup Final in Milan, Celtic lost 2-1 to Feyenoord of Holland after extra time despite having taken the lead through Tommy Gemmell.

Back in Scotland, however, Celtic were still the team to beat, though few did. They won the League Championship for the 25th time in their history and the League Cup for the fifth time in a row, beating St Johnstone 1-0 in the Final.

Celtic were denied another treble by Aberdeen, who beat them 3-1 in the Final of the Scottish FA Cup.

Aberdeen - who had finished second in the League - had not won the Scottish FA Cup since 1947. Their goals in the Final were scored by Joe Harper from the penalty spot and two from Derek McKay. Celtic's goal was scored by Bobby Lennox.

In 1970, Arsenal won their first trophy since the League Championship in 1953 when they beat Anderlecht of Belgium 4-3 on aggregate in the Final of the Inter-Cities Fairs Cup.

The Sixties

Facts

The Home International Championship was a three-way tie between England, Scotland and Wales. The England v Northern Ireland match was Bobby Charlton's 100th international cap. The Scotland v England match at Hampden Park on April 25, 1970, was the first 0-0 draw since the inaugural meeting of the old enemies in 1872.

Two founder members of the Football League - Aston Villa and Preston North End - were relegated to the Third Division for the first time in their history.

Bradford Park Avenue failed to gain re-election after finishing bottom of the Fourth Division. Their place in the League was taken by Cambridge United.

Martin Peters moved from West Ham United to Tottenham Hotspur for a British record fee of £200,000. Part of the amount was made up with the transfer in the opposite direction of the once-great Jimmy Greaves, now a victim of alcoholism and - as a player, at least - a mere shadow of his former self.

In the build-up to the 1970 World Cup, El Salvador and Honduras fought a four-day war which was at least partly sparked by animosity generated between the two countries when they met in the qualifying tournament.

The 1970 World Cup finals were held in Mexico. The choice of venue was controversial - the 1968 Olympic Games had been held here and many of the competing athletes had experienced severe problems with the intense heat and the altitude.

During a pre-tournament acclimatisation tour of South America, England captain Bobby Moore was arrested in Bogota and charged with stealing an emerald bracelet worth £600 from a hotel jewellery shop in the Colombian capital.

 **Facts** The Sixties

Moore was placed under house arrest while the rest of the squad went off to beat Ecuador 2-0 in Quito. When they came back to Colombia, the charges were dropped and Moore was exonerated.

Later, the whole incident was convincingly shown to have been an attempt to frame the England captain. Bobby Moore himself remarked: 'The fact that they accused Bobby Charlton of sheltering me while I stole a bracelet proves I'm innocent. Bobby has never done a dishonest thing in his life'.

The 16 finalists in the 1970 World Cup were Belgium, Brazil, Bulgaria, Czechoslovakia, El Salvador, England, Israel, Italy, Mexico, Morocco, Peru, Romania, Sweden, Uruguay, the USSR and West Germany.

Holders England were drawn in the same group as Brazil, Czechoslovakia and Romania. Their matches were played in Guadalajara, where the altitude was lower than in Mexico City but where the daytime temperatures typically reached close to 100°F.

The first of many great matches in this World Cup was the meeting between England and Brazil. England lost 1-0 to a goal by Jairzinho, but the match is best remembered for the save Gordon Banks made from a header by Pele.

The last eight in the 1970 World Cup were Brazil, England, Italy, Mexico, Peru, Uruguay, the USSR and West Germany. The four quarter final matches produced 17 goals.

The tie of the round was the meeting in Leon between England and West Germany, a repeat of the 1966 Final.

The Sixties

Gordon Banks had to miss this match with a stomach upset, and Peter Bonetti of Chelsea took his place in goal. England took a two-goal lead through Alan Mullery and Martin Peters, then Franz Beckenbauer pulled one back for the Germans. The game looked like England's, and manager Alf Ramsey took the historic decision to take off Peters and Bobby Charlton and replace them with Francis Lee and Norman Hunter. This changed the balance of the side and the course of the match - shortly after the twin substitution, Uwe Seeler equalised for West Germany. In extra time, Geoff Hurst had an effort disallowed before Gerd Muller scored the winner.

In the semi-finals, Italy beat West Germany 4-3 after extra time and Brazil beat Uruguay 3-1.

The 1970 World Cup Final between Brazil and Italy was held in the Aztec Stadium, Mexico City on June 21 before a crowd of 107,000.

BRAZIL: Felix, Carlos Alberto, Brito, Piazza, Everaldo, Clodoaldo, Gerson, Jairzinho, Tostao, Pele, Rivelino
ITALY: Albertosi, Burgnich, Facchetti, Cera, Rosato, Bertini (sub: Juliano), Riva, Domenghini, Mazzola, De Sisti, Boninsegna (sub: Rivera)

In the first half, Pele headed Brazil into an early lead, but a defensive disaster allowed Boninsegna to equalise. In the second half Brazil took control and showed themselves to be the outstanding team of the tournament. They scored again through Gerson, Jairzinho and captain Carlos Alberto.

This was Brazil's third World Cup triumph and they thus kept the Jules Rimet Trophy.

The leading scorer in the 1970 World Cup finals was Gerd Muller of West Germany, with 10 goals in the tournament. Brazil's Jairzinho was second with seven and the veteran Peruvian Teofilo Cubillas third, with five goals.

Jairzinho also became the only player in the 20th century to score in every round of the World Cup finals.

THE SEVENTIES

The Seventies

Facts

In 1971, Arsenal became only the second club this century - after fierce local rivals Tottenham Hotspur - to win the League and FA Cup double.

Arsenal's manager was Bertie Mee, their captain Frank McLintock.

Runners-up were Leeds United - their 64 points in the season was the highest number of points that had ever failed to secure the Championship.

Fifth-placed Liverpool conceded only 24 goals in the 1970-71 season - an all-time low.

The First Division's leading scorer was Tony Brown, with 28 goals for 17th-placed West Bromwich Albion.

In the FA Cup Final, Arsenal beat Liverpool 2-1 after extra time. Liverpool went ahead with a goal from Steve Heighway, and then Eddie Kelly became the first substitute ever to score in an FA Cup Final. The winner came eight minutes from time - scorer Charlie George.

Among the giant-killers in this season's FA Cup were Barnet - then a non-League club - who beat Fourth Division Newport County 6-1.

 **Facts**   The Seventies

Tottenham Hotspur won the League Cup. They beat Aston Villa 2-0 in the Final, both their goals being scored by Martin Chivers, their record signing from Southampton in 1968.

The season was a disaster for the 'B's of Lancashire - Burnley and Blackpool were relegated from the First Division, Blackpool after only a year back in it; Blackburn Rovers and Bolton Wanderers - founder members of the League - were relegated to the Third Division for the first time in their histories.

North of the border, Celtic did the League and FA Cup double for the third time in five seasons. Their - and Scotland's - leading scorer was Harry Hood, with 22 goals in the season.

Rangers prevented Celtic from doing the treble by beating them 1-0 in the Final of the Scottish League Cup. It was five years since Rangers had won a trophy - their last success had been in the 1966 FA Cup Final. This was the longest barren period in their history.

This season, the Scottish League introduced goal difference instead of goal average as a means of separating teams level on points.

Ajax of Amsterdam won the European Cup for the first time, beating Greek League Champions Panathinaikos 2-0 in the Final at Wembley.

Chelsea won the Cup Winners' Cup, beating Real Madrid 2-1 after extra time in the Final replay after the first match had been drawn 1-1. Peter Osgood scored in both games; Chelsea's other goal came from John Dempsey. Both games were played in Athens.

In the semi-final of the Cup Winners' Cup, Chelsea had eliminated the holders, Manchester City, 1-0 on aggregate.

The Seventies

Facts

Leeds United finally won a trophy - the Inter-Cities Fairs Cup for the second time. They drew with Juventus 3-3 in the Final, but took the Cup on away goals after their 2-2 draw in the first leg in Turin.

This was the last season of the Inter-Cities Fairs Cup. The following year it was replaced by the UEFA Cup. It was also the fourth year running that it had been won by an English club.

The 1972 English First Division Championship was won by Derby County, the first League title in their history.

Derby had finished the 1966-67 season in 17th place in Division Two. But then Brian Clough and Peter Taylor took over the management of the club and the upturn in their fortunes began. They won the Second Division Championship in 1969, then came fourth in the First Division in 1970 and ninth in 1971.

The First Division's leading scorer was Francis Lee of Manchester City. Of his 33 League goals, 13 were penalties - an all-time record. Many of these spot kicks were the result of fouls on the player himself - this gave rise to his Oriental-sounding nickname Lee Won Pen.

 **The Seventies**

Leeds United won the 100th FA Cup, beating the holders, Arsenal, 1-0 in the Final with a goal from Allan Clarke.

Arsenal reached Wembley the hard way - for the second season running, they did not have a single home draw in the competition.

FA Cup giantkillers of the season were Hereford United - then still a non-League club - who drew 2-2 with First Division Newcastle United at St James' Park and then beat them 2-1 at Edgar Street with goals from Ronnie Radford and Ricky George.

Leeds were again runners-up in the First Division. This was despite having been ordered to play their first four home matches away from Elland Road - a punishment for a pitch invasion in April.

This was the year in which Leeds almost bought Asa Hartford from West Bromwich Albion, but pulled out of the deal after a medical examination revealed that the player had a hole in his heart. Despite this condition, Hartford went on to play with great distinction for several clubs, including Manchester City - where he won two League Cup winner's medals - and 50 times for Scotland.

Stoke City won the League Cup - the first trophy in their history - beating Chelsea 2-1 in the Final at Wembley. Their goals were scored by Terry Conroy and veteran George Eastham, aged 35. Chelsea's goal was scored by Peter Osgood.

The great match of the season's League Cup was Stoke's epic semi-final against West Ham United. Stoke lost the first leg 2-1 but levelled the tie at Upton Park. Then, with three minutes of extra time remaining, Stoke's England keeper Gordon Banks saved a penalty from Geoff Hurst.

The Seventies

Facts

The first West Ham v Stoke play-off, at Hillsborough, ended goalless, so a second replay was held at Old Trafford. West Ham's keeper Bobby Ferguson was hurt in this match and had to leave the field. His place in goal was taken by captain Bobby Moore, who saved a penalty, but Mike Bernard scored from the rebound.

West Ham plugged on with 10 men - they expected Ferguson to return - and took the lead with goals by Billy Bonds and Trevor Brooking. But Stoke equalised through Peter Dobing and scored the winner shortly after half time through Terry Conroy.

In Scotland, Celtic again did the double. They won the League Championship by 10 points from second-placed Aberdeen and beat Hibernian 6-1 in the Final of the FA Cup.

Surprisingly, however, Celtic were beaten 4-1 in the League Cup Final by unfancied Partick Thistle. This was only Thistle's second trophy - their previous triumph had been in the 1921 FA Cup.

Partick Thistle's goals came in the first 37 minutes through Alex Rae, Bobby Lawrie, Denis McQuade and Jimmy Bone. Celtic's reply was scored by Kenny Dalglish.

Ajax Amsterdam retained the European Cup, beating Inter Milan 2-0 in the Final in Rotterdam. Star of the match was European Footballer of the Year Johan Cruyff.

Rangers won the Cup Winners' Cup, for which they had only qualified as losing FA Cup finalists because Celtic did the double and went into the European Cup. They beat Moscow Dynamo 3-2 in the Final in Barcelona, with one goal from Colin Stein and two from Willie Johnston.

Rangers never defended their trophy. The match was marred by pitch invasions by their fans, and as a result the club was banned from European competition for a year.

 **Facts**

The Seventies

The first UEFA Cup Final was an all-England affair, Tottenham Hotspur beating Wolverhampton Wanderers 3-2 on aggregate. They won the first leg at Molineux 2-1, with two goals by Martin Chivers. Wolves' scorer was Jim McCalliog. At White Hart Lane, Alan Mullery increased the London club's lead, but David Wagstaffe equalised for Wolves. Spurs thus became the first English club to win two different European trophies - they had lifted the Cup Winners' Cup in 1963.

In the European Championship, England were eliminated by West Germany after losing 3-1 at Wembley. The German star was Gunter Netzer, who scored from a penalty and set up two goals for Gerd Muller. In the second leg, although England brought in Norman Hunter to neutralise Netzer, they could only draw 0-0 and were knocked out.

The semi-finals and Final of the 1972 European Championship were held in Belgium. West Germany beat the hosts 2-1, while in the other match the USSR beat Hungary 1-0.

The Final was held in Brussels on June 18, 1972. West Germany beat the USSR 3-0 with another two goals from Muller and one from Wimmer.

In 1973, Liverpool won the League Championship for a record eighth time.

The First Division's leading scorer was Bryan 'Pop' Robson, with 28 goals for West Ham United.

The Champions of all four Divisions of the Football League came from Lancashire - Liverpool won the First Division, Burnley the Second, Bolton Wanderers the Third and Southport the Fourth.

The Seventies

Facts

Sunderland became the first Second Division side to win the FA Cup since West Bromwich Albion in 1931 when they beat Leeds United 1-0 in the Final at Wembley with a goal from Ian Porterfield. Thereafter, Jim Montgomery held Leeds at bay almost singlehandedly with a magnificent display in goal.

Tottenham Hotspur won the League Cup, beating Norwich City 1-0 in the Final. Spurs' winner was scored by Ralph Coates.

In May 1973, Derby County bought Leicester City full back David Nish for £225,000, a British record transfer fee.

Huddersfield Town - three times League Champions - were relegated to the Third Division for the first time in their history.

In Scotland, Celtic won the League Championship and finished runners-up in both the Cups.

Rangers took the Scottish FA Cup in their centenary year, beating Celtic 3-2 in the Final with goals from Parlane, Conn and Forsyth. Celtic opened the scoring through Dalglish, and later brought the game back to 2-2 with a penalty scored by Scottish Footballer of the Year George Connelly.

Hibernian won the Scottish League Cup, beating Celtic 2-1 in the Final.

Ajax of Amsterdam won the European Cup for the third year in succession, beating Juventus 1-0 in the Final in Belgrade.

AC Milan won the Cup Winners' Cup, beating Leeds United 1-0 in the Final in Salonika. Yet again, Leeds finished empty-handed a season that had promised so much - they had nearly won the League, but finished third, lost in the FA Cup Final to unfancied opposition, and now this defeat by an Italian team they outplayed for much of the match.

 **Facts**   **The Seventies**

Liverpool won the 1973 UEFA Cup, beating Borussia Moenchengladbach 3-2 on aggregate in the Final.

Leeds United won the League Championship in 1974 for the second time in their history. At the start of the season, they went 23 matches without defeat - a record.

Promotion and relegation changed from two- to three-up and down between the First and Second and the Second and Third Divisions. The first club to be relegated from the First Division after finishing 20th out of 22 was Southampton.

The First Division's leading scorer was Mike Channon, with 21 goals for relegated Southampton.

Manchester United finished 21st (next to last) and were relegated - they had been in the First Division since 1938. Their final match was at home to local rivals Manchester City - they lost 1-0, and the goal was scored by ex-United hero Denis Law. Shortly afterwards, a massive pitch invasion led the referee to abandon the match on the advice of police, but the result stood.

In his first season as a manager, England World Cup hero Jack Charlton guided Middlesbrough to the Second Division Championship, thus getting them back into the top flight for the first time since 1954.

On September 22, 1973, three Notts County players missed the same penalty in their Second Division match against Portsmouth at Fratton Park.

The Eagles of Crystal Palace went into a free fall, as they were relegated from the First to the Third Division of the League in successive seasons.

The Seventies

Facts

Fourth Division Exeter City unilaterally cancelled their League match against Scunthorpe United because they had nine players unfit. In doing this, they risked expulsion from the League, but escaped with a fine of £5000 and two points (the League awarded the game to Scunthorpe).

League runners-up Liverpool won the FA Cup, beating Newcastle United 3-0 in the Final. Their goals were scored by Kevin Keegan (2) and Steve Heighway.

At 11 o'clock on the morning of January 6, 1974, professional football was played on Sunday in England for the first time - Cambridge United drew 2-2 with Oldham Athletic in the third round of the FA Cup.

Wolverhampton Wanderers won the League Cup Final, beating Manchester City 2-1 in the Final.

Plymouth Argyle of the Third Division reached the League Cup semi-finals. En route, they beat three First Division clubs away - Burnley, Queen's Park Rangers and Birmingham City - before losing 3-1 on aggregate to Manchester City, the eventual runners-up.

Celtic won the Scottish Championship for the ninth year in a row. They also did the double, beating Dundee United 3-0 in the Final of the Scottish FA Cup.

Celtic's - and the Scottish First Division's - leading scorer was Dixie Deans, with 24 goals.

Dundee won the Scottish League Cup was won by Dundee, who beat Celtic 1-0 in the Final.

In the first European Cup Final to require a replay, Bayern Munich eventually beat Atletico Madrid 4-1 after the first match had been drawn 1-1. Both games were played in Brussels.

 **Facts**   **The Seventies**

Feyenoord of Rotterdam made it a double Dutch Cup celebration when they beat Tottenham Hotspur 4-2 on aggregate in the Final of the UEFA Cup. The second leg was marred by Spurs fans who rioted in the stadium and had to be dispersed by Dutch police.

FC Magdeburg of East Germany won the Cup Winners' Cup, beating AC Milan 2-0 in the Final in Rotterdam.

On September 26, 1973, Trevor Hockey of Aston Villa became the first Welsh player to be sent off in an international during his country's 3-0 defeat by Poland in Katowice in the World Cup qualifying match.

England were knocked out of the World Cup when they finished behind Poland in their qualifying group. The killer blow came when the Poles came to Wembley and went ahead through Domarski who shot under Peter Shilton's body after 58 minutes. The rest of the match was sustained England pressure, and although they salvaged a draw with a penalty from Allan Clarke, the home team were denied the win they needed by Polish keeper Jan Tomaszewski, memorably - but inaccurately - described by Brian Clough on television as 'a clown'.

In the aftermath of England's failure to reach the World Cup finals, the FA sacked Sir Alf Ramsey. Of their 113 matches under Ramsey, England had won 69 and drawn 27 and one of these victories had been their greatest triumph - the 1966 World Cup Final. There was widespread distaste that, given his distinguished record, Sir Alf had not been given the opportunity to resign.

Sir Alf Ramsey was replaced by Joe Mercer, who took over as England caretaker-manager while a long-term successor was sought.

Three days before the opening ceremony of the 1974 World Cup finals, Brazilian Joao Havelange replaced Sir Stanley Rous as President of FIFA.

The Seventies

The 1974 World Cup finals were held in West Germany. The 16 qualifying nations were Argentina, Australia, Brazil, Bulgaria, Chile, East Germany, Haiti, Holland, Italy, Poland, Scotland, Sweden, Uruguay, West Germany, Yugoslavia and Zaire.

In a departure from the practice in previous tournaments, goal difference was brought in for the first time to separate teams equal on points in the qualifying groups.

In another change to previous formats, the top two teams in each of the four qualifying groups were to progress into two more groups of four - the winners of these two groups would contest the Final, which would thus become the only true knockout match in the entire tournament.

Scotland went out in the group stage, but only because they scored one goal fewer than Brazil against Zaire. Quite how close they came to reaching the second stage may be seen from the Group Two Final Table:

	P	W	D	L	F	A	Pts
Yugoslavia	3	1	2	0	10	1	4
Brazil	3	1	2	0	3	0	4
Scotland	3	1	2	0	3	1	4
Zaire	3	0	0	3	0	14	0

The shock of round one was the 1-0 defeat of hosts and favourites West Germany by their neighbours East Germany.

Poland - who had been regarded as no-hopers, even after they had qualified at England's expense - won Group Four at a canter, with maximum points against Argentina, Italy and Haiti. They eventually finished third in the tournament and had the two leading scorers - Grzegorz Lato with seven goals and Andrzej Szarmach with five.

 **Facts**   **The Seventies**

In the second round, Group A contained Argentina, Brazil, East
Germany and Holland; in Group B were Poland, Sweden, West
Germany and Yugoslavia.

The winners of these groups were West Germany and Holland, each with
hundred per cent records.

**The 1974 World Cup Final was played at the Olympic Stadium,
Munich, on July 7, 1974, before a crowd of 77,833.**

West Germany: Maier, Vogts, Schwarzenbeck, Beckenbauer, Breitner,
Hoeness, Bonhof, Overath, Grabowski, Muller, Holzenbein
Holland: Jongbloed, Suurbier, Rijsbergen (sub: De Jong), Haan, Krol, Jansen,
Neeskens, Van Hanegem, Rep, Cruyff, Rensenbrink (sub: R. Van Der Kerkhof)

**Holland scored before a German had touched the ball when Uli
Hoeness fouled Johann Cruyff inside the penalty area and Johan
Neeskens scored from the spot.**

This was the first penalty in a World Cup Final. The referee who awarded it
was Englishman Jack Taylor.

**The second penalty in a World Cup Final came less than 25
minutes later. This time, it went to West Germany after
Holzenbein had been fouled in the box. Paul Breitner took the
spot kick and made the score 1-1.**

Two minutes before half-time, Bonhof fed Gerd Muller in the area - he
swivelled and scored what turned out to be the World Cup-winning goal for
West Germany.

The Seventies

Facts

The 1974-75 season began with the unprecedented spectacle of a double sending-off in the Charity Shield match between last year's Champions Leeds United and the FA Cup winners Liverpool. The two to get their marching orders for fighting were no less than the international stars Billy Bremner and Kevin Keegan - the first Britons ever to be sent off at Wembley. They were later fined £500 each and banned for what turned out to be 11 matches.

Derby County won the League Championship for the second time in four years, this time under the management of Dave Mackay.

Brian Clough and Peter Taylor had quit Derby after the former had refused to accept an ultimatum from the club that he stop writing for the newspapers and appearing on television. Derby chairman Sam Longston was particularly concerned about Clough's accusation that some of his own players were giving less than one hundred per cent.

The First Division's leading scorer in 1974-75 was Malcolm Macdonald, with 21 goals for Newcastle United.

Malcolm Macdonald also became the only player to score five goals in a Wembley international when England beat Cyprus 5-0 in the European Championships.

Manchester United came straight back up, winning the Second Division Championship at their first attempt.

West Ham United won the FA Cup in 1975, beating Fulham 2-0 in the Final. Both their Wembley goals were scored by Alan Taylor.

 **Facts** The Seventies

Taylor - purchased from Rochdale shortly before Christmas - had also scored two goals for West Ham in the sixth round versus Arsenal and in the semi-final replay versus Ipswich Town.

Playing for Fulham in that Final was West Ham's former captain and greatest legend - Bobby Moore.

The 1975 League Cup was won by Aston Villa, who beat Norwich City 1-0 in the Final. This was Norwich's second defeat at Wembley in this competition - they had been beaten by Spurs in the 1973 Final.

For Villa manager Ron Saunders, it was third time lucky - this was his third consecutive match in charge of a League Cup finalist, but on the two previous occasions he had seen his team lose - with Manchester City in 1974 and the year before with Norwich.

In Scotland, Celtic's great run of victories came to an end after nine League titles in a row - Rangers won their first title since 1964.

The joint leading scorers in the Scottish First Division were Andy Gray of Dundee United and Willie Pettigrew of Motherwell, each with 20 goals.

Celtic won the 1975 Scottish FA Cup, beating Airdrieonians 3-1 in the Final, which was European Cup-winning captain Billy McNeill's swansong for the club as a player.

The League Cup also went to Celtic, who beat Hibernian 6-3 in the Final.

The Seventies

Facts

Bayern Munich won the European Cup for the second year running, beating Leeds United 2-0 in the Final in Paris. The English Champions were incredibly unlucky in this match - they had two legitimate-looking penalty appeals against Beckenbauer turned down by French referee Kitabdjian, and a second-half goal by Peter Lorimer disallowed for offside. The Leeds fans rioted. There have since been strong and persistent rumours that the result was somehow fixed.

In an all-Eastern European Final, Dynamo Kiev of the USSR beat Ferencvaros of Hungary 2-0 to win the Cup Winners' Cup.

Borussia Moenchengladbach (West Germany) won the UEFA Cup, beating Twente Enschede (Holland) 5-1 on aggregate in the Final.

On July 4, 1974, the FA announced the appointment of Leeds United boss Don Revie as Sir Alf Ramsey's permanent successor as England manager.

Revie was succeeded at Leeds by Brian Clough, the man who had taken Derby County to their first League title and then taken over at Brighton and Hove Albion. He lasted only 43 days in the post, unable to make an impact on the well-established cliques among the senior players in the Leeds dressing room.

During the 1974-75 season, three England international players went absent without leave - Kevin Keegan, Stan Bowles and Kevin Beattie.

After 15 years in charge at Anfield, Bill Shankly announced that he was stepping down as manager of Liverpool. Under him, Liverpool won the Second Division in 1962, the League Championship in 1964, 1966 and 1973, the FA Cup in 1965 and 1974, and the UEFA Cup in 1973.

 **Facts**   **The Seventies**

Bill Nicholson, for 38 years a Tottenham Hotspur employee and their manager since 1958, also announced his retirement. He gave as his reason the unreasonable demands and expectations of modern players. Under Nicholson, Spurs had won the double in 1961, two more FA Cups in 1962 and 1967, the Cup Winners' Cup in 1963 and the UEFA Cup in 1972.

In 1975-76, Liverpool won the League Championship for a record ninth time and the first time under Bob Paisley in his first season as manager in succession to Bill Shankly. They pipped Queen's Park Rangers to the title by a single point.

The First Division's leading scorer in 1975-76 was Ted MacDougall, with 23 goals for 16th-placed Norwich City.

Second Division Southampton won the 1976 FA Cup - the first major honour in their history - beating the favourites Manchester United 1-0 in the Final. The winning goal was scored by Bobby Stokes.

Manchester City won the League Cup for the second time, beating Newcastle United 2-1 in the Final. Peter Barnes and Denis Tueart scored for the winners; Alan Gowling replied for the Magpies.

In Scotland, the League was reorganised yet again. The two old Divisions - the First of 18 clubs the Second of 20 - were changed into a Premier League of 10 clubs and a First and Second Division, each of 14 clubs.

Rangers did the treble, winning the League, the Cup and the League Cup. They retained the Championship and thus became the first winners of the new Premier League. They beat Heart of Midlothian 3-1 in the FA Cup Final and Celtic 1-0 in the League Cup Final.

The leading scorer in the Scottish Premier Division was Kenny Dalglish, with 24 goals for Celtic.

The Seventies

Facts

Bayern Munich won the European Cup for the third time running, beating St Etienne of France 1-0 in the Final.

Anderlecht of Belgium won the Cup Winners' Cup, beating West Ham United 4-2 in the Final in Brussels.

West Ham United came close to repeating their 1965 Cup Winners' Cup triumph. They went ahead with a goal from Pat Holland and were on top until Frank Lampard injured himself while trying to pass back to keeper Mervyn Day - the ball fell short and Dutch international Robbie Rensenbrink scored easily. In the second half, Anderlecht took the lead with a goal from François Van Der Elst, but West Ham got back on level terms with a goal from 'Pop' Robson. But after that, Anderlecht took charge - Holland brought down Rensenbrink, who scored from the penalty spot, and then Van der Elst broke through on his own, rounded the West Ham right back and keeper and scored a brilliant individual clinching goal.

League Champions Liverpool did a unique double by also winning the UEFA Cup, beating FC Bruges of Belgium 4-3 on aggregate in the Final. This was Liverpool's second UEFA Cup in four years.

The semi-finals and Final of the 1976 European Championship were held in Yugoslavia. In the semi-finals, Czechoslovakia beat Holland 3-1 and West Germany beat Yugoslavia 4-2.

The Final between Czechoslovakia and West Germany, the holders and World Champions, was played in Belgrade on June 20, 1976, in front of 45,000 spectators. The Czechs went two up with goals from Svehlik and Dobias; the Germans pulled one back through Dieter Muller and equalised through Holzenbein in the dying seconds of normal time. The score remained unchanged at the end of extra time and the Championship had to be decided on a penalty shoot-out, which the Czechs won 5-3.

 **Facts**   The Seventies

At the start of the 1976-77 season, the English Football League abolished goal average - from now on, teams equal on points would be separated by goal difference (the number of goals they had conceded subtracted from the number of goals they had scored).

1976-77 was the first League season in which yellow and red cards replaced (respectively) the notebook and the finger pointed towards the tunnel.

Liverpool retained the League Championship, a point ahead of Manchester City in second place.

Joint leading scorers with 25 in the First Division were Malcolm Macdonald, formerly of Newcastle United but now of eighth-placed Arsenal, and Andy Gray of fourth-placed Aston Villa.

Manchester United won the FA Cup, beating Liverpool 2-1 in the Final. Stuart Pearson scored the first, Jimmy Case equalised for Liverpool and then Jimmy Greenhoff scored the winner with a fluke as he tried to get out of the way of a shot from Lou Macari.

Aston Villa won the League Cup after a marathon Final against Everton. The first match finished 0-0; the replay was 1-1 after extra time. The second replay went to extra time before Villa clinched it 3-2, with two goals from Brian Little and another by Chris Nicholl. Everton's replies came from Bob Latchford and Mick Lyons.

Terry Paine of Southampton retired at the end of the season after 824 League appearances - a record.

Bobby Moore - now of Fulham, but famously of West Ham and England - retired at the end of his 1000th first class match on May 14 at Blackburn.

The Seventies

Facts

After finishing bottom of the Fourth Division for the second year running - and next to bottom in both previous seasons - Workington failed to win re-election. Their place in the Football League was taken by Wimbledon.

In Scotland, Celtic did the double. They won the Premier Division by nine points from second-placed Rangers and beat the same club 1-0 in the Final of the FA Cup.

Celtic's dreams of another treble were shattered by a 2-1 defeat by Aberdeen in the Final of the League Cup.

Liverpool more than made up for their FA Cup Final disappointment by beating Borussia Moenchengladbach 3-1 in the European Cup Final in Rome. Their goals were scored by Terry McDermott, Tommy Smith and Phil Neal (penalty). The German team's replay was scored by Danish international Allan Simonsen.

SV Hamburg won the Cup Winners' Cup, beating the holders Anderlecht 2-0 in the Final in Amsterdam.

Hamburg captured another prize at the end of the season - they bought Kevin Keegan from Liverpool for £500,000.

Juventus won the UEFA Cup on away goals after drawing 2-2 on aggregate in the Final with Athletic Bilbao.

Scotland won the Home International Championship and Wales won at Wembley for the first time in their history.

 **Facts**   The Seventies

After three years in which the national team won only 14 times in 29 internationals, Don Revie resigned as England manager on July 12, 1977, and took a £60,000-a-year job as coach to the United Arab Emirates.

In July 1977, former West Ham manager Ron Greenwood took over from Revie as England manager. The appointment was temporary at first, but was soon extended to the end of the 1980 European Championship.

In his first match in charge - a 0-0 draw against Switzerland at Wembley on September 7 - Greenwood picked six Liverpool players plus a seventh - Kevin Keegan - who had been at the club until the end of last season. This was the highest number of players from a single club to represent England since seven Arsenal players took the field against Italy on November 14, 1934 - the notorious match that became known as The Battle of Highbury.

Shortly after selling Kevin Keegan to Hamburg, on August 10, 1977, Liverpool spent £400,000 on a replacement - 27-year-old Kenny Dalglish of Celtic.

Tommy Docherty was sacked as manager of Manchester United only six weeks after leading them to victory in the FA Cup Final because of tabloid revelations about his love affair with the wife of Laurie Brown, the Old Trafford club's physiotherapist .

Scotland qualified for the World Cup Finals in Argentina with a 2-0 victory over Wales in a play-off at neutral Anfield. The first goal was scored by Don Masson from a penalty which television replays showed should not have been awarded - the handler was not a Welshman but Scotland's Joe Jordan. The clincher was scored after 87 minutes by Kenny Dalglish with a header.

Liverpool were denied a third consecutive League title by Nottingham Forest, who won the Championship in their first season back in the First Division.

The Seventies

Facts

Among Forest's stars were goalkeeper Peter Shilton - the club's record £250,000 buy from Stoke City - and defender Kenny Burns, a player with a reputation as a wild man whom manager Brian Clough bought from Birmingham City for £150,000 and promptly made club captain. At the end of the season, Shilton was voted the PFA Player of the year; Burns won the Football Writers' award.

Having won the League with Derby County in 1972, Brian Clough now became only the second manager to lead two different clubs to the English Championship - the other was Herbert Chapman, who won it with Huddersfield Town and Arsenal in the 1930s.

Leading scorer in the First Division was Bob Latchford, with 30 goals for third-placed Everton.

On February 9, 1978, Manchester United bought Scottish international defender Gordon McQueen from Leeds United for a British record fee of £495,000.

Nottingham Forest did the so-called 'New Double' by winning the League Cup as well as the League. They drew 0-0 with Liverpool after extra time in the Wembley Final and then scraped home 1-0 in the replay at Old Trafford with a penalty by John Robertson.

In both the Final matches, Forest's goalkeeper was Chris Woods, who played because first choice Peter Shilton was Cup-tied.

Ipswich Town won the 1978 FA Cup, beating Arsenal 1-0 in the Final with a goal by Roger Osborne.

In Scotland, Rangers did the treble for the second time in three seasons. They won the League by two points from runners-up Aberdeen, beat them again in the FA Cup Final, by two goals to one, and beat Celtic 2-1 after extra time in the League Cup Final.

 **Facts**   **The Seventies**

Rangers' - and the Scottish First Division's - leading scorer was Derek Johnstone, with 25 goals.

Liverpool retained the European Cup, beating FC Bruges in the Final at Wembley. The only goal of the game was scored in the 66th minute by Kenny Dalglish.

Anderlecht made it two Cup Winners' Cups in three years, beating Austria/WAC 4-0 in the Final in Paris.

PSV Eindhoven of Holland won the UEFA Cup, beating Bastia of France 3-0 on aggregate in the Final.

The 1978 World Cup finals were held in Argentina. The 16 qualifying nations were Argentina, Austria, Brazil, France, Holland, Hungary, Iran, Italy, Mexico, Peru, Poland, Scotland, Spain, Sweden, Tunisia and West Germany.

Scotland - Britain's only representatives in Argentina - had been enormously hyped in the build-up to the finals, especially by their manager, Ally MacLeod. This made their performance all the more of a let-down - they lost their opening group match 3-1 to Peru and then almost guaranteed elimination by managing only a 1-1 draw with widely unfancied Iran. In between these matches, Willie Johnston failed a drugs test and was sent home in disgrace.

The Seventies

Facts

The Scots almost retrieved the situation with a 3-1 victory in their final group match against Holland. This was a magnificent performance, which owed much to Graeme Souness and Archie Gemmill, but it was too little, too late.

The eight nations who went through to the second round of the finals were Argentina, Austria, Brazil, Holland, Italy, Peru, Poland and West Germany.

Holland won Group A, beating Austria and Italy and drawing with West Germany, the holders.

Argentina won Group B, with victories over Poland and Peru and a draw with Brazil.

The 1978 World Cup Final was held in the River Plate Stadium, Buenos Aires on June 25, 1978 in front of a crowd of 77,260.

ARGENTINA: Fillol, Olguin, Galvan, Passarella, Tarantini, Ardiles (sub: Larrosa), Gallego, Kempes, Bertoni, Luque, Ortiz (sub: Houseman)
HOLLAND: Jongbloed, Poortvliet, Krol, Brandts, Jansen (sub: Suurbier), Neeskens, Haan, W. Van Der Kerkhof, R. Van Der Kerkhof, Rep (Sub: Nanninga), Rensenbrink

Mario Kempes, the tournament's leading scorer, put Argentina ahead after 38 minutes, but Holland equalised after 82 minutes through a header from Dirk Manninga, who had come on as substitute for Johnny Rep. Argentina pulled away in extra time, with another goal from Kempes and a clincher from Ricardo Bertoni after 115 minutes.

Just over a fortnight after winning the 1978 World Cup, two of Argentina's squad were signed by Tottenham Hotspur. Osvaldo Ardiles and Riccardo Villa came from Huracan and Racing Club respectively for a combined total of £750,000. The deal was brokered on Spurs' behalf by Sheffield United manager Harry Haslam.

 **Facts**   **The Seventies**

Liverpool regained the League Championship, eight points ahead of last year's title-winners Nottingham Forest in second place. Their points total - 68- was a new record for the 22-club First Division under two points for a win. They also conceded only 16 goals in the season - an all-time low.

When Forest lost 2-0 at Liverpool on December 9, 1978, it was their first League defeat in 42 matches over one year and 13 days - the longest unbeaten run in the history of the Football League.

The First Division's leading scorer in 1978-79 was Frank Worthington of 17th-placed Bolton Wanderers.

Nottingham Forest had the consolation of retaining the League Cup, beating Southampton 3-2 in the 1979 Final. Forest's Wembley goals came from Garry Birtles (2) and Tony Woodcock; Southampton replied through David Peach and Nick Holmes.

Arsenal won the 1979 FA Cup, beating Manchester United 3-2 in one of the most exciting Finals for years. They went ahead in the first half with a goal by Brian Talbot, but then United scored twice in two minutes through Gordon McQueen and Sammy McIlroy. With a minute to go, Frank Stapleton levelled the scores again. Then, just as the crowd was preparing for extra time, Liam Brady broke down the left for Arsenal, then passed to Graham Rix who centred for Alan Sunderland to score the winner.

In Scotland, Celtic won the League Championship, finishing three points ahead of Rangers in second place.

Rangers did a Cup double. They won the Scottish FA Cup - beating Hibernian 3-2 in a second Final replay after the first two matches had ended goalless - and the League Cup with a 2-1 victory in the Final over Aberdeen.

The Seventies

Facts

Leading scorer in the Scottish Premier Division was Andy Ritchie, with 22 goals for seventh-placed Morton.

A new British transfer record was set in February 1979 - Trevor Francis became the first million-pound player when he moved from Birmingham City to Nottingham Forest.

The European Cup remained in England but moved from Liverpool to Nottingham. Forest beat FC Malmo in the Final in Munich. The only goal of the game was scored by million-pound man Trevor Francis.

European Cup holders Liverpool were knocked out in the second round of the 1978-79 competition by Nottingham Forest, the current English Champions and eventual winners of the Cup. Barcelona won the Cup Winners' Cup, beating Fortuna Dusseldorf 4-3 after extra time in the Final.

Borussia Moenchengladbach won the UEFA Cup, beating Red Star Belgrade 2-1 on aggregate in the Final.

On November 29, 1978, Viv Anderson of Nottingham Forest became the first black man to play for England in their 1-0 victory over Czechoslovakia in a friendly at Wembley.

Don Revie was banned for 10 years by the FA for walking out of his job as England manager in July 1977 to coach the United Arab Emirates. However, this ruling was later overturned by the High Court, which suggested that the football authorities might have been biased against their former employee.

In 1979-80, Liverpool won the League Championship for the second year running. This was their 12th title - a record.

The First Division's leading scorer was Phil Boyer, with 23 goals for eighth-placed Southampton.

Facts

The Seventies

West Ham United - currently a Second Division side - won the FA Cup for the third time in their history. Runners-up Arsenal were appearing in their third consecutive Final. The only goal at Wembley came from a first-half header by Trevor Brooking.

Wolverhampton Wanderers won the League Cup. They beat Nottingham Forest 1-0 in the Final with a goal from record signing Andy Gray after Forest defender David Needham collided with Peter Shilton after failing to hear the keeper's call.

Nottingham Forest retained the European Cup. In the Final in Madrid they won 1-0 against an SV Hamburg side that included Kevin Keegan. The winning goal was scored by John Robertson.

Valencia won the Cup Winners' Cup, beating Arsenal 5-4 on penalties after the Final had ended 0-0 after extra time. This was the first major Final to be decided by this method.

Eintracht Frankfurt won the UEFA Cup, beating the holders, Borussia Moenchengladbach in the Final on away goals after the two legs had finished 3-3 on aggregate.

In September 1979, the British transfer record was smashed twice in quick succession - first when Malcolm Allison of Manchester City signed Steve Daley of Wolverhampton Wanderers for £1,437,500, and again shortly afterwards when Wolves spent £1,469,000 on Aston Villa striker Andy Gray.

In February 1980, it was announced that next season European Footballer of the Year Kevin Keegan would be playing for Southampton after three years at Hamburg. The £400,000 transfer fee would almost certainly have been immensely higher had there not been an EEC-imposed limit of £500,000 on international transfers between clubs in different member states.

The Seventies

Facts

In Scotland, there was an unfamiliar name on the honours board as Aberdeen won the League Championship for only the second time in their history (the previous occasion had been in 1955).

The leading scorer in the Scottish Premier Division was Doug Somner, with 25 goals for third-placed St Mirren.

Celtic won the 1980 FA Cup, beating Rangers 1-0 after extra time in the Final.

Dundee United won their first major honour when they beat Aberdeen 3-0 in the 1980 League Cup Final replay at Dens Park, Dundee. The first match at Hampden had ended in a 0-0 draw after extra time. The Terrors' goals were scored by Willie Pettigrew (2) and Paul Sturrock.

Northern Ireland won the Home International Championship outright for the first time since 1914. They beat Wales 1-0 in Wrexham, drew 1-1 with England at Wembley and won 1-0 against Scotland in Belfast.

The 1980 European Championship was held in Italy. The eight qualifying nations were Belgium, Czechoslovakia, England, Greece, Holland, Italy, Spain and West Germany.

West Germany won the European Championship for the third time running when they beat Belgium in the Final in Rome on June 22, 1980. Horst Hrubesch scored both their goals in a 2-1 victory in front of 47,864 spectators.

THE EIGHTIES

The Eighties

Facts

In 1980-81, the FA stopped the red and yellow card system that had been introduced in 1976.

In 1981, Aston Villa won the League Championship for the seventh time in their history but the first time since 1910. They used only 14 players throughout the 42-match season.

With 20 goals apiece, joint leading scorers in the First Division were Steve Archibald of Tottenham Hotspur and Peter Withe of Aston Villa.

When they lost 2-1 at home to Leicester City on January 31, 1981, Liverpool suffered their first defeat at Anfield for three years and 10 days (85 matches in all competitions).

Tottenham Hotspur won the FA Cup for the sixth time in their history, beating Manchester City 3-2 in a replay after the first match - the 100th FA Cup Final - had finished 1-1 after extra time. In the first Final, City's Tommy Hutchison had scored for both sides - but not, as he has since been quick to point out to anyone who uses the wrong phrase, at both ends - his goal for City came in the first half and his own goal was scored in the second.

The hero of the replay - again held at Wembley - was Argentine Ricardo Villa, who had been substituted in the first match. He scored twice for Spurs, the second time after a fantastic dribble through a crowded City penalty area. Spurs' other goal was scored by Garth Crooks; City's goals came from Steve Mackenzie and a Kevin Reeves penalty.

Liverpool won the League Cup - the only domestic trophy that had previously eluded them - beating Second Division West Ham United 2-1 in a replay at Villa Park after the Wembley Final had ended 1-1 after extra time.

 **Facts**   **The Eighties**

Liverpool regained the European Cup in 1981 after a two-year gap, beating Real Madrid in the Final in Paris with a goal by Alan Kennedy. This was Liverpool's third triumph in the competition and the fifth time running that the Cup had been won by an English club. One of the stars of the Real Madrid team was England international Laurie Cunningham.

Dynamo Tbilisi of the USSR won the Cup Winners' Cup, beating Carl Zeiss Jena of East Germany 2-1 in the Final in Dusseldorf.

In the second round of the Cup Winners' Cup, West Ham United had been forced to play the second leg of their match against Castilla of Spain behind closed doors after crowd trouble during the first match in Madrid.

Ipswich Town won the UEFA Cup, beating AZ 67 Alkmaar of Holland 5-4 on aggregate in the Final.

John Trollope of Swindon Town retired in November shortly after setting a new record for the number of League appearances for a single club - 770 since 1960. The previous record-holder had been Jimmy Dickinson, who played 764 games for Portsmouth between 1946 and 1965.

Celtic won the Scottish Premier Division - their 32nd League Championship. Their forward Frank McGarvey was the leading scorer, with 23 goals.

Rangers won the FA Cup, beating Dundee United 4-1 in a Final replay after the first match had ended goalless.

Dundee United retained the League Cup, beating Dundee 3-0 in the Final.

At the start of the 1981-82 season, the English Football League instituted three points for a win.

The Eighties

Facts

Second Division Queen's Park Rangers became the first English League club to install a plastic pitch. The material used was marketed under the name Omniturf.

The English transfer market boomed - enormous fees were paid for Justin Fashanu, who moved from Norwich City to Nottingham Forest for £1 million, Trevor Francis (£1.2 million from Nottingham Forest to Manchester City) and Frank Stapleton (Arsenal to Manchester United for £1.1 million). The biggest of the lot, however, was Bryan Robson, whose £1.7 million move from West Bromwich Albion to Manchester United was a new British record.

Liverpool won the League Championship for a record 13th time - their fifth title in seven seasons.

Liverpool also retained the League Cup (now renamed the Milk Cup), beating Tottenham Hotspur 3-1 after extra time in the 1982 Final. Their goals came from Ronnie Whelan (2) and Ian Rush; Spurs' reply came from Steve Archibald.

The First Division's leading scorer was Liverpool old boy Kevin Keegan, with 26 goals for his new club, Southampton.

Tottenham Hotspur retained the FA Cup, beating Second Division Queen's Park Rangers 1-0 in the Final replay after the first match had been drawn 1-1. Both Spurs' goals were scored by Glenn Hoddle, the second from the penalty spot.

Aston Villa won the 1982 European Cup, making it six in a row for English teams in this competition. They beat Bayern Munich in the Final in Rotterdam with a goal by Peter Withe.

Villa's victory came less than four months after Tony Barton had taken over as manager from Ron Saunders.

 **Facts**   **The Eighties**

First-choice Villa keeper Jimmy Rimmer had to leave the field after only nine minutes of the Final because of a neck injury sustained during the pre-match warm-up. His place in goal was taken by Nigel Spink, playing in only his second game for the first team.

Barcelona won the Cup Winners' Cup in their own stadium, where they beat Standard Liege 2-1 in the Final.

IFK Gothenburg won the UEFA Cup, beating SV Hamburg 4-0 on aggregate in the Final.

In Scotland, Celtic won the League Championship. Their striker George McCluskey was the Premier Division's leading scorer, with 21 goals.

Aberdeen won the FA Cup, beating Rangers 4-1 in the Final after extra time.

Rangers won the League Cup, beating Dundee United 2-1 in the Final.

The 1982 World Cup finals were held in Spain. The tournament was now expanded to include 24 countries for the first time. The competing nations were Algeria, Argentina, Austria, Belgium, Brazil, Cameroon, Chile, Czechoslovakia, El Salvador, England, France, Honduras, Hungary, Italy, Kuwait, New Zealand, Northern Ireland, Peru, Poland, Scotland, Spain, the USSR, West Germany and Yugoslavia.

The surprise package in the first round of group matches was Cameroon, playing in their first finals. They were unbeaten against Italy, Peru and Poland and went out of the competition only because they had scored fewer goals than the Italians. Their stars were captain and keeper Thomas N'Kono and striker Roger Milla.

England had a hundred per cent record in the first round, beating France 3-1, Czechoslovakia 2-0 and Kuwait 1-0.

The Eighties

Facts

Scotland began the tournament by taking the lead against Brazil, but eventually lost 4-1. They then drew 2-2 with the USSR and, although they scored five goals against New Zealand, they carelessly conceded two - because of this they went out of the competition when a clean sheet would have seen them through to the second round.

Northern Ireland topped their group after drawing 0-0 with Yugoslavia and 1-1 with Honduras and then beating the hosts, Sapin, 1-0 with a goal by Gerry Armstrong.

The 12 countries that went forward to the second round of group matches were Argentina, Austria, Belgium, Brazil, England, France, Italy, Northern Ireland, Poland, Spain, the USSR and West Germany.

Most of the games between the three countries in each of the four groups were marred by defensive-mindedness. England drew their matches against Spain and West Germany and thus went out of the competition without having lost a match.

Northern Ireland drew with Austria but were soundly beaten 4-1 by France.

The four group winners - France, Italy, Poland and West Germany - went forward to the semi-finals, the first knockout matches of the 1982 tournament.

Italy beat Poland 2-0 and then France and West Germany drew 3-3 after extra time before the Germans won 5-4 on penalties.

 **Facts** The Eighties

The 1982 World Cup Final between Italy and West Germany was held in the Santiago Bernabeu Stadium, Madrid, on July 11 in front of 90,000 spectators.

ITALY: Zoff, Gentile, Collovati, Scirea, Cabrini, Conti, Oriali, Bergomi, Tardelli, Rossi, Graziani (subs: Altobelli, then Causio)
WEST GERMANY: Schumacher, Kaltz, K-H. Forster, Stielike, B. Forster, Briegel, Breitner, Dremmler (sub: Hrubesch), Littbarski, Fischer, Rummenigge (sub: Muller)

The main talking-point in the first half of the World Cup Final was a penalty miss by Cabrini. Italy eventually took the lead after 57 minutes with a goal by Paolo Rossi and then Marco Tardelli and Alessandro Altobelli made the Cup safe for Italy before West Germany's Paul Breitner became the first man to score in two World Cup Finals.

Paolo Rossi was the leading scorer in the 1982 World Cup finals, with six goals for Italy.

Shortly before the 1982 World Cup Final, the FA announced that the new England manager in succession to Ron Greenwood would be Bobby Robson of Ipswich Town.

In 1983, Liverpool won the Championship for the second year in succession and the sixth time in eight years. It was the 14th title in their history.

Runners-up were Watford, their highest ever League position in the year after they won promotion. Their leading scorer - and the First Division's - was Luther Blissett, with 27 goals.

Manchester United won the FA Cup in 1983 for the fifth time in their history, beating Brighton and Hove Albion 4-0 in the Final replay, with goals from Bryan Robson (2), Norman Whiteside and Arnold Muhren (penalty).

The Eighties

Facts

The first FA Cup Final had been drawn 2-2 - Frank Stapleton and Ray Wilkins scored for United, Gordon Smith and Gary Stevens for Brighton.

Brighton were also relegated in 1983, after three years in the First Division.

Liverpool retained the League (Milk) Cup, beating Manchester United 2-1 in the 1983 Final. United took the lead after 12 minutes with a goal by Norman Whiteside, but Liverpool fought back, drawing level with a goal by Alan Kennedy. Ronnie Whelan scored the winning goal in extra time.

On his 12th and final visit to Wembley, Bob Paisley became the first manager to lead his team up and collect a major trophy.

In Scotland, Dundee United won the League for the first time in their history under the management of Jim McLean.

Leading scorer was Charlie Nicholas, with 29 goals for second-placed Celtic.

Aberdeen became the first Scottish club this century other than Celtic and Rangers to retain the FA Cup, beating Rangers 1-0 after extra time in the Final. They then proceeded to do a Cup double, beating Real Madrid 2-1 in the Final of the Cup Winners' Cup in Gothenburg, Sweden.

Celtic won the League Cup, beating Rangers 2-1 in the Final.

SV Hamburg won the European Cup, beating Juventus 1-0 in the Final in Athens.

Anderlecht won the 1983 UEFA Cup, beating Benfica 2-1 on aggregate in the Final over two legs.

 **Facts** The Eighties

In 1983-84, for the first time in its history, the English First Division had a commercial sponsor - the Japanese-based camera-makers Canon.

Liverpool - now under the management of Joe Fagan - won the League Championship for the 15th time. This was one of three major trophies lifted by Liverpool this season. They also retained the Milk Cup, beating Everton 1-0 in the Final replay after the first match had been drawn 0-0. Then they won the European Cup for the fourth time, beating AS Roma 4-2 on penalties after the match had ended 1-1.

Liverpool's - and the First Division's, and Europe's leading scorer - was Ian Rush, with 32 goals.

Everton won the FA Cup, beating Watford 2-0 in the Final with goals by Graeme Sharp and Andy Gray.

The season's great giantkillers were both from the Third Division - Plymouth Argyle reached the semi-final of the FA Cup and Walsall reached the same stage of the Milk Cup.

In Scotland, Aberdeen did the double. They won the League Championship for the third time in their history - their previous victories had been in 1955 and 1980. They also became the first club other than Rangers to win the FA Cup three years running, beating Celtic 2-1 in the 1984 Final. Like their two previous Cup wins, this one was achieved after extra time.

Rangers won the League Cup, beating Celtic 3-2 after extra time in the Final.

Juventus won the 1984 Cup Winners' Cup Final, beating FC Porto 2-1 in the Final in Basle.

Tottenham Hotspur won the UEFA Cup 5-4 in a penalty shoot-out at White Hart Lane after each leg had been drawn 1-1.

The Eighties

Facts

Northern Ireland won the last Home International Championship on goal difference after all four countries finished with three points. The competition was not held again after England and Scotland withdrew because of fears for their safety in Belfast.

The finals of the 1984 European Championship were held in France. The eight qualifying nations were Belgium, Denmark, France, Portugal, Romania, Spain, West Germany and Yugoslavia.

France beat Portugal 3-2 in one semi-final; the other, between Denmark and Spain, finished 1-1 after extra time but Spain won the penalty shoot-out 5-4.

The European Championship Final was held at the Parc des Princes, Paris on June 27, 1984, in front of 80,000 spectators. France, the hosts, won the competition for the first time, beating Spain 2-0 with goals by Platini and Bellone.

The 1984-85 season was overshadowed by two great tragedies - the Bradford fire and the Heysel Stadium disaster.

On May 11, 1985, 56 people were burned to death, 70 more detained in hospital with severe burns, and a further 211 supporters and police injured when a timber stand caught fire at Bradford City's Valley Parade ground during an end-of-season match against Lincoln City. The game was fairly well attended, because Bradford had just ensured promotion from the old English Third Division, and many fans had come to celebrate.

The fire began amid rubbish which had accumulated beneath the stand over a long period and had never been swept up. Turnstiles had been locked to prevent latecomers getting in without paying. To make matters worse, there were no fire extinguishers in this part of the ground: they had been removed and stored in a room in the clubhouse because during previous games they been set off and used as missiles by unruly fans.

 **Facts**   **The Eighties**

**The Heysel Stadium disaster took place on May 29, 1985 just
before the kick-off in the European Cup Final between Juventus
and Liverpool in Brussels, Belgium. Thirty-nine people - most of
them Italians - were killed and 454 others injured, many seriously,
when groups of rival supporters charged each other through Block
Z, which had been reserved for neutral spectators. Contributory
factors included the easy availability of alcohol, poor segregation
and inadequate safety barriers.**

The League Championship moved across Stanley Park from Anfield to
Goodison Park. It was the eighth title in Everton's history.

**Everton also won the 1985 Cup Winners' Cup, beating Rapid
Vienna 3-1 in the Final in Rotterdam.**

With 24 goals apiece, the joint leading scorers in the First Division were
Kerry Dixon of sixth-placed Chelsea and Gary Lineker of 15th-placed
Leicester City.

**Manchester United prevented a Goodison double by beating
Everton 1-0 in the FA Cup Final. The winning goal was scored by
Norman Whiteside.**

Kevin Moran of Manchester United became the first player ever to be sent
off in an FA Cup Final when he was dismissed by referee Peter Willis for a
foul on Peter Reid.

**Norwich City won the 1985 League Cup, beating Sunderland 1-0 in
the Final. Both clubs were relegated from Division One at the end
of the season.**

Aberdeen retained the Scottish League Championship, finishing on 59 points,
seven ahead of runners-up Celtic. Their leading scorer - and Scotland's - was
Frank McDougall, with 24 goals.

The Eighties

Facts

Rangers won the 1985 League Cup - now renamed the Skol Cup - with a 1-0 Final victory over Dundee United.

Dundee United were again unlucky in the FA Cup, losing 2-1 in the Final to Celtic.

Real Madrid won the 1985 UEFA Cup, beating Videoton of Hungary 3-1 on aggregate in the Final.

Queen's Park Rangers - who qualified for the UEFA Cup by finishing fifth in 1984 - had to play their home matches in the competition at Highbury because UEFA refused to allow them to play on the synthetic pitch they had installed in 1981.

In the UEFA Cup second round, first leg, Queen's Park Rangers beat Partizan Belgrade 6-2 but lost the return 4-0 and went out of the competition.

In spite of the Heysel Stadium disaster, the European Cup Final went ahead as scheduled, kicking off 85 minutes late. Juventus won 1-0, the winning goal coming from a penalty by Michel Platini.

In the aftermath of Heysel, all English clubs were banned from European competitions. None was allowed back until 1990; Liverpool were readmitted in 1991. Joe Fagan stepped down and handed over to Kenny Dalglish, who became Liverpool's first player-manager.

In 1985-86, Liverpool won the double. Their League Championship was their eighth in 11 seasons and the 16th in their history. They finished two points ahead of last year's Champions, Everton, who came second.

Liverpool also beat Everton in the FA Cup Final. The score in the first ever Merseyside Cup Final was 3-1 - Liverpool's goals came from Ian Rush (2) and Craig Johnston.

 **Facts**   The Eighties

Everton's goal in the 1986 FA Cup Final was scored by Footballer of the Year Gary Lineker. Lineker was also the First Division's leading scorer, with 30 goals.

A year after winning the Second Division Championship, Oxford United won the League (Milk) Cup, beating Queen's Park Rangers 3-0 in the Final with goals by Trevor Hebberd, Ray Houghton and Jeremy Charles.

On their way to the Third Division Championship, Reading created a new League record by winning their first 13 games of the season.

In Scotland, Celtic won the League Championship for the 34th time, finishing ahead of second-placed Heart of Midlothian on goal difference.

Scottish Premier Division 1985-86 Top of Table

	P	W	D	L	F	A	Pts
Celtic	36	20	10	6	67	38	50
Heart of Midlothian	36	20	10	6	59	33	50

Fifth-placed Rangers announced the appointment of Graeme Souness as player-manager in succession to Jock Wallace. The former Middlesbrough, Liverpool and Sampdoria midfielder had played 54 times for Scotland.

Aberdeen did a domestic double, winning both the FA Cup and the League Cup. They beat Heart of Midlothian 3-0 in the FA Cup Final, with two goals from John Hewitt and one from John Stark. In the League Cup Final, they beat Hibernian by the same score, two of their goals this time coming from Eric Black and another from John Stark.

Steua Bucharest of Romania won the European Cup, beating Barcelona 2-0 on penalties after the Final in Seville had finished 0-0 after extra time.

The Eighties

Facts

Dynamo Kiev won the Cup Winners' Cup, beating Atletico Madrid 3-0 in the Final in Lyon.

Real Madrid won the UEFA Cup, beating Cologne 5-3 on aggregate in the Final.

The 1986 World Cup was held in Mexico, which thus became the first country to stage the tournament twice. It had originally been awarded to Colombia, but it was subsequently decided that the country was too politically and socially unstable, and that the personal safety of those attending could not be guaranteed.

The 24 nations that reached this stage of the competition were Algeria, Argentina, Belgium, Brazil, Bulgaria, Canada, Denmark, England, France, Hungary, Iraq, Italy, Mexico, Morocco, Northern Ireland, Paraguay, Poland, Portugal, Scotland, South Korea, Spain, Uruguay, the USSR and West Germany.

England lost their opening match 1-0 to Portugal, then drew 0-0 with Morocco in a match in which Ray Wilkins was sent off for throwing the ball at the referee.

England came good in their final group match. Captain Bryan Robson's shoulder injury forced manager Bobby Robson to rejig his team's formation - Peter Beardsley replaced Mark Hateley up front; Gary Lineker responded by scoring all the goals in their 3-0 victory over Poland.

Scotland lost their first two matches - 1-0 to Denmark and 2-1 to West Germany. After less than a minute of their final game, Jose Batista of their opponents Uruguay was sent off. But the Scots could not capitalise on their numerical advantage - a 0-0 draw was not enough to keep them in the World Cup.

 **Facts**   **The Eighties**

Northern Ireland found themselves in the what was probably the toughest group of the finals. They drew their opening game against Algeria but lost 2-1 to Spain and 3-0 to Brazil.

FIFA again altered the format of the World Cup finals. Although commencing the knockout stage in the second round was preferable to the stultifying groups of three there had been in Spain in 1982, the problem was how to reduce 24 finalists to 16. The solution - taking the top two in each group of four and adding the four best-place third teams - was unsatisfactory.

Belgium and Poland clearly deserved to go through to the next stage of the competition, finishing third in their groups with three points each. But although both Bulgaria and Portugal finished with two points and a goal difference of minus two, only Bulgaria went through. Uruguay took the 16th second round berth simply because they had finished third in their group - the fact that they had two points and a goal difference of minus five - inferior to Portugal's record - was discounted, and it was the Portuguese who went home.

In the second round of the 1986 World Cup finals, England beat Paraguay 3-0 (two more for Lineker) and Argentina beat Uruguay 1-0. The two victorious nations then met each other in one of the greatest - and most controversial - matches in the history of the World Cup.

Argentina's opening goal in the quarter-final was scored by Diego Maradona with his hand. This was clearly visible on television, but the linesman's view was obstructed by Peter Shilton, whose outstretched arm fortuitously eclipsed that of the Argentine striker - from behind the England keeper, Maradona appeared to have won the ball fairly with his head. Maradona then clinched it for Argentina with a run from his own half which cut through the heart of the by no means absent England defence - this was undeniably a good goal in both senses. England rallied and pulled a goal back through Gary Lineker, who later had a chance to bring the scores back level. But Argentina won 2-1.

The Eighties

Facts

Afterwards, Maradona said his first goal was 'A little bit the head of Maradona, a little bit the hand of God' - the irony of which has never been much appreciated in England.

Brazil were widely fancied to repeat their 1970 success in the previous Mexico World Cup, but they went out on penalties in the quarter-final to France.

West Germany progressed quietly to the semi-finals, beating Morocco 1-0 and Mexico 4-1 on penalties after their quarter-final finished goalless after extra time.

Belgium progressed by beating the USSR 4-3 and then Spain 5-4 on penalties in the quarter-final after the match had been drawn 1-1.

In the semi-finals, Argentina beat Belgium 2-0 and West Germany beat France 2-0.

The 1986 World Cup Final was held in the Aztec Stadium, Mexico City on June 29, 1986 in front of a crowd of 114,590.

ARGENTINA: Pumpido, Cuciuffo, Brown, Ruggeri, Olarticoechea, Giusti, Batista, Burruchaga (sub: Trubbiani), Enrique, Maradona, Valdano
WEST GERMANY: Schumacher, Berthold, Briegel, Jakobs, Forster, Eder, Brehme, Matthaus, Allofs (sub: Voller), Magath (sub: Hoeness), Rummenigge

Argentina went two up with a first half goal by José Luis Brown and another after 56 minutes by Jorge Valdano. But the Germans clawed their way back to 2-2, with goals by Karl-Heinz Rummenigge and substitute Rudi Voller. Then, six minutes from time, Maradona released Jorge Burruchaga who raced away to leave the final score Argentina 3 West Germany 2.

 **Facts**   **The Eighties**

The leading scorer in the 1986 World Cup finals was England's Gary Lineker, with six goals. Three players scored five - Emilio Butragueno (Spain), Diego Maradona (Argentina) and Careca (Brazil).

During the close season, Everton sold England striker Gary Lineker to Barcelona for £4,262,000. The Spanish club was managed by Terry Venables.

In 1987, Everton won the League Championship for the ninth time.

The leading scorer in the First Division was Clive Allen, with 33 goals in the season for third-placed Tottenham Hotspur.

Coventry City won the 1987 FA Cup, their first major honour since they entered the Football League in 1919. They beat Tottenham Hotspur 3-2 after extra time in the Final, with goals by Dave Bennett and Keith Houchen and an own goal by Spurs' Gary Mabbutt. Mabbutt also played a major part in his own side's second goal, when his shot was deflected in off Coventry defender Brian Kilcline. Spurs had opened the scoring through Clive Allen but had been pulled back to 1-1.

The Littlewoods Cup (as the League Cup was now named, after its new sponsor) was won by Arsenal, who beat Liverpool 2-1 in the Final. Both Gunners Wembley goals were scored by Charlie Nicholas. This was the first match in which Ian Rush had scored for Liverpool and finished on the losing side.

After five years at Old Trafford, Ron Atkinson was sacked as manager of Manchester United on November 6 despite having led the club to two FA Cup triumphs and never finishing lower than fourth in the League. His successor was Aberdeen's title-winning manager Alex Ferguson.

Fulham and Queen's Park Rangers announced plans to merge, but the scheme was rejected by the Football League.

The Eighties

At the end of the season, the English First Division was reduced from 22 to 21 clubs and the Second Division increased from 22 to 23.

The final promotion and relegation places in England were decided for the first time by play-offs. Under the new system, the three teams just below the automatic promotion places played off against each other and against the club that finished just above the automatic relegation positions in the division above.

There was also to be automatic relegation to the Conference for the team finishing bottom of the Fourth Division. The first team to suffer this fate were Lincoln City.

The Scottish Premier Division was increased from 10 clubs to 12 and the First Division reduced from 14 clubs to 12.

Rangers won the Scottish League Championship. This was Graeme Souness's first season as player-manager. He was sent off on his debut, leaving the field at the same time as the victim of his tackle, George McCluskey of Hibernian, was carried off. Rangers lost the match 2-1.

Rangers also won the 1987 League Cup, beating Celtic 2-1 in the Final. This was Souness's first trophy with his new club, but the sweetness of victory was soured by a nasty match in which nine players were booked and Celtic's Mo Johnston was sent off.

Rangers were knocked out of the UEFA Cup in the second round by Borussia Moenchengladbach. Two Rangers players were sent off during the second leg in Germany.

 **Facts**

The Eighties

Leading scorer in the Scottish First Division was Brain McClair, with 35 goals for second-placed Celtic.

St Mirren won the Scottish FA Cup for the third time in their history, beating Dundee United 1-0 after extra time in the Final.

Porto won the 1987 European Cup, beating Bayern 1987 Munich 2-1 in the Final in Vienna.

Ajax won the Cup Winners' Cup, beating Lokomotiv Leipzig 1-0 in the Final in Athens.

IFK Gothenburg won the UEFA Cup, beating Dundee United 2-1 on aggregate in the Final. Dundee's disappointment came only four days after their defeat in the Scottish FA Cup Final.

In 1987-88, for the first time, the Football League permitted two substitutes per team per match.

Liverpool won the 1988 Championship in the Football League's centenary year. Manchester United were runners-up.

With 26 goals for the Champions, the First Division's leading scorer was John Aldridge.

After only 11 years in the Football League, Wimbledon won the FA Cup, beating Liverpool 1-0 in the 1988 Final. Lawrie Sanchez scored the winner in the first half and after 61 minutes Dons' keeper Dave Beasant saved a penalty from John Aldridge.

Luton Town won the Littlewoods Cup (formerly the League Cup), beating Arsenal 3-2 in the Final. Much of the credit for capturing their first major trophy went to two-goal Brian Stein.

The Eighties

On October 23, 1987, David Pleat resigned as manager of Tottenham Hotspur after tabloid press allegations about his private life.

On April 9, 1988, at the age of 17 years 240 days, Alan Shearer became the youngest player ever to score a hat-trick in the First Division in Southampton's 4-2 defeat of Arsenal.

On April 14, 1988, Chris Kamara of Swindon Town appeared in court where he was fined £1200 and ordered to pay £250 compensation for causing grievous bodily harm on the field of play to Shrewsbury Town striker Jim Melrose.

Chelsea became the first - and as it turned out, the only - team ever to be relegated from the First Division after a play-off. They lost their top-flight status after finishing 18th and then losing to Middlesbrough, who came third in the Second Division.

In Scotland, Celtic did the double, winning the League Championship for the 35th time and the FA Cup for the 28th time.

The leading scorer in the Scottish Premier Division was Tommy Coyne, with 33 goals for seventh-placed Dundee.

The Scottish League Cup went to Rangers, who beat Aberdeen 5-3 on penalties in the Final after the match ended 3-3 after extra time. This was the first time a major British trophy had been decided by a shoot-out.

 **Facts**   **The Eighties**

Less than a week before this Final, Rangers' player-manager Graeme Souness had been suspended for five matches after his third sending-off in 14 months for fouling Billy Stark of Celtic.

There was more trouble for Rangers in April 1988, when Glasgow Sheriff Court fined England internationals Terry Butcher and Chris Woods for disorderly conduct and a breach of the peace on the field of play. The incident had occurred during an Old Firm match the previous October. Frank McAvennie, the only Celtic player charged, was acquitted. The case against another Rangers and England player, Graham Roberts, was not proven.

The Finals of all three major European Cup competitions in 1988 were decided on penalties.

PSV Eindhoven of Holland won the European Cup, beating Benfica 6-5 on penalties after the Final in Stuttgart had been drawn 0-0.

Mechelen of Belgium won the Cup Winners' Cup in their first ever season in European competition. They beat Ajax 1-0 in the Final in Strasbourg.

Bayer Leverkusen of West Germany won the UEFA Cup, beating Espanol of Spain 3-2 on penalties in front of their home crowd after the scores had finished 3-3 on aggregate over two legs.

The finals of the 1988 European Championship were held in West Germany. The eight qualifying nations were Denmark, England, Holland, Italy, the Republic of Ireland, Spain, the USSR and West Germany.

The Republic of Ireland and England were quickly eliminated after finishing third and fourth respectively in the group that also contained the USSR and Holland.

In the semi-finals, Holland beat the hosts, West Germany 2-1 and the USSR beat Italy 2-0.

The Eighties

Facts

The 1988 European Championship Final between Holland and the USSR was held in the Olympic Stadium, Munich on June 25 in front of 72,308 spectators.

The Dutch won their first major international trophy 2-0 thanks to goals by Marco Van Basten and Ruud Gullit and a penalty save by Hans Van Breukelen.

1989 was the year of the Hillsborough disaster, the worst tragedy in the history of British football. On April 15, 95 spectators were crushed to death and 170 injured shortly before the start of the FA Cup semi-final between Liverpool and Nottingham Forest. The Leppings Lane enclosure became swamped with Liverpool supporters who kept coming in, pressing those at the front up against the fencing which had been erected around the perimeter to prevent pitch invasions. The match kicked off on time and was six minutes old before the authorities realised that the activity behind the goal was not routine unrest but the unfolding of a major disaster.

Arsenal won the League Championship for the first time in 18 years. In the final game of the season, they went to Anfield needing to win by two goals - anything less, and the title would go to Liverpool. And that is exactly what they did, with goals by Alan Smith and Michael Thomas.

 Facts   The Eighties

League Division One 1988-89 - Top of Final Table

	P	W	D	L	F	A	Pts
Arsenal	38	22	10	6	73	36	76
Liverpool	38	22	10	6	65	28	76

Alan Smith was the First Division's leading scorer, with 23 goals in the season.

In the aftermath of Hillsborough, there were calls for the FA Cup to be held over for a year as a mark of respect to the victims of the tragedy. But eventually the Liverpool v Nottingham Forest semi-final was replayed and won 3-1 by Liverpool, who went on to win the trophy with a 3-2 extra time Final victory over Everton. John Aldridge and Ian Rush (2) scored for Liverpool; both Everton's goals came from substitute Stuart McCall.

Nottingham Forest won the Littlewoods (League) Cup, beating Luton Town 3-1 in the Final with two goals from Nigel Clough (one of them a penalty) and one from Neil Webb. Ray Harford scored for Luton.

After the crowd trouble that had marred the previous season's First/Second Division play-off between Chelsea and Middlesbrough, the format of these games was altered. From now on, only the teams seeking promotion would be involved.

In May, 1989, former Leeds United and England manager Don Revie died after a long battle against motor neurone disease.

On June 7, 1989, Peter Shilton became England's most capped player when he made his 109th appearance against Denmark. The previous record holder, with 108 caps, had been Bobby Moore.

On June 20, Gary Lineker returned to England from Barcelona - where he had moved after the 1986 World Cup finals - when he signed for Tottenham Hotspur.

The Eighties

Facts

The Scottish League was restructured again - the Premier Division reverted to 10 clubs and the First Division to 14.

Rangers won the Scottish League Championship and began their sequence of nine titles in a row which equalled Celtic's record achievement of 1966-74. They also took the League Cup, beating Aberdeen 3-2 in the Final.

Joint leading scorers in the Scottish Premier Division were Charlie Nicholas of Aberdeen and Mark McGhee of Celtic, each with 16 goals.

Celtic won the Scottish FA Cup, beating Rangers 1-0 in the Final.

AC Milan won the 1989 European Cup, beating Steua Bucharest 4-0 in the Final in Barcelona.

Barcelona won the Cup Winners' Cup, beating Sampdoria 2-0 in the Final in Berne.

Napoli of Italy beat Stuttgart of West Germany 5-4 on aggregate in the Final of the UEFA Cup.

Lord Justice Peter Taylor's Report on the 1989 Hillsborough disaster was published on January 29, 1990. His findings were severely critical of the squalid condition of many grounds and led directly to the introduction of all-seater stadiums.

In 1990, Liverpool won the League Championship for the 18th time.

The First Division's leading scorer was Gary Lineker, with 24 goals for his new club, Tottenham Hotspur.

Manchester United won the FA Cup for the seventh time, beating Crystal Palace 1-0 in the 1990 Final replay after the first match had been drawn 3-3.

 **Facts**   **The Eighties**

Nottingham Forest retained the Littlewoods (League) Cup, beating Oldham Athletic 1-0 in the 1990 Final with a goal by Nigel Jemson.

Tottenham Hotspur sold England international Chris Waddle to Olympique Marseilles for £4.5 million.

Second Division Oldham were Cup club of the season, reaching both the League Cup Final and the semi-final of the FA Cup. The Lancastrians went 32 matches without defeat on their widely-loathed plastic pitch at Boundary Park.

On May 28, Swindon Town won promotion to the First Division when they beat Sunderland in the play-offs. Less than two weeks later, the club was relegated to the Third Division after admitting a catalogue of financial irregularities since 1985. The club later won an appeal against this demotion, and eventually played the 1990-91 season in the Second Division.

Rangers won the Scottish Championship for the second year in succession. It was a remarkable year for them in another way, too - when they bought Mo Johnston from Nantes in July, the former Celtic striker became the first high-profile Roman Catholic ever to sign for the strongly Protestant Gers.

The leading scorer in the Scottish Premier Division was John Robertson, with 17 goals for Heart of Midlothian.

Aberdeen did a domestic Cup double - they beat Rangers 2-1 after extra time in the Final of the League Cup, then beat Celtic 9-8 on penalties in the FA Cup Final which had remained goalless at the end of extra time.

AC Milan retained the European Cup, beating Benfica 1-0 in the 1990 Final in Vienna.

The Eighties

Facts

Sampdoria won the Cup Winners' Cup, beating Anderlecht 2-0 after extra time in the Final in Gothenburg.

The UEFA Cup Final was an all-Italian affair in which Juventus beat Fiorentina 3-1 on aggregate.

The 1990 World Cup finals were held in Italy. The 24 qualifying nations were Argentina, Austria, Belgium, Brazil, Cameroon, Colombia, Costa Rica, Czechoslovakia, Egypt, England, Holland, Italy, the Republic of Ireland, Romania, Scotland, South Korea, Spain, Sweden, the United Arab Emirates, Uruguay, the USA, the USSR, West Germany and Yugoslavia.

England topped their group after drawing 1-1 with the Republic of Ireland, 0-0 with Holland and beating Egypt 1-0.

The Republic of Ireland came second in this group after drawing all three of their games. Holland also qualified for the second round, despite coming third in their group.

Scotland beat Sweden 2-1 in their group, but the loss of their two previous games - 1-0 to Costa Rica and 1-0 to Brazil - condemned them to another early exit from the finals.

The top two teams in each of the six groups of four went through automatically to the second round. They were Belgium, Brazil, Cameroon, Costa Rica, Czechoslovakia, England, Italy, the Republic of Ireland, Romania, Spain, West Germany and Yugoslavia. These 12 countries were joined by the four best third-placed teams - Argentina, Colombia, Holland and Uruguay.

In the second round, the 1990 World Cup finals became a knockout competition. England beat Belgium 1-0 with a goal by David Platt seconds before the referee was about to blow for the end of extra time. The Republic of Ireland beat Romania 5-4 on penalties after the two countries had played out a 0-0 draw.

 **Facts** The Eighties

In the quarter-finals, England took the lead against Cameroon, but later found themselves 2-1 down with eight minutes left in normal time. But Lineker was fouled twice in the area and scored himself from each of the resulting penalties - final score after extra time: England 3 Cameroon 2.

The Republic of Ireland reached the end of the road, losing 1-0 to the host nation, Italy.

The 1990 World Cup semi-finals - Argentina v Italy and West Germany v England - were both decided on penalty shoot-outs after both games ended 1-1 after extra time.

The goals in open play in the West Germany v England game were scored by Andreas Brehme and Gary Lineker. Then Stuart Pearce and Chris Waddle missed their spot kicks and West Germany went forward to the Final.

The 1990 World Cup Final was held in the Stadio Olimpico, Rome, on July 8, 1990, in front of 73,603 spectators.

WEST GERMANY: Iligner, Berthold (sub: Reuter), Kohler, Augenthaler, Buchwald, Brehme, Littbarski, Hassler, Matthaus, Voller, Klinsmann
ARGENTINA: Goycochea, Lorenzo, Serrizuela, Sensini, Ruggeri (sub: Monzoni), Simon, Basualdo, Burruchaga (sub: Calderon), Maradona, Troglio, Dezotti

West Germany won 1-0 with a penalty awarded - probably unjustly - for a foul by Sensini on Voller six minutes from time. Brehme scored from the spot. In the 64th minute, after fouling Klinsmann, Monzon became the first player to be sent off in a World Cup Final. There was but a short time to wait for the second dismissal - two minutes after the penalty, Dezotti was directed to the tunnel after trying to drag the ball away from a timewasting German.

The Eighties

Facts

Franz Beckenbauer became the first man ever to have both captained and managed World Cup-winning sides.

Although some matches in the knockout stages of the 1990 World Cup finals were exciting - particularly for supporters of England - many believed that the tournament had been seriously weakened as a spectacle by the paucity of goals - only 115 in 52 matches - and by the high number of cautions (164) and sendings-off (16).

Worst of all was the number of matches that had been decided either by penalties or by penalty shoot-outs. Of the last seven matches, from the quarter finals to the Final, only two had been settled in open play without a goal from the penalty spot.

One of these was the third place play-off, in which Italy beat England 2-1 in normal time.

THE NINETIES

The Nineties

Facts

The 1990-91 season was the first in which English clubs other than Liverpool were allowed back into Europe after the ban that had been imposed on them in the wake of the Heysel tragedy on May 29, 1985.

Thus the season started with a note of optimism. The total attendance at League matches on the first day of the season was the highest since the start of 1981-82.

At half time in Everton's first game of the season, goalkeeper Neville Southall refused to go back to the dressing room to discuss tactics. He was fined a week's wages by manager Howard Kendall.

On September 8, York City forward David Longhurst collapsed and died from a heart attack during the match against Lincoln City.

Peter Taylor - Brian Clough's managerial assistant in the great days at Derby County - died on October 5 after a long illness at the age of 62.

Arsenal won their 10th League Championship. Their leading scorer - and the First Division's - was Alan Smith, with 23 goals.

Arsenal won the title despite having had two points deducted from their total after a players' brawl during a League game at Old Trafford. Manchester United were docked one point for their involvement in the same incident. Both clubs were fined £50,000.

Liverpool led the table for much of the season, but were stunned by the resignation of manager Kenny Dalglish on February 22, 1991 after 14 years at the club.

Dalglish announced his decision just after Liverpool had drawn 4-4 with local rivals Everton.

Facts   **The Nineties**

The reasons for Dalglish's departure were not made entirely clear, but he was thought to have become sick of the stress of such a high-profile job. However, there must have been some compensations to being a successful manager of England's most successful club. Leeds United manager Howard Wilkinson expressed the thoughts of many when he said: 'If he has resigned because of pressures, the rest of us have no chance'.

Over the next seven weeks, Liverpool lost the League leadership and saw Arsenal move five points ahead of them at the top of the table. On April 16, the Anfield board announced that Dalglish's successor would be Graeme Souness, their former player who was currently manager of Rangers.

Another famous figure who seemed to have grown tired of the game was rock star Elton John, who in August sold his stake in Watford to Jack Petchey for £6 million.

Former Liverpool and Wales forward John Toshack was sacked as manager of Real Madrid despite the club having suffered only eight defeats during his 64 matches in charge.

During the 1990-91 season, Atletico Madrid goalkeeper Abel Resino went more than 14 matches (1275 minutes) without conceding a goal - a new world record.

On January 1, 1991, Paul Gascoigne became the first player to be sent off on live British television when he got his marching orders for dissent during Tottenham Hotspur's League game against Manchester United.

In recognition of the fact that he had never been booked or sent off in his career, FIFA awarded Gary Lineker their Fair Play prize, worth £20,000.

UEFA announced that, from the start of the 1991-92 season, clubs would be allowed to field up to five foreign players in domestic League games.

The Nineties

Facts

Tottenham Hotspur won the FA Cup, beating Nottingham Forest 2-1 after extra time in the 1991 Final. This was the match in which Paul Gascoigne was stretchered off after a quarter of an hour with a serious knee injury after launching a high, illegal tackle on Forest's Garry Parker. Stuart Pearce scored from the resulting free kick, but Spurs equalised through Paul Stewart. The Londoners should have gone ahead when they were awarded a penalty, but Mark Crossley saved Gary Lineker's spot kick. The winner eventually came from a headed own goal by Forest's Des Walker.

The semi-final between Tottenham and Arsenal had been played at Wembley - the first time an FA Cup tie other than the Final had been held at the stadium. Spurs won 3-1 with one goal from Gascoigne and two from Lineker. Arsenal's goal was scored by Alan Smith.

The injured Gascoigne spent the next year in limbo, uncertain of whether he would remain at Spurs or if he would even play again. At the end of the following season, however, he eventually completed his expected £8.5 million transfer to Lazio of Italy.

Sheffield Wednesday won the 1991 League Cup, which had now been renamed the Rumbelows Cup after its new sponsor. They beat Manchester United 1-0 in the Final with a goal by John Sheridan. The victory was particularly sweet for Wednesday manager Ron Atkinson, who had been sacked by United in 1986.

Wednesday also won promotion back from the Second Division, to which they had been relegated at the end of 1989-90.

Torquay United became the first team to win promotion on penalties. Their play-off final against Blackpool ended 2-2 after extra time and the Devon club won the shoot-out 5-4.

Despite losing their manager, Graeme Souness, to Liverpool, Rangers won the Scottish Championship for the third year running. They also won the League Cup, beating Celtic 2-1 after extra time in the Final.

 **Facts**   **The Nineties**

The leading scorer in the Scottish Premier Division was Tommy Coyne, with 18 goals for third-placed Celtic.

Red Star Belgrade won the European Cup, beating Marseille 5-3 on penalties after the Final in Bari, Italy, had finished goalless at the end of extra time.

Manchester United won the 1991 Cup Winners' Cup, beating Barcelona 2-1 in the Final in Rotterdam. Both United's goals were scored by Mark Hughes, who had returned to Old Trafford in 1988 after spending the least successful period of his career with the Spanish club. Barcelona's goal was scored by Dutch international Ronald Koeman.

Manchester United manager Alex Ferguson thus became the second man after Johann Cruyff to manage two Cup Winners' Cup-winning sides, having previously lifted the trophy with Aberdeen.

In another all-Italian UEFA Cup Final, Inter Milan beat Roma 2-1 on aggregate.

Leeds United won the First Division Championship in 1992, the last year before it became the Premiership. This was the third title in their history.

The leading scorer in the First Division was Ian Wright, with 29 goals in the season. Five of them were scored for Crystal Palace; the other 24 came after his mid-season transfer to Arsenal.

Liverpool won the FA Cup for the fifth time, beating Second Division 2-0 in the Final with goals by Michael Thomas and Ian Rush.

In a departure from tradition, this year's FA Cup runners-up went up the steps first. But, owing to a mix-up, Sunderland were mistakenly given the winners' medals.

Cup-winning manager Graeme Souness was just recovering from major heart surgery.

The Nineties

One of the results of the Taylor Report on the Hillsborough disaster was that there could no longer be an infinite number of Cup replays, partly because of the difficulty of organising security and policing at the grounds. Henceforth, if two clubs were still level after extra time in the first replay, ties would be decided by a penalty shoot-out. Manchester United became the first First Division club to go out of the FA Cup on penalties when they lost in the fourth round in 1992 to Southampton.

Manchester United won the League Cup in its second and last year under the aegis of Rumbelows. They beat Nottingham Forest 1-0 in the Final with a goal by Brian McClair.

On February 5, 1992, Newcastle United, languishing near the bottom of the Second Division, sacked manager Ossie Ardiles and appointed Kevin Keegan to replace him.

Seven months after leaving Liverpool, Kenny Dalglish took over as manager of Blackburn Rovers. Under his guidance, Rovers returned to the top flight of English football after a 26-year absence when they beat Leicester City in the Second Division play-off final at Wembley.

In Scotland, Rangers did the double. They won their fourth consecutive Scottish League title and beat Airdrieonians 2-1 in the Final of the FA Cup.

The Premier Division's leading scorer was Ally McCoist, with 34 goals for Rangers.

Hibernian won the League Cup, beating Dunfermline Athletic 2-0 in the Final.

Barcelona won the European Cup, beating Sampdoria 1-0 after extra time in the 1992 Final at Wembley.

 **Facts**   **The Nineties**

Werder Bremen won the Cup Winners' Cup, beating Monaco 2-0 in the Final in Lisbon.

Ajax Amsterdam won the UEFA Cup, beating Torino on away goals after the Final had finished 2-2 on aggregate.

The 1992 European Championships were held in Sweden. The eight competing nations were the CIS (a team representing the new republics of the former USSR), Denmark, England, France, Germany (the old East and West Germany had now been reunified), Holland, Scotland and Sweden.

Denmark appeared in the finals despite having failed to qualify when Yugoslavia were expelled from the tournament because of civil war in the disintegrating federation.

England performed disappointingly, drawing 0-0 with Denmark and France and losing 2-1 to Sweden in the group stage.

In the closing stages of the match against Sweden, England manager Graham Taylor controversially substituted Gary Lineker when the striker needed just one more goal to equal Bobby Charlton's England record of 49. This turned out to be Lineker's last international appearance.

Scotland also went out in the group stage - although they beat the CIS 2-0, they lost 1-0 to Holland and 2-0 to Germany.

In the semi-finals, Germany beat the hosts, Sweden, 3-2. Denmark drew 2-2 with Holland after extra time but went through 5-4 on penalties.

The 1992 European Championship Final was held on June 26, 1992 in Gothenburg in front of a crowd of 37,800. Rank outsiders Denmark beat red-hot favourites Germany 2-0, with goals by John Jensen and Kim Vilfort.

The Nineties

Facts

In 1992-93, the Football League disbanded after 104 years and re-formed as the FA Premier League, the first main commercial sponsor of which was Barclays Bank. The Premier League will carry on with 22 clubs for this season, and then reduce its size to 20 by the end of 1994-95. The old Second Division would henceforth be known as the First Division and there would be three-up, three-down between it and the Premiership.

The first FA Premier League Champions were Manchester United.

Alex Ferguson thus became only the third British manager to win a League title with two different clubs - the other two were Herbert Chapman (Huddersfield Town and Arsenal) and Brian Clough (Derby County and Nottingham Forest).

One of the main contributory factors to United's success was their capture of Eric Cantona, who they bought for about £1.5 million on November 26 after the French striker had fallen out with his previous boss, Howard Wilkinson of Leeds United.

Teddy Sheringham was the Premiership's leading scorer, with 22 goals (one for Nottingham Forest, 21 for Tottenham Hotspur).

 **Facts**

The Nineties

WEMBLEY

Arsenal did a Cup double, beating Sheffield Wednesday 2-1 in both Finals. They won the FA Cup, beating the Owls 2-1 in a replay after the first match had finished 1-1 after extra time. Ian Wright scored for Arsenal in both games.

In the Final of the League Cup (which was now known as the Coca-Cola Cup), the Arsenal scorers were Paul Merson and Steve Morrow. Morrow then broke his arm when he fell off Tony Adams during celebrations after the final whistle.

The FA Cup semi-finals were both local derbies - Sheffield Wednesday v Sheffield United and Arsenal v Tottenham Hotspur - and were both played at Wembley.

On February 24, 1993, England's World Cup-winning captain, Bobby Moore, died of cancer at the age of 51.

On May 1, 1993, Brian Clough retired after 18 years as manager of Nottingham Forest. Under him, Forest had won the League Championship in 1978, the European Cup in 1979 and 1980 and the League Cup in 1978, 1979, 1989 and 1990. The only trophy to have eluded Clough throughout his career was the FA Cup.

On May 14, 1993, Terry Venables was sacked as chief executive of Tottenham Hotspur by the club chairman, Alan Sugar.

The Nineties

Facts

Kevin Keegan guided Newcastle United to the Championship of the First Division (the old League Division Two).

Maidstone United of Division Three were declared bankrupt and went out of the Football League.

In Scotland, Rangers did the treble. They won their fifth consecutive League title and for the second year running their leading scorer was Ally McCoist, again with 34 goals.

Rangers also won the FA Cup and the League Cup, beating Aberdeen 2-1 in both Finals (the League Cup after extra time).

Olympique Marseille won the 1993 European Cup Final, beating AC Milan 1-0 in Munich, but they were stripped of the title the following year when it emerged that they had fixed a French league fixture against Valenciennes. Their chairman, Bernard Tapie, was charged with corruption and suborning witnesses and ordered to give up ownership of the club. He was subsequently sentenced to two years' imprisonment. The team was relegated to the Second Division.

Parma won the European Cup Winners' Cup, beating Royal Antwerp 3-1 in the Final at Wembley.

Juventus won the UEFA Cup, beating Borussia Dortmund 6-1 on aggregate in the Final.

In 1994, Manchester United did the double. They won the FA Premiership again and beat Chelsea 4-0 in the FA Cup Final thanks to two penalties by Eric Cantona and two goals by Mark Hughes and Brian McClair.

The leading scorer in the Premier League was Andy Cole, with 34 goals for newly-promoted Newcastle United, who finished third.

 **Facts**　　　　　　　　　　　**The Nineties**

United nearly did an unprecedented treble, but lost 3-1 to Aston Villa in the Final of the League (Coca-Cola) Cup. Villa's goals in this match were scored by Dalian Atkinson and Dean Saunders (two - one penalty). United's scorer was Mark Hughes.

On January 20, 1994, Sir Matt Busby, president of Manchester United, died at the age of 84.

Graeme Souness resigned as Liverpool manager after his team was knocked out of the FA Cup by First Division Bristol City. He was succeeded by Roy Evans.

The penalties imposed on Tottenham Hotspur for illegal loans to players in the 1980s were unprecedented in their severity - they were fined £1.5 million, banned from the 1994-95 FA Cup and docked six League points. These were later overturned by the English courts.

Wycombe Wanderers took Maidstone United's place in the Football League. They finished fourth in their first season in the Third Division and then won promotion through the play-offs, beating Preston North End in the Final at Wembley.

A week after England's failure to qualify for the 1994 World Cup finals, their much-maligned manager Graham Taylor resigned and the FA announced that his successor would be Terry Venables. The former Tottenham chief executive would be known as coach rather than as manager.

Wales also failed to qualify for the World Cup finals, and this meant the end for their manager, Terry Yorath. His replacement, John Toshack, was taken on part-time so that he could continue in charge of the Spanish club Real Sociedad. This was such an unpopular move that Toshack resigned after only 47 days in charge of the national side.

The Nineties

Facts

In Scotland, Rangers won the Premier Division for the sixth time in a row and also took the League Cup, beating Hibernian 2-1 in the Final.

Leading scorer in Scotland was Rangers' England international Mark Hateley, with 24 goals.

Dundee United won the FA Cup for the first time in their history, beating Rangers 1-0 in the Final. The Terrors had been losing finalists six times since 1974.

Italians AC Milan won the European Cup, beating Barcelona 4-0 in the Final in Athens.

Arsenal won the Cup Winners' Cup, beating Parma 1-0 in the Final in Copenhagen. The winning goal was scored by Alan Smith.

Inter Milan won the 1994 UEFA Cup, beating Salzburg 2-0 on aggregate in the Final.

The 1994 World Cup finals were held in the USA. The 24 qualifying nations were Argentina, Belgium, Bolivia, Brazil, Bulgaria, Cameroon, Colombia, Germany, Greece, Holland, Italy, Mexico, Morocco, Nigeria, Norway, Republic of Ireland, Romania, Russia, Saudi Arabia, South Korea, Spain, Sweden, Switzerland and the USA.

Andres Escobar, the Colombian defender who scored an own goal in his country's 2-1 defeat by the hosts, was shot dead on his return home.

Diego Maradona failed a random drugs test after Argentina's second match against Nigeria and was sent home in disgrace.

The Nineties

The top two countries in each group went through to the second, knockout, phase. These were Brazil, Bulgaria, Germany, Holland, Mexico, Nigeria, Republic of Ireland, Romania, Saudi Arabia, Spain, Sweden and Switzerland.

They were joined in the knockout stage by the four best third-placed teams - Argentina, Belgium, Italy and the USA.

The Republic of Ireland went through to the second phase after winning one, drawing one and losing one of their three group matches. Their 1-0 victory over Italy came after a shot by Ray Houghton deceived the Italian keeper in the air.

Holland beat the Republic of Ireland 2-0 in the last 16 match at Orlando, Florida.

Germany beat Belgium 3-2 but the result might have been different if the Belgians had not had a penalty turned down by Swiss referee Kurt Rothlisberger. The official admitted his mistake after seeing the video replay and was not used again in the tournament.

Nigeria led for much of their game against Italy, who had Gianfranco Zola sent off. But then in the 88th minute Roberto Baggio equalised and then scored the winner in extra time from the penalty spot.

In the other second phase matches, Spain beat Switzerland 3-0, Sweden beat Saudi Arabia 3-1, Romania beat Argentina 3-2, Brazil beat the USA 1-0 and Bulgaria beat Mexico 5-4 on penalties after the two countries had finished 1-1 after extra time.

The Nineties

Facts

In the quarter-finals, Brazil beat Holland 3-2 after throwing away a two-goal lead; Romania went out on penalties for the second World Cup in succession, losing 5-4 to Sweden after a 2-2 draw, and Italy beat Spain 2-1. But the performance of the round was Bulgaria's 2-1 defeat of Germany, who were widely regarded as the holders even though they had won the World Cup in 1990 as West Germany.

Roberto Baggio scored both Italy's goals as they eliminated Bulgaria in one semi-final; in the other, Brazil beat Sweden 1-0 thanks to an 81st minute goal from Romario.

The 1994 World Cup Final was held on July 17 at the Pasadena Rose Bowl, Los Angeles, California, in front of 94,194 spectators.

BRAZIL: Taffarel, Jorginho (sub: Cafu), Aldair, Marcio Santos, Branco, Mauro Silva, Dunga, Mazinho, Zinho (sub: Viola), Babeto, Romario
ITALY: Pagliuca, Mussi (sub: Apolloni), Baresi, Maldini, Benarrivo, Berti, Albertini, D. Baggio (sub: Evani), Donadoni, R. Baggio, Massaro

The Final finished 0-0 after extra time and so for the first time the World Cup was decided on penalties.

Baresi missed the first kick; Pagliuca saved from Marcio Santos; Albertini scored; Romario scored; Evani scored; Branco scored; Taffarel saved the fourth Italian penalty from Massaro; Dunga scored; Roberto Baggio fired over the bar.

Brazil won the 1994 World Cup 3-2 on penalties.

The joint leading scorers in the 1994 World Cup were Salenko of Russia and Stoichkov of Bulgaria, each with six goals.

The tournament was the best-attended of all 15 World Cups, with an average gate of 68,592.

 **Facts**   The Nineties

At the start of the 1994-95 season, Tottenham Hotspur swooped on three World Cup stars - Jurgen Klinsmann of Germany and Ilie Dumitrescu and Gica Popescu of Romania. Then, in October, they sacked manager Ossie Ardiles and replaced him with Gerry Francis.

In the close season, Liverpool paid Nottingham Forest £8.5 million for Stan Collymore and Arsenal bought Dennis Bergkamp from Inter Milan for the same amount and then David Platt from Sampdoria for £4.75 million. Manchester United sold Paul Ince to Inter Milan for £7.5 million.

Newcastle United bought Les Ferdinand from Queen's Park Rangers for £6 million, Warren Barton for £4 million from Wimbledon and David Ginola for £2.5 million from Paris St Germain.

Aston Villa bought Gareth Southgate from relegated Crystal Palace for £2.5 million, Savo Milosevic from Partizan Belgrade for £3.5 million, and Mark Draper from Leicester City for the same amount.

Blackburn Rovers won the 1994-95 FA Premier League Championship, finishing a point ahead of Manchester United in second place. This was the third League title in their history, but their first since 1914.

Kenny Dalglish thus joined Herbert Chapman, Brian Clough and Alex Ferguson in the select band of managers who had won a League championship with two clubs.

Everton won the FA Cup for the fifth time, beating Manchester United 1-0 in the 1995 Final through a goal by Paul Rideout.

Liverpool won the Coca-Cola Cup, beating Bolton Wanderers 2-1 in the Final. Steve McManaman scored both Liverpool's goals.

The Nineties

Facts

Crystal Palace reached the semi-finals of both the FA and the League (Coca-Cola) Cups and were then relegated form the Premier Division.

Eric Cantona was sent off while playing for Manchester United at Crystal Palace. On his way to the dressing room, the Frenchman attacked a spectator who had been hurling abuse at him.

Cantona was subsequently banned by the FA until the following season and a magistrate sentenced him to two weeks' imprisonment (although the judgment was overturned on appeal, and Cantona had to do 120 hours' community service.

Bruce Grobbelaar (Southampton), John Fashanu (Aston Villa) and Hans Segers (Wimbledon) were charged by the police with match-fixing.

George Graham, manager of Arsenal since 1986, was sacked by the club when a Premier League inquiry revealed that he had received a total of £425,000 in 'bungs' for himself when he signed John Jensen and Pal Lydersen in 1991 and 1992.

Scotland went over for the first time to the three-points-for-a-win system. The Scottish League was also restructured and increased in size from 38 to 40 clubs. From now on, there were to be four divisions, rather than three. The two new clubs were Caledonian Thistle and Ross County.

In 1995, Rangers won their seventh League Championship in a row, the 45th in their history.

After six years without a trophy, Celtic ended the drought when they beat Airdrieonians 1-0 in the Final of the FA Cup. The winning goal was scored by Dutchman Pierre Van Hooijdonk.

 **Facts** **The Nineties**

The Scottish League Cup was won by Raith Rovers, who beat Celtic 6-5 on penalties after the match had finished 2-2 after extra time. This was the first major trophy in the history of the Kirkcaldy club.

Ajax Amsterdam won the European Cup, beating AC Milan 1-0 in the Final in Vienna.

Zaragoza won the Cup Winners' Cup, beating Arsenal 2-1 after extra time in the Final in Paris. The winning goal came less than a minute before the final whistle would have signalled a penalty shoot-out. Nayim - an ex-Spur whose real name is Mohamed Ali Amar - lifted the ball over Arsenal keeper David Seaman from the halfway line.

In an all-Italian Final, Parma won the UEFA Cup, beating Juventus 2-1 on aggregate.

In December 1995, the European Court of Justice made a historic ruling which had seismic repercussions throughout British and continental football.

The judgment concerned a Belgian player named Jean-Marc Bosman who had signed for RFC Liège in 1988. Two years later, when his contract expired, he was offered a new deal with the club but at less than half his previous wage. He said he would prefer a transfer to Dunkerque, who had expressed an interest in him, but Liège blocked this by putting him on the market at more than twice what Dunkerque were prepared to pay.

Bosman claimed that this was in restraint of trade and the European Court of Justice supported him. In their view, existing football transfer rules were in breach of EEC laws governing free movement of labour within all member states. They also ruled that restrictions on the number of foreign players in a team were likewise unlawful.

The Nineties

Facts

As a result of the Bosman Ruling, any player who is out of contract is a free agent, and his present club can no longer expect anything from another club who buys his services. Today, more players than ever before are transferred when they are in the middle of a contract, so that the selling club can make money on the deal.

Manchester United won both the League and the FA Cup for the second time in three years and thus became the first English team ever to do a double double. They won the Premier League with 82 points, four points ahead of second-placed Newcastle United, and beat Liverpool 1-0 in the FA Cup Final with a goal by Eric Cantona.

Premiership leading scorer Alan Shearer of Blackburn Rovers became the first player ever to score more than 30 goals in three consecutive seasons.

Aston Villa won the League (Coca-Cola) Cup, beating Leeds United 3-0 in the Final with goals by Savo Milosevic, Ian Taylor and Dwight Yorke.

Terry Venables announced that he would not continue as England coach after the end of the 1996 European Championships (Euro '96). The FA appointed as his successor Glenn Hoddle, the former Tottenham Hotspur and England player who was currently manager of Chelsea.

First Division Leicester City lost their second manager in less than a year. Aston Villa had taken Brian Little from them in 1994, and in December, 1995, his replacement, Mark McGhee, was poached by Wolverhampton Wanderers. The parting was extremely acrimonious, but the club soon replaced him with Martin O'Neill, who led them to promotion through the play-offs at the end of the 1995-96 season.

 **Facts**

The Nineties

Chelsea appointed former Dutch international Ruud Gullit as player-manager in succession to Hoddle.

Bob Paisley died on February 14, 1996 at the age of 77. He was manager of Liverpool from 1974-83, during which time the club won the European Cup three times, the UEFA Cup once, the League Championship six times and the League Cup three times.

In Scotland, Rangers did the double, winning their eighth League Championship in a row and the FA Cup, beating Heart of Midlothian 5-1 in the Final with two goals from Brian Laudrup and three from Gordon Durie.

The Nineteen

Facts

Aberdeen won the the League Cup, beating Dundee 2-0 in the 1996 Final.

Juventus won the European Cup, beating Ajax 4-2 on penalties after the Final in Rome had been drawn 1-1.

Paris St Germain became the first French club to win the Cup Winners' Cup, beating Rapid Vienna 1-0 in the Final in Brussels.

Bayern Munich won the UEFA Cup, beating Bordeaux 5-1 on aggregate in the 1996 Final.

Euro '96 - the 1996 European Championships - were held in England. There were 16 qualifying nations, twice as many as in Sweden in 1992. They were Bulgaria, the Czech Republic, Croatia, Denmark, England, France, Germany, Holland, Italy, Portugal, Russia, Scotland, Spain, Switzerland and Turkey.

England topped their group, drawing 1-1 with Switzerland and beating Scotland 2-0 and Holland 4-1.

The seven other countries that joined England in the quarter-finals were the Czech Republic, Croatia, France, Germany, Holland, Portugal and Spain.

England were lucky to draw 0-0 with Spain, who had a goal wrongly disallowed for offside. Then keeper David Seaman excelled himself in the penalty shoot-out, which England won 4-2.

In the other three matches, Germany beat Croatia 2-1, France beat Holland 5-4 on penalties after a 0-0 draw, and the Czech Republic beat Portugal 1-0.

Both semi-finals were decided on penalties. England took the lead against Germany after three minutes through Alan Shearer, but Stefan Kuntz equalised after 16. Both sides scored with their first five penalties, and then Gareth Southgate had England's sixth saved. Andreas Moller made no mistake with Germany's reply, to take them through 6-5.

 **Facts** The Nineties

The Czech Republic and France drew 0-0 after extra time, then won the penalty shoot-out 6-5.

The Euro '96 Final was played at Wembley in front of 73,611 spectators. The Czech Republic took the lead after 59 minutes when Karel Poborsky was fouled in the area and Patrik Berger scored from the penalty.

German manager Berti Vogts then brought on Oliver Bierhoff, who brought the scores level after 73 minutes.

Bierhoff scored again after five minutes of extra time - that was the end of the match, because Euro '96 was the first tournament in which the first team to score in extra time won the match - the so-called 'golden goal'.

Manchester United won the FA Carling Premiership in 1996-97 for the fourth time in five years. Their leading scorer, with 19 goals, was the Norwegian Ole Gunnar Solskjaer.

For the second year running, the leading scorer in the Premiership was Alan Shearer, with 25 goals for his new club, Newcastle United.

Chelsea won the FA Cup for the second time in their history. They beat Middlesbrough 2-0 in the Final with goals from Roberto Di Matteo and Eddie Newton.

Di Matteo's goal was the fastest in Cup Final history - he scored after only 43 seconds, thus beating the previous record set by Jackie Milburn, who scored after 45 seconds of the 1955 Cup Final for Newcastle United against Manchester City.

Leicester City won the League (Coca-Cola Cup), beating Middlesbrough 1-0 in the Final replay at Hillsborough with a goal by Steve Claridge.

The Nineties

Facts

Giantkillers of the year were Second Division Chesterfield, who reached the semi-final of the FA Cup.

The Wembley Coca-Cola Cup Final had ended 1-1 after extra time. Emile Heskey scored for Leicester and Fabrizio Ravanelli for Middlesbrough.

Middlesbrough achieved a unique and unwanted treble - they were beaten finalists in both Cups and were relegated from the Premiership. They would have avoided the drop had they not had three points deducted for cancelling a Premiership fixture against Blackburn Rovers without sufficient notice.

Kevin Keegan left his job as manager of Newcastle United in mid-season when his team were second in the Premiership. The club announced plans to become a public company and then, on January 14, 1997, appointed Kenny Dalglish as manager.

After eight years in charge, Howard Wilkinson was sacked as manager of Leeds United. He was later appointed Technical Director of the FA.

Former Arsenal manager George Graham replaced Howard Wilkinson at Elland Road after 18 months out of the game.

Macclesfield Town won the GM Vauxhall Conference and gained entry to the Football league for the first time. Their manager was former Manchester United and Northern Ireland international Sammy McIlroy.

Queen's Park Rangers were bought by music entrepreneur Chris Wright for £10 million.

Former England coach Terry Venables became Director of Football at First Division Portsmouth. He later also took on a part-time job as manager of Australia.

 **Facts**   **The Nineties**

Bruce Rioch was sacked as Arsenal manager after 61 weeks in the job. His replacement was Arsène Wenger, a Frenchman who had previously been coach at Grampus Eight in Japan.

In August 1996, Alan Ball resigned as manager of Manchester City. Six weeks later, the Maine Road board announced his replacement - Steve Coppell, formerly manager of Crystal Palace. Coppell lasted 33 days before resigning 'for health reasons'. He was replaced in December by Frank Clark, who had been manager of Nottingham Forest since 1993.

In Guatemala, 80 people were killed at a football match due to overcrowding in a stadium.

Chelsea director Matthew Harding was killed in a helicopter crash on his way back from watching his team's Coca-Cola Cup match at Bolton Wanderers.

Ray Harford resigned as manager of Blackburn Rovers. The club then announced that his replacement next season would be Sven Goran Eriksson, but he never came and they hired Roy Hodgson instead.

On December 22, 1996, Peter Shilton made his 1000th League appearance for Third Division Leyton Orient.

In Scotland, Rangers won the Premier League for the ninth year in succession, thus equalling Celtic's record of 1966-1974. They also won the League Cup, beating Heart of Midlothian 4-3 in the Final.

Kilmarnock won the 1997 Scottish FA Cup for the third time in their history, beating Falkirk 1-0 in the Final.

Alex Miller resigned as manager of Hibernian after 10 years in charge.

Borussia Dortmund won the European Cup, beating Juventus 3-1 in the Final in Munich.

The Nineties

Barcelona won the Cup Winners' Cup, beating Paris St Germain 1-0 in the Final in Rotterdam.

Schalke won the UEFA Cup, beating Inter Milan 4-1 on penalties after the Final had finished 1-1 on aggregate.

Arsenal won the FA Carling Premiership in 1997-98 - this was the 11th title in their history.

Frenchman Arsène Wenger thus became the first non-British manager to win the English League.

Arsenal completed the Double by winning the FA Cup, beating Newcastle United 2-0 in the Final at Wembley.

Arsenal's goals in the Final were scored by Marc Overmars and Nicolas Anelka.

The Premiership's leading scorer was Andy Cole, with 25 goals in all competitions.

Aston Villa sold controversial and disaffected Yugoslav striker Savo Milosevic to Real Zaragoza for a reported £3.5 million.

Chelsea won the League (Coca-Cola Cup), beating First Division Middlesbrough 2-0 in the Final with goals by Frank Sinclair and Roberto di Matteo.

All three of the clubs promoted to the Premiership at the end of the 1997 season were relegated from it again at the end of 1998 - Bolton Wanderers, Barnsley and Crystal Palace.

Crystal Palace let themselves down badly at home, where they won only one game. This was against Sheffield Wednesday, the only team from whom they took six points in the season.

 **Facts**   **The Nineties**

Everton flirted dangerously with relegation and only ensured safety through a 1-1 draw with Coventry City on the last day of the season.

Promoted automatically from the Nationwide Division One were Nottingham Forest (Champions) and Middlesbrough.

They were joined in the Premiership by Charlton who beat Sunderland 7-6 on penalties after the play-off Final at Wembley had ended 4-4 after extra time. Clive Mendonca scored a hat trick for Charlton in this match.

Kevin Phillips scored one of Sunderland's Wembley goals. It was his 35th of the season, making him the club's all-time leading marksman.

The crucial penalty was taken by Sunderland's Michael Gray and saved by Charlton keeper Sasa Ilic.

Celtic won the Scottish Premier League - their first championship since 1988. Their manager, Wim Jansen, then resigned, it is thought because of disagreements with club chairman Fergus McCann.

Tom Boyd became the first Celtic captain to lift the Premier League trophy for 10 years.

Heart of Midlothian won the Scottish FA Cup, beating Rangers 2-1 in the Final with goals by Colin Cameron (penalty) and Stephane Adam. Ally McCoist scored for Rangers.

Celtic won the Scottish League Cup, beating Dundee United 3-0 in the Final. Their goals were scored by Marc Rieper, Henrik Larsson and Craig Burley.

This was the first season since 1986 that Rangers had failed to win any of the major domestic trophies.

The Nineties

Facts

Real Madrid won the European Cup, beating Juventus 1-0 in the Final in the new Amsterdam ArenA. The winning goal was scored after 67 minutes by Montenegran international Predrag Mijatovic.

This was Real's seventh European Cup triumph, but their first since 1966.

Real's German coach, Jupp Heynckes, was thought to be in imminent danger of losing his job.

Chelsea won the 1998 Cup Winners' Cup, beating Stuttgart 1-0 in the Final in Stockholm. The only goal of the game was scored by substitute Gianfranco Zola.

This was the eighth time that a club from England had won the trophy - more than any other nation.

Chelsea's Gianluca Vialli became the first player-manager to win a major European trophy.

Two players were sent off in the Cup Winners' Cup Final - Dan Petrescu of Chelsea and Gerhard Poschner of Stuttgart.

For the first time since 1965, the UEFA Cup Final was a one-off, rather than a two-legged affair. Inter Milan beat Lazio 3-0 in the Parc des Princes, Paris, with goals by Zamorano, Zanetti and Ronaldo.

In the close season it was announced that outgoing Rangers manager Walter Smith would take over at Everton the following season. Smith had been thought to have wanted a rest.

THE 1998
WORLD CUP

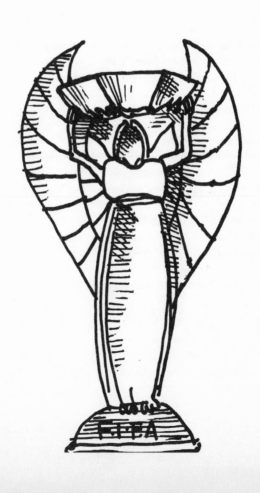

The 1998 World Cup

The 1998 World Cup finals were held in France, which thus became the second country to host the tournament twice (the other was Mexico in 1970 and 1986). The French had previously hosted the tournament in 1938.

There were 32 finalists, as follows: Argentina, Austria, Belgium, Brazil, Bulgaria, Cameroon, Chile, Colombia, Croatia, Denmark, England, France, Germany, Holland, Iran, Italy, Jamaica, Japan, Mexico, Morocco, Nigeria, Norway, Paraguay, Romania, Saudi Arabia, Scotland, South Africa, South Korea, Spain, Tunisia, the United States and Yugoslavia.

Matches were played in 10 centres across the country. There were two stadia in Paris - the existing Parc des Princes and the new Stade de France at St Denis on the western edge of the city centre. Other venues were Bordeaux, Lens, Lyons, Marseilles, Montpellier, Nantes, Saint-Etienne and Toulouse.

The countries were divided into eight groups, each of four teams. When the draw was made, there were eight top seeds, eight second seeds, eight third seeds and eight fourth seeds.

The eight top seeds were Argentina, Brazil (the holders), France, Germany, Holland, Italy, Romania and Spain.

England had only a moderate build-up to the finals, losing to Chile and drawing with Saudi Arabia and Belgium. The only real source of encouragement was a win over Portugal.

In the run-up to the finals, Scotland drew three and lost two of their try-out games.

The squads of each participating nation were as follows:

 **Facts**   The 1998 World Cup

Group A

	Brazil			Scotland
I	Taffarel		I	Jim Leighton
2	Cafu		2	Jackie Mcnamara
3	Aldair		3	Tommy Boyd
4	Junior Baiano		4	Colin Calderwood
5	Cesar Sampaio		5	Colin Hendry
6	Roberto Carlos		6	Tosh McKinlay
7	Giovanni		7	Kevin Gallacher
8	Dunga		8	Craig Burley
9	Ronaldo		9	Gordon Durie
10	Rivaldo		10	Darren Jackson
11	Emerson Ferreira		11	John Collins
12	Carlos Germano		12	Neil Sullivan
13	Ze Roberto		13	Simon Donnelly
14	Goncalves		14	Paul Lambert
15	Andre Cruz		15	Scott Gemmill
16	Ze Roberto		16	David Weir
17	Doriva		17	Billy McKinlay
18	Leonardo		18	Matt Elliott
19	Denilson		19	Derek Whyte
20	Bebeto		20	Scott Booth
21	Edmundo		21	Jonathan Gould
22	Dida		22	Christian Dailly
Coach:	Mario Zagalo		Coach:	Craig Brown

The 1998 World Cup

Facts

Group A

Norway		Morocco	
1	Frode Grodas	1	**Abdelkader El Brazi**
2	Gunnar Halle	2	**Abdelilah Saber**
3	Ronny Johnsen	3	**Abdelkrim El Hadrioui**
4	Henning Berg	4	**Youssef Rossi**
5	Stig Inge Bjornebye	5	**Smahi Triki**
6	Stale Solbakken	6	**Noureddine Naybet**
7	Erik Mykland	7	**Mustapha Hadji**
8	Oyvind Leonhardsen	8	**Said Chiba**
9	Tore Andre Flo	9	**Abdeljalil Hadda**
10	Kjetil Rekdal	10	**Abderrahim Ouakili**
11	Jahn Ivar Jakobsen	11	**Ali El Khattabi**
12	Thomas Myhre	12	**Driss Benzekri**
13	Espen Baardsen	13	**Rachid Nehrouz**
14	Vegard Heggem	14	**Salaheddine Bassir**
15	Dan Eggen	15	**Lahcen Abrami**
16	Jostein Flo	16	**Rachid Azzouzi**
17	Havard Flo	17	**Gharib Amzine**
18	Egil Ostenstad	18	**Youssef Chippo**
19	Erik Hoftun	19	**Jamal Sellami**
20	Ole Gunnar Solskjaer	20	**Taher El Lakhlej**
21	Vidar Riseth	21	**Rachid Roki**
22	Roar Strand	22	**Mustapha Chadli**
Coach:	Egil Olsen	Coach:	**Henri Michel**

 **Facts**

The 1998 World Cup

Group B

Italy		Chile	
1	Francesco Toldo	1	**Nelson Tapia**
2	Guiseppe Bergomi	2	**Cristian Castaneda**
3	Paolo Maldini	3	**Ronaldo Fuentes**
4	Fabio Cannavaro	4	**Francisco Rojas**
5	Alessandro Costacurta	5	**Javier Margas**
6	Alessandro Nesta	6	**Pedro Reyes**
7	Gianluca Pessotto	7	**Nelson Parraguez**
8	Moreno Torricelli	8	**Clarence Acuna**
9	Demetrio Albertini	9	**Ivan Zamorano**
10	Allesandro Del Piero	10	**Jose Luis Sierra**
11	Dino Baggio	11	**Marcelo Salas**
12	Gianluca Pagliuca	12	**Marcelo Ramirez**
13	Allesandro Cois	13	**Manuel Neira**
14	Luigi Di Biagio	14	**Miguel Ramirez**
15	Angelo Di Livio	15	**Moises Villarroel**
16	Roberto Di Matteo	16	**Mauricio Aros**
17	Francesco Moriero	17	**Marcelo Vega**
18	Roberto Baggio	18	**Luis Musrri**
19	Filippo Inzaghi	19	**Fernando Cornejo**
20	Fabrizio Ravanelli	20	**Fabian Estay**
21	Christian Vieri	21	**Rodrigo Barrera**
22	Gianluigi Buffon	22	**Carlos Tejas**
Coach:	Cesare Maldini	Coach:	**Nelson Acosta**

The 1998 World Cup  Facts

Group B

Cameroon		Austria	
1	Jacques Songo'o	1	Michael Konsel
2	Joseph Elanga	2	Markus Schopp
3	Pierre Wome	3	Peter Schottel
4	Rigobert Song	4	Anton Pfeffer
5	Raymond Kalla Nkongo	5	Wolfgang Feiersinger
6	Pierre Njanka	6	Walter Kogler
7	François Omam-Biyick	7	Mario Haas
8	Didier Angibeaud	8	Heimo Pfeifenberger
9	Alphonse Tchami	9	Ivica Vastic
10	Patrick Mboma	10	Andreas Herzog
11	Samule Eto'o	11	Martin Amerhauser
12	Jean-Jacques Etame	12	Martin Hiden
13	Serge Kwetche	13	Harald Cerny
14	Augustine Simo	14	Hannes Reinmayer
15	Joseph Ndo	15	Arnold Wetl
16	William Andem	16	Franz Wohlfahrt
17	Michel Pensee	17	Roman Mahlich
18	Samuel Ipoua	18	Peter Stoger
19	Marcel Mahouve	19	Toni Polster
20	Salomon Olembe	20	Andreas Heraf
21	Joseph-Desire Job	21	Wolfgang Knaller
22	Alioum Boukar	22	Dietmar Kuhbauer
Coach:	Claude Le Roy	Coach:	Herbert Prohaska

 **Facts**　　　　　The 1998 World Cup

Group C

France		Denmark	
1	Bernard Lama	1	Peter Schmeichel
2	Vincent Candela	2	Michael Schjonberg
3	Bixente Lizarazu	3	Marc Rieper
4	Patrick Vieira	4	Jes Hogh
5	Laurent Blanc	5	Jan Heintze
6	Youri Djorkaeff	6	Thomas Helveg
7	Didier Deschamps	7	Allan Neilsen
8	Marcel Desailly	8	Per Frandsen
9	Stephane Guivarc'h	9	Miklos Molnar
10	Zindine Zidane	10	Michael Laudrup
11	Robert Pires	11	Brian Laudrup
12	Thierry Henry	12	Soren Colding
13	Bernard Diomede	13	Jacob Laursen
14	Alain Boghossian	14	Morten Wieghorst
15	Lilian Thuram	15	Stig Tofting
16	Fabien Barthez	16	Mogens Krogh
17	Emmanuel Petit	17	Bjarne Goldbaek
18	Frank Lebouef	18	Peter Moller
19	Christian Karembeu	19	Ebbe Sand
20	David Trezeguet	20	Rene Henriksen
21	Christophe Dugarry	21	Martin Jorgensen
22	Lionel Charbonnier	22	Peter Kjaer
Coach:	Aime Jacquet	Coach:	Bo Johansson

The 1998 World Cup  Facts

Group C

South Africa		Saudi Arabia	
1	Hans Vonk	1	Mohammed Al-Deayea
2	Themba Mnguni	2	Mohammed Al-Jahani
3	David Nyathi	3	Mohammed Al-Khilaiwi
4	Willem Jackson	4	Abdullah Zubramwi
5	Mark Fish	5	Ahmed Madani
6	Phil Masinga	6	Fuad Amin
7	Quinton Fortune	7	Ibrahim Al-Shahrani
8	Alfred Phiri	8	Obeid Al-Dosari
9	Shaun Bartlett	9	Sami Al-Jaber
10	John Moshoeu	10	Saeed Al-Owairan
11	Helman Mkhalele	11	Fahd Al-Mehallel
12	Brendan Augustine	12	Ibrahim Al-Harbi
13	Delron Buckley	13	Hussain Sulimani
14	Jerry Sikhosana	14	Khalid Al-Muwalid
15	Doctor Khumalo	15	Youssef Al-Thyniyan
16	Brian Baloyi	16	Khamis Al-Owairan
17	Benni McCarthy	17	Ahmed Al-Dosari
18	Lebogang Morula	18	Nawaf Al-Temiyat
19	Lucas Radebe	19	Abdel Aziz Al-Janoubi
20	Naughty Mokoena	20	Hamza Saleh
21	Pierre Issa	21	Hussein Al-Sadiq
22	Andre Arendse	22	Tisir Al-Antarif
Coach:	Philippe Troussier	Coach:	Carlos Alberto Parreira

 **Facts**   The 1998 World Cup

Group D

Spain		Nigeria	
1	Andoni Zubizarreta	1	Peter Rufai
2	Albert Ferrer	2	Jero Shakpoke
3	Agustin Aranzabal	3	Celestine Babayaro
4	Rafael Alkorta	4	Nwankwo Kanu
5	Abelardo	5	Uche Okechukwu
6	Fernando Hierro	6	Taribo West
7	Fernando Morientes	7	Finidi George
8	Julen Guerrero	8	Mutiu Adepoju
9	Juan Pizzi	9	Rashidi Yekini
10	Raul Gonzalez	10	Jay-Jay Okocha
11	Alfonso Perez	11	Garba Lawal
12	Sergi Barjuan	12	Willy Okpara
13	Santiago Canizares	13	Tijani Babangida
14	Ivan Campo	14	Daniel Amokachi
15	Carlos Aguilera	15	Sunday Oliseh
16	Alberto Celades	16	Uche Okafor
17	Joseba Etxeberria	17	Augustine Eguavoen
18	Guillermo Amor	18	Wilson Oruma
19	Narvaez Kiko	19	Ben Iroha
20	Miguel Nadal	20	Victor Ikpeba
21	Luis Enrique Martinex	21	Godwin Okpara
22	Jose Molina	22	Abiodun Baruwa
Coach:	Javier Clemente	Coach:	Bora Milutinovic

The 1998 World Cup Facts

Group D

Paraguay		Bulgaria	
1	Jose Chilavert	1	Zdravko Zdravkov
2	Francisco Arce	2	Radostin Kisishev
3	Catalino Rivarola	3	Trifon Ivanov
4	Carlos Gamarra	4	Ivailo Petkov
5	Celso Ayala	5	Ivailo Iordanov
6	Edgar Aguilera	6	Zlatko Yankov
7	Juan Carlos Yegros	7	Emil Kostadinov
8	Aristides Rojas	8	Hristo Stoichkov
9	Jose Cardozo	9	Luboslav Penev
10	Roberto Acuna	10	Krassimir Balakov
11	Pedro Sarabia	11	Ilian Iliev
12	Danilo Aceval	12	Borislav Mihailov
13	Carlos Paredes	13	Gosho Ginchev
14	Ricardo Rojas	14	Marian Hristov
15	Miguel Benitez	15	Adalbert Zafirov
16	Julio Cesar Enciso	16	Anatoli Nankov
17	Hugo Brizuela	17	Stoicho Stoilov
18	Cesar Ramirez	18	Daniel Borimirov
19	Carlos Morales	19	Georgi Bachev
20	Denis Caniza	20	Georgi Kirilov
21	Jorge Campos	21	Rosen Kirilov
22	Ruben Ruiz Diaz	22	Milen Petkov
Coach:	Paulo Cesar Carpeggiani	Coach:	Hristo Bonev

 **Facts** The 1998 World Cup

Group E

Netherlands		Belgium	
1	Edwin van der Sar	1	**Filip de Wilde**
2	Michael Reiziger	2	**Bertrand Crasson**
3	Jaap Stam	3	**Lorenzo Staelens**
4	Frank de Boer	4	**Gordan Vidovic**
5	Arthur Numan	5	**Vital Borkelmans**
6	Wim Jonk	6	**Franky van der Elst**
7	Ronald de Boer	7	**Marc Wilmots**
8	Dennis Bergkamp	8	**Luis Oliveira**
9	Patrick Kluivert	9	**Mbo Mpenza**
10	Clarence Seedorf	10	**Luc Nilis**
11	Phillip Cocu	11	**Nico van Kerckhoven**
12	Boudewijn Zenden	12	**Philippe van de Walle**
13	Andre Ooijer	13	**Dany Verlinden**
14	Marc Overmars	14	**Enzo Scifo**
15	Winston Bogarde	15	**Philippe Clement**
16	Edgar Davids	16	**Glen de Boeck**
17	Pierre van Hooijdonk	17	**Mike Vestraeten**
18	Ed de Goey	18	**Gert Verheyen**
19	Giovanni van Bronckhorst	19	**Eric van Meir**
20	Aron Winter	20	**Emile Mpenza**
21	Jimmy Floyd Hasselbaink	21	**Danny Boffin**
22	Ruud Hesp	22	**Eric Deflandre**
Coach:	Guus Hiddink	Coach:	**Georges Leekens**

The 1998 World Cup Facts

Group E

South Korea		Mexico	
I	Kim Byung-ji	I	**Jorge Campos**
2	Choi Sung-yong	2	**Claudio Suarez**
3	Lee Lim-saeng	3	**Joel Sanchez**
4	Choi Young-il	4	**German Villa**
5	Lee Min-sung		**Castenada**
6	Yoo Sang-chul	5	**Diulio Davino**
7	Kim Doh-keun	6	**Marcelino Bernal**
8	Noh Jung-yoon	7	**Ramon Ramirez**
9	Kim Do-hoon	8	**Alberto Garcia Aspe**
10	Choi Yong-soo	9	**Ricardo Pelaez**
I I	Seo Jung-won	10	**Luis Garcia**
12	Lee Sang-hun	I I	**Cuauhtemoc Blanco**
13	Kim Tae-young	12	**Osvaldo Sanchez**
14	Ko Jong-soo	13	**Pavel Pardo**
15	Lee Sang-yoon	14	**Raul Lara**
16	Jang Hyung-seok	15	**Luis Hernandez**
17	Ha Seok-ju	16	**Isaac Terrazas**
18	Hwang Sun-hong	17	**Francisco Palencia**
19	Jang Dae il	18	**Salvador Carmona**
20	Hong Myung-bo	19	**Braulio Luna**
21	Lee Dong-gook	20	**Jaime Ordiales**
22	Seo Dong-myung	21	**Jesus Arellano**
Coach:	Cha Bum-kun	22	**Oscar Perez**
		Coach:	**Manuel Lapuente**

 Facts The 1998 World Cup

Group F

Germany		Yugoslavia	
1	Andreas Kopke	1	Ivica Kralj
2	Christian Worns	2	Zoran Mirkovic
3	Jorg Heinrich	3	Goran Djorovic
4	Jurgen Kohler	4	Slavisa Jokanovic
5	Thomas Helmer	5	Miroslav Djukic
6	Olaf Thon	6	Branko Brnovic
7	Andreas Moller	7	Vladimir Jugovic
8	Lothar Matthaus	8	Dejan Savicevic
9	Ulf Kirsten	9	Predrag Mijatovic
10	Thomas Hassler	10	Dragan Stojkovic
11	Olaf Marschall	11	Sinisa Mihajlovic
12	Oliver Kahn	12	Dragoje Lekovic
13	Jens Jeremies	13	Slobodan Komljenovic
14	Markus Babbel	14	Nisa Saveljic
15	Steffen Freund	15	Ljubinko Drulovic
16	Dietmar Hamann	16	Zeljko Petrovic
17	Christian Ziege	17	Savo Milosevic
18	Jurgen Klinsmann	18	Dejan Govedarica
19	Stefan Reuter	19	Miroslav Stevic
20	Oliver Bierhoff	20	Dejan Stankovic
21	Michael Tarnat	21	Perica Ognjenovic
22	Jens Lehmann	22	Darko Kovacevic
Coach:	Berti Vogts	Coach:	Slobadan Santrac

The 1998 World Cup

Facts

Group F

The USA		Iran	
1	Brad Friedel	1	Ahmadreza Abedzadeh
2	Frankie Hejduk	2	Mehdi Mahdavikia
3	Eddie Pope	3	Naeem Saadavi
4	Mike Burns	4	Mohammad Khakpour
5	Thomas Dooley	5	Mohammad Ali
6	David Regis		Peyrovani
7	Roy Wegerle	6	Karim Bagheri
8	Ernie Stewart	7	Alireza Mansourian
9	Joe-Max Moore	8	Sirous
10	Tab Ramos		Deenmohammadi
11	Eric Wynalda	9	Hamid Estili
12	Jeff Agoos	10	Ali Daei
13	Cobi Jones	11	Khodadad Azizi
14	Preki Radosavljevic	12	Nima Nakisa
15	Chad Deering	13	Ali Latifi
16	Jurgen Sommer	14	Nader
17	Marcelo Balboa		Mohammadkhani
18	Kasey Keller	15	Ali Ostadasadli
19	Brian Maisonneuve	16	Reza Shahroudi
20	Brian McBride	17	Javad Zarrincheh
21	Claudio Reyna	18	Satar Hamedani
22	Alexi Lalas	19	Behnam Seraj
Coach:	Steve Sampson	20	Mehdi Pashazadeh
		21	Mehrdad Minavand
		22	Parviz Boromand
		Coach:	Jalal Talebi

 Facts   The 1998 World Cup

Group G

Romania		Colombia	
1	Dumitru Stingaciu	1	Oscar Cordoba
2	Dan Petrescu	2	Ivan Ramiro Cordoba
3	Christian Dulca	3	Ever Palacios
4	Anton Dobos	4	Jose Santa
5	Constantin Galca	5	Jorge Bermudez
6	Gheorge Popescu	6	Maurizio Serna
7	Marius Lacatus	7	Antony de Avila
8	Dorinel Munteanu	8	Harold Lozano
9	Viorel Moldovan	9	Adolfo Valencia
10	Gheorge Hagi	10	Carlos Valderrama
11	Adrian Ilie	11	Faustino Asprilla
12	Bogdan Stelea	12	Miguel Calero
13	Liviu Ciobotariu	13	Wilmer Calero
14	Radu Niculescu	14	Jorge Bolano
15	Lucian Marinescu	15	Victor Aristizabal
16	Gabriel Popescu	16	Antonio Moreno
17	Ilie Dumitrescu	17	Andres Estrada
18	Iulian Filipescu	18	John Perez
19	Ovidiu Stinga	19	Freddy Rincon
20	Tibor Selymes	20	Hamilton Ricard
21	Gheorge Craioveanu	21	Leider Preciado
22	Florian Prunea	22	Farid Mondragon
Coach:	Anghel Iordanescu	Coach:	Hernan Dario Gomez

The 1998 World Cup

Facts

Group G

England		Tunisia	
1	David Seaman	1	Chokri el Ouaer
2	Sol Campbell	2	Imed Ben Younes
3	Graeme Le Saux	3	Sami Trabelsi
4	Paul Ince	4	Mounir Boukadida
5	Tony Adams	5	Hatem Trabelsi
6	Gareth Southgate	6	Ferid Chouchane
7	David Beckham	7	Tarek Thabet
8	David Batty	8	Zoubeir Beya
9	Alan Shearer	9	Riadh Jelassi
10	Teddy Sheringham	10	Kaies Ghodbane
11	Steve McManaman	11	Adel Sellimi
12	Gary Neville	12	Mourad Melki
13	Nigel Martyn	13	Riadh Bouazizi
14	Darren Anderton	14	Sirajeddine Chihi
15	Paul Merson	15	Skander Souyah
16	Paul Scholes	16	Radhouane Salhi
17	Robert Lee	17	Jose Clayton
18	Martin Keown	18	Mehdi Ben Slimane
19	Les Ferdinand	19	Faycal Ben Ahmed
20	Michael Owen	20	Sabri Jaballah
21	Rio Ferdinand	21	Khaled Badra
22	Tim Flowers	22	Ali Boumnijel
Coach:	Glenn Hoddle	Coach:	Henry Kasperczak

 **Facts**   The 1998 World Cup

Group H

Argentina		Croatia	
I	CArlos Roa	I	**Drazen Ladic**
2	Roberto Ayala	2	**Petar Krpan**
3	Jose Chamot	3	**Ante Seric**
4	Hector Pineda	4	**Igor Stimac**
5	Matias Almeyda	5	**Goran Juric**
6	Nestor Sensini	6	**Slaven Bilic**
7	Claudio Lopez	7	**Aljosa Asanovic**
8	Diego Simeone	8	**Robert Prosinecki**
9	Gabriel Batistuta	9	**Davor Suker**
10	Ariel Ortega	10	**Zvonimir Boban**
11	Juan Veron	11	**Silvio Maric**
12	German Burgos	12	**Marijan Mrmic**
13	Pablo Paz	13	**Mario Stanic**
14	Nelson Vivas	14	**Zvonimir Soldo**
15	Leonardo Astrada	15	**Igor Tudor**
16	Sergio Berti	16	**Ardijan Kozniku**
17	Pablo Cavallero	17	**Robert Jarni**
18	Abel Balbo	18	**Zoran Mamic**
19	Hernan Crespo	19	**Goran Vlaovic**
20	Marcelo Gallardo	20	**Dario Simic**
21	Marcelo Delgado	21	**Krunoslav Jurcic**
22	Javier Zanetti	22	**Vladimir Vasilj**
Coach:	Daniel Passarella	**Coach:**	**Miroslav Blazevic**

The 1998 World Cup

Facts

Group H

Japan		Jamaica	
1	Nobuyuki Kojima	1	**Warren Barrett**
2	Akira Narahashi	2	**Steven Malcolm**
3	Naoki Soma	3	**Christopher Dawes**
4	Masami Ihara	4	**Linval Dixon**
5	Norio Omura	5	**Ian Goodison**
6	Motohiro Yamaguchi	6	**Fitzroy Simpson**
7	Teruyoshi Ito	7	**Peter Cargill**
8	Hidetoshi Nakata	8	**Marcus Gayle**
9	Masashi Nakayama	9	**Andy Williams**
10	Hiroshi Nanami	10	**Walter Boyd**
11	Shinji Ono	11	**Theodore Whitmore**
12	Wagner Lopes	12	**Dean Sewell**
13	Toshihiro Hattori	13	**Aaron Lawrence**
14	Masayuki Okano	14	**Donovan Ricketts**
15	Hiroaki Morishima	15	**Ricardo Gardner**
16	Toshihide Saito	16	**Robbie Earle**
17	Yutaka Akita	17	**Onandi Lowe**
18	Shoji Jo	18	**Deon Burton**
19	Eisuke Nakanishi	19	**Frank Sinclair**
20	Yoshikatsu Kawaguchi	20	**Darryl Powell**
21	Seigo Narazaki	21	**Durrant Brown**
22	Takashi Hirano	22	**Paul Hall**
Coach:	Takeshi Okada	Coach:	**Rene Simoes**

 **Facts** The 1998 World Cup

The final tables of each group were as follows:

	P	W	D	L	F	A	Pts
Group A							
Brazil	3	2	0	1	6	3	6
Norway	3	1	2	0	5	4	5
Morocco	3	1	1	1	5	5	4
Scotland	3	0	1	2	2	6	1
Group B							
Italy	3	2	1	0	7	3	7
Chile	3	0	3	0	4	4	3
Austria	3	0	2	1	3	4	2
Cameroon	3	0	2	1	2	5	2
Group C							
France	3	3	0	0	9	1	9
Denmark	3	1	1	1	3	3	4
South Africa	3	0	2	1	3	6	2
Saudi Arabia	3	0	1	2	2	7	1
Group D							
Nigeria	3	2	0	1	5	5	6
Paraguay	3	1	2	0	3	1	5
Spain	3	1	1	1	8	4	4
Bulgaria	3	0	1	2	1	7	1
Group E							
Holland	3	1	2	0	7	2	5
Mexico	3	1	2	0	7	5	5
Belgium	3	0	3	0	3	3	3
South Korea	3	0	1	2	2	9	1

The 1998 World Cup

Facts

	P	W	D	L	F	A	Pts
Group F							
Germany	3	2	1	0	6	2	7
Yugoslavia	3	2	1	0	4	2	7
Iran	3	1	0	2	2	4	3
USA	3	0	0	3	1	5	0
Group G							
Romania	3	2	1	0	4	2	7
England	3	2	0	1	5	2	6
Colombia	3	1	0	2	1	3	3
Tunisia	3	0	1	2	1	4	1
Group H							
Argentina	3	3	0	0	7	0	9
Croatia	3	2	0	1	4	2	6
Jamaica	3	1	0	2	3	9	3
Japan	3	0	0	3	1	4	0

Scotland played in the opening match of the tournament against the holders, Brazil. The champions went ahead after four minutes through Cesar Sampaio, but Scotland got back on terms through a penalty by John Collins. The Scots were unlucky to lose through an own goal when an attempted clearance bounced in off Boyd.

England began their campaign with a 2-0 victory over Tunisia. Their first came from captain Alan Shearer after 42 minutes, the second from Paul Scholes in injury time.

Scotland drew their second game against Norway 1-1, a goal by Craig Burley cancelling out one by Tore Andre Flo immediately after the start of the second half.

 **Facts**   The 1998 World Cup

England lost their second game to Romania, the top seeds in their group. Both Romanian goals came from players based in England - Viorel Moldovan of Coventry City scored the first, which was pulled back in the 83rd minute by substitute Michael Owen. Just as both sides seemed to have settled for a draw, Dan Petrescu of Chelsea stuck his foot between Graeme Le Saux and goalkeeper David Seaman to grab all three points.

The eight games in the second round of the 1998 World Cup finals turned out as follows:

Italy *Vieri*	1	Norway	0
Brazil *Cesar Sampaio (2),* *Ronaldo (2, 1 penalty)*	4	**Chile** *Salas*	1
France *Blanc*	1	Paraguay	0
Nigeria *Babangida*	1	**Denmark** *Moller, Brian Laudrup, Sand,* *Helveg*	4
Germany *Klinsmann, Bierhoff*	2	Mexico *Hernandez*	1
Holland *Bergkamp, Davids*	2	**Yugoslavia** *Komljenovic*	1
Romania	0	Croatia *Suker (penalty)*	1
Argentina *Batistuta (penalty), Zanetti*	2	**England** *Shearer (penalty), Owen*	2

The 1998 World Cup

The match between France and Paraguay was the first in the history of the World Cup to be decided by the 'golden goal' method. Under this system, previously used in Euro '96, the team that wins is the one that scores first in extra time.

Germany left it very late against Mexico, after going behind in the 47th minute. Although they came through in the end, the Germans were widely thought to be struggling to paper the cracks in an old side - average age 31. Klinsmann gave everything, but the question remained: did he have enough left to get his side through another three high-pressure matches?

Holland almost lost to Yugoslavia, who were awarded a penalty but hit the crossbar with the kick. Edgar Davids' winner came in the last minute of normal time.

Croatia beat Romania thanks to Davor Suker, who remained calm when he had to retake his penalty kick because of encroachment in the area. He put the ball in the net both times.

The tie of the round was the match between Argentina and England. The South Americans went ahead through a penalty awarded against Seaman after six minutes, but England equalised four minutes later after Michael Owen was impeded in the Argentine area. Shearer scored from the resulting penalty.

England then took the lead with a goal from Owen, but Argentina made it 2-2 at half time when a cleverly worked free kick just outside the area was played through to Javier Zanetti.

At the start of the second half, David Beckham was sent off for retaliation after he had been fouled by Diego Simeone. The loss of a man greatly restricted England's capacity to attack, but they held out and seven minutes from time even had the ball in the Argentine net, but Sol Campbell's header was disallowed for a foul by Shearer on goalkeeper Carlos Roa.

 **Facts**   The 1998 World Cup

After extra time produced no golden goal, the tie was decided on penalties. Argentina took the first and scored through Berti; Shearer made it 1-1, then Crespo's shot was saved by Seaman. Ince had the chance to make it 2-1 to England, but Roas saved his effort. Then Veron and Merson both scored to make it 2-2, and they were followed by Gallardo and Owen (3-3). Ayala made it 4-3 to Argentina and then David Batty's shot was saved by Roas. England were eliminated.

The quarter finals of the 1998 World Cup were between Holland and Argentina, Germany and Croatia, Italy and France and Brazil and Denmark.

Holland beat Argentina 2-1, with a goal by Patrick Kluivert after 12 minutes and a winner by Dennis Bergkamp from virtually the last kick of the game. In the meantime, the South Americans had equalised through Claudio Lopez.

Croatia beat a weary-looking Germany 3-0. Their goals were scored by Robert Jarni, Goran Vlaovic and Davor Suker. Germany had Christian Worns sent off.

Neither Italy nor France looked as if they would ever score, and they didn't. The tie was decided when Di Biagio missed in the penalty shoot-out.

Denmark took the lead against the favourites, Brazil, with a goal by Martin Jorgensen after two minutes. Brazil hit back through Bebeto and Rivaldo to take a half-time lead, but the Danes equalised after the break with a goal by Brian Laudrup. Brazil's winner was another goal for Rivaldo, whose speculative shot from outside the box evaded the dive of Peter Schmeichel.

In the first World Cup semi-final, Brazil beat Holland 4-2 on penalties after their match had ended 1-1 after extra time. Ronaldo had given Brazil the lead at the start of the second half, but Patrick Kluivert equalised three minutes from the end of normal time.

The 1998 World Cup   Facts

In the second semi-final, France came from a goal down to beat Croatia 2-1. Davor Suker gave the Croats the lead straight after half time but Lilian Thuram equalised immediately and then scored the winner in the 70th minute. France had Laurent Blanc sent off for hitting Slaven Bilic. Television replays suggested that although the Frenchman raised his hand and did make contact with his opponent, Bilic seemed to have made the most of the moment, as if wishing to draw the referee's attention to it.

The 1998 World Cup Final between the holders Brazil and the hosts France was held at the Stade de France, St Denis, Paris on July 12, 1998 in front of 80,000 spectators.

Brazil: Taffarel, Cafu, Aldair, Junior Baiano, Roberto Carlos, Leonardo (sub: Denilson), Cesar Sampaio (sub: Edmundo), Dunga, Rivaldo, Ronaldo, Bebeto
France: Barthez, Thuram, Desailly, Leboeuf, Lizarazu, Karembeu (sub: Boghossian), Deschamps, Petit, Zidane, Djorkaeff (sub: Vieira), Guivarc'h (sub: Dugarry)

Ronaldo had been unsure of his place until the last minute because of illness. He is thought to have suffered a fit on the morning of the match. His performance was subdued to say the least, and the French won 3-0 with two goals by Zinedine Zidane and one in the last minute by Emmanuel Petit. Marcel Desailly was sent off for two bookable offences.

Leading scorer in the 1998 World Cup finals was Davor Suker, with six goals for Croatia, who finished in third place.

Suker's closest challengers for the Golden Boot were Gabriel Batistuta of Argentina and Christian Vieri of Italy, who both finished the tournament with five goals. Ronaldo of Brazil, Marcelo Salas of Chile and Luis Hernandez of Mexico all scored four.

QUIZ SCORE SHEET

QUIZ SCORE SHEET

QUIZ SCORE SHEET

QUIZ SCORE SHEET

QUIZ SCORE SHEET

QUIZ SCORE SHEET